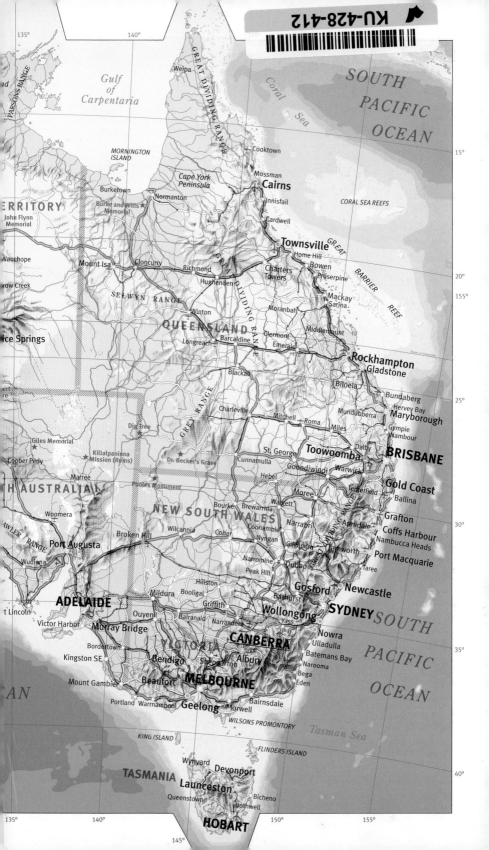

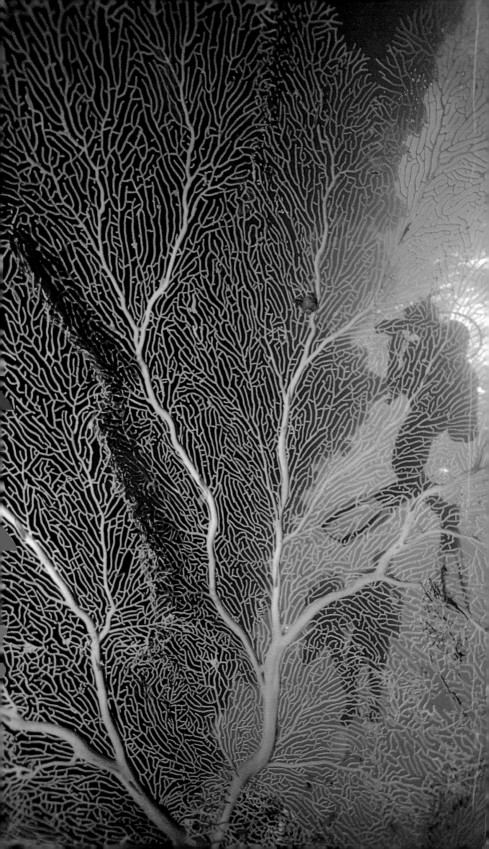

FIELDING'S DIVING AUSTRALIA

FIELDING'S IN-DEPTH GUIDE TO DIVING DOWN UNDER

NEVILLE COLEMAN
AND
NIGEL MARSH

EDITED BY ROD RITCHIE
AND JULIA WALKDEN

PERIPLUS EDITIONS

Fielding Worldwide, Inc.
308 South Catalina Avenue
Redondo Beach, California 90277 U.S.A.

FIELDING WORLDWIDE INC.

PUBLISHER AND CEO	**Robert Young Pelton**
GENERAL MANAGER	**John Guillebeaux**
OPERATIONS DIRECTOR	**George Posanke**
ELECTRONIC PUBLISHING DIRECTOR	**Larry E. Hart**
PUBLIC RELATIONS DIRECTOR	**Beverly Riess**
ACCOUNT SERVICES MANAGER	**Cindy Henrichon**
PROJECT MANAGER	**Chris Snyder**
MANAGING EDITOR	**Amanda K. Knoles**

EDITORS

Rod Ritchie   **Julia Walkden**

COVER DESIGNED BY	**Digital Artists, Inc.**
COVER PHOTOGRAPHERS—Front cover	**Douglas David Selfert, Earth Water**
Back cover	**Chris A. Crumley, Earth Water**

Inquiries should be addressed to: Fielding Worldwide, Inc., 308 South Catalina
Ave., Redondo Beach, California 90277 U.S.A., Telephone *(310) 372-4474*,
Facsimile *(310) 376-8064*, 8:30 a.m.–5:30 p.m. Pacific Standard Time.
Web site: http://www.fieldingtravel.com
e-mail: fielding@fieldingtravel.com

ISBN 1-56952-139-5

CONTENTS

Diving with a bot-
tlenose dolphin.
Neville Coleman

DIVING AUSTRALIA

Vermilion biscuit star. *Neville Coleman*

New South Wales

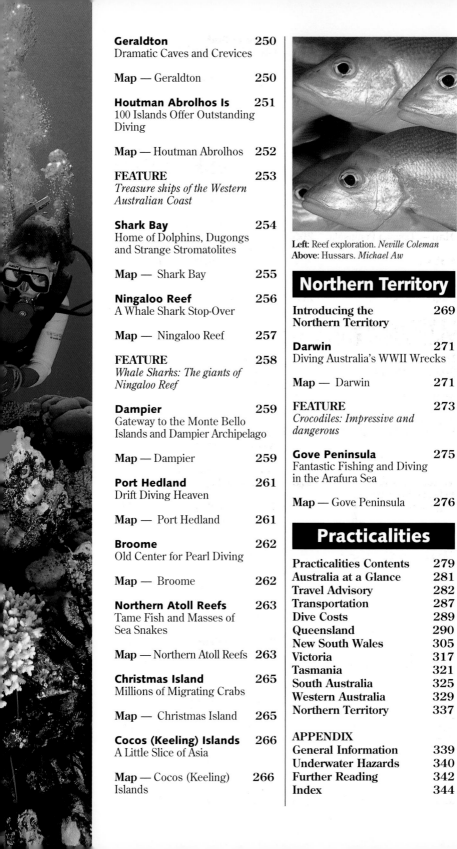

Left: Reef exploration. *Neville Coleman*
Above: Hussars. *Michael Aw*

Northern Territory

Practicalities

THE AUTHORS

NEVILLE COLEMAN has recorded Australia's marine fauna and flora and dived the continent's waters for 34 years, discovering over 450 new marine species. A versatile photo-journalist, he has produced 150 books and countless magazine articles on underwater natural history. World-renown as a marine ecologist, and patron of the Australian Marine Conservation Society, Neville is at the forefront of underwater exploration.

NIGEL MARSH is a Brisbane-based underwater photographer and photo-journalist whose work has been published in many magazines, newspapers and books, both in Australia and abroad. This is the second book he has co-authored with Neville Coleman. Nigel has dived extensively around the Australian coastline and throughout Asia and the Pacific and he has won a number of photographic competitions.

Dedication
To a new age of discovery...and discoverers

Authors' Acknowledgments

A book of this size and scope would not be possible without the help and information of many people. The authors would like to thank everybody who assisted including the following dive operators for up-to-date information about their dive sites. **Queensland**: Graham McCallum (Auriga Bay II), John McGregor (Undersea Explorer), Quicksilver Diving Services, Wayne Inglis (Rum Runner), Pro Dive Townsville, Tony Fontes (Great Barrier Reef Diving Services), Vince O'Hagan (Keppel Island Dive Centre), Darren Newton (Slaty's Dive Team), Owen Griffith (Dive Boatique), Bill Elliot (Suncoast Fundive). **New South Wales**: Alan Jarrett (Alan Jarrett's Divers World), Roger Newman (Brooms Head Dive Centre), John (Roy) Stewart (Cool D Dive Shop), Bob Diaz (Pro Dive Central Coast), Adam Donaldson (Sea Trek). **Victoria**: Lex Thorbeckle (LT Divers), Phillip Doak & Alistair MacDonald (Schomberg Dive Services), Bill Karoly (Warrnambool Diving Services), Frank Zeigler (Professional Diving Services). **Tasmania**: Jason Griffith (Scuba Centre), Colin Lester (East Coast Scuba Centre), Ian Palmer (The Dive Shop Hobart). **South Australia**: Ian Lewis (Cave Divers Association of Australia), Victor Marine & Watersport. **Western Australia**: Scott & Colleen Wuillemin (Jurien Bay Dive & Hire), Ian Stiles (Beagle Island Dive Company), Jenny (Batavia Coast Dive Academy), Graeme Wignell (Big Blue Dive), Jo Bostock (Workline Divers Supply), Cliff Campbell & Leanne Hamence (Indian Ocean Diving Academy); Ron Moore (Albany Dive Centre) and Jeff Mullins. **Northern Territory**: Rick Weiss (Cullen Bay Dive Centre) Lorraine Chidgey and Russell Butel (Gove Diving Academy). We would also like to thank the following for information contained in this book; Julie & Victoria (Genesis Travel), Wendy Roil-Stoker (Greyhound-Pioneer), Rail Australia, McCafferty's, Lisa Harris (Ansett Australia) and Juliana Stehn (Qantas Airways).

We would also like to thank Tom Byron, Peter Stone, John Wright and Jeff Mullins, whose guides to dive sites were of great assistance. Last, but not least, there are those people close to us that deserve special mention, Helen Rose and Karen Handley.

Most of the **photographs** in this book are from the files of the **Australasian Marine Photographic Index** (AMPI), which contains color transparencies of animals and plants, cross-referenced against identified specimens housed in museums and scientific institutions. The Index also covers related marine activities. The project is housed at Sea Australia Resource Centre, under the network of educational services offered by Neville Coleman's Underwater Geographic Pty Ltd. Nigel Marsh's extensive photolibrary is also housed at the centre.

Introducing Australia

Often referred to as the "Wide Brown Land", much of Australia is a harsh, waterless outback, where personal survival cannot be taken lightly. On the other hand, the eastern coastal districts and the island of Tasmania are relatively fertile, with mountain ranges causing moderate to high rainfalls, and river systems draining the land forms to the sea.

With warm currents descending along both the east and west coasts, and cold currents sweeping up from the south, almost every type of weather is experienced. Monsoonal influences cause winds and currents to change direction often, depending on the season. Extreme seasonal fluctuations unleash some of nature's mightiest forces—floods, cyclones, fire and drought are all part of the weather equation.

The governing climatic factors are Australia's position on the Tropic of Capricorn, the influence of the Asian land masses to the north, and the surrounding physiography. The northern part of the continent is subject to wet northwest monsoons in summer and the southeast trade winds in winter. Due to the warming of the surrounding oceans, this influence has extended south over the past 50 years. In general, the southern part of Australia experiences moist, westerly air streams during winter. Between these two systems is a subtropical high pressure belt which brings about a drying influence west to east across southern Australia in the summer, and across northern Australia in the winter.

Most of Australia's average rainfall of 1000 mm falls on the northern and eastern coasts (less than 7 per cent of the nation), while inland, the second driest continent in the world (after Antarctica), receives less than 250 mm per year over the majority of its land mass. At least 70 per cent of the entire country can expect less than 500 mm of rainfall per year.

Australia's plant life is rich and diverse with many unique species, the result of isolation from other continents. Its wide variety of habitats include alpine areas, rainforests, open forests, monsoon forests, heath, desert, and mangrove forests. However, savanna-mallee species cover the greatest expanse of the country, because of the poor nutrient soils, heat, drought and reduced rainfall which occur away from the coast.

The dominant tree type is the eucalypt, with over 500 species. These grow almost everywhere on the continent, from the arid interior, to the wet coastal forests, and high above the snowline. Eucalypts are the world's tallest hardwoods, growing more than 60 m, and they make up 90 per cent of all forests.

Australia's unique marsupials (pouched mammals such as koalas, kangaroos, wombats and possums) have evolved during long periods of continental isolation and in response to the varied geography. Likewise the monotremes (egg-laying mammals such as the platypus and the echidna) are often described as living fossils. In the past, this isolation

Opposite: The famous rock formations, known as the "Olgas", out of Alice Springs in the Northern Territory, are surrounded by mulga trees and spinifex grass, typical of outback Australia.
Neville Coleman

Below: In contrast to the arid interior, Australia's rugged Great Dividing Range on the east coast has remnants of the ancient rainforest which was the dominant vegetation millions of years ago. Today the forests are home to the graceful tree frog (*Litoria gracilenta*).
Neville Coleman

Above: With such a huge coastline, Australia has so much to offer divers; from the temperate south to the tropical north, the sheer diversity brings visitors from the world over. Shown here is Cape du Comedic on Kangaroo Island, one of South Australia's top diving destinations. *Michael Aw*

prevented more advanced species from eradicating the native fauna by more effective competition. However, the white settlers introduced species such as rabbits, and these became so numerous that they decimated ground cover and plants over millions of hectares, making survival difficult for native species.

Around 750 bird species can be found in Australia, from the world's second largest (the emu) down to the smaller wrens and finches. Of these, around 600 species breed on the mainland and offshore islands. Huge numbers of birds, particularly the waders and shore feeding species, visit Australia each year as a feeding stopover during the harsh Northern Hemisphere winter.

Reptiles are also well represented in Australia, with more than 400 recorded species—from the tiny gecko lizards to giant saltwater crocodiles and amazing creatures such as the outback's thorny devil and the frill-necked lizard. Over 60 venomous land snakes exist—many capable of killing humans.

The Aborigines, Australia's first settlers who arrived over 60,000 years ago, have one of the oldest known cultures. Due to its isolated location and its geographical position deep in the Southern Hemisphere, Australia was the last great land mass to be settled by Europeans (1788). The new settlers quickly spread fatal diseases and dispossessed the Aborigines, who lost out in the struggle with people determined to forge new frontiers in their quest for land. Even today, Aborigines have a lower than average life expectancy, although a policy of reconciliation and some newly won native title land rights have given new hope to the descendants of the indigenous inhabitants.

In the past, Australia depended on produce from the land such as wool, wheat and beef to bolster its exports. However, over the past few decades, huge deposits of minerals have been developed along with natural gas and extensive reserves of coal and bauxite. These underground riches now contribute more to the national economy than agriculture. Even manufacturing has lost much of its economic importance, and tourism is forging ahead, with Australia's reputation as a holiday destination growing each year.

Visitors come to Australia to enjoy the natural beauty of this vast continent, to marvel at its unique plants and animals (both terrestrial and marine) and to visit its cosmopolitan cities. Australia has an excellent tourism infrastructure, with tours and services to suit every taste, and a wide range of transport and accommodation.

Most commerce and industry have developed on the eastern seaboard and on the southwest coast of the continent. Railway systems run from Cairns, south to Melbourne and thence west to Perth, with shorter lines branching out into the interior. Around the coastal fringes and extending into the interior, a vast network of roads links cities, communities, towns and stations. Although the roads are sealed between most towns, many inland and outback roads are made of gravel, soil, sand or dust, which can become impassable during the wet season.

A sealed highway links Darwin in the north to the Red Centre of Australia and on to Adelaide, however, the only roads which cross from east to west are those traversing the coast or linking the inland rural communities. Vast distances separate many towns, especially in Western Australia, and many roads have no services along the way, so all survival necessities must be carried. Rented cars and campervans are available from most of the larger towns, and an excellent range of bus services covers the entire coast.

Airline services are available throughout most of Australia, although the less populated areas may only be reached through secondary services. Domestic flights are reliable, but often subject to modifications to flight times due to increased air traffic during school holidays, especially over summer. Major international airports are Sydney, Brisbane, Cairns, Melbourne, Perth, Adelaide and Darwin.

Australia's population now exceeds 17 million. Over the last 20 years a multicultural community has developed, which increases each year, due to the government's active immigration policies. In the past decade, an influx of Asian immigrants has joined the many Europeans who arrived after World War II, making Australia one of the most multicultural nations in the world.

Below: Kangaroos (such as these grey kangaroos from the Snowy Mountains in New South Wales) can be seen in every state in Australia in the wild, or in many superb wildlife parks.
Neville Coleman

The World's Most Diverse Diving

The seas surrounding Australia have much to offer—countless fantastic dive sites, thousands of reefs still unexplored, many new species yet undiscovered, and marine life unlike any in the world.

The Great Barrier Reef has always been one of the world's most popular dive destinations. However Australia offers many other unusual dive sites—the temperate sponge gardens and kelp forests in southern waters, the amazing underwater cave systems of Mount Gambier and the Nullabor Plain, the reef systems in the Coral Sea, and the subtropical coral reefs fringing the coasts of Queensland, New South Wales and Western Australia.

Around this island continent the diver can experience the entire range of tropical and temperate habitats. Diving in Australian waters is almost always adventure diving, and is often a challenge, since the wind rarely lets up. Consequently, during most offshore diving, ocean swells and surface wave chop are an integral part of the scene.

Diving should not be a haphazard event carried out on the spur of the moment. Most places (except the west coast of Tasmania) have seasons when the winds are not so strong and the seas are relatively calm, so trips can be planned to coincide with these periods. Diving requires forethought, planning and a commonsense approach to be enjoyed to its fullest.

Australia's Dive Sites

The following are Australia's main dive destinations, served by dive shops which provide compressors, hire gear, retail gear and charter boats. The order of appearance is the same as in the main text of this book, clockwise around the continent, starting with Queensland.

Queensland

Queensland is the most popular dive destination. Although the Great Barrier Reef and Coral Sea areas are the most heavily visited, excellent diving can also be enjoyed on the reefs in the south of the state.

Northern Queensland

Stretching from Bundaberg to Papua New Guinea, the thousands of reefs that make up the Great Barrier Reef offer a wealth of exciting experiences. Our exploration of the Great Barrier Reef begins on the **Far Northern Reefs**, an area still largely unexplored, with deep drop-offs, brilliant corals and good populations of pelagic fish and sharks. **Lizard Island**, the location of one of the most exclusive resorts on the reef, is close to the **Ribbon Reefs**, a chain of reefs dotted with pinnacles and coral gardens, and

Below: While the Ningaloo Reefs off Exmouth, Western Australia are not as extensive or well known as the Great Barrier Reef, they are easier to get to, and the only site in Australia that can, in season, guarantee whale sharks.
Neville Coleman

home to a wonderful diversity of marine life. Here divers can explore the Cod Hole and Dynamite Pass. Live-aboard boats from Cairns and Port Douglas offer trips to the Ribbon Reefs. These trips are generally combined with a few days at **Osprey Reef**, a reef located in the Coral Sea renowned for its wall diving and sharks. The reefs close to **Cairns and Port Douglas** are generally dived on day trips, and although hundreds of divers may be in Cairns at any one time, the diving is still excellent, the reefs quite healthy and the fish life prolific. Cairns is also the gateway to **Holmes Reef**, a Coral Sea reef where there are plenty of sharks, schooling pelagic fish, reef fish, invertebrates and corals.

Off **Townsville** lies a fine selection of reefs that can be visited on day trips or by live-aboard boat, however its most famous dive site is the *Yongala* shipwreck. Townsville live-aboard boats also travel to **Flinders Reef**, one of the most popular Coral Sea reefs, which features famous sites like Watanabee Bommie and Scuba Zoo. Deeper into the **Coral Sea** are many other reefs that are only occasionally visited. Lihous and Dart Reefs offer exploratory diving on walls and pinnacles, and the chance of seeing sharks, pelagic fish and incredible coral growths.

The **Whitsunday Islands**, many of which have resorts, are popular holiday destinations. The diving can be excellent around the islands, but most dive boats head out on day trips to the nearby reefs. Accessible only by live-aboard boat, the **Swain Reefs** are made up of hundreds of tightly packed reefs that provide outstanding diving. Beyond the Swain Reefs are a number of reef systems in the **Southern Coral Sea** that see few divers. These reefs are quite different from the more popular northern Coral Sea reefs, but are no less exciting with sharks, pelagic fish and numerous sea snakes seen on most dives.

Positioned inside the Barrier Reef, off Rockhampton, the **Keppel** Islands (a group of continental islands) are surrounded with fringing reefs which support prolific fish communities, sea snakes and a diverse range of invertebrates. The **Capricorn and Bunker Groups** are the southernmost reefs on the Great Barrier Reef. Two popular island resorts are found in these groups, and a number of the coral cays have camping areas, but perhaps the easiest way to explore these reefs is by live-aboard boat.

One of the most popular resort islands on the Great Barrier Reef, **Heron Island** offers excellent diving and a great diversity of marine life. **Lady Elliot Island** is the last stop on the Great Barrier Reef, and one of the best. Incredible dive sites surround the island, and manta rays, turtles, sharks and pelagic fish are common dive companions.

Southern Queensland

Although overlooked by many visitors from overseas, some of the most interesting diving in Queensland is found in the areas south of the Great Barrier Reef. Around **Bundaberg** and **Hervey Bay** are numerous offshore reefs featuring gropers, sea snakes, masses of fish and manta rays.

The **Sunshine Coast** has a wealth of hidden offshore reefs. Off **Brisbane**, the capital of Queensland, divers will find many reefs and wrecks, inhabited by gropers, sharks, rays, reef fish, pelagic fish, turtles and often manta rays. The

Above: Bottom-dwelling wobbegong sharks usually sleep during the day. Particular species inhabit tropical and temperate reefs right around the Australian mainland.
Nigel Marsh

GLOBAL WARMING
A danger to the reefs

SINCE THE EARLY 1980s, ABNORMALLY HIGH SEA-water temperatures have resulted in mass mortality of corals on many of the world's reefs. The most significant factor causing this rise in temperature is a phenomenon known as "global warming". Over the past century, the industrial nations of the world have released billions of tonnes of pollutants into the air, particularly carbon dioxide, through the burning of fossil fuels in refineries, chemical production and coal-fired electricity generators. These accumulating pollutants, known as 'greenhouse' gases, trap the heat radiating from the earth's surface, which results in the overall warming of the earth's atmosphere.

Bleaching in this staghorn coral has been caused by an increase in sea surface temperatures. If this rise is sustained, the entire colony will die. *Neville Coleman*

There is no doubt that the earth's climate is changing. In many areas prolonged droughts, drier conditions and acid rain have had a devastating effect on wildlife. Populations of many species have been greatly reduced, and a large number of species are threatened with extinction.

Elevated levels of ultraviolet radiation, now able to reach the earth's surface due to the depletion of the ozone layer by CFC gases, may also prove damaging to the earth's ecosystems. However studies have shown that the depletion of the ozone layer is not the main cause of coral bleaching.

Hard and soft corals, sea anemones, hydrozoan corals, ascidians, clams and some sponges contain microscopic, single-celled, dinoflagellate algae called zooxanthellae in their tissues.

The symbiotic relationship of zooxanthellae to corals is mutualistic—the coral provides inorganic nutrients such as phosphate ions and ammonium to the zooxanthellae, in return for hydrocarbons (such as sugars, amino acids and glycerol) provided by the photosynthetic process. The association is essential to the corals' high productivity and calcifying ability, and is known to be the basis for the success of reef-building corals, which flourish in low-nutrient tropical waters.

In most cases, the pigmented zooxanthellae provide color to the host corals, which appear white (bleached), when the zooxanthellae are absent. Although corals can survive for some time without zooxanthellae in their tissues, mass mortality often results if the sea temperature remains even one degree above optimum temperatures (25–29°C).

Consequences

Since the early 1980s, the consequences of sustained increases in sea-surface temperature have been unprecedented. In 1983, 90 percent of corals bleached and died on many reefs in the Galapagos Islands. In 1990, the temperature of Caribbean waters increased dramatically, and huge areas of coral reef bleached and died. The event was considered an ecological disaster by leading coral experts.

By 1991, nearly every coral reef system in the world was affected by bleaching, in most cases due to higher than normal sea-surface temperatures. Coral reefs off Australia, China, Japan, Panama, the Philippines, India, Indonesia, Malaysia, Thailand, Kenya, the Red Sea states, Puerto Rico, Jamaica and the Bahamas all showed signs of major distress, with widespread bleaching.

From 1994–96, significant warming caused massive devastation to many of the coral reefs in the northern Milne Bay area of Papua New Guinea, and throughout the Bismarck and Solomon seas. Greenpeace reported severe bleaching in French Polynesia, with over 70 per cent of live corals bleached down to 25 m. American and Western Samoa and the Cook Islands also reported massive die-off of corals.

At least 70 per cent of the world's coral reefs are threatened by global warming. If the trend is not reversed, the world's coral reefs—the second most diverse ecosystem on earth—may be doomed.

Gold Coast, a popular and glitzy holiday region, has plenty of off-shore reefs along its coastline.

New South Wales

The coast of New South Wales offers some of the most varied diving in the country. Many excellent shore and boat dives are available, from coral gardens in the north, to dense sponge gardens in the south.

Northern New South Wales

Dive sites in the north of New South Wales are generally on rich coral gardens surrounding islands and reefs. Turtles, sharks, rays, gropers, pelagic and reef fish are all commonly seen, as well as numerous colorful invertebrates. **Byron Bay** is a popular destination for divers—just offshore are several fine dive sites, around the Julian Rocks Marine Reserve. Off the coast of **Ballina,** often overlooked by divers, are a range of exciting reefs. Just opened up to diving, **Brooms Head** supports a wealth of marine life, and is proving to be a popular destination. **Coffs Harbour** is the gateway to the many islands and reefs of the Solitary Island Marine Reserve, while around **South West Rocks** are found many fascinating dive sites, none more so than the famous Fish Rock Cave. **Port Macquarie**, one of the most popular holiday destinations on the coast, is the launching place for a range of off-shore reefs.

Central New South Wales

The dive sites of central New South Wales are likely to be covered in colorful sponges, but many plate and soft corals are still seen. This area is famous for its large populations of grey nurse sharks and other shark species, although turtles, gropers, rays, reef fish and pelagic fish are also numerous. **North Haven** has a brilliant range of reefs and wrecks, including the wreck of the *Titan*, the largest floating industrial crane in the Southern Hemisphere.

Forster/Tuncurry, Seal Rocks and the many hundreds of reefs in the area are well known as great places to observe grey nurse sharks and an excellent range of marine life.

Around **Port Stephens** are some of the best shore dives in the country. The area also offers many opportunities to dive on shipwrecks, offshore islands and reefs. **Newcastle** and **Swansea** are famous for the large number of shipwrecks in the area. Off the coast lie plenty of reefs to explore. The **Central Coast** is a very popular holiday area, and a favorite with divers as well, providing an interesting variety of reefs and wrecks.

Southern New South Wales

From Sydney south, the multi-hued sponge gardens found on most reefs become more prolific, as do sea horses, sea dragons, stingrays, giant cuttlefish and Port Jackson sharks. Fur seals are sometimes seen, as well as several varieties of reef and pelagic fish. **Sydney**, a most exciting dive destination, has shipwrecks in shallow and deep water, pinnacles, bays and many other unusual areas. Wonderful shore diving on rocky reefs, piers and caves can be found at **Wollongong** and **Bass Point**, as well as boat trips to a range of island and reef dive sites offshore. **Jervis Bay**, one of the most popular dive destinations in Australia, has many brilliant sites. The best are found outside the bay and include caves, reefs and walls.

Ulladulla, a busy fishing port, offers a diverse range of dive experi-

Above: Most of Australia's 85 known leatherjacket species are found in temperate water. They tend to be secretive, hiding among algae, reef corals or in sea-grass meadows. Shown here is the Pygmy leatherjacket (Brachaluteres jacksonianus). Michael Aw

ences just minutes from its harbor and the dozens of offshore islands and reefs off **Batemans Bay** are packed with marine life. **Montague Island** is home to a colony of fur seals that obviously enjoy frolicking with divers on a range of spectacular dive sites, while further down the coast, **Tathra** offers both shore and boat dives. **Merimbula** and **Eden** are popular destinations, with reefs that can be dived from shore or boat, and a number of wreck dives.

Island Territories

Off the New South Wales coastline, deep in the South Pacific Ocean, lie two island territories that are increasingly popular with tourists and divers. **Norfolk Island**, a former penal colony, has wonderful reefs offshore, inhabited by turtles, pelagic fish, sharks, reef fish and a diverse range of invertebrates. Northeast of Sydney, **Lord Howe Island**, surrounded by the southernmost coral reefs in the world, is famous for its spectacular diving. Its reefs and drop-offs support excellent populations of reef fish invertebrates, reef sharks, turtles and schools of pelagic fish.

Victoria

In Victoria the diver has a wide variety of sites to choose from. The numerous reefs and shipwrecks are packed with sponges and other invertebrates. Curious fur seals accompany divers, and rays, sea drag-

ons, dolphins, pelagic fish, catsharks and various colorful reef fish are part of the dive scene. The rugged peninsula of **Wilsons Promontory** is known for its drop-offs, caves, islands, hidden reefs and clear water, while **Melbourne** offers a diverse range of dive sites—shipwrecks, piers, drop-offs, channel markers, dense sponge gardens, and exhilarating dolphin and seal dives. **Port Campbell**, famous for its shipwrecks, also has many popular reef dive sites. At **Warrnambool**, a good variety of reef fish are found on the accessible reefs along the shore. Sponge gardens, kelp beds, caves and a number of shipwrecks are easily accessed off **Portland**.

Tasmania

The waters surrounding Tasmania contain some of the richest kelp forests and sponge gardens in the world. The cool, southern waters abound with marine life—sea dragons, rays, catsharks, fur seals, reef fish, invertebrates and pelagic fish. Local charter boats and dive shops offer trips to the interesting sites in their areas, but not all of Tasmania's coastline is accessible to divers.

The **Bass Strait Islands** have claimed many a good ship. These shipwrecks and the numerous reefs around the islands provide wonderful diving. **Wynyard**, the only area on the north coast that is regularly dived, offers a range of excellent

Below: Generally found in waters below 20 m on the Great Barrier Reef, the long-nosed hawkfish *(Oxycirrhites typus)* is often associated with gorgonian sea fans and black corals.
Neville Coleman

shore and boat dives. Offshore from **St Helens** lie many islands and reefs harboring a rich variety of marine life. **Bicheno**, by far the most popular dive destination in Tasmania, is famous for its incredible sponge gardens and dense kelp forests. Diving off the **Tasman Peninsula** is particularly rewarding. Highlights include fur seals, caves, kelp forests, sponge gardens and the *Nord* shipwreck. Off the coast of **Hobart**, the state's capital, are found a diverse range of sites, including shore, wreck, reef and kelp forest dives.

South Australia

Great white sharks are the most famous inhabitants of the waters off South Australia. However these creatures are rarely seen, even on cage diving trips, so divers can relax and enjoy the numerous underwater attractions. Interesting dive destinations include freshwater caves and sinkholes, offshore islands and reefs, shipwrecks and piers. Fur seal and seal lion colonies are located along the coast, and dolphins, sea dragons, invertebrates, reef fish, pelagic fish, rays and catsharks are regularly sighted on marine dives.

Mount Gambier is renowned for its incredible freshwater caves and sinkholes with excellent visibility. However, these challenging caves should only be dived by qualified cave divers. **Victor**

Harbour embraces many granite islands and reefs packed with sponges, invertebrates and reef fish. Offshore, **Kangaroo Island** provides a variety of experiences, the highlight being dives with the seal population.

Adelaide, the state capital, has interesting artificial reefs, shipwrecks and piers and many rocky reefs. Diving the spectacular dive sites in the **Yorke Peninsula** area is possible from the shore or by boat. Some of South Australia's best diving is found in the island groups of the **Spencer Gulf**, which are most easily explored from a live-aboard boat. Plenty of marine life can be seen on the various reefs and islands that lie off **Port Lincoln**.

Western Australia

Lapped by the waters of the Indian Ocean, Western Australia provides some of the most diverse diving in Australia. The many unique sea creatures and interesting dive locations continue to attract an increasing number of divers to the state.

Southern Western Australia

The reefs off southern Western Australia support dense sponge gardens, and numerous hard and soft corals. Invertebrates, reef fish, rays, seals, sharks, pelagic fish and sea dragons are common and even the occasional turtle can be seen.

The Western Australian section begins in the desert, with dives in

Above: Both in and out of the water, Australian sea lions attract a lot of human attention at particular haul-out sites. Divers are careful not to approach large bulls during the mating season.
Nigel Marsh

Above: At 30 m the reefs around Rottnest Island, Western Australia, are a mass of colorful sponges, ascidians, sea fans and bryozoans.
Neville Coleman

the underground caves of the **Nullarbor Plain**, where freshwater caves, devoid of animal life, provide some of the most fantastic cave diving in the world. Hundreds of islands and reefs can be visited from **Esperance**, while **Albany** offers wonderful shore and boat dives to offshore islands and reefs. **Augusta** boasts a wealth of exciting exploration diving.

A spectacular pier dive and excellent dive sites on coral and boulder reefs are found around **Geographe Bay**. Numerous limestone reefs, which have claimed many ships, lie off the coastline of **Perth**. The most popular dives are around these shipwrecks, with their incredible populations of resident marine life. Also just off Perth is the picturesque **Rottnest Island**, with a range of excellent dive sites. Both **Jurien Bay** and **Leeman** provide a seemingly endless selection of reefs to explore.

Northern Western Australia

As we move north along the coast of Western Australia, coral growth becomes more dense. On these coral reefs live plenty of reef and pelagic fish, turtles, manta rays, reef sharks, rays and, in a few locations, whale sharks. Good numbers and varieties of fish and invertebrates are found on **Geraldton's** nearby limestone reefs. Off Geraldton's coastline are located the **Houtman Abrolhos Islands**, most fringed by coral reefs.

Naturally **Shark Bay** is a good place to see sharks, as well as dugongs, dolphins and turtles.

Most famous for its whale sharks, **Ningaloo Reef** stretches from Coral Bay to Exmouth, and is home to many other marine creatures as well. Although the inshore diving around **Dampier** is rather murky, wonderful diving can be experienced on the two island groups offshore. Although both **Port Hedland** and **Broome** are affected by big tides and murky water, abundant marine life can be found on the many reefs offshore. Some of the most spectacular diving off Western Australia—which rivals diving on the Coral Sea reefs—is found on the remote **Northern Atoll Reefs**. Sea snakes, reef and pelagic fish, reef sharks, manta rays and many other creatures are usually part of the underwater spectacle.

Island Territories

Far off the north coast of Western Australia, closer to Indonesia than Australia, lie the island territories of Christmas Island and the Cocos (Keeling) Islands. Both are accessible by flights from Perth and both offer excellent diving. **Christmas Island**, rising dramatically from the sea, is surrounded by steep dropoffs, and colorful walls where pelagic fish, turtles, reef fish, reef sharks and whale sharks gather. The **Cocos (Keeling) Islands** are two coral atolls providing fantastic diving among reef and pelagic fish, reef sharks and manta rays.

Northern Territory

Diving in the Northern Territory is limited to two locations at present, but both of these spots offer an incredible range of adventure dives. A wide variety of reefs and World War II shipwrecks can be reached from **Darwin**, the Territory's capital. Although the water can be murky for most of the year, corals, sponges, invertebrates, reef and pelagic fish, gropers and other prolific marine life can be found. The **Gove Peninsula** gives divers access to incredible offshore islands and coral reefs, sheltering manta rays, turtles, reef and pelagic fish, and sometimes whale sharks.

Conditions

Divers will generally find the best time to dive northern Australia is over winter, and southern Australia over summer. But this rule is not to be taken too seriously—refer to the practicalities section for a guide to the best time to visit each area. Water temperatures vary across the country. A lycra suit may be fine in the north over summer, however you may need a 5 mm suit when diving the same area in winter, mainly because of cooler winds. In southern Australia, 5 mm suits are used over summer, but most divers prefer 7 mm or drysuits over winter.

Dive Shops

There are hundreds of dive shops operating right around the coast of Australia. The great majority run charter boats or can organize trips and offer dive courses, retail dive gear, hire gear, air fills and gear servicing. A current C card or certificate from a recognised training agency is required before gear can be hired, tanks filled or a dive undertaken.

Dive Boats

A range of dive boats operate around the country, from large catamarans that run day trips to the Great Barrier Reef, to small "tinnies" that take out a handful of divers to a local reef or wreck. All charter boats in Australia have to be in survey to take paying passengers, which means they must carry a radio and safety equipment. Boats must be operated by ticketed skippers and most boat crews are trained in first aid and are qualified divers. Live-aboard boats are generally the best value for money, with tanks, weights, meals, linen, and accommodation included in the cost. While most day trip boats operating on the Great Barrier Reef include all gear as part of the price, when doing boat dives in other parts of the country, you will have to hire your dive equipment.

Below: Dive boats in Australia come in many shapes and sizes, from rubber "ducks" to giant catamarans. One thing is certain, always be prepared for changes in the weather. Wind chop and/or swells are an integral part of getting to most dive sites by boat, even if the dive site itself is in sheltered water behind an island or reef.
Neville Coleman

Australia's Marine Environment

The incredible diversity of marine habitats established along the Australian coastline is largely due to the massive size of the island continent, and its proximity to four seas and three major ocean systems. Hundreds of endemic plant and animal species have evolved in these species-rich habitats—which range from warm tropical to cool temperate.

Within the Australian fishing zone—from the shoreline to the depths of the deepest ocean floor—almost every major and micro habitat is represented. Four major habitats have been identified: (1) open ocean, (2) reef, (3) coastal, and (4) estuarine. Each of these contain many other micro habitats, depending on depth, salinity, currents, nutrients, substrate, bottom configuration and temperature. Within these habitats live the majority of all Australia's marine flora and fauna.

Much faunal composition and distribution is related to ocean currents caused by winds, the result of the earth's rotation and the moon's gravitational pull. However tides usually influence currents locally, whereas most ocean currents are largely influenced by the wind, modified by the earth's rotation, the topography of the ocean floor, water temperature and salinity.

Five major current systems influence the Australian marine environment. The **South Equatorial Current** flows south from Indonesia, then west towards Christmas Island in the north Indian Ocean. The **Leeuwin Current** also originates in Indonesian waters and flows southward to an area off the coast of Dampier on the northwest coast, eddies around the Carnarvon area off Cape Leeuwin, Albany and Ceduna, and then trickles off into the vastness of the Great Australian Bight. This warm current travels the length of Western Australia for several months of the year, and is the reason that the enormous variety of marine life, especially the large coral bommies, survive along the temperate southwestern coast of Australia. The **West Wind Drift** travels on through the Southern Ocean, from west to east, south of Tasmania and

Below: Turbidity often hampers diving along the shallow Queensland Coast. The silty shoreline associated with numerous creeks and rivers is easily disturbed by wave action and tidal movement. *Neville Coleman*

AUSTRALIAN FISHERIES
Balancing on a razor's edge

AUSTRALIA'S FISHING ZONE IS THE THIRD LARGEST in the world, covering an area of some 9 million square kilometers. Although approximately 3600 species of fish have been recorded in Australian waters, less that 20 species make up 80 per cent of the commercial catch. About 200 species are utilized overall.

Most of the fishing fleet (close to 10,000 fishing vessels) now use satellite imagery and sea surface temperatures to find schools of fish. This ability to catch large numbers of fish has not been balanced with ecologically sustainable management of target species. As a result, some fisheries have ceased to exist, due to over-exploitation.

This short-sighted management has left Australia in the unenviable position of having to import fish to service local demand. However, in all ports around the coast, local seafood is still available in restaurants and hotels, with most of the imports being used for processing and fast food outlets.

Most commercial fish are taken by trawling, gill nets, haul nets, sine nets, traps, set lines and long lines, trap nets and tunnel nets. Many of these systems incur huge incidental catches, a great deal of which is unfortunately discarded.

A wide range of fish and marine invertebrates are exploited for food, bait, pet food, fertilizer, and stock feed. These include more than 60 species of crustaceans, 30 species of molluscs and several echinoderms. Almost half of the commercially-fished molluscs and crustaceans, and about 25 per cent of the fish, are endemic to Australian waters.

Rock lobsters, crabs and octopi are taken in traps, dillies or snares, while prawns, bugs (shovelnose lobsters) and scallops are trawled and dredged. Oysters, mussels and some scallops are commercially farmed, while abalone is harvested from reefs by licensed divers.

Almost 80 per cent of Australians live along the coastal fringe, so it isn't any wonder that a huge recreational fishing industry exists, with one-third of the population over the age of 10 years going fishing each year. Yet, it has taken some 200 years for this very large group of people to come to terms with its responsibility—to bring about a greater awareness regarding preservation of fish habitats and nursery areas. Mangrove forests and sea grass meadows have been decimated throughout Australia by coastal development

Moves implemented by the Australian Marine Conservation Society and other influential groups are making inroads into the re-education of decision-makers. Commonwealth and State Governments are developing a national fishing policy, whereby management of all resources will be based on

With close to 10,000 professional fishing boats working around Australia using the latest technology, we can now catch more than is left. Many fisheries have ceased to be commercially viable, and according to fisheries reports, many more will collapse by the year 2000 unless steps are taken. *Michael Aw*

both commercial and amateur access to available stocks.

In all states, fishing permits are required for inland waters, with bag limits and minimum size laws. Some states have restrictions and limitations on recreational marine fisheries, especially on laws relating to the taking of various species by scuba divers for the aquarium market or spearfishing using scuba or hookah equipment. It is an offence to remove or kill sea creatures in most marine and aquatic parks, or reserves.

A wide network of reserves and parks has been created in Australia, and although many of these were slow in being established, their acceptance is now nationwide, as people have realized the necessity of these all-important protective sites.

on to New Zealand's South Island. The **Flinders Current** flows northwesterly, from southwest Tasmania into the Great Australian Bight. Originating in the northern Coral Sea, the **East Australian Current** flows north to the tip of Papua New Guinea, then south along the east coast of Australia to the North Island of New Zealand. Large eddies of cooler water from the Tasman Sea occur off the south coast of Australia from Jervis Bay down to southern Tasmania.

Studies of these basic current flows, which depend on various environmental factors from year to year for their direction, show how the present day marine flora and fauna have been distributed, and how many unique species have evolved.

Since current patterns determine the zoological distribution of marine plants and animals, it seems appropriate to describe the biogeographical provinces as follows:

Warm Tropical: From the tip of Cape York (Queensland) to the west, following the coast south and around to Geraldton in Western Australia.

Western Warm Temperate: From Shark Bay off central Western Australia to the south, then east along the southwestern coast of Australia, along the coasts of South Australia and Victoria to Warrnambool, and finally south to the northwestern coast of Tasmania.

Cool Temperate: From around about Eyre on the southwestern side of the Great Australian Bight, east along the coastline to Cape Howe on the south-east coast, and then southward, encompassing all of Tasmania.

Eastern Warm Temperate: From Warrnambool in western Victoria, east and then north to just below Fraser Island, near Hervey Bay in Queensland.

Tropical: From Brisbane in southern Queensland, north to the tip of Cape York, taking in the entire Great Barrier Reef.

A certain amount of overlapping of faunal regions takes place. In some areas, animals inhabit waters around reefs and offshore islands, but are not found on the fringing coastal reefs. Even then, these may be present one year, and gone the next. Depending on temperature and currents, tropical larvae may invade temperate waters as far south as 1000 km, develop and thrive, only to succumb to winter temperatures. A description of the origins of Australian species, specific faunal regions, and their overlapping relationships and geographics are beyond the scope of this book.

To present a simplified overview, the authors have separated the marine environment into two main faunal regions—**Tropical** and **Temperate**. To define these regions we will assume a diagonal line along the 30° parallel just south of Geraldton in Western Australia, across the continent to a point slightly north of Coffs Harbour in New South Wales.

Temperate Marine Environment

Most southern shorelines are dominated by rugged cliffs, headlands, bays and long sandy beaches pounded by high-energy swells which sweep in from across the surrounding oceans to constantly reshape the coastline. Life in temperate waters is characterized by constant water movement, with most diving carried out in swell conditions.

The temperate marine environ-

Below: Many temperate water reefs are dominated by the brown kelp (*Ecklonia radiata*) which sways with the motion of the water during swell conditions. Penetration diving should only be attempted by experienced divers.
Neville Coleman

ment (largely established on coastal and offshore rocky reefs and islands), is dominated by marine plants known as algae. Algae of all descriptions (from pink, paint-like, rock-encrusting lithothamnians to giant forest kelps 25 m in length) flourish in the clear, cool, nutrient-laden seas—from the intertidal zone, down to 30 m and beyond.

Some of the more common marine plants are the sea lettuce (*Ulva*), the short-stalked kelps (*Ecklonia*), the massive strap kelps (*Durvillia*) and the giant forest kelps (*Macrocystus*) of southern Tasmania. Many of the animals (especially the invertebrates) are not as easily seen as their counterparts on coral reefs, because of the sometimes extensive coverage of the kelp forests.

In the deeper waters—in caves, on ledges and along cliff faces—invertebrates are dominant. Incredible sponge gardens are often interspersed with soft corals and sea fans in every color imaginable. Huge clumps of sea tulips (ascidians) sway in the unceasing movement of the swells, while fish dart in and out of cover, chasing food or seeking shelter from predators.

The coastal substrates are mostly sandstone, basalts, limestone and granite, therefore most sand is made up of minerals, mixed with disintegrating skeletons of animals such as forams, bryozoa, shells, echinoderms and coralline algae. Deep water sand tends to be largely shell grit, while sand which is cast up on coastal beaches has more mineral content.

Huge banks of dead sea grass and kelp wash up on many coastal beaches, especially after storms, and slowly decay. Beaches all along the major embayments have permanent mats of dead sea grass, inhabited by thousands of small crustaceans (isopods and amphipods), which help to break the mat down. These crustaceans also feed on any dead or decaying animal tissue that washes up. Both tropical and temperate regions contain representatives of all major phyla.

Tropical Marine Environment

Coral reefs occur inshore and offshore right around the top half of Australia, north of the 30° parallel. Some are true coral reef structures built by coral polyps over many ages, others are rocky reefs and outcrops covered with the corals and other animals and plants usually found on true coral reefs. Reefs located just off mainland beaches and around continental islands are known as fringing reefs.

In Western Australia, at places like Port Gregory and Quobba, coral reefs grow along the shoreline along the lower intertidal zone. Ningaloo Reefs form a barrier along the coast all the way to Exmouth Gulf. The lagoonal conditions between this barrier and the coast are optimum for the growth of coral and associated fauna.

The offshore islands all the way to Dampier are fringed with coral reefs, as most of the islands in the Dampier Archipelago, although over the past two decades many inshore reefs have been destroyed by siltation from dredging.

Top: Photographers should take care not to damage the fragile coral formations. *Michael Aw*

Above: Delicate feather stars, close relatives of the starfish, sea cucumbers and sea urchins, often shelter under large plate corals and other overhangs during the day. *Michael Aw*

Above: Off Rottnest Island, Western Australia, corals, sponges, sea fans, ascidians and bryozoans live side by side in dimly lit caves at 20 m.
Neville Coleman

Extensive coral reefs exist off northwest Australia at Rowley Shoals, the Monte Bello Islands and Scott Reefs, although the inshore reefs around the north coast to Darwin are very muddy because of the huge estuarine embayments and mangroves. Fringing reefs exist all along the northern coasts into the Gulf of Carpentaria, across to and down the eastern side of Cape York, and all the way down the Queensland coast.

The Great Barrier Reef, the largest tropical coral reef system in the world, is made up of several types of reef: mainly barrier reefs, fringing reefs, atolls and patch reefs. Scattered amongst these are thousands of coral pinnacles, or bommies, rising from the sea floor—sometimes from as deep as 50 m—to within meters of the surface. These coral pinnacles provide the most fantastic dives—with undercuts, caves, giant sea whips and fans, hard and soft corals, and incredible numbers of colorful fish and invertebrates everywhere. Opinion varies as to the age of the Reef. Corals may have lived in the area since Pre-Cambrian times, perhaps 4.5 million years ago,

and some estimates suggest that the Great Barrier Reef has been in existence for as long as 30 million years.

The Coral Sea has independent coral reefs, giant bastions with only a sand cay here and there to hint at their presence. These coral cays provide some of the last safe nesting grounds for huge numbers of sea birds.

A coral reef may be comprised of many hundreds of coral species, many similar in shape—others singularly characteristic, which live from mid-tide level down to about 50 m. Colonies vary in size from several millimeters to massive monoliths 5–10 m across. Most coral polyps are nocturnal, but when the skies are overcast many feed during the daylight hours.

The low-tide fossicker sees only a small fraction of these, for the majority of corals live subtidally. The snorkeler or scuba diver has the greatest opportunity to observe the reef and its inhabitants.

The majority of reef-building corals are colonial, however each polyp acts independently, even though it is linked to its relations by common body cells. Therefore, a coral head is a single object, made up of thousands of connected polyps all contributing to the colony as a whole. The food caught and eaten by each polyp helps to sustain the entire group. The general life history of the more common corals is well-known throughout the world, and the Australian forms differ little from these (refer to Feature—A Sea of Pink: The annual coral spawning).

Coral colonies increase in size in various ways. One of the most common is by budding—the formation of smaller corallites at the sides of larger ones. Staghorn corals use this method of reproduction. Polyp division is another way of increasing colony size, but is usually restricted to the larger corals. The polyp divides, and as growth proceeds, separate corallites are formed.

The colors of the stony, reef-building corals are due to the pigments found in the thousands of zooxanthellae (minute single-celled marine plants) embedded in the tissue of each polyp. During the daylight hours, the algae provide the coral with supplies of oxygen and hydrocarbons, and absorb some of the excess carbon dioxide given off by the polyps. At night, when the coral polyps feed, they obtain oxygen directly from the water passing over or through their tissues.

All corals are carnivores, and feed mainly on planktonic organisms which either drift or are directed towards the tentacles. Each tentacle is armed with batteries of nematocyst pods. These pods contain a small, coiled spring, tipped with a barbed dart resembling minute oval balloons filled with venom. The instant a small animal brushes past the tentacles, it is transfixed by these poisonous darts. The tentacles then move the prey towards the mouth, which enlarges and engulfs the animal. Digestion begins immediately and when the meal is finished, the refuse is released from the mouth.

Corals are the main contributors to the bulk of the reef, however other organisms (the coralline algae) cement the reef together. Many different species of this important group occur on the Great Barrier Reef. These coralline algae, often referred to as lithothamnians, are able to extract calcium carbonate from sea water. Found all over coral reefs, they are especially prevalent on the weather edge, where they form hard encrusting layers, cementing the living and dead corals together to form protective ramparts against the tireless, erosive ocean.

Below: Some of the most brilliantly colored corals are the staghorns (*Acropora* sp.). However, in many cases these colors can only be appreciated to their fullest when they are viewed at close range.
Neville Coleman

Australia's Sea Creatures

Australia's marine environment includes both temperate and tropical habitats, which support an enormous array of marine organisms. This is a general introduction to the plants and animals found in Australian waters, although the authors have not attempted to separate specific faunal regional inhabitants.

Phytoplankton

Marine plants, known as phytoplankton (mostly single-celled microscopic algae), inhabit the sunlit layer of the ocean. One liter of sea water may contain up to 20 million individuals, representing dozens of different species. The best-known of the many phytoplankton species are the diatoms and dinoflagellates.

Often referred to as the pastures of the sea, these marine plants use the energy of sunlight to convert carbon dioxide and water into carbohydrates (sugars and starches). A by-product of this photosynthetic process is oxygen. It has been calculated that phytoplankton alone produce up to 60 per cent of the earth's oxygen.

Groups of transitional creatures exist that often bear features of both the phytoplankton (plants) and zooplankton (animals). One of these groups is the foraminifera, of which there are approximately 30 pelagic species worldwide. Twenty or so species live on tropical reefs, and some cold-water species are found at both the North and South Poles.

A few of the benthic, shallow water foraminifera in tropical seas are quite large—one tropical species, *Marginopora*, grows to 20 mm in width. Most are smaller, and their calcareous star-shaped skeletons can be seen in the form of "star sand".

Zooplankton

While most phytoplankton are microscopic in size, zooplankton range from protozoans of 0.01mm, to giant salps and sea jellies, over 2 m in length.

Below: Typical sea-grass meadow (*Posidonia*) in the shallow waters of Cockburn Sound, Fremantle, Western Australia. The sandy hole behind has become eroded due to damage by boat anchors.
Neville Coleman

The tiny zooplankton, however, are important to the ocean food chain. Zooplankton feed on phytoplankton and convert their vegetable matter into animal protein. Two of the most important converters are the copepods and euphausiids or krill (planktonic crustaceans). These

Opposite: Divers will find a great variety of marine life co-existing on the coral bommies found in warm tropical waters.
Michael Aw

two groups exist in such huge numbers, and are so efficient at harvesting phytoplankton, that they may one day be a source of food.

Sea Grasses

In the open ocean phytoplankton provide the initial resource for the offshore food chains, while within the inshore coastal environment, sea grasses and algae are by far the greatest primary producers.

About 50 species of sea grasses or phanerogams (land plants that have returned to the marine environment and have re-adapted to life in the sea) are found throughout the world. Sea grasses have roots and flowers, although the flowers look more like seed pods than the colorful blooms of land plants and also reproduce sexually. They also increase by vegetative growth, producing runners under the sand from which rhizomes grow and produce more runners.

The best-known sea grasses of southern Australian seas are *Posidonia* (strapweed), *Amphibolis* (wire weed) and *Zostera* (eelgrass). Strapweed, often more than a meter in length, forms dense underwater meadows around some islands. Eelgrass generally prefers a more muddy substrate than other sea grasses, and can often be seen in estuaries or on tidal mudflats.

Many coastal sea grass beds are being decimated by dredging and sewage pollution. Each year, thousands of hectares of coastal seagrass is destroyed, and as a result, hundreds of dugong die annually from starvation. Sea grasses are of vital importance to the coastal food chain and must be protected at all cost. They provide food and shelter for juveniles of commercial and recreational fish species. A reduction in this resource will lead to reduced catches.

Algae

More than 9000 species of algae live in the world's oceans. Of these, the largest and most dominant occur in temperate waters. Southern Australia boasts several hundred species of marine algae, which occur high in the intertidal zone, down to at least 70 m in clear water. Australian algae range from filamentous turfs only millimeters in height, to giant kelps which can be 30 m long and can sometimes grow at the rate of half a meter a day.

Whereas land plants have leaves that extract carbon dioxide from air, and roots that absorb moisture and minerals from soil, algae have no true roots—their "holdfasts" simply anchor them to the bottom. Nor do they have flowers, but reproduce by way of spores, and in many cases the reproductive cycle includes both sexual and asexual plants.

Like all plants, algae need light to enable them to photosynthesize (convert carbon dioxide to starch and sugars), and although they may have many shapes and structures, their general subdivision is based on color. The algae that dominate the rocky reefs of southern Australia are browns (kelps, sargassums and bladder weeds) and reds (coralline algae that cover rocks with pink encrustations, especially along the New South Wales and eastern Victorian coasts).

Sponges

Sponges are considered by some to be the first multicellular animals; their fossil remains have been traced back to the Precambrian era, some 650 million years ago. These simple, primitive life forms are widespread throughout the temperate and tropical seas, with about 15,000 species recognized worldwide.

Although tropical seas support a number of specifically shaped (and therefore easily recognized) sponges, their greatest diversity in shape, color and species occurs in temperate waters. Temperate sponges exhibit every color of the rainbow, and their shapes are as flamboyant as their hues.

Sponges usually have a fibrous skeleton, made up of a keratin-like

material called spongin, which is only found in sponges. To identify these animals, taxonomists rely on microscopic examination of their internal skeleton and spicules. These spicules can be either calcareous or siliceous, and in most cases are minute.

The anatomy of a sponge is complex. The body is perforated by many small inhalant pores called ostia, and one or a few large exhalant pores called oscula (singular: osculum). The ostia lead to the oscula via converging channels passing through the sponge tissue. These channels are wholly or partially lined by special cells called collar cells, thus named because of their shape when seen under the microscope. Each collar cell bears a single filament, or flagellum, which whips back and forth. The combined effect of the beating flagella of the collar cells drives a stream of water through the sponge body. Fine protoplasmic extensions on the collars of the cells trap suspended fragments of food, which are then ingested. The stream of water supplies the sponge with oxygen and removes waste carbon dioxide. A small sponge, no bigger than a clenched fist, is able to filter its own body volume of water every 4 to 20 seconds, which amounts to about 5000 liters in one day.

Over the last 10 years, a great deal of work has been done on Australian sponges. Hundreds of new species have been discovered and cross-referenced with underwater photographs (a system pioneered by the author). Dr John Hooper, from the Queensland Museum, has discovered, and is in the process of describing, hundreds of new sponges, and his huge visual reference system enables him to recognize a large number, which makes the work of preparing fauna surveys and monitoring species simpler.

Cnidarians

In the past all animals with radial symmetry and simple sac-like bodies were included in the phylum Coelenterata. Today scientists recognize two separate phyla at this level: Cnidaria and Ctenophora.

All the animals described in this section belong to the larger of the two, the phylum Cnidaria. The term "Cnidaria" refers to the power to sting—a feature of these invertebrates, which have special stinging cells in their bodies.

The basic structural unit of a typical cnidarian is a flower-like polyp. This polyp has no breathing mechanism, no blood and no excretory system. In short, it is a sac-like organism with an opening at one end surrounded by one or more circlets of tentacles. The vital functions of respiration, excretion and food distribution are achieved by simple diffusion.

The tentacles are hollow, connected to the gut, and are armed with cells called cnidoblasts, which

Above: The giant, bull kelp (*Durvillea potatorum*) at St Helens in Tasmania. This species is very common in cool temperate waters where it lives at the fringe of the intertidal zone. This algae is so thickly massed that it is often very difficult to get in and out of the water at some shore dive locations. *Neville Coleman*

house multiple numbers of stinging nematocysts.

Once the prey is subdued, the tentacles manoeuvre it to the mouth. It then passes to the stomach where it is digested and the useful products are absorbed. The refuse is regurgitated and ejected via the mouth.There are estimated to be 9000 species of Cnidarians living in the world's oceans.

As the life cycles of Cnidarians are often varied and complex, the following is only a general description. Within the phylum Cnidaria, there are two main body forms—free swimming medusae (sea jellies, also known as jellyfish) and stationary polyps (hydroids, corals and sea-anemones)—both radially symmetrical, with the mouth located at the center. One of the major differences between the free-swimming medusa and the stationary polyp is their orientation. Most medusa swim with the mouth and tentacles facing downwards, while the stationary polyp is attached to a substrate, with the mouth and tentacles facing upwards, outwards or downwards. One important feature of Cnidarians is their ability to form colonies.

Although all cnidarians possess nematocysts, only a few have the capacity to harm humans. Some hydroids, fire corals, sea jellies and sea anemones can inflict a painful sting, and a few—mostly the tropical box jellies—have caused the deaths of swimmers.

Below: Violet hydrocoral (*Distichopora violacea*) is often found beneath ledges along the Great Barrier Reef. *Michael Aw*

Sea ferns, hydrocorals, fire corals, Portuguese man-of-war

The order Hydroidea (sea ferns) is one of the few Cnidarian groups that is more diverse in temperate waters than in tropical seas. Although very common, hydroids are not familiar to most divers. The majority are low-profile clusters of fine, fern-like structures that tend to blend in, rather than stand out. Many species are very small, and may live on other organisms, like seaweeds, sponges and molluscs. However those in tropical waters, such as *Agliophena* and *Lytocarpus*, grow in large clumps and sting virulently. In contrast, the colonial hydrocorals and fire corals have massive, hard, calcified structures. The fire corals have powerful nematocysts which can inflict severe stings.

Sea jellies

Sea jellies are also Cnidarians. The first, temporary stage of their life cycle is a stationary polyp, however the medusa phase is dominant. The identification of the sedentary polyp phase is very difficult. The anatomy of the sea jelly is quite complex—transfer of food from the digestive areas to the tissues takes place via a system of canals, and balance organs assist in swimming. Pulses of contraction sweep over the muscles of the bell, causing the characteristic beats which enable the animal to propel itself through the water.

Box jellies

Box jellies are among the most venomous animals in the world. Although tropical in their distribution, the largest and most dangerous occur in the waters of the southern hemisphere. The common term, "box jelly", describes this group admirably. The body, a box-like, four-sided bell, has a tough, gelatinous composition. One or more tentacles are attached to each corner. The edges of the bell curve underneath, forming a "skirt". Sense organs—a balance mechanism and an eye—are situated on each of the four sides, usually on the central perpendicular axis

towards the base of the bell. Under the bell, hanging from the top, is the stomach and tubular mouth.

Box jellies are made up of two families: members of Corybdeidae have four single tentacles and are mild stingers, while the Chirodropidae have four clusters of tentacles. Some species are deadly to humans.

Black corals

Black corals are commonly found in both shallow and deep tropical waters. In temperate seas, they are not commonly seen by divers in usual dive locations, as they grow beyond the recreational diver depth recommended (40 m).

At least 15 species of black coral are found in Australian waters, and *Antipathes* is the dominant genus. In temperate seas there appear to be fewer species. Living black corals are covered by a fleshy skin which may be white, pink, yellow, brown, orange or green. The polyps have six tentacles that do not retract into the skeleton, although they may shrink when disturbed.

The inner skeleton is a black, extremely tough and tremendously pliable protein secreted by the polyps. Most black coral forests have been decimated due to their reputation as a "precious" coral, which at one time brought high prices in the semi-precious jewellery markets.

In Australia, huge quantities were harvested from the shallow waters of the Great Barrier Reef. When the skeletons of the shallow water species cracked during drying, entrepreneurs filled up the cracks with silver solder and sold the polished results as silver-inlaid black coral.

Tube anemones

At the time of writing, only one genus *Cerianthus* has been found in the Indo-Pacific region, occurring in both tropical and temperate waters. However, new species have recently been described from various regions.

These anemones are inhabitants of soft sediments from low tide level down to 50 m. Each animal constructs a protective, soft mucus tube in the mud, in which the anemone lives. Tube anemones have two rings of tentacles around the mouth, with the outer ring tentacles being much longer than the inner tentacles.

Although they are able to stun small fish, most of their food is plankton caught at night, or on dark overcast days, when the tentacles are expanded. Tentacle colors may be yellow, pink, brown, white, mauve or grey.

Soft corals

Both the soft corals and gorgonians (sea fans) are known as octocorals, they belong to the class Alcyonaria, which are distinguished from other members of the Cnidarian phylum by their eight-tentacled polyps and fringed tentacles.

With the exception of the genera *Tubipora* and *Heliopora* most soft corals have no true skeleton. Their soft bodies are flexible and various species may be soft and squelchy (*Xenia*) or firm and leathery (*Sarcophyton*). Others (*Dendronephthya*) hold themselves erect by pumping water into their interconnecting body cavities. No matter how soft or pliable, all species contain minute spicules of silica or calcium which in many cases help to strengthen the body walls. Scientists use these spicules to describe species of alcyonarians, and in the genus *Dendro-*

Above: Found in relatively shallow waters in the tropics (around 10 to 25 m) the sea fan genus *Melithaea* grows into smaller colonies than many of its relations living in deeper waters.
Neville Coleman

nephthya some types of these spicules can be clearly seen in the body walls.

Soft corals have nematocysts in their polyps which sting and capture planktonic food, however these do not affect humans. Some of the spiky soft corals *(Dendronephthya)* have protective spikes arranged around their polyp clumps, which act in a similar fashion to the thorns on rose bushes, and help protect the soft coral from browsing nudibranchs or cowry shells.

Soft corals also have extremely potent chemical defences—some even produce chemicals which attack and kill other organisms inhabiting nearby territory. Many of these substances are being investigated by biochemists for properties which will inhibit cancer and other diseases. Those soft corals which live in shallow, sunlit waters have symbiotic zooxanthellae living in their tissues.

Gorgonians (sea fans)

On deeper parts of the reefs, the polyps of gorgonians and sea whips can be seen out feeding during the day, especially in areas of strong current or on the incoming tide.

Most gorgonians have strong wire-like central skeletons and are quite flexible, although a few are very brittle. More species of gorgonians (and soft corals) are found in tropical waters than in temperate, although in both areas they exhibit extremely brilliant colors and intricate growth patterns. The polyps secrete a special skeletal protein called gorgonin, which is embedded with the spicules and hard to the touch. Many species build their fans at right angles to the prevailing currents, and in deep waters or in quiet lagoons have been known to reach a height of 3 m and a width of 4 m. On some deep-water Coral Sea reefs, gardens of gorgonian fans run like giant, netted fences along the tops of the ridges for as far as the eye can see, at depths from 50 m downward.

Sea pens

Sea pens are quill-shaped, octocoral colonies which live in soft-bottomed areas of sand or mud, where there are moderate currents (channel bottoms). One specialised polyp supports the body, which is able to expand or retract into the sand, and most have an internal skeleton. Common in some areas of tropical and temperate waters, sea pens appear to be sensitive to light, and divers tend to see more feeding at night. Some species give off bioluminescent light when disturbed or touched.

Stony corals

Although stony corals do exist in temperate waters, it is in tropical seas that the true reef-building corals flourish. Tropical reefs carry about 400 species. While temperate seas support about 20 species, some form large plate-like formations as deep as 65 m in very clear water.

Some genera, such as the staghorn corals *(Acropora),* may have as many as 100 different species, however some of these may be the same species exhibiting a different growth form in response to a difference in micro habitats. Extensive underwater photography of corals and specimen collection (pioneered by the author) has led to a visual identification system of corals. Scientists have expanded this concept and are able to identify the majority of corals (at least to genera) by observing photographs. However, many species remain difficult to identify.

Australia's tropical coral reefs are dominated by the many growth forms of the staghorn corals *(Acropora),* while in the shallow waters, warty corals *(Pocillopora)* and needle corals *(Seriatopora)* are very common.

Large, often circular, flat-topped coral colonies may be seen at low tide in the shallow water of lagoons and reef flats. These modified *Porites* colonies, known as micro-atolls, are dead skeleton surrounded by living coral on the outside, formed as the colonies grow vertically to the level of low tide and die, but continue their horizontal growth. Thus the height of the atoll corresponds to the low tide level in the lagoon. In general, the more robust corals live on the exposed situations, and are smaller and stouter than their counterparts living in deeper water or sheltered lagoons.

The polyps of stony corals have six, or multiples of six, unfringed tentacles. The majority of tropical hard corals are colonial, building their massive structures by budding or splitting (asexual reproduction). A few are solitary, some of the largest being the mushroom corals *(Fungia* and *Heliofugia)*. *Heliofungia actiniformis* extends its feeding tentacles during the day, and looks very much like an anemone.

Temperate waters have beautiful little solitary corals, such as the bright green *Scolymia,* and the *Balanophyllia,* found in deeper water, with florescent symbiotic bacteria living around its mouth.

The best way to see corals is during night dives, as the polyps all have their tentacles extended, capturing plankton. One of the most brilliantly-colored coral polyps is Faulkner's coral *(Tubastrea),* which grows on the roofs and sides of caves and under ledges, in small fist-sized clumps. Sometimes these can be seen feeding during the day, when the sky is cloudy or on the incoming tide.

Anemones

Well represented in Australia's tropical and temperate seas, anemones vary in size from the giant tropical forms *(Heteractis* and *Stichodactyla)* which may grow to one meter across, down to the small jewel anemones *(Corynactis)* which carpet many southern areas in their brilliant colors.

Many tropical anemones contain microscopic zooxanthellae algae in their tissues, which give the anemones a green or brown coloration. Some have extraordinary shapes and patterns, and a few tropical species *(Dofleina* and *Actinodendron)* have virulent stings, caus-

ing intense pain and tissue damage on contact with bare skin.

Those tropical species which provide a safe haven for commensal clown and anemonefish are well known, however the temperate species have not been as well described, and a number remain as new discoveries without names. In addition to the well-publicized partnerships between anemones and anemonefish, a number of species of commensal shrimps, porcellanid crabs, portunid crabs and even brittle stars make their homes in sea anemones.

Zoanthids

Zoanthids are best described as communal coral-like animals, without skeletons, which feed on plankton. On tropical reefs, colonies are often seen at low tide in the shallow water of the reef flat, covering extensive areas in sheets of tightly-packed individuals, usually with polyps retracted during the day. The best known is the intertidal species *Palythoa*. In temperate seas, strange sausage-like specimens of the genus *Zoanthus* grow in clumps on reefs, in depths down to 60 m. The most colorful zoanthids are

Above: A cool temperate species occurring right around southern Australia, the yellow zoanthid *(Parazoanthus* sp.) is usually found on sponges and is without doubt the most attractive of its kind. *Neville Coleman*

those from the genus *Parazoanthus*, which live on and in sponges, mostly in temperate seas, forming intricate patterns on the sponge surface. In the deeper waters of southern New South Wales, Victoria and Tasmania, the bright yellow *Parazoanthus* sp. is one of the most prominent cnidarians. With the exception of the more colorful species, zoanthids often go unnoticed by divers.

Corallimorphs

Looking for all the world like small beaded carpets of flat anemones, corallimorphs occur in a host of brilliant pinks, blues and greens. They live mostly in large colonies, with individual polyps up to 50 to 70 mm across; however the giant balloon corallimorph (*Amplexidiscus* sp) may grow to 30 cm across. Most species are tropical.

Flatworms

Few divers recognize flatworms, or if they do, generally only notice the more brightly-colored species. Often flatworms are confused with nudibranchs (shell-less molluscs). Although many tropical species may be found in the open during the day, temperate species are less obvious, living beneath rocks and stones, or hidden among the folds of an invertebrate host, as does the flatworm (*Pseudoceros colemani*),

which lives on the ascidian *Sycozoa*. The greater number of marine flatworms are grouped in the Order Polycladida. The term "flatworm" includes the turbellarians (free-living flatworms), parasitic flukes and tapeworms, but is used here to refer to the turbellarians only.

In most cases, a close inspection will reveal the difference between a flatworm and a nudibranch. Flatworms have no external gills (unlike most nudibranchs), but some have marginal tentacles at the "head" end which may contain simple eyes, and other species may have dorsal tentacles issuing from the back near the "head".

Flatworms are hermaphrodites, having complex male and female sex organs. Mating and cross-fertilization occur between two individuals. Eggs are laid on the substrate in spirals, similar to an open-ended circle.

Most marine species are predatory and carnivorous. In the author's experience, many southern temperate and tropical flatworms feed on colonial ascidians. Only a few species show any specific body color patterns that relate to the markings of the species on which they feed.

Segmented Worms

The phylum Annelida, the segmented worms, is one of the major groupings of the animal kingdom.

Below: An inhabitant of coral reefs, the flatworm (*Pseudocerous ferrugineus*) has a very distinctive and easily recognized color pattern. This species is found over a wide area of the Indo-Pacific. *Michael Aw*

There are more than 12,000 species and 70 families worldwide, although comparatively little is known of the natural history or distribution of this diverse phylum. There are two groups of segmented worms: the active, mobile, foraging Polychaetes, and the Terebellids—the sedentary, burrowing (or tube-dwelling), suspension or detrital feeders.

Most of the Polychaete worms commonly seen underwater are the larger, roving bristle worms, scale worms and "sea mice", or the stationary deposit-feeding worms, the fan worms and tube worms whose brightly-colored feeding tentacles often reveal their presence. Because the spiral "fan" is the only part of the worm's body that is usually seen, many snorkelers and divers fail to realise that the mystery object is part of a worm.

Terebellid worms inhabit sand or mud tubes on the bottom or beneath rocks, and radiate their many retractable tentacles over the substrate to collect food. Serpulid worms build a hard, calcareous tube, either alone or within a colony. Serpulids are filter feeders; most have a small, stalked operculum that acts as a trapdoor to seal the tube after the worm retracts.

Reproductive techniques of Polychaete worms are as diverse as their lifestyles, and vary from shedding eggs and sperm into the sea, to incubating their young in brood chambers. Some carry their developing young on their backs, and others carry their eggs only until they hatch, releasing the larvae into the sea where they develop as members of the zooplankton until they are ready to settle and metamorphose.

Sea Mosses

The Bryozoa are a fascinating group largely unknown to the layman. Although a microscope is necessary to make out details of the individuals (known as zooids), their colonies are easily seen by eye. About 3500 species exist, mostly marine, and many more are known

from the fossil record.

All bryozoans and polyzoans are colonial, and grow in an amazing array of shapes and configurations—from small, circular, encrusting formations, to intricate lace-like structures and plant-like tufts, to large clumps of coral-like colonies several meters in circumference.

Some species are known to produce larvae by sexual reproduction, however most are hermaphrodites. Some release eggs into the sea, and others pass the fertilized eggs into brood chambers.

Most bryozoan colonies, or "sea mosses", grow on and cover non-living surfaces or organisms, just as moss sometimes grows on wood or rocks.

Crustaceans

Crustaceans are by far the most numerous animals in the sea. Almost 40,000 species are found throughout the world, some of these species occurring in fresh water. Although they vary in superficial structure and habitat, most have a basic design: jointed legs and a jointed, armor-like outer casing (exoskeleton) that protects their soft parts. The segmented body is bilaterally symmetrical, with a head, nervous system and sensory organs that are usually well-developed. Many crustaceans have remarkably acute eyesight.

Above: Occurring in both muddy coastal waters and the clean clear depths of the barrier reefs throughout tropical Australia, the magnificent tube worm (*Protula magnifica*) may have a tube up to 300 mm in length. *Neville Coleman*

Divers often see the larger crustaceans such as rock lobsters, shovelnose lobsters, blue swimmer crabs and prawns, however the smaller crustaceans are less familiar. Color photography of living or recently dead specimens can aid identification of many species. It is usually possible to identify crustaceans in the field, although colors and patterns vary, external features on juveniles and adults may differ, and sexual dimorphism often occurs.

Crustaceans feed on a variety of organisms: bacteria, plankton, sediment, suspended particles, algae, molluscs, fish, worms, and other crustaceans and carrion.

The sexes are generally separate. After mating, the female lays eggs that are carried beneath the abdominal flaps (of crabs), on the modified swimmerets (of rock lobsters and shrimps) and on the chests (of mantis shrimps). On hatching, the larvae join the plankton, and pass through a series of free-swimming stages, before settling to the bottom where they metamorphose into juveniles.

Crustaceans are found in most marine habitats. They live in burrows in sand and mud, among rubble and on reefs—in caves and under ledges and rocks. Some bury by day and emerge at night. Some carry shells over their heads and others live in them. Some are permanent swimmers in the vast ocean spaces. There are species only millimeters in size, carried about in the water column as plankton, and giants weighing 15 kg that crawl about on rocky reefs 100 m below the surface.

Barnacles

Very few divers recognize barnacles as crustaceans. After all, who would imagine that a swift-footed rock crab would be related to a small volcano-shaped bunch of shelly plates glued to a rock? Almost all species of barnacles are hermaphrodites, although cross fertilization usually occurs. The eggs hatch into planktonic larvae, which—unlike their parents—are immediately recognizable as crustaceans.

Rock lobsters

During the day divers may see some of the larger, more obvious species of crustaceans such as crayfish, rock lobsters, slipper lobsters and crabs beneath ledges; however most of the small and more colorful species of reef shrimp and crab venture forth at night. Nocturnal activity is a survival technique, for just as humans enjoy eating prawns, rock lobsters and crabs, so do predatory fish and birds, but most of these larger carnivores are only active during the day.

Tropical waters support far more species than temperate waters, but the colder waters produce the largest species. The giant deep water Tasmanian crabs can measure over a meter across the nippers, and weigh over 15 kg. Giant packhorse rock lobsters (genus *Jasus*) also grow to mammoth proportions (up to 10 kg).

Most of the more common species of larger tropical rock lobsters belong to the genus *Panulirus*. These spectacular crustaceans venture out from under their ledges and caves at night to feed and seek mates. They have long, spined antennae, and powerful tail and abdominal muscles, which can propel them backward at a fair speed.

Below: Always found in relation to a cnidarian host, the commensal shrimp (*Periclimenes venustus*) is a tropical species which is seen here on the soft coral *Sarcophytum* sp. Neville Coleman

Shrimps

More shrimp species are found on tropical reefs than on reefs in temperate regions. During the day, commensal shrimps can be observed easily on their hosts—usually sea anemones, gorgonian sea fans, corals or black corals. At cleaning stations, cleaner shrimps remove parasites from fish which, under other circumstances, would eat them. At night some of the most beautiful shrimps (especially *Saron*) emerge onto the reef to feed.

The imperial shrimps *(Periclimenes ornatus)* live on nudibranchs, sea cucumbers and sea stars. Some in the genus *Rhynchocinetes* are found in both tropical and temperate waters; all have extremely attractive patterns and can be identified by their coloration.

Generally found in pairs, pistol shrimps belong to the genus *Alpheus* and usually live in burrows. Some pistol shrimps are found in commensal relationships with small fish known as gobies. These shrimps are known as "pistol" shrimps because some species have the ability to produce loud clicks with their large nipper.

Crabs

Most crabs are nocturnal, although in some areas along the tropical and temperate coast, rock crabs can be seen foraging during the day at the low tide level. However many are taken by sea birds.

Hermit crabs

The hermit crab has no hard, exterior carapace covering its abdomen, and uses uninhabited mollusc shells as protection from predators. The largest, *Dardanus*, is bright red and lives on tropical reefs. Some crabs place living anemones on their shells as camouflage and protection. Two species of land hermit crabs (*Coenobita*) are found on the coast and offshore islands of northern Australia.

Decorator crabs

These spider crabs camouflage themselves by fixing sea weed, sponges, soft corals and sea squirts to their backs and legs, to fool predators. However the Pacific gull from southern shores—which walks along on reefs at low tide looking for crabs—is not deceived no matter how much marine life the crabs wear. Large populations of giant spider crabs occur in Victorian and Tasmanian waters where they congregate to mate.

Poisonous reef crabs

Some tropical reef crabs with black tips on their nippers are poisonous (*Etisus* and *Lophozozymus*). These crabs are very colorful and make excellent photo subjects—however they must not be eaten.

Above: Living in temperate seas at depths below 50 m, the giant crab (*Pseudocarcinus gigas*) grows to 400 mm across the carapace and may weigh up to 15 kg. *Neville Coleman*

Molluscs

A major component of the world's marine invertebrate fauna are molluscs. At least 112,000 species are known, and no doubt many more remain to be discovered. The word mollusc means "soft-bodied", and most members of this phylum are protected by a hard calcareous shell, with the exception of the cephlapods (octopi, squid and cuttlefish) and nudibranchs.

The most ancient group of molluscs that divers are likely to see are chitons, which belong to the class Polyplacophora. Chitons are sometimes called "coat-of-mail" shells because of their eight-valved shells which are set in a tough, leathery girdle similar to armor worn by ancient soldiers. Chitons can roll up into a ball when disturbed, a defence mechanism somewhat similar to that displayed by the South American armadillo. Chitons are all marine, and most species are intertidal. Subtidal forms live beneath rocks and dead coral, are slow moving, and able to clamp their bodies to the substrate so tightly that it is difficult to remove them without damaging the animal.

Gastropoda is the largest class of molluscs, and includes those animals which have a single shell for at least part of their life cycles. The gastropods include cone shells, cowries, murex shells, volutes, tritons, nudibranchs and sea hares—to name a few familiar individuals.

Bivalves belong to the class Pelecypoda, and all have two-part shells. The second-largest mollusc in the world—the giant clam *(Tridacna gigas)*—belongs to this class, which contains other well-known edible bivalves such as oysters, mussels, cockles, scallops and pearl oysters.

A lesser-known group of bivalves are the tusk shells (Scaphopoda), which live beneath the sand and mud. The shells of this class are all shaped like an elephant's tusk, hence their common name. The most common genus is called *Dentalium*.

By far the most interesting and highly-intelligent molluscs belong to the class Cephalopoda (meaning head-footed). Meeting a giant cuttlefish is one of the highlights of any diver's experience. These playful and inquisitive molluscs are well known for delightful and fascinating displays of alterations to their color and shape.

Gastropods

Cowries: Well over 100 species of cowrie are found in the seas surrounding Australia. Some of the most extravagant and rare species are found here, ranging in size from the tropical *Cypraea fimbriata*, only 12 mm long, to the giant tiger cowrie *Cypraea tigris*, which sometimes grows to 120 mm in northern New South Wales and southern Queensland.

Although tropical waters have both the largest and the smallest cowries in Australia, the southern temperate waters contain the endemic, rare species. Most cowries belong to the genus *Cypraea*. Rossell's cowrie *(Cypraea rosselli)* and the margin cowrie *(Cypraea marginata)* are highly prized and many deep-water species sell for thousands of dollars. Most cowries browse on sedentary animals such as soft corals, sponges and bryozoans, or on encrusting algae, which is scraped from surfaces with a sharp-toothed, file-like device called the radula.

The shell of the cowrie is shiny and smooth, protected by its living mantle, which usually covers the entire shell and does not allow foreign organisms to settle on it.

Cone shells: The shells of these cone-shaped molluscs display an amazing array of intricate patterns. These beautiful animals can be found from low tide level, to depths of hundreds of meters, and are mostly nocturnal. During daylight hours they remain hidden beneath dead coral boulders, or lie buried in sandy pockets on the reef. The textile cone *(Conus textile)*,

AUSTRALIAN WATERS
Home to rare and unusual species

MOST ANIMAL PHYLA FOUND ON SPECIFIC TROPICAL coral reefs are represented on tropical coral reefs all over the world. Although families, genera and species may differ in specific groups, for the most part the groups are very similar.

Tropical species are thought to have originated in the seas around Indonesia, and spread from there across the oceans. The larvae of many tropical marine animals are transported from reef to reef by ocean currents, a mechanism known as planktonic lar-

In southern temperate waters, many of Australia's unique marine species have evolved in relative isolation. A number of new species have been discovered around Lord Howe Island over the last few years—the Lord Howe Island coralfish, the Lord Howe hydrocoral, the *Coleman's Phyllodesmium* nudibranch, the Ballina angelfish (of which only three specimens have ever been seen alive), the splendid hawkfish, and the half-banded angelfish, just to name a few.

Endemic to subtropical and tropical seas off Western Australia, Rossel's cowrie (*Cypraea rosselli)* is still considered a rare find. It lives and feeds on sponges in depths from 20 to 100 m. *Neville Coleman*

val dispersal. The eggs are laid directly into the water and externally fertilized, then the eggs, and later the hatched larvae, drift along with the current until the juvenile is ready to swim down from the surface and settle on a new reef.

Thus most tropical species are widely distributed, and few are rare, or endemic to one reef or geographical location. Of course exceptions are found, such as a species of cowrie which lives completely on hosts exclusive to a particular area of coastal fringing reef.

Also, the reproductive cycles of many species found in temperate waters includes an element of parental care. The eggs are fertilized internally or externally, and after being laid by the female, are tended until they hatch. In many cases the hatchlings are miniature replicas of their parents. Eggs destined to be tended are generally fewer and larger than those produced to spend weeks drifting with the ocean currents.

Many marine species are unique to Australia—the leafy and weedy sea dragons, a range of sea horses, southern cowries, volutes, murex, sea stars, corals and hundreds of fish species, crustaceans, nudibranchs and sponges.

the cat cone *(Conus cattus)*, the geography cone *(Conus geographus)* and the striated cone *(Conus striatus)* are among the 15 species of cones known to be dangerous to humans. Divers sometimes pick up these pretty shells, and put them in their wet suits or hold them in their hands. Sensing danger, the animal extends its proboscis, and shoots out a little venomous dart (normally used to paralyze prey) into whatever is holding it. The dart, which is a modified tooth, contains a neuro-toxin which can paralyze, or even kill humans. The species which feed on fish and other molluscs are the most dangerous; however, a sting from those species that feed on worms may also have adverse effects, so it is best not to handle them.

Trochus shells:Belonging to the Trochidae family, all trochus (also known as top shells) are spiral-shaped, with a flat, round base diminishing to a pointed apex. Most species are large (about 8 cm in height) and fairly smooth, although some are flatter and have knobs or spikes. The trochus shell *(Tectus niloticus)* is the largest member of the family, growing to 150 mm. Usually collected by Aboriginal and Torres Strait islanders, the trochus is still used in the shell ornament and pearl button industry to some extent, and its meat is cooked and smoked for export.

Triton and frog shells: The giant triton *(Charonia tritonis)* is not a common shell in tropical waters, although it occurs from Lady Elliot Island on the Great Barrier Reef, north and around to the Houtman Abroholos off Geraldton in Western Australia. The giant triton grows to 460 mm and feeds on sea stars and sea urchins, including the crown-of-thorns starfish, especially when they are in plague proportions.

Heavy collecting by early trochus, pearl shell and sea cucumber divers may have led to the reduced population of this animal. Although the triton is fully protected in Australian waters, these animals are still collected from reefs around third world countries, and the shells imported and sold in Australian tourist shops.

Triton and frog shells belong to the family Ranellidae. Most frog shells are fairly small (up to 75 mm), but some may reach over 200 mm, such as the red-mouthed frog shell *(Bursa lissostoma)*.

Nudibranchs: Nudibranch means "naked gill", a reference to the extended gill "plumes" generally seen on the backs of most nudibranchs. Newly-hatched, planktonic nudibranchs have a shell, which is discarded when they settle to the reef to metamorphose into the shell-less adult. From then on they survive by camouflage or by using as a defense the distasteful chemicals in their food supply, the stinging cells in hydroids, or in some cases manufacturing their own chemicals.

Adults may range in size from only a few millimeters, to the giant Spanish dancer *(Hexabranchus sanguineus)*, which can grow to over 300 mm.

There are thought to be about 1000 species of nudibranch-like molluscs in Australian waters, many awaiting scientific description and others yet to be discovered. Although there are more species of nudibranchs in tropical waters, large numbers live in temperate seas. Even southern Tasmania has

Below: The red-lined flabellina nudibranch *(Flabellina rubrolineata)* grows to 42 mm and can be seen in depths of 2–32 m from the Great Barrier Reef south to Sydney, New South Wales. *Neville Coleman*

extremely colorful and interesting nudibranchs.

Most nudibranchs are carnivorous, feeding on sponges, soft corals, corals, hydroids, gorgonian sea fans, sea whips, sea pens and anemones. Some species have been known to eat other nudibranchs, bubble shells, sea hares, amphipods and bryozoans—even nudibranch eggs.

Some nudibranchs blend into their prey species so well that they are almost impossible to detect. Others are so brightly patterned that they would be difficult to miss. The bright colors are thought to act as a warning to predators that they are poisonous, and should be left alone. Species that feed on hydroids are able to store ingested undischarged nematocysts in the tips of the cerata on their backs, using these effective weapons as a defence. *Pteraeolidia* can sting a human.

Bivalves

Oysters: Several species of oyster are found along Australia's coastline, including the cock's comb oyster (*Lopha cristagalli*)—usually covered with sponges; winged pearl oysters—attached to gorgonians and black corals; transparent window pane oysters—living on mud; and of course the many edible species found clinging to the rocks along the shores.

Perhaps the most well known are the pearl shell oysters (*Pinctada maxima* and *P. margaritifera*), which have been farmed to produce millions of dollars worth of giant pearls. The giant thorny oysters (*Spondylus*), often seen on drop-offs or wrecks, are usually covered in encrusting growths. When open and feeding they exhibit extremely colorful mantle edges, but often close before a diver can move close enough to take a photograph.

Giant clams: By far the largest bivalve is the giant reef clam (*Tridacna gigas*). This mammoth mollusc grows to over 1 m in length and may weigh several hun-

dred kilograms. From 1970–1980, reef populations of these clams were greatly reduced by Taiwanese fishermen, who fished illegally in and around the Great Barrier Reef Marine Park.

Scientists set up a successful giant clam farm at Orpheus Island Research Station off Townsville, rearing hundreds of baby giant clams, which were then transported to other parts of the Great Barrier Reef.

Millions of zooxanthellae (microscopic algae) live in the mantles of giant clams, which are exposed to sunlight in the shallow waters of the reef. The clams provide a hospitable environment for the zooxanthellae, and receive nutrients in return. Clams with zooxanthellae in their tissues seem to grow faster. The algae may assist in building the clam's massive shells in much the same way the zooxanthellae contribute to the construction of hard coral skeletons.

Top: The southern gorgonian tritonia, (*Tritonia* sp.) occurs in temperate seas off Victoria across into South Australia. It spends its entire adult life on its host sea fan. *Neville Coleman*

Above: Giant fluted clams (*Tridacna squamosa*) can be easily recognized by the patterns on their mantles, wide lips and frilled shells. Similar to all species in this genus, this clam occurs in tropical seas, usually on coral reefs. *Neville Coleman*

Other clams of the genus *Tridacana* are common on inshore and offshore reefs around tropical Australia. Several species such as *T. maxima, T. squamosa* and *T. derasa* may grow to 400 mm, while the burrowing clam, *T. crocea,* grows to just 140 mm.

Most bivalves are filter feeders, pumping water through their bodies by way of a large tube known as a "siphon". Oxygen and plankton are extracted as water passes over their gills. Many bivalves are immobile, although sand-dwelling bivalves such as cockles, or pippies, can extend part of their foot from their shells and drag or push themselves along, and dig into the sand for protection.

Cephalopods

The molluscs within this class include the nautilus, squid, octopus and cuttlefish. Although similarly "head footed" in shape, all show diverse adaptations to their different ways of life.

Pearly nautilus: The pearly or chambered nautilus (*Nautilus pompilius*) is the oldest form of cephalopod. It has a distinctive spiral-shaped shell which has many chambers connected by a tube, which enables the nautilus to alter buoyancy during its nocturnal vertical migrations, from deeper waters (below 200 m) up into the shallower depths to scavenge for food. Their tentacles are sticky, but do not have suckers like all other cephalopods, and their eyes are mere patches of pigment with no lens or pupil present. They show no reaction to a flash exposure. Some live-aboard dive boats put down traps to catch pearly nautilus, so that divers can take photographs, or observe them at close quarters.

Squid: The largest molluscs in the world are the giant deep-water squid (*Architecteuthis*), which grow to over 20 m. Several have washed up on Australian shores and are thought to have been injured by sperm whales which prey on them. The first known specimens were found in the stomachs of sperm whales, during the whaling era.

Most reef squid exist in both tropical and temperate waters, and are sometimes seen over sea grass meadows and in lagoons. They are active and most approachable at night, when most of the best photographs are taken. A squid remains stationary by rippling its mantle edges, and can move in any direction through the water by expelling a jet of water from its siphon tube. Squid undergo instant color changes through muscle-controlled chromatophore expansion

Below: The Thorny oyster *(Spondylus varius)* remains well camouflaged until the two halves of its shell open. Its rough shell surface makes a secure base for other animals. *Michael Aw*

and contraction. Their internal "shells" are made up of a very thin plastic-like strip, which runs along the back beneath the skin and is non-calcareous. Squid feed mostly on small schooling fish and shrimps, and humans catch large numbers for food (calamari).

Cuttlefish: Australian temperate seas contain the world's largest cuttlefish (*Sepia apama*), which sometimes grows in excess of 1 m in length. Cuttlefish resemble squid in shape and mode of locomotion, but cuttlefish are generally wider and larger. Although usually solitary, individuals gather together to mate. Most cuttlefish live around reefs where they hunt small fish and shrimps for food. They have excellent sight—their eyes have a structure similar to the human eye, and they are quite intelligent by invertebrate standards. They capture food by shooting out two long hunting tentacles, which are usually rolled up in pouches in their cheeks. The tentacles have pads of suckers on them (similar to squid tentacles), and once a prey has been "hit", the cuttlefish jets forward and enmeshes the animal in its other suckered arms. The prey is then held with a horny beak (shaped somewhat like a parrot's beak), while its many-toothed radula (a file-like apparatus

inside the mouth), rasps it into digestible pieces.

Cuttlefish bones—the light, shell-like, porous bone which aids the animal's buoyancy and balance—wash up on many beaches and are just one of the many mysterious objects beachcombers find. Cuttlefish bones have long been used by aviarists as a dietary aid for caged birds, and to give them—especially parrots—something to chew on, to keep their beaks from growing too long.

The name of the genus *Sepia* is derived from the "ink", released by the squid, cuttlefish and octopus, which acts as a distraction, to hide their retreat when threatened. Many historical manuscripts were written with feather quills and cephalopod ink.

Paper nautilus: Usually found in temperate waters, the paper nautilus (*Argonauta nodosa*) lives out its life in the open ocean, and only comes close to land when forced inshore by storms, or when it purposely swims into shallow waters after mating.

From the time she is born, the female argonaut builds a thin shelly cradle in which to live. After mating with an extremely small male argonaut, she then lays her eggs inside the paper nautilus shell (egg case)

Above: The egg cases of the paper nautilus (*Argonauta nodosa*) are infrequently washed ashore on beaches and into shallow bays along the coasts of Victoria and Tasmania. The female argonaut begins construction of the egg case from birth and spends all her living days in it, and the end result is a protective device for her eggs. Once they are laid and in the process of hatching, the female dies.
Neville Coleman

sion. Although some may be seen out on the reef during the day, most stay safe in their caves and hunt at night, or just before dawn.

The females of many species of octopus position themselves over the eggs to protect them. Once the young hatch, the mother dies.

Echinoderms

The term echinoderm means "spiny skin" and in this phylum there are five major classes: sea stars (also known as starfish), brittle stars, feather stars, sea urchins and sea cucumbers. Many species are brightly-colored and easily recognized. Some have sharp spines with venomous tips (sea urchins and crown-of-thorns starfish) and are best not handled. In general, their adult body shape consists of five similar sections, symmetrically arranged around a central process. There are about 600 species in Australian seas.

Sea stars (starfish)

From the intertidal zone down to and below 100 m, from coral reef to muddy bottom, sea stars inhabit almost every major habitat. While most species have a typical five-arm design, several have up to 18 arms (crown-of-thorns starfish). Even usually five-sided sea stars can be found having three to six arms on occasion.

There are two specialized groups of sea stars, those that inhabit reef, and those that live in sand or mud. While all echinoderms have tube feet modified to their way of life, the visible differences between these two groups are obvious. Reef-dwelling sea stars *(Coscinasterias)* have tube feet tipped with suckers, which enable them to hold onto reefs during rough seas, traverse any terrain (even upside down) at a fair pace, and catch and hang onto prey. In the case of bivalve prey, the suckered arms are used to open the shells enough to allow the sea star's extruded stomach to dissolve and digest the animal inside.

Above: At least three and perhaps four species of blue-ringed octopus inhabit the waters, both tropical and temperate, surrounding Australia. All blue-ringed octopus (*Hapalochlaena* sp.) are potentially deadly to any human bitten. These little molluscs are not aggressive, but when disturbed produce warning signals in the form of bright blue pulsating rings. They should not be handled.
Neville Coleman

and dies. Sometimes the egg cases wash up on the beach before the young hatch, and these are eaten by sea gulls and other predatory birds. Divers often find these beautifully sculptured empty "shells" on the bottom and collect them as souvenirs.

Octopi: The most dangerous octopi in Australian seas are the four species of blue-ringed octopus (*Hapalochlaena*), which unfortunately have caused the deaths of several people. The little octopus is not aggressive—the bites have been made when the creature has been picked up and admired. The octopus breaks through the victim's skin with its small beak, releasing a highly toxic venom (tetratoxin) into the body, which relaxes the victim's muscles and causes breathing to cease. There may be a number of octopi which have venomous salivary glands, so it is best not to handle any.

Having taste buds in the tips of their eight, long, suckered arms, octopi are excellent hunters—feeding on fish, crabs, prawns, crays, cowries, volutes, scallops and mussels. The octopus is a master of camouflage, able to alter the color and the shape of its skin. It is highly intelligent (for an invertebrate), being able to learn, make decisions, and even outwit humans on occa-

Sand-dwelling sea stars *(Astropecten)* have tube feet that are pointed and especially modified for digging. When disturbed or threatened on the surface of the sand, these sea stars can virtually melt into the sand right before a diver's eyes. This sand-dwelling sea star is able to swallow small prey whole, and may have as many as five bivalves in its mouth at once. Sea stars as a group are carnivorous (sometimes cannibalistic), herbivorous and omnivorous.

Some sea stars have long arms *(Leiaster),* and others quite short *(Tosia),* while the pincushion sea star *(Culcita)*—when fully inflated—may appear to have no arms at all.

Some tropical and temperate forms utilize planktonic larval dispersal, releasing their reproductive products into the sea. A few species from southern seas actually lay eggs and brood their young *(Tosia).* The luzon sea star *(Echinaster luzonicus)* reproduces asexually by purposely breaking off an arm, which then grows more arms to become another starfish. This behavior is common among a number of sea star species.

Many tropical varieties have small commensal shrimps *(Pericli-menes)* living on them, usually on the underside.

The most infamous sea star is undoubtedly the crown-of-thorns. Because of its dietary preference for hard corals, and population explosions on the Great Barrier Reef since the early 1960s, there has been a great deal of research into its life cycle, the recovery rates of affected reefs, and its predators (giant tritons and pufferfish).

Most of the reefs devastated by earlier crown-of-thorns outbreaks have recovered to a point where the 2 meter-high star pickets driven in as markers at some areas of infestation have all been overgrown by live corals. However, the possibility of other outbreaks is always present and scientists continue to monitor settlement and numbers of juveniles on certain reefs on a regular basis.

The crown-of-thorns starfish usually feeds during the night, and rests beneath the coral during the day. When in plague proportions, however, they feed constantly.

This sea star is best avoided, as its spines are highly venomous and any puncture causes extreme pain. Badly spined areas may ulcerate, heal slowly, and affect the body's immune system over long periods.

Below: Coleman's sea star *(Echinaster colemani)* inhabits the rocky reefs off the coast of New South Wales and is also fairly common around Norfolk Island in the South Pacific.
Neville Coleman

Brittle stars

Most animals in this class (brittle stars, serpent or snake stars, and basket stars) look like skinny-armed versions of sea stars. Locomotion is achieved by movements of their flexible arms, rather than their tube feet. The arms of brittle stars are generally edged with rows of spines, which are sometimes long and sharp. Most brittle stars cast off an arm when threatened, whereby the broken piece continues to writhe around, catching the eye of the potential predator while the brittle star scurries away to safety.

Serpent stars are more robust than brittle stars and their arms lack extensive spines. Although these animals have no eyes, they can sense shadow and once exposed always take off for the closest, darkest cover. Serpent stars are sometimes seen on gorgonians and on black corals where they help to keep the black coral "trees" clean, feeding on the rich mucus produced by the black coral.

The basket stars are the largest brittle stars by far. Although these can be found in all Australian waters, the largest live in the tropics. Totally nocturnal, these extraordinary creatures emerge from their hiding places sometime after dusk, move up onto the top of the reef, and spread out their meshed arms to catch plankton, looking for all the world like giant woven baskets.

Feather stars (crinoids)

Feather stars, with their many colorful, feathery arms, are found perched wherever plankton-rich currents occur. Most are free and mobile as adults, but the developing larvae pass through a stalked phase—part of the lifecycle which remains from a time when all species were attached to a stalk, as are the sea lilies. Some species of sea lilies still exist in deep water.

Feather stars feed by trapping plankton and suspended detritus with a thin "net" of tentacular tube feet. Food is incorporated into a mucus strand which is passed down a food groove in the arm, to the mouth which is situated on the upper surface of the body.

In temperate waters most species live beneath rocks, in crevices or among algae. In tropical waters, they are more conspicuous. The sexes are separate, sperm and ova being released into the sea where fertilization occurs. A planktonic larval phase follows and at metamorphosis the larvae settle and attach to the substrate. The developing individuals finally break free from their stalked existence, and are able to walk and swim with their long arms.

In temperate seas feather stars are poorly represented—tropical species are far more common. In some cases specific genera are common to certain substrates—

Below: Found in association with soft corals and gorgonian sea fans, this long-spined brittle star *(Ophiothrix purpurea)* is quite common at many tropical dive sites below 20 m.
Neville Coleman

some prefer sea whips and gorgonia sea fans to cling to, while others can be found on the tops of reefs, edges of channels, or bommies. All species prefer areas washed by plankton-bearing strong currents, and are difficult to identify in situ because of their varying colors, patterns and numbers of arms.

Feather stars may be inhabited by commensal shrimps, squat lobsters, brittle stars, acoelous worms, crabs and creeping ctenophores.

Sea urchins

Very common on inshore reefs right around Australia, sea urchins are well known to most scuba divers, especially in the temperate seas, where in some areas (Montague Island) they fill every crack and crevice. Ocean swells often sweep divers onto sea urchin spines, when entering or exiting from shore dives. In tropical seas, the most prominent species is the diadem sea urchin. This species, *Diademsetosum*, has long needle-like black spines and is easily recognized by its beautiful bright blue five-lined pattern and brilliant white spots. The anal bag at the top of the body is circled in bright orange. When out in the open during the day, these urchins move around in groups, while scraping algae and detritus from the rocks with a strong, sharp

chisel-like teeth arrangement known as Aristotle's lantern.

In the past, thousands of sea urchins have been broken open by divers to feed fish, and in some areas they have been all but wiped out. This practice is now discouraged, especially in marine park areas. The body shell of the sea urchin, known as a sea egg, is often washed up on beaches, and even although they are very fragile, they are often cast up by large storms without being broken.

Most sharp-spined urchins can injure a diver, and some species are highly venomous, causing serious discomfort and sometimes death. Those to be wary of are the flower urchin *(Toxopneustes pileolus)*, variable sea urchin *(Asthenosoma varins)* and the stripe-spined sea urchin *(Echinothrix calamaris)*.

Most sea urchins are nocturnal. Some of the more unusual ones—sand dollars and heart urchins—live beneath the surface of the sand in lagoons, bays, estuaries and sheltered sand flats. Some sea urchins are harvested and exported to Asiatic countries, where the roe is considered a delicacy.

Sea cucumbers

Shaped like giant cucumbers, these rather common and innocuous creatures certainly look very unlike

Above: Feather stars are far more common in the tropics and many species occur throughout northern seas. Sometimes referred to as crinoids, they have very sticky tubed feet along their arms with which they catch planktonic food. In some species they are so adhesive that if brushed by a diver's wetsuit, the attached arms break off. *Neville Coleman*

The release of Cuvier's organs are a defence mechanism, and if that does not achieve the desired result, the sea cucumber can eject their entire intestines and grow a new set. They also have the ability to heal and regrow after being bitten in half.

Trepang (or bêche-de-mer) fishing has a long history in the waters of northern Australia, but only a few local fishers exist today, which cater specifically for the Asian markets.

Sea squirts (Ascidians or Tunicates)

Adult sea squirts (also known as tunicates or ascidians) are bottle-shaped, sac-like creatures that often eject jets of water when touched—hence the name. The sea squirt may not be the most well-known of underwater creatures, yet they are the most advanced of invertebrates. The larvae are distinctly tadpole-like and possess a notochord (rudimentary backbone). The presence of these during the larval stage indicates that sea squirts are related to animals with backbones.

The name is usually used to refer to solitary ascidians, but some are colonies containing many individuals, either connected by a stalk to a common base, or embedded in a firm, jelly-like matrix. Some are beautifully colored.

There are about 1350 species of ascidians worldwide. Some species are specific in their choice of substrate, others are not. They are found on reefs, algae, sea grasses, shells, rocks, in caves, under ledges and in sand and mud. There are even pelagic ascidians that drift in ocean currents and have complex life cycles.

The adult sea squirt is round, or sac-like and is permanently anchored to the substrate. The body is enclosed in a tunic of cellulose—a rare substance in the animal kingdom. Each individual has two body openings—one is an inlet for water which brings oxygen for respiration, and food in the form of

Above: Whereas most sea cucumbers creep over the sea floor collecting detrius and settled plankton with sticky mouth pads, the stars and stripes sea cucumber (*Pseudocolochirus violaceus*) sits in one place and expands long sticky tentacles from its mouth to catch plankton passing by in the current. *Neville Coleman*

relatives of sea stars, sea urchins and brittle stars. Even though they have a long body structure, sea cucumbers are still radially symmetrical, with five body sections organized around a central cavity, and all have tube feet.

Sea cucumbers live beneath rubble or on sand or sponges. Some species use modified tube feet formed into a fine network of mouth tentacles to catch plankton; others use sticky mouth pads to pick up detritus, and pass these bottom sediments through their intestines where the organic matter is digested and the "cleaned" sediment can be expelled.

Some species have separate sexes—sperm and eggs are released into the sea on a rising tide at dusk, and others are hermaphroditic. All species have a planktonic larval dispersal.

One of the most brightly-colored of all sea creatures is the stars and stripes sea cucumber *(Pseudocolochirus)*, which lives on mainland reefs off Queensland and north Western Australia, where it expands brightly-colored mouth tentacles to catch plankton.

When molested, some tropical sea cucumbers *(Bohadschia argus)* can shoot toxic white threads (Cuvier's organs) from their anus. These are extremely sticky and can cause temporary blindness if they come in contact with the eyes. It is best not to touch eyes at all after handling or touching sea creatures.

suspended plankton and detritus, and the other is an exhalant siphon—an outlet for water bearing carbon dioxide and waste. The inhalant siphon is generally larger and nearer the top of the body. The large internal gills are ciliated and act as a pump.

Some compound ascidians may have separate intake siphons with waste products channelled into communal exhalant siphons. The tropical species *Didemnum molle* often has colonies of bright green zooxanthellae growing inside the body.

Although divers often mistake ascidians for sponges, there is one easy way to tell them apart. No matter how much a diver touches a sponge, there is no nervous system present, so it cannot react. However, ascidians have a well-developed nervous system, and when touched or even approached, their siphons will react and close.

Fishes

Fishes as a whole represent the largest group of vertebrates living on earth. They are also the most successful, dating back to the early Cambrian age, of just over 500 million years ago. They have exploited every habitat in the hydrosphere, from the tropics to the polar seas, from the ocean's surface to deepest trenches, nearly 11 km down.

Approximately 3600 species have been recorded from the seas surrounding Australia. Hundreds of these have been discovered since the advent of scuba diving some 30 years ago. Many of these species are unique, and found exclusively in the southern waters. No attempt is made to give comprehensive genera or species information. Some of the more commonly observed families are referred to.

Elasmobranchs

This group includes sharks and rays, which differ from most fishes in that they have a cartilaginous skeleton and plate-like gills. Elasmobranchs are covered by skin, which has millions of tiny teeth embedded in its surface, and somewhat resembles the texture of sandpaper. A number of gill slits are located on the sides of the head and the tail fin is asymmetrical. The sexes of elasmobranches are separate, and the females are impregnated internally.

Some varieties of shark produce a horny sac (or egg case) containing the embryo, which is usually attached to weeds or rocks, and from which hatches a juvenile shark. Other species incubate the embryos within the body of the female, which gives birth to live young.

All the species in this group are carnivorous and feed on a variety of organisms including molluscs, echinoderms, crustaceans, zooplankton, fish, turtles, sea birds and sometimes humans.

Sharks

Australia has a long history of shark attacks from bronze whalers in harbors and estuaries, to white pointers off the coast and around islands. Some attacks are fatal, and a fair few victims have never been found. While research into attacks has been going on for decades, very little information has been collated on the sharks themselves, except for the fact that sharks have been overfished (as have most commercial and recreational species in Australian waters). At this time, moves are afoot to add the white pointer to the list of sharks (two

Below: The common stingaree (*Trygonoptera testacea*) lives on the sandy bottom off southern Queensland and throughout the waters off the New South Wales coast. *Nigel Marsh*

ELASMOBRANCH ENCOUNTERS
Sharks and Rays: Where to find them

MANY SPECIES OF SHARKS AND RAYS ARE FOUND in Australia waters. When Europeans first visited the island continent, mariners made a special note of the large number of sharks and rays. In Western Australia, for instance, the Dutch recorded masses of sharks off the coastline (Shark Bay was so named because they were so prevalent) while Captain Cook first named Botany Bay, on the east coast, Stingray Bay, after the large number of rays that were seen and caught.

Today, while numbers are not nearly as plentiful as they once were due to fishing pressures and beach meshing, an impressive variety and quantity of sharks and rays can be seen when diving in Australian waters. So far over 180 species of sharks and 100 rays have been identified, but some of these still await description. While populations and distributions vary around the country, there are several places where certain species are found.

Grey Nurse Sharks The best place to see

An inhabitant of temperate seas, the southern angel shark (*Squatina australis*) is rarely seen by divers as it spends most of its time beneath the sand camouflaged, lying in wait for prey. It feeds mostly on fish and crustaceans and is not considered dangerous. *Nigel Marsh*

this species is off Forster/Tuncurry and Seal Rocks, where there are large schools, but grey nurse can also be seen north to Brisbane (over winter) and south to Montague Island (over summer).

Wobbegongs There are six species of wobbegong shark in Australia. The largest populations of spotted and ornate wobbegongs are found between Sydney and Brisbane. Off Ningaloo Reef, divers may see tasselled, northern and western wobbegongs.

Port Jackson Sharks A member of the horn shark family, the Port Jackson is most common off central and southern New South Wales, where dozens can be seen sometimes packed into caves.

Fiddler Rays One of the most strikingly patterned rays, fiddler rays are common in southern Australia. One of the biggest populations would have to be in Jervis Bay.

Electric Rays Although there are eight species of electric rays found around Australia, only two are regularly seen by divers. The Tasmanian electric ray is most common off Hobart. Divers should not settle on the sand in Jervis Bay, as they may just find a short-tailed electric ray.

Manta Rays These large rays are most common off Lady Elliot Island, Brisbane, Ningaloo Reef and the Whitsunday Islands over winter.

Whale Sharks Although occasionally seen in all tropical seas, whale sharks are usually spotted off Ningaloo Reef (in autumn), Christmas Island (in summer), and along the Gove Peninsula (in summer).

Photographing sharks and rays can be quite a challenge, as most large species are shy and very hard to approach without baits, while many small species flee when a diver approaches too close. The trick is to slow your breathing, make no sudden movement, and if possible, approach slowly from the front, to avoid startling the animal. Another trick is to remain stationary and wait for the animal to check you out, as many elasmobranchs are curious by nature. Pelagic and reef sharks are also attracted to noise, so it is possible to bring them in close by tapping your tank with a knife. The best sharks and rays to photograph are the lazy ones, such as wobbegongs and Port Jackson sharks, and shovelnose rays. You can take your time, compose your photographs and appreciate the animal as well.

grey nurse species) already fully protected in Australian waters.

Up until 1994 no scuba divers had been killed by sharks in Australia, although snorkelers and hookah divers had been taken by great whites, and spear fishermen by tiger sharks. Now it appears that, due to the huge reductions in fish populations, the traditional white shark migrations which follow the schooling fish are turning to human prey.

Wobbegong sharks These sharks are bottom-dwelling nocturnal carnivores which rest during the day in gullies, caves and under ledges. They have sharp, pointed teeth, strong jaws, excellent camouflage and are found around the full extent of the Australian coastline. The ornate wobbegong (*Orectolobus ornatus*) has been responsible for a number of serious attacks on spearfishermen, line-fishermen, snorkelers and scuba divers. However, in almost all cases the shark had previously been disturbed—either shot, caught, excited by speared or gutted fish, sat on or otherwise interferred with.

Divers should familiarize themselves with these interesting although potentially dangerous animals, and avoid handling them. Wobbegongs can be dangerous.

Once the wobbegong bites, it is

impossible to open the jaws by force; the best solution is not to panic, and hold gloved hands over, or squeeze down on the gill openings. This will interfere with its breathing and the shark must open its mouth and let go (a proven method). It is best to leave them alone. The spotted wobbegong (*Orectolobus maculatus*) is a large, territorial resident of rocky reefs, and is most common in the temperate waters off the New South Wales coastline, although also found from southern Queensland, south to Western Australian waters. Like all wobbegongs it should be treated with caution.

Tropical reef sharks The most common shallow water shark seen on tropical reefs is the whitetip reef shark (*Triaenodon obesus*). Although this shark often follows divers and snorkelers around in the shallows, it is not considered dangerous under normal circumstances. However if the white-tip is harassed, speared, caught on a hand-line, or involved in a feeding frenzy, it may bite. A shark coming in too close can be easily avoided, by pushing it off in another direction with swim fins.

The grey reef shark (*Carcharhinus amblyrhynchos*) is found in the deeper water over the reef edge. A swift, efficient predator, the grey reef shark is often ob-

Above: Well known to divers in the South Pacific, the Galapagos shark (*Carcharhinus galapagensis*) has a cosmopolitan distribution and is generally observed in small packs. The Galapagos shark is inquisitive and will approach divers, but apart from a few finchewing activities they have not proven dangerous in Australian waters. *Neville Coleman*

served by divers in the warmer oceans. Although this shark does not grow to a very large size, it does form groups, and is one of the main species used by those filming shark movies.

At times this shark will display agonistic behavior, by arching its back and erratically veering its head back and forth, with its pectoral fins lowered—this is a warning not to come any closer. Take notice of any erratic movements by sharks and respond by moving slowly away, always facing the shark. Ignored threat postures may invite an attack and any bite can be serious, even if it is only meant as a warning.

The tiger shark *(Galeocerdo cuvieri)* is very common around outer reefs, especially when the marlin fishing season is in full swing, and the turtle nesting season is on. Be warned—a big tiger shark can move at incredible speed especially when frightened. This species is probably responsible for some of the attacks credited to white pointers. Tigers are very numerous and feed on fish, birds, other sharks, turtles and mammals—they particularly enjoy sea snakes. A lot of their prey is taken in shallow water, or close to the surface. They are especially known for their scavenging roles, and consume large whales and anything dead, sick or injured that is floating near the surface.

Tiger sharks are very nervous, and take quite a while to decide to attack unless directly stimulated. Underwater they do not appear to take much notice of scuba divers on the bottom, except for a cursory surveillance. If menaced, keep cool and slowly exit the area, always facing the shark.

A species well known to divers in the South Pacific, the Galapagos shark *(Carcharhinus galapagensis),* has a cosmopolitan distribution. Most specimens encountered are about 2 m in length. Galapagos sharks appear in small groups or large schools, and at times can seem threatening. When divers are decompressing on an anchor line at 5 m and there are 30 to 40 Galapagos sharks whizzing around them at close range, the knowledge that they do not usually attack is of small consolation. Although these sharks appear menacing at times, and have been known to chew the ends of retreating divers' fins, usually they are not considered more than stimulating.

Without doubt the white pointer *(Carcharodon carcharias)* is by far the greatest danger to humans because of its huge size, intelligence and fearless nature.

A superb predator, the white pointer is cunning, strategic, highly mobile, ferocious in attack, yet surprisingly stealthy in its approach to prey. Natural food sources include sea lions, fur seals, dolphins, whales and fish. White pointer attacks on humans have been well-documented throughout the world, and because of the popular *Jaws* movies, this species is the most famous of the man-eating sharks. Yet in spite of all this publicity and interest, the shark itself has become rarer, and is now thought to be endangered.

Scuba divers have encountered white pointers, and by facing the shark, keeping their cool and staying still, were not attacked and the shark eventually went away. Unfortunately others have not been so lucky.

Due to widespread ignorance, the grey nurse shark *(Carcharias taurus)* has been wrongly labeled

Below: One of the most prettily marked larger rays, the reticulate whiptail ray (*Himantura uarnak)* may be seen around reefs, on sandy and muddy bottoms. It also inhabits estuaries and mangrove areas. This species has a large venomous spine on the tail and feeds mostly on molluscs and crustaceans.
Nigel Marsh

a ferocious man-eater—yet in reality this shark is not usually aggressive to humans unless provoked. Its long, pointed teeth are adapted to catching fast-swimming school fishes. Before the great shark slaughter of the 1960s and 1970s, schools of these sharks could be seen resting in gutters close to the bottom. Now a protected species, their numbers are on the increase. In many areas such as Terrigal, Seal Rocks, Byron Bay and Moreton Bay on Australia's east coast, large groups are once again seen as they assemble for mating during winter, spring and summer. Swimming with these sharks is an exhilarating experience.

Rays Another large group of Australia-wide elasmobranchs are stingrays (*Dasyatidae)* and stingarees (*Urolophidae*). Both these families have one or more venomous barbs on their tails, which have spined or slashed numerous reef walkers and divers. The stingrays bury themselves in sand to hide from feeding sharks and divers often fail to see the rays, which are especially difficult to see at night. It is best to stay up off the sandy bottom.

Most rays feed on molluscs and crustaceans, although some are able to catch fish. The electric ray stuns its prey with electric shocks.

Found in the tropics, the blue-spotted fantail ray *(Taeniura lymna)* is seen in shallow lagoons or along the sandy edges of drop-offs. The ray is a potential danger to waders and snorkelers because of its shallow water habitat, but, if given a chance, the ray will swim away. Reef walkers should shuffle their feet when wading in sandy pools, and snorkelers should be cautious when fossicking beneath ledges, or lifting dead coral slabs.

Encased in skin, the venomous, serrated spines of the blue-spotted fantail ray hardly appear to be the efficient weapons they are. Needle-sharp, with small knife-like serrations running down each side, the spines are designed for easy pene-

tration, to carry their venom deep into the predator's body. Once embedded, the spines break off. The shock of the wound, and the pain from the venom is instant, and the ray has a good chance of escape.

One of the largest stingrays in Australian waters is the giant 3 m Meyen's stingray *(Taeniura meyeni)*. This giant stingray glides along in the depths, looking for all the world like an interplanetary spaceship. When one swims alongside, there is an overpowering sense of wonder at being so close to such a large creature.

Never approach any stingray from above, or corner it, as most stingrays strike towards their front. Stingrays do not strike unless harassed, shot, caught on a fishing line, trawled or frightened.

Manta rays When manta rays feed near the surface, they often swim with the edge of one or both wingtips slicing the surface, and are often mistaken for sharks. Found mostly in tropical waters, this ray (*Manta birostris*) is a gentle creature that will often endure the clumsy approaches of humans. It will sometimes allow itself to be touched, and appears to be willing to "play" by taking divers for rides.

Bony fish
By far the largest group, the bony fishes have calcified skeletons and most are covered with scales. They

Above: Rarely seen out in the open during the daytime, the blind shark (*Brachaelurus waddi*) is generally observed beneath ledges or kelp forests.
Nigel Marsh

Above: Fish watching around wrecks and caves is particularly interesting since most fish allow a close approach by divers, especially those species which school.
Nigel Marsh

are among the most colorful animals in the sea. The majority have a swim bladder which acts as a buoyancy control (and hearing aid). The amount of gas it contains can be adjusted, so keeping the fish at a particular depth in the water, even when stationary. The gills open to the outside, but are covered with a body flap called the the operculum, or gill cover, which is situated behind the mouth.

Photographs of fish are useful aids to fish identification, particularly where shape and disposition of fins are concerned. However, many fish are able to change color rapidly, and the photograph available may not match all the varieties of coloration. Fish colors change with moods, reproductive and courtship cycles, and during hunting and hiding. In some cases, the fish needs to be examined for the numbers of fins, spines on the gill covers and teeth in the jaws, for precise identification.

Eels Moray eels (family Muraenidae) are common residents of tropical, subtropical, and temperate waters around Australia. Usually nocturnal, they reside in holes in the reef during the day.

Over the past two decades, morays have been hand-fed by divers and many individuals are known by pet names. However, their behavior is unpredictable, and many horrific maulings have taken place—in 1996 one diver on the Great Barrier Reef lost her entire arm.

Giant morays *(Gymnothorax)* may grow up to 2.5 m in length, although most species only reach up to 1 m. Some have very beautiful color patterns—the mosaic moray *(Enchelycore ramosa)* is a good example. Morays have an excellent sense of smell and several species feed on fish, crabs, cuttlefish and octopi. The green moray *(Gymnothorax prasinus)* is very common on the southeastern coastal reefs, and the startling, bright blue and yellow ribbon eel *(Rhinomuraena quaesita)* occurs on the Great Barrier Reef.

Seahorses, dragons and pipefish
Seahorses and pipefish belong to the family Syngnathidae. Many are very shy creatures, hiding in algae and sea grass meadows, usually close to the bottom. About 100 species of this family occur in Australian waters and some—the leafy sea dragon *(Phycodurus eques)* and the weedy sea dragon *(Phyllopteryx taeniolatus)*—are among the most bizarre of fishes. The dragons are endemic to southern Australia. Most of these fishes are cryptically colored and adopt poses and behavior which make them difficult to see in their specific habitat. However, when viewed close up, many have brilliant colors, various patterns, stripes, dots and blotches on parts of their bodies.

The most interesting feature of these animals is their unique method of reproduction. The females lay their eggs either in the abdominal pouch of male seahorses, or in the case of of male pipefishes and dragons, along the base of the tail or belly. Males incubate the embryos which develop into miniature replicas of their parents. These strange fishes feed mostly on minute crustaceans which are sucked up through their long snouts.

Pipefishes are seen on almost every dive in certain areas of the Great Barrier Reef. At night some species form groups and sleep in the same area.

Ghost pipefishes and sea moths: Ghost pipefishes (family Solenostomidae) are found on tropical reefs inshore and offshore around tropical Australia. They are difficult to find because of their head-down stance and excellent camouflage—they usually imitate sedentary marine life such as algae, sea whips or gorgonians. The ornate pipefish (*Solenostomus paradoxus*) is exquisite in its bizarre form and color. This species sometimes emulates soft corals feather stars, or behaves like floating vegetation.

Although sea moths, or dragonfish, are only a small family (Pegasidae) related to the previous families, their incredible shapes make them worthy of mention. The short dragonfish *(Eurypegasus draconis)* is the most colorful member in Australian waters. These fishes are bottom dwelling and hard to find.

Scorpionfishes All scorpionfish belong to the family Scorpaenidae. Each has venomous dorsal spines, and some species display vicious-looking head spines. Strangely enough, their flesh is considered excellent eating. A few of the best-known species are included here for reference.

Although the zebra scorpion fish *(Dendrochirus zebra)* superficially resembles other scorpionfish of the genus *Pterois,* it can be easily identified by its color pattern and the shape of its pectoral fins. This scorpionfish also differs somewhat from the *Pterois* group in its behavior. Whereas firefish are mostly seen with pectorals extended (even when on the bottom), quite often zebra scorpionfish are observed hiding among bottom growths with pectorals folded, lying in ambush. In contrast to its usual slow-swimming behavior, the zebra scorpionfish has an extremely swift hunting strike.

Known by a variety of common names—the firefish, lionfish or turkeyfish—*Pterois volitans* is found in most tropical coral reef areas. In summer it is sometimes found in temperate waters, although usually most of the sightings are juveniles. The species is easy to recognize by its unique pectoral fins and the extensive array of defensive venomous dorsal spines. These spines are long, thin and extremely sharp, and many people have been injured by them. The pain lasts about six hours, depending on the depth and position of the wound.

The ragged-finned scorpionfish *(Pterois antennata)* is far more common in the northern areas of the Great Barrier Reef and the

Below: Scorpionfish are common right around Australia. Some are easy to find (lionfish), others blend in so well that they are seldom seen by divers (Merlet's scorpionfish). The red cardinal scorpionfish (*Scorpaena cardinalis*) shown below, is a temperate water species found off southern New South Wales. *Neville Coleman*

Coral Sea, than on southern or mainland island reefs. This species, and most other scorpionfish, are not seen out in the open during the day. It resides beneath ledges and in caves and is usually observed in a head down position. Most sightings are of pairs of similar-sized fish. Although the fishes of the genus *Pterois* may all look superficially similar; they are simple to identify, by checking the shape of the pectoral fins.

The stonefish *(Synanceia horrida)* occurs on the muddy reefs of mainland estuaries, bays, inlets and lagoons, and on the fringing reefs of mainland islands. This stonefish is one of the most venomous fishes in Australian waters. Concealed in dorsal sheaths along the back are thirteen of the most efficient natural injection systems to be found in any marine animal. Hollow, needle-sharp spines, each with a twin venom sack, inflict unbearable pain and any victim must receive medical attention as soon as possible.

An absolutely magnificent southern Australian fish, the gurnard scorpionfish *(Neosebastes pandus)* is a master of the art of camouflage. It sits almost immobile, with just a hint of life coming from the barely perceptible movement of its gill covers. This species is the only gurnard scorpionfish that frequents shallow waters on inshore reefs, and even though very common, it is not often

caught on a line as it lives mainly among algae-covered reef, and normally strikes only at moving prey. The long dorsal spines inflict extremely painful wounds.

In some New South Wales estuaries, the southern fortesque *(Centropogon australis)* is so common that it is difficult to put one's hand on the bottom without having to move several of them. Surprisingly, very few divers have been stung underwater.

Exercise care when diving in estuaries, especially on soft bottom. Wear adequate footwear and gloves when netting in sandy or muddy waters.

Rock cods or groupers The family Serranidae includes the larger bottom-dwelling fishes of the genus *Epinephelus*. The giant Queensland groper *(E. lanceolatus)*, the dwarf-spotted rock cod *(E. merra)*, and the famous potato cods *(E. tukula)* found at the "Cod Hole" dive site off Cairns are members of this group, and usually inhabit tropical reefs. Only a few members of this genus are seen along the southern coasts.

Other tropical genera include *Cephalopholis,* the largest and most well known being the brightly-colored coral cod *(C. miniatus)*. This genus is easily distinguished from others by its rounded soft dorsal fin and convex tail.

The jewel-like fairy basslets *(Pseudanthias),* some of the prettiest of fishes on the reefs and every underwater photographer's challenge, also belong to the rock cod family. Fairy basslets belong to the subfamily Anthiinae; they are mostly found in groups around the tops of drop-offs and coral pinnacles, where they feed on plankton. The males have large harems of females and are distinguished from the females by color and shape. If the male is killed or dies the largest female changes into a male and takes over the harem. Some of the rarer basslets are only found in deep water at the base of drop-offs, or on the tops of sea mounts. Quite a number have been discovered and described in the last two decades. Tropical species include *P. tuka* and *P. squamipinnis,* with rarer species such as *P. pictilus* and *P. fasciatus* found only at certain reefs.

Callanthias australis, their equivalent from the splendid perch family Callanthiidae, is sometimes seen in deep southern waters.

Four species of coral trout *(Plectropomus)* occur on the Great Barrier Reef, and two species of lyre-tailed trout, *Variola*. These fish are among the most popular food fish in Australia's northern cities, and are now being exported live to Asian markets.

Trevallies or jacks Active daytime predators, trevally (family Carangidae) may be seen in huge schools, small groups, pairs or alone depending on the species. The most common in tropical waters is the big-eye trevally (*Caranx sexfasciatus*), which swims in huge schools. At Lady Elliot Island on the southern Great Barrier Reef, bottlenose dolphins (*Tursiops truncatus*) feed on these trevallies, putting on a devastating yet entertaining display.

Bluefin trevally *(Caranx melampygus)* are generally seen in pairs patrolling the reef edge, while the giant trevally *(Caranx ignobilis)* is often seen as a loner, although during the breeding season these fish school up. All trevallies have mirror-like scales, and are difficult to photograph underwater.

In temperate waters divers are often surrounded by big schools of yellow-tail kingfish *(Seriola lalandi),* especially below 20 m. Big schools of yellow-tail scad *(Trachurus novaezelandiae)* are found in shallow water and beneath jetties.

Coral snappers These large fish (family Lutjanidae) have prominent scales, big eyes and mouth, and a single dorsal fin. They are found in tropical and subtropical waters— mostly around reefs or wrecks— Many of the coral snappers—red emperor (*Lutjanus sebae*), and Mangrove Jack (*Lutjanus argentimaculatus*) are excellent eating.

However, the Bohar snapper (*Lutjanus bohar*) and the paddletail (*Lutjanus gibbus*) are known to cause ciguatera poisoning and should not be eaten.

Sweetlips Members of the family Haemulidae are large reef-dwelling fishes, many noted for their thick blubbery lips and bright colors (not all species). They are commonly seen on most tropical reefs, although a few venture into subtropical waters. One of the most spectacular is the oblique-banded sweetlip, *Plectorhynchus lineatus.* These fishes inhabit caves, ledges or cleaning stations during the day, forming small to large schools. At night they disperse into deeper waters where they feed on invertebrates in sand and rubble areas.

Snappers and bream Found in tropical and temperate waters, fishes of the family Sparidae are of significant importance to the commercial and recreational fishing industry of Australia. They can be found around inshore and offshore reefs, and enter estuaries to spawn and feed on oysters, scallops and crustaceans. The best places to see snappers and bream are marine parks or marine protected areas where the fish have had a chance to breed and are used to divers.

The snapper (*Chrysophrys auratus*), the yellow-fin bream (*Acanthopagrus australis*) and the tarwhine

Below: Hiding behind an oblique-banded sweetlips (*Plectorhinchus goldmanni*) the tropical yellow phase phase trumpetfish (*Aulostomus lineatus*), patiently awaits the approach of smaller fishes. If any stray into range, it will strike with an amazing burst of speed, swallow the small fish and resume its ruse. *Neville Coleman*

(*Rhabdosargus sarba*) are among the most well-known species.

Emperors and sea bream These medium-sized, big-eyed, heavily-scaled fish belong to the family Lethrinidae. They live in tropical and subtropical waters, and are among the most sought-after food fish by commercial and recreational fishermen. The spangled emperor (*Lethrinus nebulosus*) and red-throated emperor (*Lethrinus miniatus*) are often seen during the daylight hours in big schools around some of the day-tripper pontoons on the Great Barrier Reef, especially in areas that have been national parks for many years.

Butterflyfishes The family Chaetodontidae contains over 116 species of small, brightly-colored, delicately-patterned, deep-bodied fishes, which are very popular with underwater photographers and aquarists. Most species are confined to the tropics, but one species, the truncate coral-fish (*Chelmonops truncatus*), occurs right around southern Australia.

The three-banded coralfish (*Chaetodon tricinctus*) and the Lord Howe butterflyfish (*Amphichaetodon howensis*) are found in subtropical waters around Lord Howe and Norfolk Islands, and occasionally seen off the coast of New South Wales. Many species feed on coral polyps and mucus, others on specific marine invertebrates such as crabs, and others browse on benthic encrusting organisms. The yellow pyramid butterflyfish (*Hemitaurichthys polylepsis*) is a planktivore which often forms large schools along drop-offs.

Sometimes observed swimming in pairs, the threadfin butterflyfish *(Chaetodon auriga)* inhabits coral reef areas and is usually seen in relatively shallow depths. Most specimens are found at depths from 5–20 m. Adults are readily distinguished by the thin, black, cross-directional lines, black eye bar and characteristic black ocellus below the thread-like filament on the golden soft dorsal fin. It is easily approached underwater.

Preferring a habitat of coral slopes, the double-saddled butterflyfish *(Chaetodon ulietensis)* has a very smooth, streamlined appearance. Although much smaller in size, it is somewhat similar at first glance to the larger, lined butterflyfish *(C. lineatus)*. Underwater, the double-saddled butterflyfish is more easily approached than its relative, and can be distinguished by the bright yellow posterior third of its body, the black spot on the tail junction, the black edge of the tail and the two dark saddles. Whereas the lined butterflyfish is almost always seen in pairs, the double-saddled butterflyfish is usually seen to be solitary.

The beaked coralfish (*Chelmon rostratus*) is certainly one of the most attractive reef fish inhabiting the Great Barrier Reef waters. It is seen in pairs that "flit" around reefs, gutters and coral heads picking small organisms from the sides and roofs of coral overhangs and caves. Active during the day, it sleeps in holes and crevices at night. Usually a shallow water species, it has been recorded to 30 m.

Angelfish Most species of angelfish are brightly colored and beautifully patterned, and are sometimes confused with the butterflyfishes. The angelfish always has a spine on the lower gill cover—a simple method of telling them apart. The majority of angelfish are

Below: A resident of the tropical Australian seas, the semicircle angelfish (*Pomacanthus semicirculartis*) was originally named from its juvenile form which is ornamented with white and blue semicircles. An excellent photographic subject, this fish is easy to approach. *Michael Aw*

tropical, however the Ballina angelfish (*Chaetodontoplus ballinae*) and the conspicuous angelfish (*Chaetodontoplus conspicillatus*) are deep water species found subtropically in Australia, and around Lord Howe Island.

The semicircle angelfish *(Pomacanthus semicirculatus)* was originally named for its distinctive juvenile, which has no color and pattern resemblance to adult fish whatsoever, as is often the case with this particular group.

Most of the larger reef angelfish browse on sponges and benthic invertebrates and usually the adult males and females are similar in shape and color. However, members of the genus *Genicanthus* are planktivores and the sexes show distinctly different color patterns. In general, angelfishes are very territorial and are usually solitary, or in pairs.

Damselfish The members of the Pomacentridae family, a large group of smaller fishes, are found right around Australia. Although far more species live in tropical waters, the one-spot puller (*Chromis hypsilepsis*), which is prolific in temperate waters off the southern coast of New South Wales, can sometimes be the most common fish in the area. The larger species such as the scaly fin (*Parma victoriae*) and the white-ear (*Parma microlepis*) occur in the temperate seas.

The Pomacentrids may be planktivores or herbivores. Some even have their own algae gardens, and protect their food source from other fishes.

Many Pomacentrids are brightly colored and patterned, especially the juveniles. The specialized clown and anemonefish *(Amphiprion* and *Premnas)* are popular little Pomacentrids, and their special symbiotic relationship with stinging sea anemones is well known.

Morwongs Restricted to cool temperate waters, these larger, reef-dwelling, thick-lipped fishes belong to the family Cheilodactylidae. They have large pectoral fins, move about in large schools—especially the red morwong (*Cheilodactylus fuscus*)—and are often seen resting on the bottom during the day. They feed by sucking molluscs from rocks, and by taking in mouthfuls of detritus and sand, filtering out the edible worms, molluscs and crabs, and passing the refuse out through the rear of the gills.

Wrasses The wrasse family (Labridae) has one of the largest numbers of species in tropical waters—running second only to gobies, and numerous species are found in temperate waters as well. Wrasses

Above: The flesh of the toadfish (pufferfish) contains a poison usually lethal to humans. The star striped toadfish (*Anothron hispidus*) shown here can inflate itself with water as a defensive display.
Michael Aw

Above: The spangled emperor (*Lethrinus nebulosus*) is a popular food fish in tropical Australia. At dive sites around Heron Island, Kelso Reef and Lord Howe Island, these fish are very tame, having been fed at intervals and protected from spearfishing.
Neville Coleman

exhibit an enormous range of shapes, colors and patterns, and exploit almost every habitat—rocky and coral reefs, sea grass meadows, sand and rubble. In general, they are small and slim, but the larger ones can be deep bodied. Wrasses have individual teeth (unlike the parrotfish, a similar fish that has teeth fused into a beak) and swim with sculling movements of their pectoral fins. They range in size from the giant Maori wrasse (*Cheilinus undulatus*) which can reach a length of 229 cm, down to the small *Pseudocheilinus* sp., a mere 50 mm.

The tropical wrasses *(Thalassoma* and *Halichoeres)* and the cool temperate species *(Eupetrichthys* and *Suezichthys)* all have strikingly beautiful coloration. Without doubt, the most famous are the cleaner wrasses (*Labroides*), which set up cleaner stations at various locations on the reef, and feed on the ectoparasites and sometimes skin mucus or decayed tissue of other fishes. The food sources of some juvenile wrasses may differ from their adult diet—for example *Labropsis* act as fish cleaners when juvenile, and browse on coral polyps when older. Juveniles and adults of most species usually differ in color and pattern, and males and females also exhibit dramatic color differences. Within many genera, sex reversal occurs—all fish are born female and as they grow older, they change into males.

Parrotfish Very close relatives of the wrasses, the colorful parrotfish (family Scaridae) were named because of their obvious similarities to the brightly-colored parrots—their teeth are fused into a "beak" and they swim by "flapping" their pectoral fins. This herbivore scrapes algae from dead and living coral with its beak, and sometimes bites off coral and limestone rock. This is crushed by specially modified teeth in the throat called pharyngeal teeth. The algae is digested, and the coral and limestone rock milled into sand which is excreted back onto the reef. In many places, parrotfish are primary producers of sediment on and around tropical reefs.

All parrotfish species are of tropical origin, although some species are found in subtropical or warm temperate waters. Parrotfish juveniles rarely resemble the adults, and the differences in shapes and color between males and females of the same species often makes identification difficult.

When parrotfish first mature they can be either male or female. In this initial phase they exhibit dull colors of reds, browns or greys. Some of these initial females are able to change into brightly-colored blue-green males. The most easily recognized parrotfish are the *Scarus microrhinos*, Schlegel's parrotfish *(S. schlegeli)* and the bicolor parrotfish *Cetoscarus bicolor*. The largest species is the bumphead parrotfish *Bolbometapon muricatum,* which grows to 120 cm.

Barracudas Although the great barracuda (family Sphyraenidae) grows to 170 cm and has a fearsome reputation, it is certainly not the case in Australian waters. Most barracuda seen along the Great Barrier Reef are smaller schooling species such as the chevron barracuda (*Sphyraena putnamiae*) or Heller's barracuda (*Sphyraena helleri*). Schools of these species will often swim around divers in a huge circle, providing excellent photographic opportunities.

Surgeonfish Members of the Acanthuridae (surgeonfish and tangs) are common throughout tropical Australian waters. They are primarily herbivores, feeding on algae plucked from the substrate. Fishes of this family may swim alone or in schools. Their scales are so small that their body envelope resembles rough skin. Many have razor-sharp slashing spines which fit into grooves on each side of the tailshaft. Quite a few divers have been cut when trying to handle sleeping surgeonfish during night diving excursions.

Some of the more well-known species are worth mentioning. The most beautiful of all surgeonfish and one of the most common, the blue-lined surgeonfish *(Acanthurus lineatus)*, lives on and around the tops of reefs where it maintains a small area of algae-covered reef, surrounded by territories guarded by others of its species. This surgeonfish is a fast swimmer, found where there is considerable water movement—on headlands, seaward platforms and reef rims of reef fronts.

Dussumier's surgeonfish (*Acanthurus dussumieri*) inhabits shallow coral reef areas down to around 20 m, where it feeds on filamentous algae cropped from dead coral rubble and sandy surfaces. Preferring lagoons and the quieter water at the back of reefs, it is usually seen swimming in pairs or schools, often in the company of feeding parrotfish.

Distinctively marked and shaped, the sailfin tang *(Zebrasoma veliferum)* can be seen ranging over a large area, feeding on filamentous algae. These tangs are found from the mainland to outer barrier reefs, living in sheltered lagoons and along the terraced back edge of reefs. They are sometimes seen feeding on the shallow reef flats as the tide runs in. Pairs often spend much time chasing each other, displaying their distinctive "sails".

Triggerfish Entirely tropical, the triggerfish (family Balistidae) is a medium-sized, bottom-dwelling fish, which has a lockable dorsal spine behind the eye, hard plate-like scales (rough to touch), a small mouth and very strong jaws and teeth. Adults are often intricately patterned.

Titan triggerfish (*Balistoides viridescens*) build nests and guard their eggs vigorously, even to the point of biting divers who stray too close. The result can be a very nasty wound. If harassed, triggerfishes will flee to their "nest" hole, dive in head first and erect their dorsal spine and lock it into position, making it almost impossible to extract them. Most species feed on crabs, molluscs, echinoderms and benthic invertebrates. A few are planktivores, such as the blue triggerfish (*Odonus niger*).

Leatherjackets Most species of leatherjacket (family Monacanthidae) are found in cool, temperate Australian waters. Although related to and looking very much like triggerfishes, leatherjackets tend to be more secretive, hiding among algae, reef corals or in sea grass meadows. Australia has 85 leatherjacket species, more than any other region of the world. In

Below: More common on offshore coral reefs the chevron barracuda *(Sphyraena putmaniae)* often forms large schools which circle around divers. *Nigel Marsh*

Above: A wide-ranging southern species, the female mosaic leatherjacket *(Eubalichthys mosiacus)* blends in well with growths on the jetty pile.
Neville Coleman

general, their body shape is more compressed than triggerfishes, they have longer noses and can change their colors depending on mood or circumstance.

The largest is the scribbled leatherjacket *(Aluterus scriptus),* a tropical species growing to 750 mm. The smallest is the minute leatherjacket *(Rudarius minutus),* also found in the tropics, growing to a mere 30 mm.

One of the most unusual leatherjackets is the mimic leatherjacket *(Paraluteres prionurus)* which is almost identical in size, coloration, shape and behavior to the deadly poisonous saddled puffer *(Canthigaster valentini).*

Puffers, porcupines and boxfish

The puffers (also known as toadfish or blowfish), belong to the family Tetraodontidae, whose flesh contains a lethal poison called tetra-odontoxin. Humans usually die after eating these fish, although the toxin does not appear to have any effect on sharks. Pufferfishes are able to inflate themselves with water or air in a defensive display. Even the smaller temperate *Tetractenos* sp. and *Contusus* sp. and the small tropical sharpnose puffers *(Canthigaster)* are considered deadly poisonous to humans.

Porcupinefishes (Diodontidae) have the same toxin in their flesh and ability to inflate, as well as a body-covering armament of spines which lock into place on expansion

of the body cavity. Porcupinefishes and puffers have immensely strong jaws and sharp, fused teeth used for crushing molluscs, crabs and echinoderms. They also eat algae.

Divers must be especially careful when attempting to observe their defence mechanisms, since larger animals can easily bite off a finger. Porcupinefish bites are most painful. Most porcupinefishes are tropical *(Diodon hystrix)*. The only cool temperate species is the globefish *(Diodon nichthemerus)* which is found around the entire south coast of Australia.

Strange box-like fishes, whose scales are fused into a hard-shelled carapace, belong to the families Ostraciidae and Aracanidae, and are found in tropical and temperate Australian seas. These fishes are poisonous to eat and, within the family Ostraciidae, the species produce a toxic mucus which can be released into the surrounding water.

Marine Reptiles

Crocodiles

Throughout its range, the saltwater crocodile *Crocodylus porosus* has been responsible for hundreds of attacks on humans. Although mostly nocturnal, this stealthy, cunning opportunist is bold and fearless when hunting prey, often venturing close to human habitation. Most sightings occur in swamps and rivers, although larger adults are regularly seen in the open ocean—even on the Great Barrier Reef. After mating, females lay their eggs in a mound or below the sand onshore, and guard them until they hatch. Up to 60 young crocodiles may hatch from one nest.

Turtles

The loggerhead turtle *(Caretta caretta)* is found throughout most of the tropical waters of the world. The female lays approximately 50 eggs at a time on continental island beaches and coral cays during summer. Mating occurs at sea, either at the surface or underwater.

In the past the green turtle *(Chelonia mydas)* has been hunted ruthlessly for its shell and flesh by both professional and amateur fishermen. Even newly hatched juveniles have been collected, preserved and sold in curiosity shops. Although Australian legislation has given the green turtle some measure of protection, a great deal of exploitation still occurs in many regions of the Indo-Pacific. It is imperative that the main turtle nesting sites become established fauna reserves. The females come ashore at night on the high tides from October through to March, and lay their eggs in pits dug in the sand above the high-tide mark, which are then covered over and disguised. Hatching takes place some eight weeks later, usually at night. Refer to the feature, The Endangered Sea Turtle.

Sea snakes
Found in both the Indian and Pacific oceans, the olive sea snake *(Aipysurus laevis)*—whose color varies from brown to yellow—is without doubt the sea snake most commonly encountered by divers in tropical Australian waters. This species is active day and night, searching the crannies beneath coral and rocks for food. While awake, the olive sea snake surfaces to breathe at intervals of 10 to 20 minutes. While sleeping on the bottom, curled beneath a rock or coral, its body mechanisms are slowed, so that the snake can maintain this position for many hours, without the need to surface and breathe. Usually solitary, it becomes gregarious during the mating season. The female produces up to five live young.

Some of the so-called sea snake "attacks" are due to its very poor eyesight and curious nature. All sea snakes should be treated with much caution as they have extremely strong venom—some of the deadliest known.

Marine Mammals

Whales
Three species of right whales inhabit the world's seas. The southern right whale *(Eubalaena australis)*, which is found in the waters of the southern hemisphere, was heavily exploited in the whaling heydays and populations were drastically reduced. Numbers appear to be slowly increasing, with more sightings each year, and the protection of shallow water calving areas along the southern coast of Australia. This is significant as southern right whales only breed once in three years, the calf staying with the mother for up to 14 months. Southern right whales are fully protected in Australian waters, and even a close approach by boat or a swimmer can attract heavy fines.

Humpbacks *(Megaptera novae-angliae)* are one of the few plankton-eating whales to favor coastal areas,

Below: A relative of the toadfish family, the globefish *(Diodon nicthemerus)* is deadly poisonous and should never be eaten under any circumstances. Seen here in its normal shape, when threatened, it inflates by pumping water into its body cavity, thereby erecting its needle-sharp, defensive spines.
Neville Coleman

Above Bottlenose dolphins (*Tursiops truncatus*) are the most common cetacean observed in Australian seas. They inhabit both inshore and offshore waters, and are usually seen in groups or pods. In Moreton Bay near Brisbane, Queensland, Bunbury in south west Australia, and Monkey Mia at Shark Bay in northwest Australia, these mammals are major tourist attractions. *Neville Coleman*

Opposite: Its numbers decimated by sealers in the early days of Australia's history, the Australian sea lion (*Neophoca cinera*) now has a population which fluctuates between 3000 and 5000. They can be seen from South Australia to south Western Australia. *Neville Coleman*

which made them easy prey to shore-based whaling fleets in the past. Today, the humpback is the center of a multi-million dollar whale-watching industry in Australia, as the whales mate and give birth in the low-latitude, warmer coastal waters during the winter months. Studies have shown that numbers are now increasing.

Dolphins

Although an inhabitant of the open ocean, the bottlenose dolphin (*Tursiops truncatus*) may also be seen in bays, harbors and estuaries throughout Australia. Dolphins are social mammals and are generally seen in large groups or pods. Being mammals, they must breathe air, and therefore swim close to the surface. However, when feeding they can dive to great depths. They usually feed on schools of pelagic fishes which are found by echo-location.

Fur seals

The range of the Australian fur seal (*Arctocephalus pusillus doriferus*) is restricted to a few isolated rocky outcrops off the south/south-eastern coastline of Australia. In some of the breeding colonies there may be up to 10,000 fur seals, while other locations may only support a score or so non-breeding animals. Though totally protected by law, these animals are still shot by fishermen whose nets are occasionally robbed by the seals.

Sea lions

Although numbers of the Australian sea lion (*Neophoca cinera*) were decimated by sealers in the early days of European settlement, colonies may still be seen on the beaches and islands along south/south-western coastlines.

During the mating season, the breeding males that are strong enough to hold territories may have a harem of six to eight females. One big male may have the entire beach area as his territory and will chase off any intruder.

Dugongs

Completely protected in Australian waters, the sea cow or dugong (*Dugong dugong*) ranges from Shark Bay in Western Australia, north around to Moreton Bay in Queensland, although individuals have been sighted as far south as Port Stephens in New South Wales. In general, dugong are very shy creatures which feed mostly on sea grasses, often moving around in herds or family groups. Over the past few years, huge areas of sea grasses have been depleted on the east coast by run-off pollution, and this has led to their mass mortality. In some areas, at Hervey Bay and off Mackay, over 75 per cent of dugongs have disappeared within the last decade.

Shark Bay appears to be the only place in Australia where a snorkeler may observe a dugong in reasonably clear water. Most other coastal areas are very turbid.

Introducing Queensland

The Sunshine State

Queensland—with its balmy tropical islands, long, white sandy beaches and sunny climate—is Australia's most popular tourist destination. The Sunshine State extends from the tip of Cape York to the northern boundary of New South Wales, covering an area of 1.7 million sq km. The Great Dividing Range splits this immense, geologically ancient landscape into two regions: a large, dry plateau-plains area to the west; and a smaller, wet and relatively fertile coastal plain to the east, where the majority of Queenslanders live.

The 5,208 km coastline was first surveyed by Captain Cook in 1770. His ship, the HMS *Endeavour,* was holed when it struck the Great Barrier Reef, and Cook spent six weeks sheltering on the coast near present-day Cooktown, while his damaged ship was repaired. In 1802 the Queensland coast was extensively charted by Lieutenant Matthew Flinders, and several reefs bear his name.

The first European settlers in Queensland established a penal colony on the shores of Moreton Bay at Redcliffe, in 1824. Lack of water soon forced the relocation of the settlement to the banks of the Brisbane River, where the city of Brisbane, the capital of Queensland, is now situated. Land for pastoral purposes was offered for sale in 1842 and freehold settlers quickly followed.

Most of Queensland's three million inhabitants live in the southeast corner of the state, with close to 50 percent of the state's population in the Brisbane area. Other major population centers include Toowoomba in the south; Bundaberg, Gladstone, Rockhampton and Mackay on the central coast; Townsville and Cairns in the north; and the mining town of Mt Isa in central Queensland. Tourism, mining, farming and fishing are major industries.

Situated in a tropical to subtropical zone, Queensland's trademark is its warm, sunny weather. In the north of the state, the land temperature varies from 25–35° C, and in the south 22–30° C. In winter the overnight temperature can drop to 5° C in the southeast corner. Water temperatures vary from 23–28° C in the north, to 18–26° C in the south. While a lycra suit might be suitable during the hottest part of the year in the tropics, most of the time divers use 3–5 mm wetsuits.

Diving conditions are good all year round, but are generally more stable over winter. Cyclones, which occasionally cross the Queensland coast during the summer months, have the potential to interupt diving trips. However, they more often pass without having any effect on the diving conditions, so don't let them affect your plans, as summer can provide some of Queensland's best diving.

The state's major attraction would have to be the Great Barrier Reef, the largest coral reef system on earth. The Great Barrier Reef Region stretches for about 2000 km along the Queensland coast, from the tip of Cape York to the Tropic of Capricorn, and offers the ultimate in sensational diving on pristine dive sites. Even though 2 million people visit the Reef each year, many reefs and islands remain largely unexplored because of the incredible size and complexity of the region.

The diving industry in Queensland is booming, especially around

Opposite: Found schooling around reefs and wrecks in tropical and sub-tropical waters, hussars *(Lutjanus amabilis)* belong to a large family of fish known as coral snappers. *Michael Aw*

THE GREAT BARRIER REEF
The world's largest marine park

THE GREAT BARRIER REEF, MADE UP OF MORE THAN 2500 individual reefs and shoals, and over 900 continental and coral islands, is the largest reef system in the world. Migratory and resident seabirds breed on its tropical cays and islands, and turtles, dugongs and whales find refuge around their shores. An incredibly abundant and diverse community of marine organisms inhabits the marine park. Its reefs support over 400 species of coral, well over 1500 fish species, thousands of species of molluscs and crustaceans, 350 echinoderm species, 23 marine mammals, 16 species of sea snakes and 6 species of sea turtles.

In 1975, the Great Barrier Reef Marine Park Act was passed to protect and manage the Great Barrier Reef Region, which covers an area of 349 000 sq km, and stretches for 2000 km along the Queensland coast. In recognition of its special qualities, the Region was inscribed on the UNESCO World Heritage List in 1981.

The Great Barrier Reef Marine Park is divided into the Far Northern, Cairns, Central and Mackay/Capricorn Sections, and is managed by the Great Barrier Reef Marine Park Authority, in co-operation with the Queensland National Parks and Wildlife Service. In managing this immense, complex region, the Authority endeavors to balance human needs with its obligation to conserve and protect the resources of the marine park. Zoning plans have been designed which allow multi-use of these resources, but restrict or prohibit certain activities in specified areas. General Use Zoning, that zoning applied to the majority of the marine park, allows almost all commercial activities except mineral extraction; Marine National Park Zoning restricts the removal of marine organisms, although limited fishing is allowed in some areas; and Preservation and Scientific Research Zones are off limits to all but scientists studying the reef.

The Great Barrier Reef is a sensitive ecosystem that is constantly affected by human activities and natural processes. Cyclones, crown-of-thorns starfish infestations, over-fishing, pollution, sewage, agricultural fertilisers, oil spills and boat anchors all have the potential to adversely effect the reef. While the millions of visitors a year is not without its problems, tourism could be its savior. As people gain an appreciation of the beauty, complexity and vulnerability of the Great Barrier Reef, they will understand the importance of establishing mechanisms which limit the effects of human activities, and learn to enjoy the marine park in ways that will conserve and protect its special qualities.

Cairns and Port Douglas. Diving in Queensland is regulated by legislation, which requires a high standard of safety control. All dives are logged and recorded, divers are asked to do a three-minute safety stop after each dive, and all divers must have an octopus regulator, or secondary breathing system. There is currently only one recompression chamber in Queensland, located at the Townsville General Hospital.

Dive shops and charter boats operate out of all major ports along the coast. The majority of dive shops are very professional, hire well-maintained gear, offer a good range of retail equipment, and provide excellent servicing and repairs.

Most dive sites are accessed by charter boat; some are only 5 minutes from shore, others in the Coral Sea are over 20 hours away. A handful of good shore dives are located along the coast at Bundaberg and the Gold Coast, but day trips and live-aboard boats are by far the best way to enjoy the top dive sites. When planning a trip to the Great Barrier Reef, divers have a wide choice of live-aboard and day trips, which depart from the mainland and the continental islands. Alternatively, resort accommodation is available on a handful of beautiful coral cays, where the reef is at your door step.

Divers should not neglect the dive sites off the southern coast, as many are equal to the best the Reef has to offer. Many visitors arrive in Brisbane, not realizing that the Great Barrier Reef starts 400 km to the north, or that Cairns is over 1800 km away. Air travel is the best if you're on a tight schedule, and flight costs can be reduced by pre-booking. The roads are good, if you've got plenty of time. If you are traveling on a budget, bus and train transport are comfortable and reliable.

Far Northern Reefs

The Last Frontier on the Great Barrier Reef

The Far Northern section is one of the last pristine areas of the Great Barrier Reef. Because there are hundreds of reefs that are inaccessible, the area is yet to be fully explored. Starting east of the tip of Cape York, the reefs in this section run to the northern end of the Ribbon Reefs, where most regular dive trips usually end. In recent years, however, charter boat operators have explored further north, and one in particular, Auriga Bay II, has discovered some of the most spectacular and remote dive sites on the Great Barrier Reef.

The Far Northern reefs are famous for their fantastic wall dives, pinnacles alive with fish and plenty of shark action. Reef sharks make an appearance on every dive, and turtles, stingrays, groper and manta rays are regularly seen, as well as the occasional marlin. To cut down on traveling time, charter boats run trips out of Lockhart River, a small town 500 km north of Cairns. Passen- gers are flown in, and from there the reefs are no more than a few hours" run.

Tijou Reef

Many excellent dive sites have been found around Tijou Reef, particularly the coral gardens on the inner side of the reef, and the wonderful wall dives on its outer eastern side. But the best action is at the northern tip of the reef at a site known as **Shark City**. Silvertip sharks, grey reef sharks and whitetip reef sharks are common here and will come in close to check out divers. Masses of pelagic and reef fish gather along the steep wall which is covered with an incredible variety of colorful corals and invertebrates.

Bligh Reef

Steep, dramatic walls occur around Bligh Reef, constantly swept by currents and packed with luxuriant coral growth. The currents are a rich source of planktonic food for resident bait fish and reef invertebrates, which are themselves food for the many species of larger fish also found congregating in these currents. Typical are parrotfish, trevally, surgeonfish, barracuda, batfish, groper and the giant Maori wrasse.

Below: Most of the colorful forms of hard coral (*Acropora* sp.) are to be seen in shallow water. Although hard corals grow down to and beyond 40 m, the deeper water forms are generally brown, green, blue or grey. *Neville Coleman*

Live-aboard trips up to 20 hours offshore

Generally 30–40 m

Strong currents on some reefs

Some of the richest coral growths in Australia

Wall diving, plenty of sharks

Reef and pelagic fish abundant on all reefs

Coral gardens, walls and pinnacles

wall dive that is usually done as a drift dive. The wall is packed with coral and other reef invertebrates, and manta rays feed in the current, sometimes close to the divers.

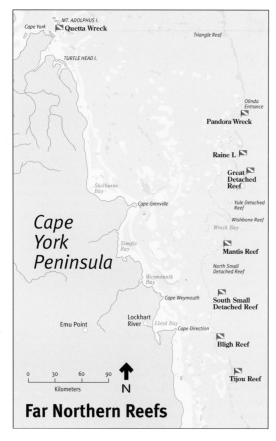

Far Northern Reefs

Southern Small Detatched Reef

Divers will see turtles, reef sharks, eagle rays, pelagic fish and occasional manta rays cruising the walls which encircle Southern Small Detatched Reef. These walls, which drop to beyond 100 m, are festooned with a spectacular array of corals, large gorgonians, long sea whips, spiky soft coral trees and sponges, which provide shelter for hosts of multicolored reef fish. All make for great photos.

Mantis Reef

Mantis is a long reef, with many fine dive sites. **Rainbow Wall** is one of the most beautiful wall dives in the area, which attracts an excellent variety of pelagic fish and reef sharks. **Martin's Mecca** is a pinnacle in 25 m that teems with fish life. **North Wall** is another brilliant

Wishbone Reef

This reef has many incredible wall dives along the outside of the reef, and dozens of large pinnacles covered in marine life throughout the lagoon. The most unique site at Wishbone Reef is the split at the **Cathedral Wall**. This site is very impressive at midday as beams of light filter through the split and light up the cave walls. Nearby is **Mobula Wall**, a wall dive where schools of mobula rays are often seen. The mobula ray is similar to a manta ray, although smaller and usually seen swimming information.

Great Detatched Reef

More breathtaking walls and huge pelagic fish can be found off Great Detached Reef. Some of the best sites include **Manta Wall** (a location where manta rays gather), and **Camel Back** (where an astonishing assortment of fish are found on two large pinnacles). At **Shark City**, the crew of *Auriga Bay II* sets out baits which attract dozens of reef whitetip and grey reef sharks, and their larger cousins, the reef silvertips. The sharks come in quite close during the feed, allowing all the action to be photographed.

Raine Island

One of the best places in the world to see turtles is Raine Island, during the nesting season. Thousands nest on the island during the night and can be seen in the water during the day, on every dive. They can be found resting in the coral gardens or swimming along the nearby drop-off, but divers should also keep an eye out for tiger sharks, as they also frequent the area, feeding on the turtles.

Lizard Island
A Secluded Resort and Excellent Dive Sites

Lizard Island Resort, which caters for a maximum of 64 guests, is one of the most upmarket, exclusive resorts on the Reef. Although basic in design, it is a real getaway and many famous visitors have enjoyed its seclusion. The resort shares the island with a marine research station which is run by the Australian Museum.

Located 240 km north of Cairns, Lizard Island is serviced regularly by a one-hour flight. Many guests come to dive, although others prefer to fish, water ski, windsurf, play golf and tennis, and enjoy nature walks along the many isolated beaches. The dive shop on the island conducts courses and runs daily boat trips to the many excellent dive sites in the area, such as **Cobia Hole**, that are well worth a dive, but trips out to the Ribbon Reefs, to famous sites such as Dynamite Pass and Cod Hole, are not to be missed.

If you are after a full-on dive hol-iday, book a live-aboard trip to the Ribbon Reefs; but if you want a diving holiday, mixed with other activities, then Lizard Island is your perfect destination.

Cobia Hole

Just off the resort in 18 m of water is a rocky reef packed with marine life, including batfish, barracuda, treval-ly, estuary cod, rabbitfish, lionfish, coral cod and baitfish. Surveying the sandy bottom around the reef, divers will find stingrays, goatfish and a number of large cobia.

Soft Coral Gardens

The western side of Lizard Island has many shallow fringing reefs in less than 10 m of water. The Soft Coral Gardens is a patchy reef with an amazing amount of coral growth and fish life. Reef inhabitants include sweetlip, parrotfish, damsels, butterflyfish, coral trout, rock

Below: Bluefin trevally *(Caranx melampygus)* and Yellowfin goatfish *(Mulloides vari-colensis)* are found on the Ribbon Reefs near Lizard Island.
Michael Aw

Boat diving up to 1 hour away

Ribbon Reefs 30 m, Lizard Island 15 m

Currents, swell, and wind chop often on Ribbon Reefs

Good coverage of hard and soft corals

Abundant reef and pelagic fish

Potato cod at Cod Hole, fish action at Cobia Hole

Coral and rocky reefs

Above: A major predator in the waters of the Great Barrier Reef, the tiger shark *Galeocerdo cuvier* may grow up to 5 m in length. It feeds on turtles, tired and injured big game fish (marlin) from the tag and release fishing programs, sea snakes, birds and fish.
Neville Coleman

cod, scorpionfish, lionfish and the occasional groper. The profusion of sea stars, brittle stars, flatworms, nudibranchs, clams, octopi, cuttlefish and crustaceans will delight the macrophotographer.

Snake Shelf

The Snake Shelf is a pinnacle in 18 m, teeming with fish life. Schools of batfish, trevally, surgeonfish, barracuda and fusiliers are regular visitors. Eagle rays patrol the top of the reef, and turtles are sometimes found on the sandy bottom. Sea snakes are common; divers will see dozens poking around the reef.

Dynamite Pass

The best way to explore Dynamite Pass, located in a channel between the Ribbon Reefs, is an action-packed drift dive. The bottom (35 m) and walls of the channel are overgrown with gorgonians, sea whips and black coral trees. Numerous fish, including groper, barracuda, trevally, mackerel and tuna gather to feed in the current. Drifting along the wall, divers will be joined by reef sharks, eagle rays and perhaps a manta ray.

Cod Hole

At the northern end of Ribbon Reef No. 10 is a patch of reef at 10–25 m that is world-famous for its fat fishy residents. The Cod Hole would be a great dive even without the potato cod. The reef is interesting to explore and populated by a diverse assortment of reef fish and invertebrates. Pelagic fish constantly sweep past the reef; barracuda, trevally and mackerel are all frequent visitors. Reef residents—moray eels, blue-spotted stingrays, estuary cod, sweetlip, sea bass, giant Maori wrasse and whitetip reef sharks—shelter in the caves and under overhangs.

Of course the potato cod are the main attraction, and do they put on a show! Up to 14 have been seen at once, but six are more usual. As soon as divers hit the water, the cod crowd around expecting food—they even push and shove each other for the best position. The cod are very aggressive when being fed, and have been known to bite hands and swallow dive gloves. Even without food being produced, the cod are approachable and can be easily photographed, reacting with each other and the divers.

Map

Lizard Island

N

0 2 4 6
Kilometers

Hicks Reef
Hilder Reef
One Mile Opening
Day Reef
Cook's Passage
Carter Reef
Underwood shoal
Half Mile Opening
Stewart Shoal
Yonge Reef
Petricola Shoal
North Reef/ Cobia Hole   Crystal Caves
Cormorant Reef
Soft Coral Gardens
MacGillivray Reef
Dynamite Pass
Lizard Island National Park
Cod Cave
LIZARD ISLAND
Cormorant Pass
EAGLE I.   PALFREY I.
SEABIRD ISLET
Snake Shelf
Cod Hole
SOUTH I.
Ribbon Reef No 10
Eyrie Reef
NORTH DIRECTION I.
Martin Reef
Kedge Reef
SOUTH DIRECTION I.
Unsurveyed
ROCKY ISLETS
Eye Reef

Ribbon Reefs and Osprey Reef
A Barrier Reef and Coral Sea Duo

One of the most popular live-aboard trips on the Great Barrier Reef is the combination visit to the Ribbon Reefs and Osprey Reef. Many charter boats offer weekly trips, which take in some of the most famous dive sites in the region such as the Cod Hole, Pixie Pinnacle, Dynamite Pass and the legendary North Horne at Osprey Reef.

some spectacular wall dives are possible along the outer edges. The inner side of the Ribbon Reefs have lush coral gardens and many spectacular pinnacles swarming with fish. Charter boats visiting this region generally depart from either Cairns or Port Douglas, and occasionally from Lizard Island, where passengers are flown in from Cairns.

Below: The potato cods (*Epinephelus tuka*) have entertained hundreds of thousands of divers at the famous cod hole at the Ribbon Reefs of the northern Great Barrier Reef.
Neville Coleman

Ribbon Reefs
The Ribbon Reefs form an almost continuous barrier north of Cairns, with over 100 km of reef bordering the Coral Sea. Due to open-water conditions, the outside of these reefs are rarely dived—most charter boats travel up the sheltered inner side of the reef; however

Temple of Doom
One of the fishiest locations on the Ribbon Reefs, the Temple of Doom absolutely pulsates with reef and pelagic fish. The site consists of a large pinnacle in 30 m of water, covered in beautiful coral growth. Invertebrate life is abundant—pho-

Live-aboard trip up to 20 hours offshore

Ribbon Reefs 30 m
Osprey Reef 45 m
plus

Slight currents, swell, wind chop

Healthy mixture of corals

Shark action at North Horne. Fish life at Temple of Doom and Cod Hole

Reef and pelagic fish abundant on all reefs

Coral gardens, walls and pinnacles

tographers will quickly run out of film. Fish species often seen on the pinnacle include trevally, tuna, goatfish, surgeonfish, stingrays, barracuda, sweetlip, angelfish, lionfish, squirrelfish, rainbow runners, fusiliers, batfish, mackerel and whitetip reef sharks.

Challenger Bay

Coral heads and coral gardens dominate the bottom of Challenger Bay. At 12 m the substrate is covered with an colorful mosaic of hard and soft corals. Macro life is superb—a stunning variety of nudibranchs, cuttlefish, flatworms, clams, feather stars, sea stars and anemones, sap suckers, molluscs, crabs and shrimps are regularly found on and around the corals. Masses of batfish, angelfish, sweetlip, gobies, damsels, wrasse, pipefish, pufferfish, filefish, rock cod and hawkfish reside around or on the reef. Look out for stingrays and large colonies of garden eels on the sandy bottom.

Pixie Pinnacle

A spectacular coral head that rises from 30 m of water to almost break the surface, Pixie Pinnacle is covered with a lovely array of hard and soft corals, gorgonians, sea whips and sponges, most of them small, but particularly colorful. Small reef fish, fairy basslets, lionfish, pipefish, anemonefish, damsels, parrotfish, hawkfish and triggerfish are all common. Pelagic fish also gather at Pixie Pinnacle. Divers often see trevally, barracuda, tuna and mackerel. This is a wonderful location for day or night photography.

Other outstanding dive sites on the Ribbon Reefs include **Steve's Bommie**, **Cod Bommie**, **Andy's Postcard**, and **Wonderland**. For details on Cod Hole and Dynamite Pass refer to the section on Lizard Island.

Osprey Reef

Osprey Reef, the most northerly of all the Coral Sea reefs, is known for its exceptional wall diving. The reef covers an area of 100 sq km and its perimeter drops vertically into 1 km of clear Coral Sea water. Exciting dives sites include **South Horne**, **Admiralty Anchor Bommies**, **Pelagic Gully** and **Flashlight Ravine**, which is most spectacular at night, when the flashlight fish are feeding. The most requested site at Osprey Reef is the North Horne.

North Horne

The North Horne is a reef shelf in depths from 20–45 m, which drops into deep water. The shelf is covered with numerous hard and soft corals, and deeper still grow large, spiky soft coral "trees" and gorgonians. This shelf attracts many reef fish, including large potato cod and schools of barracuda, trevally, tuna and mackerel. However, the North Horne is most famous for its sharks. Several resident whitetip reef sharks are constant dive companions, and grey reef and silvertip

Ribbon Reefs & Osprey Reef

sharks are generally found cruising off the wall. Schools of hammerheads are seen in winter, as well as the occasional tiger and thresher shark. The North Horne is a popular shark-feeding location, and most of the charter boats bait up for some savage shark action.

The combination trips sometimes include a stopover at **Bougainville Reef**, a small Coral Sea reef south of Osprey Reef, where wall diving is popular. Also, scattered over the top of the reef in depths from 6–18 m, is the wreck of the *Antonio Tarabocchia,* which ran aground in 1961, and now provides shelter for a variety of marine creatures.

Above: Ribbon Reef No 3 is part of the 100-km long barrier reef north of Cairns, which borders the Coral Sea. *Michael Aw*

Left: White-tipped reef sharks (*Triaenodon obesus*) are the most common of the tropical species. Although they follow divers and snorkelers around and are present at shark feeds, they are normally not aggressive. *Nigel Marsh*

Cairns and Port Douglas
Day-Tripping to the Reef

Above: Palm Beach Resort is just one of the many accommodation alternatives in the Cairns district for the dive traveler. *Michael Aw*

Live-aboard and day trips up to 3 hours offshore

Inner reefs 20 m, Outer reef 30 m

Slight currents on some reefs

Plenty of hard and soft corals, gorgonians and sea whips

Numerous good reefs close to shore

Reef and pelagic fish common

Coral gardens, drop-offs and pinnacles

The towns of Cairns and Port Douglas, with a huge range of accommodations, are popular tourist destinations attracting divers from all parts of the globe. The climate is tropical year round, and both towns offer a wealth of activities to enjoy including white-water rafting, bungy jumping, fishing, sailing, rainforest and outback tours, and of course diving. Dozens of charter boats offer live-aboard and day trips, and a large number of dive shops are located in the area. Thousands of visitors are taken out daily to snorkel and dive the large number of local reefs.

Agincourt Reefs

Two permanent pontoons, owned by Quicksilver Diving Service, are moored on the Agincourt Reefs, giving access to several excellent dive sites. **The Channels** offer interesting swim-throughs and caves, while **The Gardens** are renowned for their exceptional abundance of brightly-colored reef fish. **Blue Wonder** is a breath-taking wall dive to beyond 40 m, while **Nursery Bommie** is a spectacular pinnacle where pelagic fish gather to feed.

Norman Reef

The site of Great Adventure's pontoon, Norman Reef has many exciting dive sites along its length. Coral gardens are found in the shallows, and divers usually see reef sharks, gropers, turtles and pelagic fish patrolling the 30 m drop-off.

Saxon Reef

Saxon Reef offers many great diving and snorkeling spots. The shallows shelter a host of the ever-present reef fish—typical are anemonefish, goatfish, squirrelfish, pufferfish, damsels and butterflyfish. Dropping to 30 m are a number of walls, broken up by caves and gutters, which are covered with an incredible variety of coral and other marine invertebrates. These are good places to see turtles, reef sharks and schools of barracuda.

Hastings Reef

Pinnacles, walls, caves and coral gardens are all features of Hastings Reef. Gorgonians, soft corals and sea whips cover the walls and pinnacles. Reef and pelagic fish are numerous, and stingrays, Maori wrasse, moray eels and reef sharks are frequently seen. Photographers will find plenty of subjects, from pretty nudibranchs to schools of trevally.

Broken Patches

The pinnacles at Broken Patches, in depths from 10 to 25 m, are covered with lovely corals and masses of reef fish. A site known as **Paradise Reef** is an excellent place to see large pelagic fish and reef sharks.

Michaelmas Reef

Similar to many reefs in the area, Michaelmas Reef has extensive coral gardens and a number of pinnacles. The pinnacles, regularly visited by pelagic fish and crowded with soft corals and gorgonians, offer the best diving.

Flynn Reef

The pinnacles and hard coral gardens are popular dive sites at Flynn Reef. **Gordon's Mooring**, where a number of pinnacles attract masses of reef and pelagic fish, is one of the best.

Millin Reef

Numerous good dive sites are found at Millin Reef, a popular charter boat destination. **Whale Bommie** is an impressive pinnacle, and attractive coral gardens are found at **Club 10** and the **Swimming Pool**. Sharks, barracuda, trevally and mackerel gather at the **Three Sisters**, an assemblage of invertebrate-covered pinnacles.

Thetford Reef

Macro-photographers will find plenty of nudibranchs, tubeworms, shrimps, anemonefish, crabs, brightly-colored reef fish and pretty corals as subject matter in the coral gardens on Thetford Reef.

Moore Reef

Moore Reef has a number of beautiful hard coral gardens that are worth a visit, but the best diving is along the reef drop-off. Here an assortment of gorgonians, sea whips and soft corals clings to the wall, to depths of 30 m. A multitude of reef and pelagic fish live in the area.

Briggs Reef

The coral wall along the northern side of Briggs Reef drops into 30 m of water, and is covered in an excellent variety of corals. Along the wall

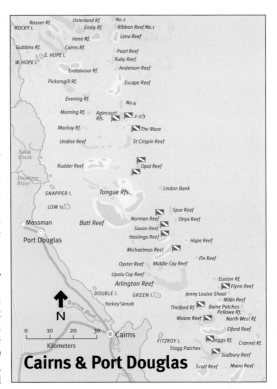

Cairns & Port Douglas

swim batfish, coral trout, sweetlips, parrotfish and the occasional pelagic fish. On top of the reef is a coral garden where lionfish, angelfish, stingrays, rabbitfish, wrasse and many other species can be found in abundance.

Sudbury Reef

Shallow coral gardens and drop-offs to 35 m can be explored on Sudbury Reef. Reef fish are prolific. You are also likely to see turtles and gropers.

Below: There are still many undiscovered nudibranch species off the shores of northern Australia. This *Chromodoris* sp. has not yet been fully described. *Neville Coleman*

A SEA OF PINK
The annual coral spawning

ONE OF THE MOST SPECTACULAR EVENTS ON the Great Barrier Reef is the annual coral spawning. Diving at night through the "snowstorm" of pink reproductive cells, as they rise to the warm surface of the sea, is an unforgettable experience.

Mass coral spawning has been observed on a number of reefs around the world, since the discovery of synchronous coral spawning by James Cook University students in 1981, on the Magnetic Island fringing reefs. Each year the scientific community turns its attention to this phenomenon, which takes place during late spring or early summer on the Great Barrier Reef, and during March and April on Ningaloo

Once fertilized, the eggs develop into free-swimming larvae which form pink "slicks" on the surface and drift with the current. After 5–20 days, the larvae descend to the reef and attach themselves to vacant sites, where they begin new coral colonies. The polyp then repeats building process and eventually thousands of individual polyps will make up the new structure. Synchronous spawning may have evolved as a survival mechanism—predators quickly get their fill with so many larvae in the water, leaving plenty of survivors to populate the reefs.

A number of charter boats co-ordinate dive trips with the coral spawning, now a popular tourist attraction. Other marine ani-

Reef off the coast of Western Australia.

Staghorn coral spawning. Over 160 species of hard corals are known to spawn at similar times at specific locations throughout the Great Barrier Reef. *Russ Babcock, AIMS*

Coral polyps ordinarily reproduce asexually by cloning, however, the annual sexual reproduction produces many more coral offspring, and distributes them over a wider area. Over 160 species of hard coral are known to spawn simultaneously, about four or five days after the full moon. Many are hermaphrodites, releasing both eggs and sperm in colorful compact bundles, which rise to the surface and then separate; the eggs chemically repel sperm from the same parent coral, while accepting sperm from another colony of the same species.

mals, such as giant clams, feather stars and sea cucumbers, spawn along with the coral, providing some very interesting night diving. Since factors such as water temperature and tidal characteristics affect the reproductive process, predicting exactly when spawning will occur is difficult. Those wishing to observe this extraordinary event must have a flexible timetable and plenty of energy for all-night vigils.

Holmes Reef
A Coral Sea Quickie

Most live-aboard trips to the Coral Sea usually take a week or longer. These trips are great if you have the time and money, but for those divers on a budget, or with limited time, there is an alternative—a Coral Sea quickie with Rum Runner Charters to Holmes Reef, a twin reef system 240 km east of Cairns. A number of other charter boats stop off at Holmes Reef, but *Rum Runner* is the most frequent visitor and runs four-day trips to the area. In two days of diving, about 8 different locations are visited. The crew of Rum Runner has pioneered several dozen dive sites around Holmes Reef, and is still exploring this 450 sq km reef system.

Nonki
This site is a complex of three huge pinnacles rising from 30 m to within 5 m of the surface. A number of caves and ledges cut into the pinnacles, each one packed with a profusion of gorgonians and soft corals. The gutters between each pinnacle are overgrown with brightly-colored corals. Small reef fish and invertebrates are common; divers will also find lionfish, angelfish, rock cod, molluscs and nudibranchs. A massive school of big eye trevally appears to be resident here, and other large pelagic fish are regularly seen.

Amazing
Dozens of caves are the main feature at Amazing, providing considerable excitement, but some of the long narrow ones should be treated with respect. Most of the caves are located in depths between 10 and 20 m, but it is possible to find some deeper. These caves are home to squirrelfish, cardinalfish and rock lobster—it is usual to find several dozen lobsters hanging off the walls. Outside the caves, the reef is superb with plenty of fish and other invertebrates.

Golden Wall
This is Coral Sea wall diving at its best—a sheer coral wall dropping into a depth of 1000 m. This wall is crammed with magnificent coral growth, large gorgonians, sea whips and masses of spiky soft

Below: This spectacular scene is typical of the Holmes Reef area—big caves, undercuts, drop-offs and crevasses. *Nigel Marsh*

Live-aboard trip over 12 hours offshore

Usually 45 m plus

Slight currents experienced

Rich variety of soft corals and gorgonians

Abundant reef and pelagic fish

Shark feed at Predators' Playground. Wall diving and spectacular corals

Coral Sea reef with walls and pinnacles

coral "trees". Small reef fish shelter along the wall, and not far off cruise the usual pelagic fish—trevally, jobfish, barracuda and mackerel. Schools of fusiliers and surgeonfish, grey reef and whitetip reef sharks are always around, and green turtles are frequently seen.

The Abyss

Another incredible wall dive! Drifting along this wall, divers feel as if they are flying, as the wall disappears into blackness in the clear water below. Photographers will find plenty of corals to photograph along the sides of the wall, and curious pelagic fish and reef sharks off the wall. Look closely, as there are many small critters to find, including shrimp, coral crabs, spider crabs, nudibranchs, sea stars, feather stars and brittle stars.

Turbo

A spectacular deep-water pinnacle in 35 m that attracts schooling fish when the current is running. Fish species regularly seen include unicornfish, barracuda, mackerel, rainbow runners, dogtooth tuna and surgeonfish. Reef sharks at the pinnacle are always fascinating to watch. The pinnacle itself is quite

beautiful, but is generally ignored among so much fish action.

Leopards Lair

Leopards Lair is a large pinnacle where harmless leopard sharks can sometimes be seen lazing on the sand during the day. The pinnacle has a good covering of hard and soft corals, gorgonians, sea whips and a variety of feather stars. Along the top of the pinnacle parrotfish can usually be found grazing in hard coral gardens.

Predators' Playground

The crew of *Rum Runner* do an exciting shark feed at Predators' Playground during each trip. They set up a large floating shark cage, where dozens of reef sharks gather. Once the divers are in the cage, baits are lowered into the water and the sharks move in. Both whitetip and grey reef sharks come in for the feed, but the whitetips are definitely the boldest.

After two days of diving around Holmes Reef, the boat does an overnight crossing back to the reefs off Cairns, where several more dive sites are explored before arriving back at Cairns harbor in the afternoon.

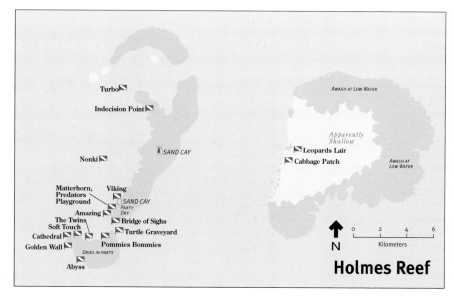

Holmes Reef

Townsville
A Rich Collection of Reefs and One Amazing Shipwreck

Divers will find a large selection of reefs to explore off Townsville. The inner reefs have extensive coral gardens and interesting drop-offs, while the outer reefs feature walls and pinnacles with a rich variety of coral and other marine life. The most exciting dive site in the Townsville area is the wreck of the SS *Yongala,* which sank during a cyclone in 1911.

Townsville is the largest city in Northern Queensland and caters well for the tourist market. Local attractions are many, and include a casino and the Great Barrier Reef Wonderland aquarium complex. A number of dive shops and charter boats are based in Townsville, including one of Australia's most well-known dive operations, Mike Ball Dive Expeditions. Day trips and extended live-aboard trips are available, but book early as there are a limited number of spaces. Those after an island getaway can stay at Magnetic Island or Orpheus Island, both of which have resorts, dive operations and a number of inshore dive sites that are rich in marine life, but good visibility depends on the weather.

ber of sites at Kelso, to dive coral gardens and a number of drop-offs. Under the pontoon is a great place to see snapper, Maori wrasse, gropers, emperor and sweetlip.

John Brewer Reef
Once the site of the world's first floating hotel, long since floated off to Vietnam, John Brewer Reef has a large lagoon and very good drop-offs to 35 m. These have an excellent coverage of corals and are frequented by reef sharks, turtles, gropers and schools of pelagic fish.

Coil Reef
An assemblage of pinnacles is found on the southern side of Coil Reef. In depths from 15–30 m divers will usually see turtles, eagle rays, stingrays, barracuda, trevally, mackerel and whitetip reef sharks.

Bowl Reef
The inner edge of Bowl Reef has many coral heads that provide interesting diving. These structures support an assortment of gorgonians, sea whips, hard and

Above: The sheltered, shallow lagoons, crammed with masses of corals, make snorkeling a treat. *Neville Coleman*

Myrmidon Reef
Located on the outer reef edge, Mymidon lies in clear water and has great coral growths, coral walls, canyons and caves. Reef fish are numerous, as are turtles, coral trout, trevally, reef sharks, stingrays, gropers and giant clams.

Kelso Reef
Pure Pleasure Cruises has a pontoon moored at Kelso Reef. The company's charter vessel *Pure Pleasure* transports divers to a num-

Live-aboard and day trips up to 6 hours offshore

Inner reefs 20 m, outer reefs 30 m

Currents experienced on some reefs

Healthy mixture of hard and soft corals

Reef and pelagic fish common

Fish life on *Yongala*

Coral gardens, drop-offs and pinnacles

Above: Giant clams (*Tridacna gigas)* can be found all along the Great Barrier Reef but are especially prevalent off Townsville reefs. *Nigel Marsh*

Chicken Reef

Giant clams are numerous on Chicken Reef. In the shallows lie dozens of these huge molluscs, some well over 1 m wide. Along many good drop-offs and in coral gardens, in less than 30 m, you will find reef sharks, groper and many invertebrate species as well as the occasional sea snake.

Broadhurst Reef

Pinnacles rising from 30 m provide great diving at Broadhurst Reef. These large bommies are packed with hard corals, sea whips, gorgonians and soft corals. The pinnacles teem with fish life. Divers will usually see barracuda, coral trout, trevally, sweetlip, lionfish, tuna and pufferfish.

soft corals, nudibranchs, moray eels, flatworms, sea stars, crustaceans and echinoderms. A large variety of reef fish and the occasional sea snake are resident on and around the heads. Pelagic fish can be quite plentiful.

Yankee Reef

On the northern side of Yankee reef are a number of pinnacles at 25 m, where large reef and pelagic fish can always be found. The reef itself has dense gardens of hard coral, and is home to many species of small, colorful reef fish and invertebrates.

Shrimp Reef

There is an exciting drop-off on the eastern side of Shrimp Reef, with plenty of corals and pelagic fish. Extensive areas of hard coral and associated reef fish and invertebrate life cover the rest of the reef.

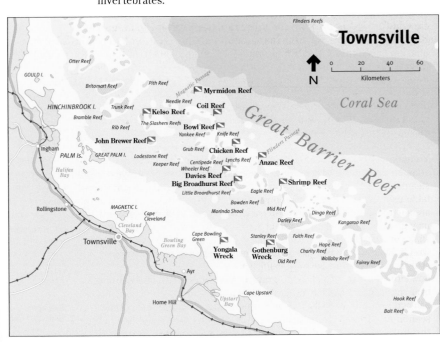

QUEENSLAND'S SHIPWRECKS

MANY HUNDREDS OF SHIPS HAVE BEEN WRECKED in the treacherous waters of the Great Barrier Reef. Most are now unrecognizable, hidden under coral or sand in shallow water. However, the following shipwrecks off the coast of Queensland are several still worth having a look at.

Quetta

The RMS *Quetta* sank off Cape York in 1890 after striking an uncharted rock. The 116 m-long ship now lies in 18 m of water and is occasionally visited by charter boats exploring the far northern reefs. Much of the wreck can still be explored. The *Quetta* shelters groper, coral trout, batfish and many pelagics.

Pandora

In 1791, on the return trip to England carrying 14 mutineers from the infamous HMS *Bounty*, the HMS *Pandora* ran aground on a reef near Raine Island and sank. The Queensland Museum is currently excavating the ship in stages, much of which lies buried in the sandy bottom. A permit is required to dive on the *Pandora*, and even though there is not much to see, its link to the *Bounty* makes it a fascinating dive.

Yongala

Descending on the wreck of the coastal steamship SS *Yongala* is always an unforgettable experience. On the way down, divers are surrounded by myriad fish. An eagle ray may glide by, followed by a curious olive sea snake or a shy turtle. Once at the top of the wreck, in 15 m, the fish life becomes especially impressive. Barracuda, queenfish, rainbow runners, black-blotched stingrays, coral trout, pufferfish, angelfish, butterflyfish, lionfish and coral cod are just a few of the species seen in and around the wreck. Dropping to the bottom, at 30 m, divers meet huge

The *Yongala* is one of the most famous wrecks in Australia, having been protected for many years. Pictured here is one of the bathroom fittings. *Nigel Marsh*

Queensland gropers, cobia, stonefish, sea snakes, estuary stingrays, tuskfish, Maori wrasse and resting turtles. There is also a wonderful variety of invertebrate marine life covering the wreck to investigate, as well as the 110 m-long shipwreck itself, which is fascinating to explore. By far, the *Yongala* would have to be the most rewarding dive off Townsville, even though the visibility is rarely over 12 m.

Gothenburg

The *Gothenburg* sank in 1875 after running aground on Old Reef off Towns-ville. The 60 m-long ship was carrying $80,000 in gold, which was salvaged soon after she sank. While the wreck is today badly broken up, it still makes for fascinating diving.

Aarhus and Marietta Dal

The iron barque *Aarhus* sank after striking Smith Rock, off Brisbane, in 1894. The remains of the *Aarhus* are now scattered at 21 m. Nearby lies what is left of the *Marietta Dal*, a 140 m-long liberty ship, which also ran aground on the rock in 1950. Wreckage is spread over a wide area.

Rufus King

Half of the *Rufus King* can be seen sitting in 8 m of water off North Stradbroke Island. This large freighter ran aground in 1942, and later her front half was towed away to be used as a machine shop during World War II. About 30 m of the ship remains, and when the seas are calm the structure can be entered and explored.

Most of the above-mentioned shipwrecks are historic shipwrecks, protected under Commonwealth law, which prohibits removal of objects from these sites. Please respect these rules.

Flinders Reef
Coral Sea Diving at Its Best

"Upon entering the water our group of divers was immediately surrounded by an enormous school of barracuda, which was quickly replaced by a massive wall of big-eye trevally. Thousands of silver bodies were flashing past us. Mixed in with the school were rainbow runners, mackerel, surgeonfish and tuna. We finally reached the top of the pinnacle in 12 m, and continued down its steep walls, passing incredible soft corals, sea whips and gorgonians. Suddenly from below two grey reef sharks shot up, charged past us, and then disappeared through the schools of fish. We descended to 40 m and then looked at the spectacle above—fish, sharks and divers all circling around this office block-sized pinnacle. It is obvious why **Watanabe Bommie**, is considered the best dive site in the Coral Sea." *Neville Coleman*

Watanabe Bommie is but one of the many fantastic dive sites that have been found around **Flinders Reef** and the nearby **Boomerang Reefs**. Located some 200 km east of Townsville, Flinders Reef is one of the most accessible and regularly visited of all the Coral Sea reefs. Almost any week of the year, you will find a charter boat heading out to the area. Conditions are good year round, although spring is considered the best time to dive anywhere in the Coral Sea.

Flinders Reef is a large circular structure and covers an area of 1000 sq km. Most of the diving is on pinnacles, but there are also superb coral gardens and walls. The Boomerang Reefs offer the more dramatic wall diving, as all sides drop steeply into 1000 m of water.

Each visiting charter boat has its own preferred dive sites, but the following, discovered by Mike Ball Dive Expeditions, are the most well-known.

Rock Arch

A wonderful wall dive with many fantastic corals. The most interesting area to explore is a shelf at the end of the wall, where numerous large coral heads interconnect to form many caves. Prolific hard corals dominate the tops of these coral heads, and the walls and caves are adorned by soft coral, sea whips and gorgonians, including one 4 m in diameter. Reef fish are very common, but divers will also see trevally, turtles, mackerel, gropers and quite a few whitetip reef sharks.

Anemone City

This site consists of five large pinnacles with their tops covered in anemones. The walls of the pinnacles are lined with gorgonians and soft coral, and darting among

Live-aboard trip over 12 hours offshore

Usually 45 m plus

Slight currents experienced

Excellent growth of hard and soft corals, gorgonians and sea whips

Shark feed at Scuba Zoo. Incredible fish life at Watanabe Bommie. Beautiful soft corals at most dive sites

Reef and pelagic fish abundant

Coral Sea reefs with sheer walls and huge pinnacles

Flinders Reef

North Reef

↑ N

Wantanabe Bommie

The Soft Spot

Flinders Reef Lagoon

Lonely Eel

Anemone City

Fan Patch

Rock Arch

FLINDERS CAY

Coral Sea

North Boomerang Reef

SAND CAY

China Wall

Cod Wall

Scuba Zoo

South Boomerang Reef

them are angelfish, fairy basslets, butterflyfish, rock cod, hawkfish and filefish. A number of caves are found on the pinnacles and one in particular is lined with beautiful pink hydroids. Pelagic fish and reef sharks sometimes cruise by, unnoticed by most divers who become totally engrossed in the anemones and their resident anemonefish.

packed shark feeds. All divers enter the cage and when in position, the crew opens a garbage bin full of fish pieces by remote control. The sharks which have gathered in the area rush in and devour the baits, giving divers a wonderful view of sharks feeding. Up to 30 sharks are frequently seen. Species include grey reef sharks, silvertips and whitetip reef sharks.

Above: Numerous silvertip sharks (*Carcharhinus albimarginatus*) reside on Flinders Reef. This species can at times be quite intimidating with its speedy approach and aggressive behavior. *Nigel Marsh.*

Soft Spot
Anyone wanting to see spectacular soft coral trees should request a dive at the Soft Spot. There are hundreds here, some 3 m long, hanging from the pinnacles that make up this site. Reef sharks, tuna, mackerel, coral trout, parrotfish, surgeonfish and invertebrates are plentiful.

Other dive sites worth a mention around Flinders Reef include the magnificent pinnacles at **Lonely Eel** and **Midnight**, a wall dive off **Flinders Cay**. Closer to the cay are wonderful coral gardens where there are plenty of turtles, stingrays and garden eels.

Scuba Zoo
Mike Ball Dive Expeditions has a large shark cage moored in 14 m of water on **Boomerang Reefs**, located where they conduct action-

China Wall
China Wall, 1000 m of vertical wall located on the **Boomerang Reefs**, is studded with gorgonians, soft coral, black corals and sea whips. Many small ledges are found along the wall, good places to see small fish and invertebrates. Grey reef sharks, barracuda, mackerel, tuna, rainbow runners, fusiliers, surgeonfish and schools of trevally cruise the currents. At the end of the dive, the coral gardens at the top are worth a close look.

Other excellent wall dives off the Boomerang Reefs include **Whaler Station** and **Cod Wall**, where you will see reef sharks, pelagic fish and a good range of corals. Exploratory dives are regularly conducted around both these reefs, and new walls and pinnacles are constantly being discovered by adventurous divers.

Outer Coral Sea Reefs
Exploring the Heart of the Coral Sea

Exploratory trips are a real diving adventure. Although some of the Coral Sea reefs have been regularly dived for over 10 years, most are still largely unexplored and offer extraordinary diving opportunities.

Over a dozen reef systems are found in the Coral Sea. Some are only 1 km in diameter, while others

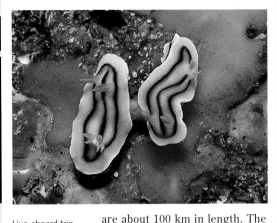

Live-aboard trip over 12 hours offshore

Usually 45 m plus

Slight currents

Rich collection of corals

Shark action and spectacular wall dives

Reef and pelagic fish abundant

Walls and pinnacles

are about 100 km in length. The closest of these reefs are 12 hours from the mainland by boat, while the furthest are another 12 hours away. A number of charter boats run regular trips to Coral Sea reefs such as Holmes, Osprey and Flinders. They also run charters to other inner Coral Sea reefs such as Flora Reef, Herald Cays, Abington Reef, Malay Reef, Herald Surprise and Dart Reef. Each charter boat crew has its own special dive sites, which they don't like to reveal, mainly to protect the sites from fishermen who also operate in the area.

The outer reefs, including Moore Reefs, Willis Islets, Diane Banks, Chilcott Islet, Magdeliance Cays, Lihou Reefs, Tregrosse Reefs and Diamond Islets also have a number of popular spots, but remain essentially pristine and unexplored.

All offer basically the same type

of diving: action-packed pinnacles and exciting sheer coral walls. So rather than relate similar types of dives on different reefs, the two basic dive types will be described.

Pinnacle Diving

Pinnacles dot the lagoons of many reefs in the Coral Sea. These towers of coral rise from the depths to sometimes break the surface, but the best ones lie hidden under the waves and are harder to find. Almost all are covered in fantastic coral growths, long sea whips, intricate gorgonians and massive soft coral "trees", some well over 2 m long. Invertebrates abound on these pinnacles, but are sometimes overlooked in the general profusion of marine life. Clams, nudibranchs, flatworms, hermit crabs, coral crabs, shrimps and echinoderms are everywhere. Especially striking are the multicolored feather stars which crowd together on the gorgonians.

Among the hard corals on top of the pinnacles is the best place to see the spectacular display of small, multicolored reef fish. Common varieties include lionfish, rock cod, fairy basslets, filefish, boxfish, blennies, damsels, squirrelfish, butterflyfish, wrasse and anemonefish. Other marine animals found around the pinnacles include turtles, stingrays, tawny nurse sharks, rock lobster, octopi, squid, tasseled wobbegongs, moray eels and eagle rays—and on the sand, occasional colonies of garden eels.

Pelagic fish gather around the pinnacles to feed. Some sites are circled by schools of trevally and barracuda, while mackerel, tuna and bonito cut through the swirling mass. Reef sharks are particularly common in the Coral Sea, and

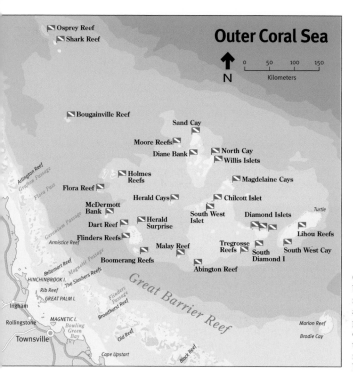

Outer Coral Sea

Osprey Reef
Shark Reef

N

0   50   100   150
Kilometers

Bougainville Reef

Sand Cay

Moore Reefs
Diane Bank

North Cay
Willis Islets

Arlington Reef
Grafton Passage

Flora Pass

Holmes Reefs

Magdelaine Cays

Flora Reef

Herald Cays

Chilcott Islet

McDermott Bank

South West Islet

Diamond Islets

Turtle

Geranium Passage

Dart Reef

Herald Surprise

Flinders Reefs

Lihou Reefs

Armistice Reef

Magnetic Passage

Malay Reef

Tregrosse Reefs

South Diamond I

South West Cay

Britomart Reef

Boomerang Reefs

Abington Reef

HINCHINBROOK I.

The Slashers Reefs

Rib Reef

GREAT PALM I.

Flinders Passage

Great Barrier Reef

Ingham

Broadhurst Reef

MAGNETIC I.

Rollingstone

Bowling Green Bay

Old Reef

Marion Reef

Townsville

Brodie Cay

Cape Upstart

Black Reef

they seem to be bolder here than on the inner reefs. Whitetip and grey reef sharks will swim right up beside divers.

Wall Diving

The best wall dives in the world are found in the Coral Sea. Most walls drop from the surface to a depth of more than 1 km, and all that can be seen is blackness below when swimming along them. The reefs are constantly washed by currents which provide food and oxygen for the prolific variety of invertebrates that grow along the wall. Black coral trees, sponges, sea whips, gorgonians, hydroid corals and large soft coral trees all make for wonderful photo subjects.

Ledges and caves riddle these walls and provide shelter for reef fish and a host of invertebrates. While not always seen in large numbers, pelagic fish usually sweep along the wall and will sometimes zoom in to feed on smaller fish. On almost every wall divers will encounter whitetip and grey reef sharks and the larger silvertip

sharks. Hammerhead, tiger and thresher sharks, bottlenose dolphins, manta rays, minke whales and even marlin have been seen swimming near the walls.

Most of these reefs have shallow coral gardens and sheltered lagoons that provide safe overnight anchorages. Coral cays, definitely worth a side visit, are found on a number of the reefs. However, most are home to nesting sea birds at certain times of the year, so do not walk through a nesting site where eggs and young are present.

Opposite: Nudibranchs are hermaphrodites and pass sperm packets to each other through their necks, (as males) after which both separate and lay their own egg girdles (as females). Two Loch's nudibranchs (*Chromodoris lochi*) are shown mating here. *Neville Coleman*

Below: Huge gorgonians and giant soft corals are features all along the outer Great Barrier Reef, especially on Coral Sea reefs beyond depths of 25 m. *Nigel Marsh*

Whitsunday Islands
Excellent Diving and World-Class Resorts

Below: Male blotched fairy basslets (*Pseudanthias pleurotaenia*), have a different coloration from the females, which are usually orange or yellow.
Neville Coleman

Reef trips up to 2 hours offshore

Around islands 10 m, on offshore reefs 25 m

Strong currents around some islands

Gardens of hard and soft corals

Manta rays in winter

Reef fish abundant, pelagic fish often seen

Rocky and coral gardens, walls and pinnacles

The Whitsunday Islands are beautiful continental islands lying off the coast, east of Proserpine. Over 150 islands are scattered throughout the region and most can only be explored by those prepared to sail these waters. However six of the islands (South Molle, Long, Hayman, Hamilton, Daydream and Brampton) have world-class resorts on them that offer the visitor a range of water sport activities, including diving.

For the more adventurous, camping is possible. Divers have the choice of staying at one of the island resorts or on the mainland, as a number of dive shops and charter boats are based on the islands as well as around Airlie Beach and Mackay.

Diving around the Whitsunday Islands can be excellent. The reefs are rich in marine life, however the visibility can be poor on occasion. For consistently clear water, the local charter boats run day trips to the main reef, which is about 2 hours from the islands.

Hayman Island
There are a number of pretty rocky reefs around Hayman Island in depths of 6–16 m. These reefs have a good coverage of hard and soft corals, and in places there are gorgonians, black corals and sea whips. The variety of reef fish and invertebrate life is particularly impressive. Molluscs, nudibranchs, flatworms, clams, gobies, blennies, damsels, lionfish, scorpionfish, butterflyfish, tubeworms, sea stars and feather stars are all common.

Hook Island
Hook Island has the best marine life and range of dive sites of any island in the Whitsunday Group. **The Pinnacles**, off the northeastern corner of the island, are a number of large coral heads. They sit in 18 m of water, and attract numerous reef and pelagic fish. Nearby, **The Woodpile** is a rocky wall covered in exceptional coral growth to 30 m. On a close inspection of the wall you will find many small tropical fish and invertebrate species, so don't forget your macro lens for this dive. **Manta Ray Bay** has a good coverage of hard and soft corals. In only 15 m of water lives abundant marine life and even manta rays over the winter months.

Fairey Reef
Fairey Reef has a number of dive sites featuring pinnacles, coral gardens and walls, mostly between 15 and 30 m. Marine life around Fairey Reef includes reef sharks, turtles, parrotfish, angelfish, batfish, coral trout, sweetlip, stingrays, moray eels and giant clams.

Bait Reef
At the southern end of Bait Reef is a spectacular wall dive known as

Manta Ray Drop-off. As on many dive sites in the area, manta rays are found cruising the wall in winter, but at any time of the year reef sharks and pelagics are common. The wall, which drops to 36 m, is covered with gorgonians, soft coral trees, sponges and sea whips. **The Stepping Stones** are made up of a series of large pinnacles with many caves and ledges in between, lined with a wonderful assortment of invertebrates. The Stepping Stones are a good place to see gropers, sweetlips, coral trout, lionfish, moray eels, anemonefish, stingrays and the occasional manta ray.

Hardy Reef

Many of the local charter boats regularly visit Hardy Reef as it has a well-balanced range of dive sites for any level of experience. There are shallow areas with hard and soft coral, alive with reef fish, typically: butterflyfish, wrasse, angelfish, damsels, pufferfish, triggerfish, filefish, boxfish, pipefish, gobies, lionfish and anemonefish. Nearby are drop-offs to 30 m with sea whips, black coral trees, sponges, ascidians and soft corals. Along these drop-offs are turtles, reef sharks, gropers and the occasional school of trevally and barracuda. Hardy Reef is the site of the Fantasea Reef World pontoon, where fish are fed regularly. Trevally, coral trout, snapper, Maori wrasse and one huge Queensland groper about 2 m long usually congregate at the pontoon for a free feed.

Line Reef, Sinker Reef, Hook Reef, Black Reef and several others in the area are also often dived. A couple of boats now offer liveaboard trips to the reefs off the Whitsundays and further afield.

Above: The spiny squirrelfish (*Sargocentron spinifer*), which inhabits caves, labyrinths and ledges, is rarely seen in the open. *Neville Coleman*

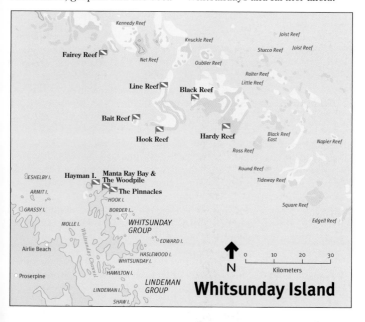

CROWN-OF-THORNS STARFISH
A prickly problem

THE CORAL-EATING CROWN-OF-THORNS STARFISH is a unique member of the starfish family. Venomous, sharp spines cover the upper surface of its grey-green/reddish-brown body, which can grow to over 80 cm in diameter. Preferring a steady diet of hard corals, the starfish feeds mainly at night by extruding its stomach over the coral polyps, releasing its digestive enzymes, and finally absorbing the "digested" food. When hard coral is scarce, the crown-of-thorns will feed on soft corals and certain algae.

During an infestation, the starfish feeds during the day and often starves to death once the food source is depleted. However it has been known to live up to 14 years under optimum conditions. Males and females gather to spawn in mid-summer. When the water surface temperature reaches about 28° C, over 20 million eggs may be released by a single female. The fertilized eggs quickly develop into planktonic larvae which are carried by ocean currents for several weeks before settling on the reef, to metamorphose into juvenile starfish.

Large numbers of the starfish were first observed in 1962, feeding on corals around Green Island, east of Cairns. Over the next two years, more than 27,000 starfish were destroyed in an attempt to protect the area, but within two years, the northern patches were devastated. By 1965, a much wider area of the Great Barrier Reef was known to be affected—entire reefs, not just isolated patches, and the problem wasn't unique to Australia. Outbreaks were discovered at the same time on the reefs around Japan, Southeast Asia, the Maldives, Samoa, Micronesia, the Red Sea, Cook Island, Fiji, Hawaii and many reefs in the Indo-Pacific region. Since then, a second outbreak was observed in 1979 on the Green Island reef, and only recently a third in the same locality.

Between 13 and 28 percent of the Great

Crown-of-thorns starfish. *Nigel Marsh*

Barrier Reef has been affected by outbreaks and considerable scientific research has been undertaken in an attempt to understand the reasons for the population explosions and whether or not they constitute a danger to the reef. Scientists have found that the infestations appear to originate north of the Cairns area and spread south at a rate of about 200 km every five years. By the time the outbreak reaches the reefs off the Whitsunday Islands, 10–12 years later, the northern reefs are well on their way to recovery. Often remnants of hard coral colonies survive, and recolonisation of the devastated areas begins after coral spawning in October-November. The fast-growing corals such as staghorns and tabular corals usually provide good coral cover within 10–20 years.

Operators have been trained to control populations in areas important to tourism or science, using a sodium bisulphate injection, which is harmless to marine life nearby. Dive operators on the reef are part of an observer network, set up to monitor crown-of-thorns activity. Any visiting diver can help by filling in sighting reports. New research programs involving DNA sampling will help determine the origin of the population explosions.

Although outbreaks occur every fifteen years or so, we still do not know whether this is a natural event or a result of man's inflence on the reef environment. Nutrient-rich runoff from nearby agricultural areas, removal of the natural predators of the starfish, overfishing and/or other disturbances to the reef system all have the potential to kick-start an outbreak.

While the crown-of-thorns starfish may be the destroyer of corals, its reputation as destroyer of the Great Barrier Reef may be undeserved, as many of the reefs severely affected in the past by its predations have recovered to such an extent that they are now attracting visitors.

Swain Reefs

Exceptional Diving on Hundreds of Small Reefs

Before the Coral Sea reefs became a regular live-aboard destination, the Swain Reefs were the most popular live-aboard trip on the Great Barrier Reef. Hundreds of reefs, most known only by a number, make up this system which covers an area of over 15,000 sq km.

The Swain Reefs are now mainly visited by fishermen, but dive charter boats still run regular trips if they can get the numbers. Boats based in Gladstone, Bundaberg and Hervey Bay usually explore the southern end of the reef system, but groups can set their own itineraries.

Most of the Swain Reefs are small and offer great diving along reef walls or around dense coral gardens. A number also have sheltered lagoons, which provide safe anchorages and good night diving.

Hixson Cay

Exceptional diving can be enjoyed right around Hixson Cay, with coral gardens in the shallows and exciting wall diving at the southern end of the reef. This wall drops beyond 60 m and is a multi-hued mass of sea whips, gorgonians and soft corals with mackerel, rainbow runners, jobfish and reef sharks.

Sandshoe Reef

Photographers will be delighted with Sandshoe Reef. At 10–30 m lie extensive fields of hard coral, home to a fantastic range of invertebrates and reef fish, including sea stars, brittle stars, feather stars, cuttlefish, clams, flatworms, nudibranchs, shrimps, anemonefish, damsels, gobies, filefish, boxfish, triggerfish and wrasse.

Sinker Reef

Deep gutters cut into the coral at Sinker Reef and form a fantastic maze. Lionfish, butterflyfish, anemonefish and angelfish are common, as well as gropers, sea snakes, trevally, batfish and barracuda—and all in less than 20 m of water.

Hook Reef

Parrotfish, scorpionfish, lionfish, gropers, batfish, surgeonfish and sweetlips are but a few of the fish species found amid the coral gardens at Hook Reef. At less than 20 m divers will encounter stingrays, reef sharks, sea snakes and a multitude of invertebrate species.

Horseshoe Reef

Several popular dive sites are found around Horseshoe Reef, which has a large lagoon with the safest anchorage in the area. The best dive site is along the wall, which

Live-aboard trip over 12 hours offshore

Varies from 15 to 30 m

Strong currents between reefs

Good hard and soft coral, gorgonians and sea whips

Reef and pelagic fish abundant

Spectacular drop-offs and coral gardens

Coral gardens, walls and pinnacles

Previous page
Orange Daisy Coral
*(Tubastraea faulk-
neri)* is usually seen
below 10–15 m.
Always a favorite
subject for photog-
raphers, the bright
orange polyps are
often found in
wrecks and caves.
Michael Aw

Opposite
Operating between
Cairns and Osprey
Reef, the *Taka II* is
just one of many
liveaboard boats
that offer the best
way to get to dive
sites on the Great
Barrier Reef.
Michael Aw

drops to 35 m on the southern side of the reef, coated with soft corals and large gorgonians. Tasselled wobbegongs, rock lobster and the occasional tawny nurse shark can be found on a number of ledges along the wall. Near the drop-off, you are likely to see pelagic fish, sea snakes, reef sharks and turtles.

Gannet Cay
A wonderful pinnacle off the southern side of Gannet Cay sits in 35 m of water. Circling this coral-encrusted structure are masses of reef and pelagic fish, including barracuda and trevally. Many invertebrate species can be found among the coral.

Snake Reef
Drop-offs to 40 m make Snake Reef special. These walls, over-grown with coral, shelter many small invertebrates. Reef sharks, trevally, barracuda, batfish, sur-

geonfish and sea snakes tour the wall, searching for food.

Central Reef
Excellent diving can be found around Central Reef at all depths. Photographers will find many sub-jects—schools of trevally, plenty of corals and other invebrates, reef fish and beautiful little nudibranchs.

Mystery Cay
Many coral heads rise in 20 m of water, on the southern side of Mystery Cay. Populated with a rich assortment of marine life, they are regularly visited by manta rays that come to the pinnacles to feed and be serviced by the cleaner wrasses.

Lavers Cay
There are many ledges and gutters on the northern side of Lavers Cay that are home to an interesting vari-ety of marine life. Along these gut-

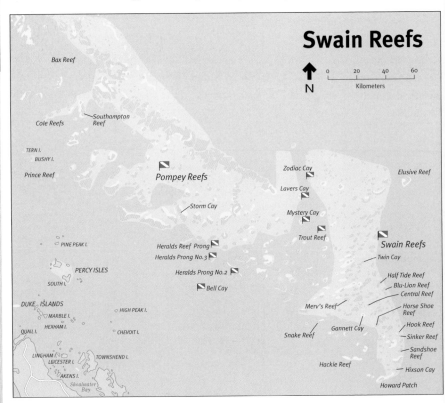

Above: The White lined grouper *(Anyperudon leuogrammicus)* inhabits coral-rich areas of clear lagoon and protected seaward reefs, feeding mainly on small fishes. Juveniles mimic herbivorous wrasses to get closer to their prey.
Michael Aw

ters divers will see trevally, batfish, sea snakes, rock lobster, reef sharks and a number of huge resident Queensland gropers, almost 2 m in length.

Pompey Reefs

The Pompey Reefs are a continuation of the northern end of the Swain Reefs. This area offers exciting wall dives and healthy populations of fish and corals, but is rarely dived. New Blue Hole is 100 m in diameter. Its sheer walls, lined with small corals, drop straight down into 90 m of water. A mixture of reef and pelagic fish enters the hole over the reef top.

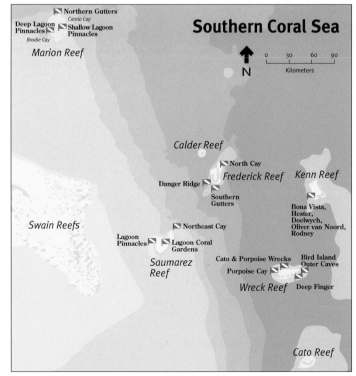

Southern Coral Sea Reefs
The Kingdom of the Sea Snake

On reefs in the Southern Coral Sea divers will particularly notice the sea snakes—hundreds of them! The reefs in this area support several species of these reptiles, the most common being the olive sea snake. Every dive is full of encounters—they swim around your legs, peer into your mask and even get amorous with your regulator hoses. Although venomous, sea snakes are not aggressive, and will leave you alone after satisfying their curiosity. All the attention may be unnerving at first, but divers soon become used to the snakes and can then concentrate on observing the other interesting marine life in the Southern Coral Sea.

None of the reefs in the area are regularly dived. To explore these remote reefs, you will have to find a group advertising a trip, or organize one. This is true live-aboard diving, as all the reefs are well over 12 hours from the closest port. Charter boats departing from Airlie Beach, Mackay, Gladstone and Hervey Bay are in the best position to visit these reefs, so they should be contacted about trips on offer.

The reefs of the Southern Coral Sea differ from their northern neighbors. The corals are generally smaller and not as colorful, there are fewer walls, and most of the diving is on pinnacles and coral gardens. However, plenty of marine life inhabits the reefs besides the sea snakes—an abundance of turtles, stingrays, reef sharks, gropers, reef and pelagic fish, and invertebrates.

Marion Reef
Marion Reef is a large atoll some 30 km in diameter, located over 400 km from the mainland. Its large lagoon offers a safe anchorage at the center with hundreds of pinnacles scattered in depths from 10–60 m. These pinnacles make for great diving and those in deep water have healthy growths of corals. Reef fish are plentiful and pelagic fish such as trevally, barracuda, mackerel and tuna circle the pinnacles. Reef sharks and sea snakes are often seen, and some sharks will come in close for great photos.

Marion Reef also has some exciting wall dives along the outer edge of the reef. These walls have a good coverage of soft corals, gorgonians, sponges and sea whips. The pelagic fish and reef sharks are not usually far off.

Frederick Reef
Frederick Reef is approximately 10 km in length and has extensive coral gardens on the northern side. The hard corals that dominate are very prolific and shelter a multitude of small reef fish and invertebrates. Jobfish, gropers, turtles, stingrays, whitetip reef sharks, trevally, shovelnose rays and barracuda are also found in the vicinity of these superb stands of coral.

Many pinnacles are found in the lagoon on the northern side of Frederick Reef, in depths from 10–30 m. Sea whips and gorgonians cling to the sides of the pinnacles, and big volcano sponges surround the bases. Pelagic and reef fish, and various species of shark swarm around these outcrops.

Saumarez Reefs
Saumarez is the most popular reef with both divers and fishermen. The reef structure is some 30 km in length and about 300 km from the mainland. The northern side of the

Live-aboard trips over 16 hours offshore

About 45 m plus

Slight currents

Hard corals dominate; also soft corals and gorgonians

Reef and pelagic fish are numerous

Rich marine life on the pinnacles at all the reefs. Abundance of sea snakes

Coral reefs, pinnacles and the occasional wall

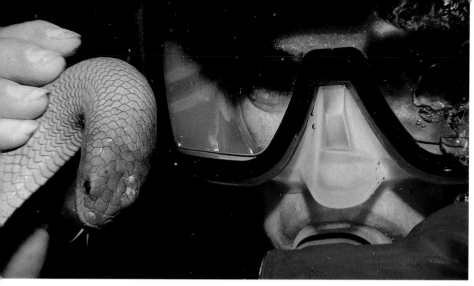

Above: Although sea snakes are potentially the most venomous snakes in the world, they are more curious than aggressive towards divers. The snake shown here is very docile, but it is not a recommended practice to handle any venomous snakes.
Nigel Marsh

Below Even from the air, it is hard to comprehend the size of a single reef, let alone thousands of square kilometers of reefs.
Neville Coleman

reef offers good anchorages and has the best dive sites. One of the most interesting sites is the coral gardens of **North East Cay**. In the gutters and caves running thoughout the reefs, at depths from 6–20 m, are numerous reef fish and sea snakes. Explore the small caves to find stingrays, tawny nurse sharks, wobbegongs, rock lobster and resting turtles. Pelagic fish constantly sweep over the reef, joined by eagle rays and reef sharks.

As with the other reefs in this region, hundreds of pinnacles rise from the lagoon floor. The best coral growth is found on these pinnacles, and gathered around them are the usual reef sharks, reef and pelagic fish, and sea snakes.

Wreck Reef

Wreck Reef is about 30 km long and is, as the name implies, scattered with the remains of many a ship. Divers will find debris from several wrecks on the reef and in the lagoon. The most spectacular dive site at Wreck Reef is a wall dive off Bird Island, that drops from 10–200 m. Soft corals, sea whips, sponges and gorgonians grow along the wall. Out in the deeper water you will see the big stuff—schools of barracuda and trevally, lone mackerel and tuna. Around these circle whitetip and grey reef sharks, and down deeper, tiger sharks.

Cato and Kenn Reefs

The two smallest and most remote reefs in the Southern Coral Sea are Cato and Kenn Reefs. Neither of these reefs has been extensively dived, and so, along with the other reefs in this region, offer the diver wonderful exploration diving.

Keppel Islands
Island Diving Inside the Reef

The Keppel Islands, located only 10 km off the coast of Yeppoon, are a popular holiday destination for fishermen, sailors and divers. The largest island, Great Keppel, is the most developed. Divers can stay at either the Great Keppel Island Resort, the cheaper Keppel Haven Resort or on the mainland where there is a good range of accommodation and a number of dive shops and charter boats. The dive operator on Great Keppel Island, Keppel Island Dive Centre, is in the best position to organize trips to the dozens of dive sites found in the area.

The Keppel Group offers excellent diving, which may surprise some, since the islands are located well inside the Great Barrier Reef, and the adjacent coastline is lined with mangroves. Around each island are rocky reefs covered in hard and soft corals, which support a fascinating mixture of invertebrates, reef fish and sea snakes. While the visibility might not be as good as the Great Barrier Reef, the great number and variety of marine creatures make the Keppel Group an excellent dive destination.

Man and Wife Rocks

Wobbegongs, turtles, batfish, reef sharks, angelfish, stingrays, trevally, parrotfish and sea snakes are regularly sighted on the reef around Man and Wife Rocks. The best diving is from 15–20 m, where there is good coverage of hard corals, gorgonians, sponges and soft corals.

Below: The exquisite, unique little toe-nail cowrie (*Calpurnus verrucosus)* spends its entire life on its food source host the soft coral *Sarcophytum.* *Neville Coleman*

Boat diving up to 1 hour away

Usually 10 –20 m

Common around the islands

Dense gardens of hard and soft corals

Reef fish abundant, pelagics also seen

A rich diversity of life, especially invertebrates

Coral and rocky reefs

Above Hussars
(Lutjanus amabilis)
form impressive,
large schools on
shallow coastal
rocky reefs, in
lagoons around
bommies and off
seaward reefs.
At night they dis-
perse to feed.
Michael Aw

Miall Island

An interesting sloping reef wall,
which drops to 15 m, is located on
the northern side of Miall Island.
This reef has plenty of small reef
fish and enough invertebrates to
keep a macro photographer busy.
Look out for the flatworms, nudibranchs and fan worms. Where
the current is strongest, on the
deep, sandy fringe, live groves of
sea whips.

Middle Island

Similar to most of the islands in
the Keppel Group, Middle Island
has good fringing reef right
around its shores. At the Underwater Observatory, you will find
large numbers of fish in only 6 m
of water. Commonly seen are estuary gropers, batfish, sweetlip,
trevally, rabbitfish, moray eels and
lionfish. You can get quite close to
tame cod here, while the Barrier
Reef chromies, common throughout the Keppels, are plentiful.

Great Keppel Island

A number of excellent sites around
Great Keppel Island can be dived
and snorkeled from the beach or
by boat. **Parkers Bommies**, one
of the best sites in the area, has
coral heads covered with gorgonians, soft corals and sea whips,
located in 18 m of water at the
southern end of the island. An
excellent range of marine life is
attracted to the bommies, which
team with fish life.

Halfway Island

Halfway Island has many sheltered
coral gardens found in 5–10 m of
water. The coral growth here is
exceptionally good and divers will
see many reef fish, sea snakes and
moray eels on its fringing reef.

Humpy Island

On the eastern side of Humpy Island
is a dive site called Cathedral Rock.
Although it has only fair fish life and
coral growths, the many caves,

ledges and gutters make for interesting diving in only 12 m of water.

Barren Island

Surrounded by pretty coral gardens, Barren Island is a great place to see plate, brain, staghorn and other hard and soft corals. The sheltered southern side is the best place for inexperienced divers and is home to interesting marine life in a diverse range of habitats. Usually found at depths to 15 m, are lionfish, coral trout, sea snakes, stingrays, sweetlips, angelfish, butterflyfish, gobies, wrasse, anemonefish, scorpionfish, moray eels and leatherjackets. The invertebrate life is exceptionally diverse. Egg cowries, clams, shrimp, hermit crabs, coral crabs, sea stars, feather stars, brittle stars, flatworms and a variety of nudibranchs are all common.

Child Island

Located between Child and Barren Islands is a deep channel to 30 m known as The Gulch. Its walls are lined with small colorful invertebrates including ascidians, sponges, sea fans and forests of sea whips. Current and surge are common in the channel, but the movement of water attracts masses of fish. On a good dive, gropers, barracuda, trevally, stingrays, wobbegongs, cobia and surgeonfish can be seen.

Egg Rock

Egg Rock is a tiny monolith surrounded by an excellent fringing reef. A good range of small tropical fish and invertebrates are found in less than 15 m of water, as well as moray eels, gropers, sea snakes, anemones, clams, trevally, turtles, and wobbegongs.

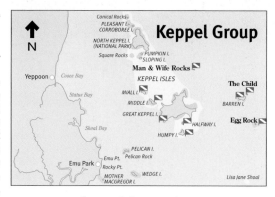

Keppel Group

Below: A massive soft coral *(Dendronephthya* sp.) found on Holmes Reef in the Coral Sea. *Michael Aw*

Capricorn and Bunker Groups
Idyllic Coral Cays, Fantastic Reefs

Live-aboard trips up to 6 hours offshore

Usually 20–30 m

Common around the islands

Healthy gardens of hard and soft corals

Manta rays, turtles, reef sharks and fish on most reefs

Reef and pelagic fish are common

Coral reefs and pinnacles

The reefs known as the Capricorn and Bunker Groups straddle the Tropic of Capricorn, just off Gladstone. The groups include several vegetated coral cays inhabited by thousands of sea birds. Each summer turtles lay their eggs in the warm sands of these islands. Heron and Lady Elliot Islands are the most famous for their excellent dive sites, but fantastic coral gardens, pinnacles and drop-offs populated with reef and pelagic fish, manta rays, turtles, reef sharks and countless varieties of invertebrates can be found on the rest of the reefs as well.

Divers can stay at the resorts on Heron and Lady Elliot, and explore the rest of the Capricorn and Bunker Groups by charter boat, or camp on one of the coral cays.

Island Camping
Camping is an inexpensive way to see the reef. Permits and regulations can be obtained from the Queensland Department of Environment for stays on Lady Musgrave, Masthead, North West and Tryon Islands. Camping on these islands can be quite an adventure, as you must bring all your own food and equipment, and arrange to be dropped off and picked up again by a charter boat. Compressors are only allowed on Lady Musgrave and North West Island, which makes snorkeling the only feasible option on the other cays. A number of dive shops used to take groups on camping safaris, but this has become less popular as the islands are far easier to visit on a live-aboard vessel.

Live-aboard trips
The most convenient way to see the best of the Capricorn and Bunker Groups is from a live-aboard vessel. A number of charter boats run 5- to 7-day trips from Gladstone, Bundaberg and Hervey Bay. In a week of diving you will be able to visit many of the cays and reefs.

North Reef
Manta rays gather above the coral heads found on the northern side of North Reef. In depths from 10–18 m are whitetip reef sharks, gropers, turtles, wobbegong, moray eels and the occasional pelagic fish. Hard and soft corals dominate the reef, small reef fish are very plentiful and a good range of invertebrate life can be found here.

Sykes Reef
A number of gutters lie in depths from 6–15 m, at the northern end of Sykes Reef. These gutters attract a variety of marine life, including baitfish, coral trout, gropers, Maori wrasse, turtles, moray eels, stingrays, batfish, trevally, parrotfish, surgeonfish, tawny nurse sharks and wobbegongs. Whitetip, blacktip and grey reef sharks gather here to feed on the abundant fish life.

Polmaise Reef
On a flat exposed reef on the western side of Polmaise Reef are a number of small pinnacles in only 9 m of water. These pinnacles are alive with schools of barracuda, trevally and batfish, sweetlip, gropers, coral trout, angelfish and lionfish. In a number of small caves that cut into the pinnacles hide wobbegong, colorful shrimp and rock lobster. Sea snakes can be seen among the coral.

Fairfax Island

Numerous pinnacles are located in depths of 10–17 m on the northern side of Fairfax Island. One in particular, which stands 8 m high, provides some incredible diving. This pinnacle is riddled with caves where hosts of small baitfish congregate which attract trevally, coral trout, lionfish and rainbow runners. The caves also shelter tasselled wobbegongs and moray eels. Around the pinnacles, you will see turtles, shovelnose rays, manta rays, stingrays, reef sharks and leopard sharks.

Lady Musgrave Island

Just two hours from Bundaberg, this island is most popular with campers, and is visited regularly by day-trippers from Bundaberg as well. The MV *Lady Musgrave* trav-els to the island four times a week, and daily during school holidays. Once on Lady Musgrave, you can explore the cay, snorkel the lagoon or reef, enjoy glass-bottom boat tours, or dive on the number of excellent dive sites located around the reef. Even the large lagoon makes for good diving as there are hundreds of coral heads (bommies) found at depths ranging from 5–8 m.

The northern side of the island has pretty coral gardens, small pinnacles and plenty of marine life, including manta rays, reef sharks and turtles. The most exciting diving is found on the southern side of the island where the reef drops from 12–21 m. Many ledges, with wobbegongs, turtles, stingrays and rock lobster, undercut this drop-off. Pelagic fish and reef sharks cruise the area, and sea snakes are often seen.

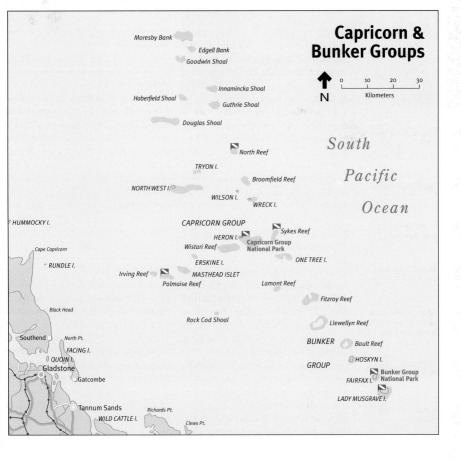

Heron Island
The Oldest Resort on the Reef

Below: As the day fades, the noddy terns (*Anous minutus*) return in their thousands from the day's fishing to roost in the she-oaks. *Neville Coleman*

Up to 20 minutes by boat

Usually 15 m

Slight currents are common

Hard and soft corals

The fish life at the Heron Bommies and other dive sites

Plentiful populations of reef and pelagic fish

Coral reefs and pinnacles

Located among the magnificent cays and reefs of the Capricorn Group, Heron Island can be reached easily by helicopter, ferry or charter boat from Gladstone. A true coral cay, the island's beaches are white coral sand, where thousands of green and loggerhead turtles lay their eggs during the summer months. The marine life on the surrounding reefs is some of the most interesting in the area.

The island supports a marine research station, run by the University of Queensland, and a resort which, until 1932, was a turtle soup factory. Since that time the resort has grown, and now offers a range of accommodation and excellent facilities, including a pool, bar, dining area, games room and shops. Package deals are available which include diving, accommodation and meals. Free diving is offered sometimes in the off season. The dive shop organizes trips to the many excellent dive sites around Heron and to nearby islands and reefs.

Heron Island Bommies
Located at depths from 8–17 m, the famous Heron Island Bommies (pinnacles) might be devoid of dramatic coral growth, but compensate for this by supporting a profusion of fish and other marine life. On a typical dive it is not uncommon to see batfish, barracuda, tuskfish, estuary cod, lionfish, trevally, angelfish, sweetlips, fusiliers, baitfish, rainbow runners, butterflyfish, rock cod, parrotfishs, and surgeonfish, as well as a host of sharks, rays and reptiles. Moray eels, stingrays, tasselled wobbegongs, eagle rays and manta rays are regularly seen around the bommies. Turtles are especially common all around Heron Island during the summer months.

Gorgonia Hole
This is a good area for macro-photographers as the gutters and reef walls are covered with a vast array of sea stars, feather stars, nudibranchs, flatworms, shrimp, crabs, brittle stars and other small reef creatures. A maximum depth of 16 m gives divers plenty of time to explore the reef. Hard coral growth is moderate, but there are plenty of small gorgonians and soft corals. Resident reef fish include angelfish, butterflyfish, blennies, goatfish, sweetlips, lionfish, damsels, filefish, triggerfish, hawkfish and rock cods.

Blue Pools
Divers exploring the Blue Pools will find a great selection of fish in depths from 5–20 m. Semicircle angelfish are common and very friendly (great fish portraits) and other resident fish include gropers, coral trout, batfish, lionfish, wrasse, parrotfish, surgeonfish and a variety of butterflyfish. Invertebrate life around the corals is impressive, and

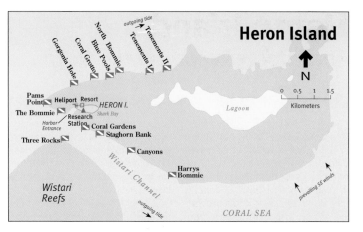

a number of nudibranch and flatworm species are common. Here the reef forms a bowl shape, like a protected swimming pool, and offers an easy, relaxing dive.

Pams Point

This coral wall is the best place to see manta rays at Heron Island. They feed just off the point and can be seen swimming past with their mouths open to collect plankton. When a slight current is running, pelagic fish and reef sharks also gather here, making it one of the best dive sites at Heron Island.

Coral Gardens

The Coral Gardens is made up of a sloping reef of staghorn and other hard corals that drops into 20 m of water. Fish life is very prolific in this area and divers will regularly see lionfish, moray eels, flutemouths, stingrays, coral trout, trevally, barracuda, anemonefish, surgeonfish, tuskfish and gropers. This is also a good place to find turtles, reef sharks and manta rays, which cruise the channel between Heron Island and Wistari Reef.

Many other good dive sites are located around Heron Island, such as the **Tenements**, **Harry's Bommie**, **North Bommie** and **The Canyons**. If you have the time, book an adventure dive to some of the other lovely cays and reefs of the Capricorn and Bunker Groups.

Wistari Reef

A number of dive sites are popular along the drop-off on the north side of Wistari Reef. Here the reef drops to 25 m and has some of the best coral growth in the area—large soft corals, gorgonians and sea whips. A number of coral heads that rise from the sandy sea floor at the base of the wall are well worth a look, as they shelter an interesting assortment of reef fish and invertebrate life. Off the wall you will find coral trout, gropers, reef sharks, sweetlips, flutemouth, scorpionfish, turtles and the occasional school of pelagic fish.

Below: Heron Island, a top diving destination, and the place where thousands of green and loggerhead turtles come to lay eggs during the warmer summer months. *Michael Aw*

Lady Elliot Island
An Unforgettable Coral Cay

Below: Common on many inshore and offshore reefs off Queensland, the manta ray (*Manta birostris*) is one of the few rays which does not have a venomous barb in its tail. These gentle giants spend hours playing and courting during the spring and summer months and often interact with divers—a wonderful experience.
Nigel Marsh

Sites accessible from shore and boat

Usually 20–30 m

Common around the island

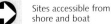
Good hard and soft corals

Manta rays, leopard sharks, reef sharks and spectacular pinnacles

Abundant reef and pelagic fish

Coral reefs and pinnacles

When first visited in the early 1980s, accommodation on Lady Elliot Island was tent style—meals were taken under the trees, and there were few facilities. Today the resort on the island boasts excellent facilities, but in all this time one thing that hasn't changed—the diving is still spectacular.

After boarding a flight in Bundaberg, it is a quick 30 minutes to Lady Elliot Island. That first view of the island is unforgettable. Peering from the window you see a 42-hectare coral cay, bisected by a grassy runway, surrounded by many patches of reef. Lady Elliot Island is at the southern-most end of the Great Barrier Reef, and being close to the continental shelf, is blessed with clear water and an impressive array of marine life. Manta rays are the most famous residents of the area, as dozens can be seen feeding around the island throughout the year.

The dive shop on the island conducts three trips daily. Over 20 sites are regularly dived, both from the shore and by boat. Currents are common around the island, so most dives are done as drift dives. The sites on the western side of the reef are accessible from the shore and numerous pinnacles offer the best diving. The rest of the reef is bordered by an exciting drop-off.

Lady Elliot Island Resort offers two types of accommodation—cabins or large safari tents—and package deals on meals, accommodation and diving. Facilities at the resort include a marine education center, bar, pool, gift shop and a large dining-room complex. As well, guests can relax on the beach, or observe and photograph the many thousands of sea birds that nest on the island.

Blow Hole

This large tube-like cave, 6 m in diameter, cuts into the reef wall and exits on the top of the reef. Inside live many fish species, including squirrelfish, lionfish, bannerfish, rock cod, coral trout, sweetlips, butterflyfish and many thousands of baitfish. The cave walls are lined with tubastrea corals and small soft corals. Look closely and you may find shrimp, crabs and cowries. The Blow Hole is also a popular hangout for wobbegongs, blotched

stingrays, old turtles and the occasional tawny nurse shark.

Gropers Grovel

Gropers Grovel is off the northern end of the island. Here numerous caves and ledges are found along the reef wall. Coral growth is extremely prolific—sea whips, gorgonians, sponges, ascidians, soft corals and tubastrea corals cover the reef. Pelagic fish are everywhere—barracuda, trevally, rainbow runners and fusiliers. A giant Queensland groper is occasionally seen in the area. Regulars are reef sharks, eagle rays, turtles and silvertip sharks that zoom in to check out divers and disappear just as quickly.

Anchor Bommie

This towering coral head, which stands 7 m tall in 20 m of water, is cut by many small caves where baitfish, squirrelfish and wobbegongs hide. Small reef fish dart in and out of the corals along the sides and top of the bommie, while schools of barracuda and trevally circle the structure. Manta rays often visit, and will sometimes glide around the bommie, seeming to check out the humans. Divers will also see turtles, sea snakes, gropers, reef sharks, stingrays, leopard sharks, eagle rays, and shovelnose rays. Colonies of garden eels can be found on the sand at the base of the bommie.

Lighthouse Bommies

Lighthouse Bommie, a group of small coral heads in 15 m, is definitely the best place to enjoy the company of manta rays. Manta rays constantly cruise the area, sometimes playing follow the leader, other times feeding on plankton. They also come in to be cleaned by the resident cleaner wrasse. Around the Lighthouse Bommies you are likely to see leopard sharks, stingrays, sea snakes, moray eels, reef sharks, mackerel, trevally, gropers, Maori wrasse, shovelnose rays, reef fish,

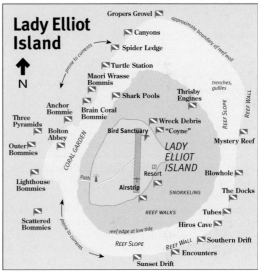

invertebrates and turtles—and all this is accessible from the shore.

Many other excellent shore dives are located on the western side of the island, including the **Outer Bommies**, **Three Pyramids** and **Maori Wrasse Bommie** where manta rays and other marine life can be seen. **The Shark Pools** are best snorkeled during summer, as reef sharks gather here to hunt along the reef flats. Dozens of whitetips, blacktips and grey reef sharks congregate in 3–8 m of water. Other popular boat diving sites include **Sunset Drift**, **Southern Drift**, **Hiro's Cave**, **The Canyons**, and **Turtle Station**. At every site, divers will see turtles, sharks, schools of fish and manta rays.

Above: Widespread from the southern Great Barrier Reef well into the South Pacific, Elizabeth's chromodoris (*Chromodoris elizabethina*) has an easily recognized combination of pattern and colors.
Neville Coleman

ENDANGERED SEA TURTLES

ENCOUNTERS WITH SEA TURTLES, THE MOST common marine reptile found in Great Barrier Reef waters, are among the diver's most memorable experiences. During the summer breeding season, these giant reptiles are often found resting in the calm waters of the lagoon, or under coral ledges. While the majority of encounters are brief, occasionally an inquisitive individual will hang around and accompany a diver over the reef flat, where it forages for food.

Of the six species of sea turtle inhabiting Australian waters, the green turtle *(Chelonia mydas)* and loggerhead turtle *(Caretta caretta)* found along coastal New South Wales, Queensland, the Northern Territory and Western Australia, are most regularly seen by divers. The pretty hawksbill turtle *(Eretmochelys imbricata)* is

Loggerhead turtle hatchlings. *Neville Coleman*

common on some coral reefs, while the flatback turtle *(Chelonia depressa)* and Pacific ridley *(Lepidochelys olivacea)* are rarely sighted. The giant leatherback turtle *(Dermochelys coriacea)* is found occasionally off the east coast, but is generally considered to be rare in the area, feeding on jellyfish and other soft-bodied invertebrates in the open ocean. Of the six species of turtle found in Australian waters, five are listed as either endangered or vulnerable by the government.

Summer is the best season to observe turtles on the Great Barrier Reef. From October to February, males and females gather on their "home" reefs surrounding sandy cays, such as those found in the Capricorn and Bunker Groups and around Raine Island. Divers often see turtles mating in shallow pools along the lee edge of the reef. After dark, on the incoming tide, the females drag their large bodies from the sea and lay their round eggs in the warm sand. Over 10,000 nesting turtles have been recorded in a single night on Raine Island, located in the Far Northern section of the Great Barrier Reef Marine Park. Turtle watching is very popular at both Heron Island

and Lady Elliot Island, however strict rules prevent the turtles being disturbed. Turtles may return to the sea distressed, if upset by lights, noise or movement before laying has begun, but once the ping pong-ball size eggs start to fall, torches and flash photos are allowed.

For decades researchers from the Queensland National Parks and Wildlife Service have been tagging and monitoring the hatchlings and adult turtles at Mon Repos, Bundaberg and Heron Island. They 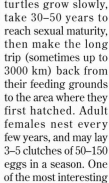 have discovered that turtles grow slowly, take 30–50 years to reach sexual maturity, then make the long trip (sometimes up to 3000 km) back from their feeding grounds to the area where they first hatched. Adult females nest every few years, and may lay 3–5 clutches of 50–150 eggs in a season. One of the most interesting times to visit the islands of the Capricorn and Bunker Groups is from January to March, when turtle hatchlings break through the sand at night and make a mad dash for the ocean. They are wonderful to watch, like tiny wind-up toys, but due to high predator pressure, few of these will reach maturity.

Even though turtles are protected in Australian waters, man's activities are a continual threat to their survival. Many die accidentally in shark and trawler nets, however the main threat is the degradation of important turtle habitats, especially inshore sea grass beds, mangrove forests, coral reefs and nesting beaches. A number are allowed to be taken by Aborigines and Torres Strait Islanders each year. Those tagged in Australia have been found in the waters of Papua New Guinea and Indonesia, where turtle eggs and meat are considered a delicacy—up to 40,000 turtles a year are consumed by the Balinese alone. Without protection throughout the Indo-Pacific, and improved netting techniques within our own waters, the long-term survival of this marine giant seems exceedingly unlikely.

Bundaberg and Hervey Bay
Diving the Whales' Playground

Left: All turtles are fully protected throughout Australian waters. The green turtle (*Chelonia mydas*) is the one usually seen by divers, particularly during the summer months when they congregate around coral cays for the breeding season. *Neville Coleman*

Roy Rufus Artificial Reef, the largest artificial reef in the Southern Hemisphere, is one of the most popular dive sites in the Bundaberg and Hervey Bay area. Since 1968, members of Maryborough Skindivers Inc. have been sinking old ships, concrete blocks, car bodies and tires to create this haven for fish and other marine life in 18 m of water. The effort has been very successful: masses of fish congregate on and in the wreckage—gropers, coral trout, rock cod, bream, kingfish, trevally, angelfish, scorpionfish, butterflyfish, sweetlips and surgeonfish.

Other marine life observed on the artificial reef includes sea snakes, wobbegongs, stingrays, turtles and even dugongs. Divers will find the shipwrecks the most interesting areas to explore. With a little care they can be safely entered, so remember to bring a torch. The only thing to watch out for when diving the reef is stonefish.

There are many other excellent dive sites accessible from Bundaberg and Hervey Bay, including **Two Mile Rock**, **Four Mile Reef**, **Rooney Point** and **Moon Ledge**. Most of the dives sites offer good

diving all year round, and even in rough conditions Fraser Island shelters many of them from all but the worst weather. A number of dive shops in both Bundaberg and Hervey Bay operate charter trips to the best sites in the area, and will give advice on shore diving.

As the southern-most gateways to the Great Barrier Reef, Bundaberg and Hervey Bay both have a good range of accommodation and places to eat. Whale watching is definitely Hervey Bay's most popular attraction. Each winter hundreds of humpback whales rest in the bay after breeding in the northern reef waters—and each winter thousands of tourists visit Hervey Bay, hoping to catch a glimpse of these giant marine mammals.

Fraser Island, the largest sand island in the world, is a popular area for camping and 4WD adventures. Features of the island include clear lakes and streams, abundant wildlife, sand dunes, sand formations and unique rainforest.

Bundaberg Shore Dives

The rocky shore line around Bundaberg has encouraged the

Up to one hour by boat

Offshore 15–20 m Inshore 5 to 10 m

Only on exposed reefs

Rich areas of hard and soft corals

Manta rays and marine life of Evans Patch. Fish life on Roy Rufus Artificial Reef

Good mixture of reef and pelagic fish

Rocky coral reefs and pinnacles

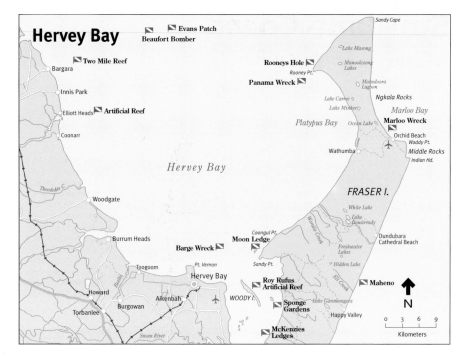

Hervey Bay

Beaufort Bomber
Evans Patch
Two Mile Reef
Bargara
Innis Park
Elliott Heads Artificial Reef
Coonarr
Rooneys Hole
Rooney Pt.
Panama Wreck
Theodolite C
Woodgate
Burrum Heads
Barge Wreck
Toogoom
Pt. Vemon
Hervey Bay
Howard
Aikenbah
WOODY I.
Burgowan
Torbanlee
Susan River
Coongul Pt.
Moon Ledge
Sandy Pt.
Roy Rufus
Artificial Reef
Sponge
Gardens
McKenzies
Ledges
Happy Valley

Sandy Cape
Lake Marong
Manooloonga
Lakes
Moondoora
Lagoon
Lake Carree
Lake Mitker
Ngkala Rocks
Marloo Bay
Marloo Wreck
Platypus Bay   Ocean Lake
Orchid Beach
Waddy Pt.
Wathumba
Middle Rocks
Indian Hd.
FRASER I.
White Lake
Lake
Bowarrady
Wungle Creek
Dundubara
Cathedral Beach
Freshwater
Lakes
Hidden Lake
Eli Creek
Lake Garawongera
Maheno

Hervey Bay

N

0   3   6   9
Kilometers

growth of many coral gardens just off it. The area from **Burnett Head** in the north, to **Elliott Head** in the south, offers dozens of fascinating shore dives in depths to 9 m. These coral gardens abound with marine life. Nudibranchs, hermit crabs, cowries, flatworms, sea stars, brittle stars, shrimp and crabs are just a few of the many invertebrates that are easily found. Small reef fish—butterflyfish, goatfish, rock cod, lionfish, angelfish, damsels and several wrasse species—are particularly common. You will also find wobbegongs, epaulette sharks, turtles, stingrays and even inquisitive sea snakes. Winter is the best season to dive the area, as the seas are calmer and the water clearer.

Evans Patch

This offshore rocky reef is small in area, but big in marine life. The reef sits in 22 m of water and can be circumnavigated many times before you run out of bottom time. Many species of fish live on this isolated patch—angelfish, kingfish, batfish, trevally, barracuda, lion-

fish, cobia, coral trout, sweetlips and moray eels. Huge schools of baitfish sometimes engulf the reef, and manta rays have been seen hovering, being cleaned by the resident cleaner wrasse. Turtles, stingrays and wobbegongs are also frequent visitors. Looking past the fish life, divers will find scattered coral growth and a mixed bag of invertebrates. This is the type of dive where a roll of film disappears quicker than your bottom time.

Beaufort Bomber

This up-turned plane wreck in 27 m makes a fascinating dive. The plane crashed in 1943, while the crew were on a training exercise. Today much of the wreckage is covered with coral, but divers can still see the cockpit area, the engines and the landing wheels. Considering the small size of the wreckage, this plane gets more than its fair share of marine life. Gropers, batfish, manta rays, stingrays, sea snakes and wobbegong sharks are just some of the species that have been observed around the wreck.

Sunshine Coast
A Diver's Surprise Package

Diving the Sunshine Coast for the first time can be quite a surprise. Some of the local reefs are so packed with hard and soft coral you would think that a section of the Great Barrier Reef had been towed south. Numerous dives are found in a relatively small area—well over a hundred have been named, and the local dive operators are finding more all the time. And finally, while fish are plentiful, it is the invertebrate life that will be long-remembered.

On every dive you will see many species of crustaceans, echinoderms and especially molluscs. Anyone with a love of nudibranchs will find dozens of species in large numbers. Some that are rare elsewhere are common here, as well as several unnamed species.

The Sunshine Coast, only 100 km north of Brisbane, is a popular holiday area stretching from Noosa in the north to Caloundra in the south. Many resorts and hotels line the beaches, where people come to swim, surf, relax or enjoy the nightclubs.

Running parallel to the coast are a number of coral reefs packed with a good variety of species of hard and soft coral. Most of these reefs are only 10 minutes from shore and are regularly visited by the dive operators in the area, who run double dive boat trips. All the dive shops are centered around **Noosa** and **Mooloolaba**, as both have accessible ports and the best dive sites on their doorsteps. Some also run trips a little further north to a popular small outcrop known as Wolf Rock.

Wolf Rock

For dramatic diving Wolf Rock is hard to beat. The rock drops straight into 25 m of water, and then slopes to 35 m and beyond. Coral growth on the rock can be brilliant. Some areas are covered with sea whips, gorgonians and black coral trees. Small reef fish

Below: During spring and summer months leopard sharks (*Stegostoma fasciatum*) congregate around the reefs and islands of southern Queensland and northern New South Wales. Sleeping during the day, these docile sharks are easily approached. *Nigel Marsh*

10 to 20 minutes by boat

Generally 12–15 m

Occasionally strong on outer reefs

Extensive gardens of hard and soft corals

Pelagic fish off Wolf Rock. Coral gardens at Jew Shoal and Gneering Reefs

A good mixture of reef and pelagic fish

Rocky coral reefs and pinnacles

are prolific, but almost forgotten when divers catch sight of the schools of barracuda, big eye trevally, fusiliers, kingfish, mackerel and bonito that gather around the rock. The occasional bronze whaler can be seen charging through the schools and may hang around to "buzz" a diver. Turtles, manta rays, wobbegongs, stingrays, eagle rays and shovelnose rays are also regulars at Wolf Rock.

Jew Shoal
One of the smaller reefs in the area, Jew Shoal is also one of the fishiest. The reef lies in 12–20 m of water and the rocky structure contains many caves, gutters and pinnacles with thick growths of hard and soft corals, sponges, ascidians, anemones and black coral trees. Small reef fish and invertebrates—

including anemonefish, lionfish, moray eels, angelfish, bullseyes, wrasse, molluscs, sea stars, brittle stars, rock lobsters and plenty of nudibranchs—are common. Pelagic fish and large reef fish are always found on the shoal, and during a good dive you will see batfish, coral trout, trevally, gropers, sweetlips, mackerel, kingfish and surgeonfish, as well as turtles, stingrays and wobbegongs. Each summer leopard sharks appear, and are usually found resting in the sandy gutters.

Inner and Outer Gneerings
Located just off Mooloolaba, the Gneering Reefs cover a wide area in depths from 10–25 m. Dozens of dive sites, found on both the inner and outer reefs, are packed with a dense covering of hard and soft corals. The terrain is extremely interesting to explore, as many gutters, caves and pinnacles are found throughout the reef area. The colors are exquisite—orange and red gorgonians, pink soft corals and white, bushy black coral trees—a photographer's field day. Anemones and their resident anemonefish are numerous, as are nudibranchs, with dozens of different species found on every dive. Also common are rock lobsters, sea urchins, sea stars and numerous species of reef fish. Pelagic fish are more plentiful on the Outer Gneerings, but turtles, stingrays and wobbegongs can be seen almost anywhere.

There are many other dive sites in the area that are worth mentioning, including **Halls Reef**, **North Reef**, **Sunshine Reef** (off Noosa), **Coolum Reef**, **Mudjimba Island** and **Murphys Reef** (off Mooloolaba). All have extensive coral gardens and an abundance of reef fish, invertebrates and other marine life. Big seas are the only restriction on diving the Sunshine Coast, as only Mudjimba Island offers any protection when the weather is rough.

Sunshine Coast

Brisbane
Rocks, Reefs and Wrecks

Brisbane is frequently over-looked as a base to dive from. Visiting divers take one look at the brown waters of the Brisbane River and automatically assume there is no good diving in the area. However, Brisbane has much to offer, with rich offshore reefs, several shipwrecks and an impressive variety of marine life. Brisbane's dive sites are located off Moreton and North Stradbroke Islands, in Moreton Bay. These dive sites are far offshore, but the water is reasonably clear year-round. Numerous dive boats operate out of Brisbane and divers have a wide choice of day trips and live-aboards. Bookings can be made through most of the dive shops in Brisbane.

For the latest information on diving conditions consult the Brisbane Coastwatch service, which provides reports on television, radio and in the newspaper each weekend.

Moreton Island
Many wonderful dive sites are located off Moreton Island. Two large artificial reefs lie along the landward side of the island, while along the seaward side are a number of shipwrecks, submerged reefs, and a true coral reef that is exposed at low tide.

Curtin Artificial Reef
Since 1968, members of the Underwater Research Group of Queensland have been sinking large vessels, cars, tires and pontoons to create the Curtin Artificial Reef. Today the reef pulsates with marine life—tropical fish, gropers, turtles, wobbegong sharks, stingrays, eagle rays, trevally and other schooling fish. Most of the wrecks have been cleared of obstructions and can be safely entered and explored.

Tangalooma Wrecks
Fifteen vessels have been sunk on the landward side of Moreton

Island to form a breakwall for small boats. These are the Tangalooma Wrecks which provide good diving in depths from 2–10 m. Even in this shallow water, the wrecks are fun to dive, and attract an amazing amount of marine life, including wobbegongs, trevally, kingfish, yellowtail and lots of tropical fish.

Flinders Reef
Located north of Moreton Island, Flinders Reef is Brisbane's only true coral reef. The diving is good all around the reef on walls, gutters, caves and pinnacles scattered in depths from 3–25 m. Lush coral growths of staghorn, brain, plate and many other hard coral species, as well as soft corals, gorgonians, sponges and sea whips are found in the shallows. You will find plenty of reef fish, and a good range of inver-

Below: The artificial reefs in Moreton Bay provide good diving and fishing to many Brisbanites, especially when the bars are too rough to get across to the outer reefs.
Nigel Marsh

Over 1 hour by boat

Offshore 15–20 m, in Moreton Bay 10 m

Only on exposed reefs

Hard and soft corals common, sea whips and black coral trees deeper
Manta rays and leopard sharks at Manta Bommies. Shipwrecks at Curtin Artificial Reef

Prolific reef and pelagic fish

Rocky coral reefs and pinnacles

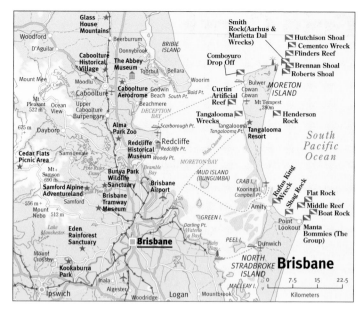

tebrates, turtles, stingrays, wobbe-gong sharks, and the occasional manta ray.

There are a number of other excellent dive sites off **Moreton Island** including **Henderson Rock**, **Smith Rock** and **Hutchison Shoal**, which all offer a good variety of marine life. The shipwrecks *Cementco* and *Aarhus* both make interesting dives.

North Stradbroke Island

Straddy, as it is affectionately known, has a number of offshore islands with good dive sites. Getting to these can be difficult sometimes as boats leaving from Brisbane must cross a large sand bar, which can be impossible in rough seas. Stradbroke Dive Centre runs an inflatable from the beach, thus avoiding the bar and taking only minutes to reach the best areas. Good dive sites off Straddy include Shag Rock, Middle Reef and Boat Rock, all of which attract an excellent range of fish and other large marine creatures.

Manta Bommies

Located off a collection of small islands known as The Group,

Manta Bommies is the best of Brisbane diving. In depths from 6–12 m lies a rocky reef with a large concentration of marine life—especially over the summer and autumn months. Up to a dozen manta rays are regularly seen cruising the reef, accompanied by schools of stingrays, eagle rays and huge shovelnose rays. Turtles are very common, and plenty of wobbegongs, catsharks and leopard sharks gather over summer. Reef fish, pelagic fishs, and an incredible range of invertebrates make this a very special dive site.

Flat Rock

Flat Rock is an island surrounded by walls, gutters, ledges and pinnacles in depths to 35 m. The coral growth is prolific, and reef fish and other marine life are plentiful. While there are dozens of good dive sites around the island, the best would have to be the **Shark Gutters** at the southern end of the island. Every winter the Shark Gutters attract grey nurse sharks, which possibly gather in the area to mate and give birth. Up to a dozen can often be seen patroling the gutters, and divers can get in quite close if they stay low on the side of the gutters.

Gold Coast
Not Just a Surfers' Paradise

The surf beaches of the Gold Coast have been a popular holiday destination for over 50 years. The numerous high-rise buildings which line the beachfront house the myriad sunseekers who flock here in the summer months. For the diver with a family and non-diving spouse, the Gold Coast is the perfect destination. There are enough activities and attractions to keep any family busy for weeks, allowing you to escape for a few quick dives on the exciting reefs in the area. The attractions include theme parks, night clubs, a casino, wildlife parks and nearby rainforests. Diving is probably the Gold Coast's least-known attraction; hidden off the famous beaches, dozens of reefs offer excellent diving year-round.

The Gold Coast tourist strip stretches from Southport in the north to Tweed Heads, New South Wales, in the south. Visitors will find a wide range of accommodation and a generous selection of shops and restaurants. A number of dive shops operate in the area,

all of which run charter boats offering morning and afternoon double-dive trips. The best range of dive sites is located around **Tweed Heads** and even the furthermost reef can be reached in under 30 minutes.

Shore Dives

Although the best reefs lie offshore, a number of interesting dive sites are found along the shore. The Southport Seaway and Tweed River are both good dives on the high tide, when reef fish, stingrays and colorful invertebrates can usually be seen. Kirra Reef is a large rocky reef that supports an impressive array of reef fish, wobbegongs, invertebrates and even turtles. All these shore dives are shallow, averaging 6 m, and visibility is usually about 10 m.

Scottish Prince Shipwreck

The 64 m-long iron barque, *Scottish Prince,* ran aground off South-

10–30 minutes by boat

Generally 12–15m

On deeper offshore reefs

Hard and soft corals, sponges, sea whips and gorgonians common

Sharks at Nine Mile Reef. Rich mixture of marine life at Cook Island

Abundant reef and pelagic fish

Rocky coral reefs and pinnacles

port in 1887. Today the hull of the historic shipwreck lies in 10 m of water and shelters a great variety of marine life. Trevally and kingfish come in to feed on the schools of bullseyes and yellowtail which swarm about the wreck. Stingrays, moray eels, wobbegongs, shovelnose rays, catsharks, turtles, lionfish and gropers are all found on or around the hull, which is fascinating to explore, as parts of the wreck can be entered. Artefacts can be found when the sands shift after storms, but since the area has been listed as an historic site, the artefacts must be left where they lie. Strong surges can sometimes make diving difficult, and divers should watch out for stonefish and little damselfish, which are aggressive if they are guarding eggs.

Palm Beach Reef

This immense reef, which varies in depth from 6–22 m, can be dived in many locations and provides consistently great diving on pinnacles, and in gutters and caves. The coral growth in the area is brilliant; plate corals, soft corals, ascidians, sponges, gorgonians and black coral trees are common. Angelfish, butterflyfish, goatfish, lionfish, rock cod, fairy basslets and damsels are just a few of the reef

Opposite: Over the past two decades underwater photography in Australia has increased in popularity and is now one of the most popular recreational diver activities.
Nigel Marsh

fish species here. Search the bottom closely and you will find nudibranchs, sea stars, feather stars, molluscs and crustaceans. Turtles, stingrays and wobbegongs are around on most dives and large schools of pelagic fish swarm over the reef at times.

Cook Island

Lying close to shore off Fingal Head, Cook Island is probably the most popular dive site on the Gold Coast. Surrounded by rocky and coral reefs in 6–20 m, Cook Island can usually be dived regardless of the prevailing conditions. Hard and soft corals cover the bottom in some areas; in others boulders form walls and caves before descending to the sandy sea floor. No matter where you dive around the island, you will find an interesting mixture of reef and pelagic fish. Pufferfish, gropers, surgeonfish, anemonefish, leatherjackets, parrotfish, trevally, bullseyes and sweetlips are regularly seen. Macro-photographers will find plenty of subjects, such as brittle stars, flatworms, shrimps and nudibranchs. Leopard sharks visit the area in large numbers over summer, however, stingrays, turtles, wobbegongs and blind sharks are permanent residents.

Nine Mile Reef

Know as a "sharky" spot by local fishermen, Nine Mile Reef certainly lives up to its reputation on some days. The rocky reef here drops from 10–30 m and is encrusted with numerous corals. Reef fish are ever present, and pelagic fish such as kingfish and trevally sometimes circle in large numbers. Turtles are regular visitors, as are stingrays, eagle rays and the occasional manta ray. Sharks resident year-round include wobbegongs and blind sharks, and bronze whalers; leopard sharks in summer; grey nurse sharks in winter; and occasional hammerheads and whale sharks.

Gold Coast

Oxenford, Paradise Point, Movie World, Wet & Wild Water Park, Seaworld, Southport Seaway, Scottish Prince Wreck, Eighty Foot Reef, Southport, Main Beach, Nerang, Surfers Paradise, Broadbeach, Mermaid Beach, Nobby Beach, Miami, Mudgeeraba, Burleigh Heads, Queensland, Neranwood, West Burleigh, Palm Beach Reef, Currumbin Bird Sanctuary, Kirra Reef, Mount Bally 489 m, Coolangatta, Tweed River, Tweed Heads, Fidos Reef, Upper Tallebudgera 640 m, New South Wales, Fingal, COOK Is., Nine Mile Reef, South Reef, 479 m, Chinderah, Tomewin, Kingscliff, Kingscliff Reef, Tumbulgum, Pacific Ocean, N, 0 5 10 15 Kilometers

Introducing New South Wales

Australia's First State

Some of Australia's most interesting and diverse diving sites are found along the 2000 km New South Wales coastline. Marine life varies from subtropical reef species in the north, to dense sponge gardens and associated organisms in the temperate waters of the south. Varied fascinating marine creatures coexist in areas where warm currents from the Great Barrier Reef meet the cooler southern waters. This mixing results in a rich diversity of species equalled by few locations in the world.

Along the state's northern coastline, divers often see turtles, tropical fish, Queensland gropers, leopard sharks and manta rays. In the south, giant cuttlefish, octopi, a wide range of invertebrate species, moray eels, weedy sea dragons, sea horses, territorial blue gropers, large pelagic fishes, and fur seals are all plentiful. Members of the shark and ray families are numerous—wobbegongs, Port Jackson sharks, grey nurse sharks, stingrays, fiddler rayss, and electric rays.

Captain Cook first sighted this rugged and varied coastline in 1770. He stepped ashore at Botany Bay, claimed the continent for England, and mapped much of the coastline. The First Fleet followed in 1788 and established a penal colony at Farm Cove at Port Jackson, one of the world's great natural deepwater harbors. The town of Sydney slowly grew into a prosperous city. Today, the city and surrounding suburbs are spread over an area of approximately 5000 sq km—home to over 4 million inhabitants.

Tourism is one of the state's strongest growth industries. The majority of international visitors to

Australia pass through Sydney at some stage during their holiday, and with Sydney hosting the Olympics in the year 2000, the tourist numbers are set to rise.

Other state attractions include deserts in the west, snow skiing in the Snowy Mountains, Canberra's museums and memorials, spectacular bushwalks in the Blue Mountains and surfing at sandy beaches along the coast.

The New South Wales diving industry has established an international reputation for excellent sites in a number of holiday areas—the southern-most coral reefs in the world around Lord Howe Island, the sponge gardens at Jervis Bay, the grey nurse sharks at Seal Rocks, and the reefs off Byron Bay and Coffs Harbour. New South Wales has several marine reserves, but many areas are threatened by over-fishing. Some dive shops run trips to areas which the dive opera-

Above: One of the most spectacular endemic Australian sea stars, the vermilion biscuit star (*Pentagonaster duebeni*) inhabits reefs from southern Queensland to south Western Australia. It has a number of color forms but that shown above is the most common. *Neville Coleman*

Opposite: An underwater photographer being "buzzed" by a couple of kingfish (*Seriola lalandi*) in the lagoon at Norfolk Island. Only 3–5 m deep, the lagoon provides excellent learning conditions for snorkeling and scuba diving. *Neville Coleman*

tors themselves have nominated for protection, and you may find that they have placed a ban on removal of anything from these reefs. Please respect these self-imposed bans to ensure the future of these areas.

Some might find the idea of shore dives unexciting, however these inexpensive dives are often some of the most interesting in the state. Off the New South Wales coastline are thousands of islands, reefs, pinnacles and shipwrecks supporting an incredible variety of marine life. Lord Howe and Norfolk Islands (Australian territories) are surrounded by superb diving sites, inhabited by many fish species endemic to these islands and the nearby Elizabeth and Middleton Reefs. West of Sydney, at Wellington and Jenolan, are a number of freshwater caves, full of spectacular limestone formations.

Another interesting dive site, located south of Canberra, is an underwater town in Lake Jindabyne, which disappeared after the construction of a dam. Divers find it an eerie experience swimming around the ruins of houses and seeing household items among the wreckage. Trips to these unusual sites are organized occasionally by dive clubs and dive operators from both Sydney and Canberra.

The climate in New South Wales varies greatly. Over summer, the daily temperature ranges from 24–29° C, with a minimum of 12° C, while winter sees daily temperatures from 12–18° C, with a minimum of 0° C. Diving conditions are generally good year round, but winter brings the most stable weather, as westerly winds flatten the seas and clear blue ocean currents sweep the coastline. Since the water temperature varies from 20–25° C over summer, 5 mm wetsuits are worn year round. A hood is needed over winter, as the water temperature can range from 12–16° C.

Visitors can explore the state by car, train or bus, and most of the major centers of population have airports which are serviced by regional airlines. Accommodation in New South Wales is of an excellent standard and caters for every budget. However, some areas are very busy during the holiday periods, so book your accommodation in advance.

Below: Sydney's magnificent harbor, showing the Opera House and Sydney Harbour Bridge; just two of the many famous landmarks found around its shores.
Neville Coleman

Byron Bay
Fantastic Diving around the Julian Rocks Marine Reserve

Byron Bay's coastline is washed by warm currents from the Great Barrier Reef, which bring an impressive assortment of tropical fish, corals and other marine invertebrates to its offshore reefs. Julian Rocks, an area of particularly rich species diversity, was listed as a marine reserve in 1982.

This lively town offers an excellent range of accommodation, including backpacker hostels. The town is usually swarming with both tourists and divers, so book your accommodation and dive trips early.

Three dive shops in Byron Bay run regular trips to the best sites in the area. Dive boats are launched from the beach, and Julian Rocks is one spot that can be enjoyed under most conditions.

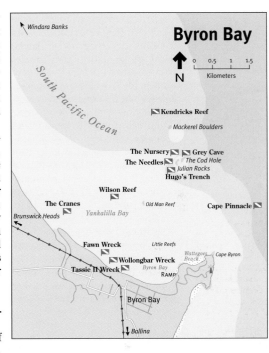

Windara Banks
This shoal is located 20 km north of Byron Bay, about 12 km offshore. This superb reef, rising from 40–16 m, has only recently been discovered. There are plenty of walls and gutters covered with beautiful corals to explore in the area, but the most exciting feature is the fish life. On a typical dive, schools of kingfish, surgeonfish, trevally, barracuda and bullseyes surround visitors. Cobia, eagle rays and sandbar sharks are common. Grey nurse sharks, wobbegongs and turtles rest in the gutters, and a great variety of tropical fish shelters among the corals on the reef.

Cape Pinnacles
Around these coral-covered pinnacles off Cape Byron, which drop from 25–40 m, are jewfish, grey nurse sharks, shovelnose rays, Queensland gropers, stingrays, kingfish and bronze whaler sharks.

Mackerel Boulders
Located at a depth of 20 m, this reef has numerous tropical fish and invertebrates. Turtles, wobbegongs, moray eels, cuttlefish, blue gropers and lionfish are some of the species found in the coral-lined gutters and caves. Pelagics cruise the open water off the reef, which is often covered in schools of bullseyes and yellowtail.

Kendricks Reef
Probably one of the most colorful reefs in the area. The best coral gardens are found at 24 m, packed with gorgonians, sea whips, soft corals, hard corals, ascidians, sponges and black coral trees. Pelagic fish are common, as well as tropical species such as fairy basslets, rock cod,

Boat dives up to 20 minutes away

Generally 15–20 m

Currents offshore at times

Good sponge and coral gardens

Fish and sharks at Julian Rocks and other dive sites

Reef and pelagic fish prolific

Rocky reefs and pinnacles

anemonefish, lionfish, gobies, blennies, wrasse, butterflyfish and angelfish. These share their territories with starfish, feather stars, crabs, cuttlefish, octopi, nudibranchs, cowries and serpent stars (usually found wrapped around branches of the black coral trees).

Julian Rocks Marine Reserve

A dozen excellent dive sites are found around the Julian Rocks Marine Reserve. **The Nursery**, a popular spot with photographers, is a shallow area on the northern edge, swarming with tropical fish and invertebrates. Anemonefish, lionfish, nudibranchs, turtles, blind sharks, cowries, moray eels, soft corals, flatworms, sea stars and many other photographic subjects can be found at depths of 6–15 m. Although the area is known as The Nursery because of its countless small resident fish, divers are also likely to see schools of large pelagics.

The **Cod Hole** is a lovely 10 m-long cave located at a depth of 21 m, lined with tubastrea coral, sponges, cowries and soft corals. A host of permanent residents, which includes moray eels, lionfish, stingrays, cuttlefish, and gropers share the cave. Grey nurse sharks and large schools of red morwong, bullseyes and sweetlips are seen occasionally. The gutters around the Cod Hole are occupied by turtles, wobbegong sharks, jewfish, manta rays, eagle rays and leopard sharks (over summer).

Hugo's Trench is a deep gutter that cuts into Julian Rocks. The gutter is at a depth of 12 m, and is often filled with bream, blue gropers, sweetlips, bullseyes and surgeonfish. There are so many fish at times that larger residents such as turtles, stingrays and large wobbegong sharks pass unnoticed. In rough weather the gutter can be quite surgey, but is always fun to dive.

The Needles offer walls and ledges in 15 m, lined with hard and soft corals and many invertebrate species. Turtles, wobbegongs, stingrays and sharks rest on the bottom, while schools of trevally and kingfish cruise above. The Needles is a good place to see angelfish, rock lobster and occasionally grey nurse sharks.

Many other gutters, caves and drop-offs are found around **Julian Rocks** at depths up to 25 m.

Tassie II Shipwreck

When the water is clear off Main Beach, the wreck of the *Tassie II* can easily be seen from the surface. This shipwreck lies in only 5 m of water. Wobbegong sharks, stingrays, cuttlefish, nudibranchs, sea stars, morwong, bream, moray eels, various tropical fish and other marine life live on and around the wreck. The remains of the *Fawn* and *Wollongbar* are found nearby.

Opposite: Clown anemonefish (*Amphiprion ocellaris*) form a symbiotic relationship with the anemone *(Heteractis manifica)* where the fish preen the tentacles in return for protection. *Michael Aw*

Below: A white-spotted shovelnose ray (*Rhynchobatus djiddensis*). *Nigel Marsh*

Ballina
Unexplored and Unspoiled

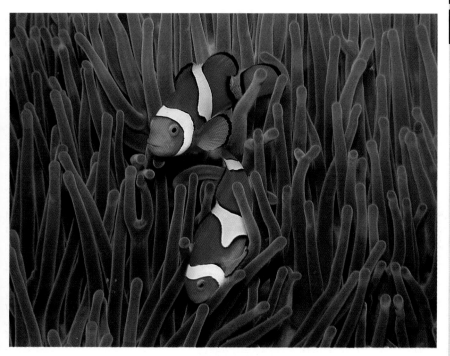

A large town at the mouth of the Richmond River, Ballina is a popular holiday destination, particularly for families. The area is not usually promoted as a dive destination, and the relatively low numbers of visiting divers means plenty of unspoiled sites offshore. A dive shop in Ballina runs trips to nearby reefs. Visitors will find there are plenty of motels and caravan parks, excellent beaches and a host of other water-based activities, including a famous waterslide. Ballina can get quite crowded during the school holidays so make a point of pre-booking accommodation if planning a visit at this time. Also, since nearby Byron Bay generally has higher prices, you might consider Ballina as a suitable base for exploring the dive sites of far northern New South Wales.

Lennox Pinnacles
A number of rocky reefs covered in kelp and sponges are located off Lennox Head, in depths of 12–15 m. A careful look will reveal nudibranchs, flatworms, sea stars, egg cowries and other molluscs. The reefs support large populations of fish—morwong, blue gropers, shovelnose rays, bullseyes, trevally, wobbegong sharks, stingrays, kingfish, bream, sweep, and an interesting assortment of tropical reef species.

Richmond River
An exceptional variety of marine and estuarine creatures can be found along the banks of the Richmond River, which floods with salt water on each high tide. Dives can be enjoyed

Boat dives up to 30 minutes away

Usually 10–15 m

Occasional offshore currents

Kelp and sponge gardens

A wealth of unexplored reefs

Reef and pelagic fish prolific

Rocky reefs and pinnacles

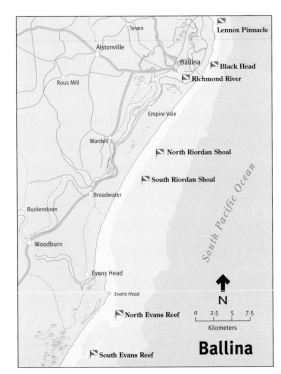

Black Head

Lobster and a variety of reef fish live on this rocky reef, located just off the mouth of the Richmond River, in depths of 8–10 m. Wobbegong sharks and stingrays are found at the base of the reef, among the kelp beds on the sea bottom.

North and South Riordan Shoals

Although the shoals are relatively unexplored, the sites dived to date have proved exciting. Pinnacles, gutters and ledges have been discovered in depths from 18–40 m, and brilliant sponge gardens further down. Reef fish and invertebrates are plentiful. Look out for blue gropers, kingfish, wobbegong sharks, moray eels and the occasional turtle.

North and South Evans Reefs

This group, featuring marine life similar to the Riordan Shoals, provides good diving in depths from 20–25 m, and also awaits further exploration. Allan Jarrett's Divers World, which services the Ballina area, offers dive courses and weekend trips to the local reefs.

Below: Although green turtles (*Chelonia mydas*) breed in the tropics they have been observed as far south as southern New South Wales. *Nigel Marsh*

anywhere along the rocky shoreline in depths from 5–10 m. Over summer large numbers of tropical fish inhabit the river, including butterflyfish, angelfish and wrasse. At other times it can be full of baitfish or huge flatheads. Divers may also be lucky enough to find many nudibranchs and other invertebrates.

Brooms Head

Pimpernel Rock: Walls, Gutters and Plenty of Sharks

Off the coast of Australia are thousands of remote reefs and pinnacles known only to fishermen or divers with their own boats. One such pinnacle is the spectacular **Pimpernel Rock**, a large rocky outcrop exploited by fishermen for years, located 6km off Brooms Head. Its walls, gutters and ledges—rising from a depth of 42 m to its shallowest point at 8 m—had not been explored by divers until recently. A resident colony of grey nurse sharks can be found in two large caves, one almost 10 m high. Up to 40 grey nurse sharks have been seen around and in the larger cave at once. Being unfamiliar with divers, the sharks will approach for wonderful photos.

Pimpernel Rock is covered in sea whips, black coral trees, gorgonians, sea tulips, ascidians, sponges and anemones. Shoals of pelagic fish circle the pinnacle—kingfish, trevally, jewfish, mackerel, yellowtail and bullseyes are all common. Resident surgeonfish, turtles, wobbegong sharks, eagle rays, stingrays, black cod, rock lobster and lionfish share the area with an impressive array of invertebrate species.

Since the recent opening of the Brooms Head Dive Centre, anyone can visit Pimpernel Rock. The dive shop runs day trips, night dives and offers holiday units at the rear of the shop. Brooms Head is centrally located between Byron Bay and Coffs Harbour, and has been a popular holiday town for many years, where visitors come to surf, fish, and enjoy the laid-back atmosphere.

Pimpernel Rock lies within the confines of the Solitary Islands Marine Reserve, but is still regularly plundered by fishermen, as it doesn't enjoy sanctuary status. The dive shop operators in the area are currently petitioning for full protection before over-fishing occurs.

The following two reefs, located off Brooms Head, also provide great diving.

Buchanan Reef

Situated in depths from 4–18 m, this shallow reef is made up of many gutters, ridges and rocky pinnacles covered with lovely hard and soft corals. Numerous reef fish and larger pelagic fish are always seen, but the reef is most famous for its invertebrate life. Macro-photographers will find plenty of nudibranchs, flatworms, shrimps, cowries, cuttlefish, hermit crabs, sea stars, brittle stars, tube worms, feather stars and octopi here.

Sandon Shoals

Exploration of this large, interesting shoal has only begun, however dive operators have already found many ledges and gutters at 9–21 m, encrusted with hard corals, sponges, ascidians, anemones, black coral trees and soft corals. Marine life includes blue devilfish, stingrays, wobbegong sharks, nudibranchs, cuttlefish, octopi, tropical fish and the occasional school of pelagics.

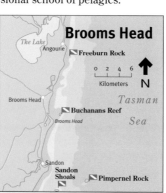

Boat dives up to 30 minutes away

Generally 15–20 m

Occasional offshore currents

Good coral gardens

Reef and pelagic fish common

Abundant marine life at Pimpernel Rock

Rocky reefs and pinnacles

Coffs Harbour
Exploring the Solitary Islands

Below: Anga's sea fan shell (*Phenacovolva angasi*) spends its entire adult life on the same gorgonian colony upon which it settles as a planktonic veliger.
Neville Coleman

The warm northerly and cooler southerly currents which mingle in the seas off the Solitary Islands have brought a fascinating mixture of tropical and temperate marine species to the islands' shores. Around the five Solitary Islands, and a few nearby rocky reefs, are gardens of hard and soft corals—some species usually found only on the Great Barrier Reef. The area surrounding these islands is so rich in marine life that it was declared a marine reserve in 1991.

The Solitary Islands are accessible from Coffs Harbour or Mullaway, both of which have dive shops. Divers can reach the northern Solitary Islands from Mullaway, and the southern islands of the group from Coffs Harbour. These islands are bathed by clear blue ocean currents most of the time and provide brilliant diving year round. The local dive operators have moorings at all their sites to prevent damage to the delicate corals.

The Coffs Harbour area is a busy holiday destination. Tourists visit the Pet Porpoise Pool and the Big Banana, enjoy whitewater rafting on the **Nymboida River**, bushwalk in the national parks, and relax on the many uncrowded beaches. The area has an extensive range of accommodation, from 4-star resorts to basic motels, and many good restaurants and take-aways.

North West Rock

The rugged terrain and currents attract masses of fish life to North West Rock. A crevice splitting the rock is fun to explore, but the best diving is in the deep gutters on the eastern side. Here you will regularly sight pelagic fish, eagle rays, wobbegongs, blue gropers, red morwong, stingrays and the occasional grey nurse shark. The western side has pretty coral gardens, with reef fish and invertebrates.

 Boat dives up to 50 minutes away

 Generally 15–20 m

 Occasional strong currents offshore

 Good hard and soft coral gardens

 Colorful reefs and a rich variety of marine life

 Reef and pelagic fish common

 Rocky reefs and pinnacles

THE BOTTOM DWELLERS
Wobbegong and Port Jackson Sharks

A VARIETY OF SHARKS ARE FOUND ALONG Australia's coastline. The more dangerous, swift, pelagic species occasionally put in an appearance, but by far the sharks most often seen are the harmless bottom-dwellers: the leopard and tawny nurse sharks, blind and angel sharks, several catshark species, and the most common of all, the wobbegong and Port Jackson sharks, affectionately known as the wobbies and PJs.

ten by wobbies than any other shark in Australia, and while there have been no fatalities, their needle-sharp teeth can cause a nasty wound. Divers who grab them by the tail or spearfish near them have been bitten, and when a wobby bites, it locks its jaw and won't let go. Many divers have returned to their boats with one locked onto an arm, leg or buttock. If not harassed, wobbies are generally harmless.

Wobbegongs

Six species of wobbegong shark, or carpet shark, are found in Australian waters. These bottom-dwellers lie motionless on the bottom, camouflaged by their ornate body coloring, waiting to ambush fish, stingrays, octopi, cuttlefish, rock lobsters, crabs, and even other sharks. They give birth to litters of as many as a dozen live young.

The tasselled wobbegong (*Eucrossorhinus dasypogon*) is common on coral reefs off Queensland, the Northern Territory and Western Australia. The northern wobbegong (*Orectolobus wardi*) is also found on coral reefs, but is rarely seen, except off Western Australia. The cobbler wobbegong (*Sutorectus tentaculatus*) is a rare species found off South and Western Australia, and the western wobbegong (*Orectolobus sp.*) is an undescribed species common off Western Australia. The most abundant of all, the spotted wobbegong (*Orectolobus maculatus*) and the ornate wobbegong (*Orectolobus ornatus*), grow to 3 m in length, and are found right around Australia.

Wobbegongs appear lazy, but move like lightning if after food or the hand of a harassing diver. More divers have been bit

Nocturnal hunters, the spotted wobbegong (*Orectolobus maculatus)* and the Port Jackson shark (*Heterodontus portusjacksoni)* often hole up in the same cave during the day. *Nigel Marsh*

Port Jackson Sharks

The Port Jackson shark (*Heterodontus portusjacksoni*) is a member of the hornshark family, one of the three species found in Australia. Although hornsharks have sharp spines in front of their dorsal fins, they are quite harmless—instead of teeth, grinding plates crush their diet of shellfish, crustaceans and small fish. Hornsharks lay cone-shaped eggs, usually under a ledge. The Port Jackson is the most common and the largest species, growing to 170 cm in length. Found along the coastline of all southern states, they are most prolific off New South Wales. The crested Port Jackson (*Heterodontus galeatus*) is smaller and less common than the Port Jackson, and is found only in New South Wales. The zebra hornshark (*Heterodontus zebra*) is a rare tropical deepwater species not seen by divers.

Sluggish and patient, PJs are fun to dive with, and will usually allow divers to pat and photograph them.

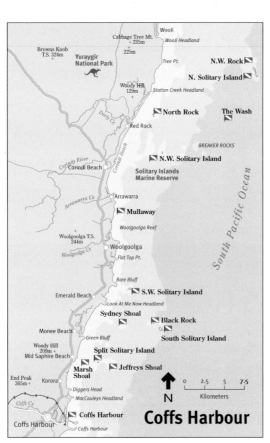

Coffs Harbour

numerous gutters covered in lush coral gardens, while the eastern and southern sides offer drop-offs, pinnacles and pelagic fish. **Anemone Bay**, at the northern end of the island, has an unusually large concentration of marine life. Here the bottom is literally carpeted with anemones, attended by three species of anemonefish. At depths of 10–20 m, divers will find abundant hard and soft corals, and masses of tropical fish. Turtles, stingrays, moray eels, wobbegongs and leopard sharks are seen in the bay during the summer months. Other sites around North Solitary feature grey nurse sharks, schools of kingfish and trevally, and eagle rays.

North West Solitary Island

Divers enjoy the gutters, caves, pinnacles and ledges at North West Solitary, but the most popular spot is **Manta Reef** on the western side of the island. Cut by a series of gutters in 6–22 m of water, this reef is covered with corals and sponges, and is home to an incredible range of invertebrates and tropical fish. Each summer manta rays visit the reef, hovering to be cleaned by the resident cleaner wrasse, and swimming circles around spellbound divers.

North Solitary Island

The terrain around North Solitary Island is very diverse. Along the western and northern sides are

Right: Although black coral (*Antipathes* sp.) is quite common in relatively shallow water (10–20 m) in northern New South Wales, on reefs further south it lives in deeper water and is regarded as rare.
Nigel Marsh

Southwest Solitary Island

Southwest Solitary, one of the least-dived islands, has some of the thickest hard coral growths of the Solitary Islands. The eastern side has many ledges and gutters inhabited by turtles and reef fish. Along the western side grows a luxuriant coral garden harboring a great variety of marine life.

Black Rock

At Black Rock, a small pinnacle of rock is all that appears above the surface. Beneath the surface, the monolith drops from 10–25 m, its walls and deep gutters are blanketed in sponges, soft corals and anemones. Blue gropers, wobbegongs, trevally, kingfish, jewfish, surgeonfish, red morwong and grey nurse sharks are just some of the marine residents.

South Solitary Island

South Solitary Island is spectacular above and below the surface. Its rocky walls drop steeply from 10–30 m, and many interesting dive sites are located along these drop-offs. The most popular site is the **Shark Gutters** at the northern end of the island, at depths between 18–23 m, where grey nurse sharks gather each winter and spring. Divers are able to get quite close to the sharks if they stay quietly at the edge of the channels. The sharks share the gutters with turtles, wobbegongs, moray eels, kingfish, jewfish, trevally, blue gropers, lionfish and eagle rays.

Marsh Shoal

One of a number of hidden reefs in the area, this boulder reef drops from 12–20 m and is covered in kelp, hard coral, soft coral, gorgonians, sponges and ascidians. Numerous small reef fish are found on the shoal. Search carefully for egg cowries, spanish dancers, shrimp, sea stars, anemones, nudibranchs, feather stars and other invertebrates.

Split Solitary Island

Split Solitary is surrounded by rocky gutters and drop-offs lined with plate corals, soft corals, sponges, gorgonians and ascidians. These coral gardens are home to tropical fish, blind sharks, red morwong, cuttlefish, octopi, moray eels, wobbegongs, nudibranchs, blue gropers and other species. Depths vary from 10–20 m, and the visibility averages about 10 m.

Above: Of tropical origins, the egg cowrie (*Ovula costellata*) seems more common around the reefs and islands of northern New South Wales than on the Great Barrier Reef.
Neville Coleman

South West Rocks
An Amazing Cave Dive and More

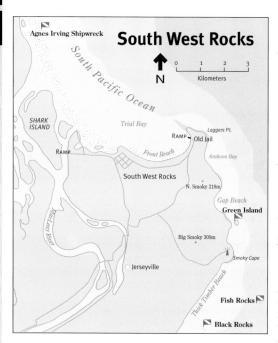

South West Rocks

N

0 1 2 3
Kilometers

Agnes Irving Shipwreck

South Pacific Ocean

SHARK ISLAND

Trial Bay

RAMP — Old Jail

RAMP

Front Beach

Laggers Pt.

Arakoon Bay

South West Rocks

N. Smoky 218m

Gap Beach

Green Island

Big Smoky 309m

Smoky Cape

Jerseyville

MacLeay River

Thick Timber Beach

Fish Rocks

Black Rocks

Boat dives up to 30 minutes away

Generally 15–20 m

Occasional strong currents offshore

Excellent sponge and coral gardens

Fish Rock Cave. Good variety of marine life at most dive sites

Reef and pelagic fish common

Rocky reefs and pinnacles

Fish Rock Cave

Although Fish Rock appears barren above the surface, its real beauty lies in the dark underwater cave that runs right through the boulder. Fish Rock Cave (120 m long), starts in a wide gutter at 10 m, and ends in another wide gutter at 24 m. Sponges, tubastrea corals and large gorgonians cover the walls, and schools of bullseyes sometimes pack both cave entrances. Wobbegongs and rock lobster are regularly found in the cave.

The journey through is a wonderful experience and requires a torch, as the passage is dark in places. Start at the deep end. The cave is narrow for the first 15 m, then rises to form a 5 m-long chute. At the end of the chute, the cave is about 6 m high, and begins to open up. At this point light can be seen coming from the shallow entrance. About 100 m further on, just near the entrance, are a number of bubble pockets where divers can talk. Swimming the length of the cave does not take long, and the swim through is quite safe for most divers.

Fish Rock

There are several other exciting dive sites around Fish Rock. Shark gutters have been discovered on the southern side, in 25 m of water, where grey nurse sharks gather over winter and spring. These gutters are lined with sponges and black coral trees, and are a great place to see wobbegongs, stingrays, blue gropers, cuttlefish and turtles—in fact one resident loggerhead turtle often tags along on the dive. The western side of the rock is overgrown with pretty coral and sponge gardens, which accommodate many species of reef fish. The most dramatic diving is on the rocky walls, which drop to 35 m on the eastern side of the island. Here pelagic fish, eagle rays and bronze whalers cruise past in the currents.

Fish Rock is one of a number of outcrops off South West Rocks —a sleepy, little town 480 km north of Sydney. An old jail stands on the shores of historic Trial Bay, built between 1877 and 1886 of local granite. The jail was abandoned 17 years later, and is now a popular tourist attraction. The area has lovely beaches and stark granite headlands, where people watch dolphins frolicking in the surf. Two dive shops based at South West Rocks run trips to the following dive sites.

Agnes Irving Shipwreck

The *Agnes Irving*, a paddle steamer, sank at the entrance to the Macleay River in 1879. The wreck now lies in 12 m of water. Visibility varies, depending on the weather, tidal conditions and movement of the sand. When visibility is good, the engines and boilers can be explored, and the paddle wheels are still recognizable. The wreckage is now encrusted with thick growths and inhabited by reef fish and invertebrates.

Green Island

Many interesting walls, gutters and ledges are found in the shallow water around Green Island. The bottom is covered in small sponges and corals, where macro-photographers will find plenty of nudibranchs, flatworms, boxfish, lionfish, moray eels, egg cowries, Spanish dancers, sea stars, feather stars and shrimp. Reef fish—cowfish, leatherjackets, morwong, wrasse, butterflyfish and pufferfish—are particularly common. Inspect the ledges, as these shelter slipper rock lobsters, blind sharks and small wobbegongs. Also regularly sighted around Green Island are stingrays, turtles, kingfish, bullseyes, sweep and drummer.

Black Rock

The best hard and soft coral growths in the area are around Black Rock, especially on the western side of the island. The bottom is covered with plate corals in depths of 8–12 m. Many species of fish congregate around Black Rock, and usually divers swim among schools of yellowtail, bullseyes, kingfish and trevally. Numerous varieties of reef fish and invertebrate species are easy to find. Divers often see turtles, cuttlefish, lionfish, wobbegongs, stingrays, and moray eels, and occasionally large, white-spotted shovelnose rays, resting on the sandy bottom near the edge of the reef.

Many other reefs and pinnacles off South West Rocks can be visited when conditions are favorable. Most of the year, clear blue water from the Great Barrier Reef reaches this area (which is only a few kilometers from the continental shelf) and brings with it an interesting assortment of tropical fish and invertebrates.

Above: The very distinctive harvest cuttlefish (*Sepia mestus*) is usually solitary, although in the breeding season they are found in groups. *Michael Aw*

Below: Mosaic seastars (*Plectaster decanus*) are found in most habitats, from coral reefs to muddy estuaries. *Michael Aw*

Port Macquarie
Shallow Reefs, Rich in Marine Life

This bustling holiday center tends to be overlooked by many divers, but it does have many reefs in shallow water, with plenty of corals, reef fish, invertebrates and pelagic fish. Port Macquarie has an excellent range of accommodation.

Ballina Shipwreck

The remains of the paddle steamer *Ballina*, which sank in 1879, rest in 10 m of water. High tide is the best time to dive on the wreck, as the water is calm and relatively clear. Movements of the sand cover and uncover the wreckage all the time.

Cod Hole

Several gutters and a large cave are located on the southern side of this pretty reef, which slopes from 9–17 m. Divers are likely to see blue gropers, wobbegongs, moray eels and a variety of reef fish.

South American Reef

This extensive reef is covered in sponges, gorgonians, sea tulips, soft corals and a few hard corals, in depths from 10–20 m. Resident reef fish include lionfish, leatherjackets, wrasse, morwong, moray eels, scorpionfish and talma.

Coral Reef

Coral Reef is one of Port Macquarie's best dives. Many fine sponges and corals cover the reef, which rises from 20 m. The reef is sometimes visited by manta rays. Schools of kingfish and drummer are common—as well as rock lobsters, wobbegongs, blue gropers and the occasional turtle.

Lighthouse Reef

This 2 km-long reef lies at depths of 11–18 m. It is great spot for photographing nudibranchs, shrimp, tubeworms, sponges, ascidians, gorgonians and corals as well as the larger reef fish, and pelagics such as kingfish, mackerel, morwong and yellowtail.

The Pinnacles

Situated at depths of 11–28 m, The Pinnacles have some of the best coral growth in the area, and attract a host of reef and pelagic fish.

 Boat dives up to 20 minutes away

 Generally 10–15 m

 Occasional currents offshore

 Sponge gardens and a few hard corals

 An interesting variety of colorful reefs close to shore

 Reef and pelagic fish common on most reefs

 Rocky reefs and pinnacles

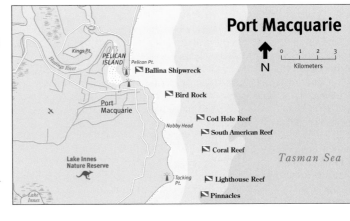

Port Macquarie

N 0 1 2 3 Kilometers

Kings Pt.
Hastings River
PELICAN ISLAND
Pelican Pt.
Ballina Shipwreck
Port Macquarie
Bird Rock
Nobby Head
Cod Hole Reef
South American Reef
Coral Reef
Lake Innes Nature Reserve
Tacking Pt.
Lighthouse Reef
Lake Innes
Pinnacles
Tasman Sea

BLUE (GROPER) WRASSE
Devil with the blue dress

A FAMILY OF BLUE GROPERS—USUALLY ABOUT A dozen animals—is found at most dive sites, but many more gather where there is plenty of food. Over a hundred are found at Latitude Rock off Forster/Tuncurry. As soon as divers hit the water, gropers appear—from behind the kelp, from small caves and over the sand—and by the time the divers reach the bottom, up to sixty blue gropers are swarming around them. The gropers circle the divers, investigate cameras and wait for a knife to be produced. One diver will usually succumb to their wishes and open a few sea urchins for the hungry mob. Then the real fun starts— divers are rammed, mugged, bailed up, bowled over and generally terrorized by the

divers will find two or three males and a dozen or so females. The closely-related western blue groper wrasse (*Achoerodus gouldii*) grows to 160 cm, and is found in South Australia and southern Western Australia. Both species are commonly called blue gropers.

Their thick lips help numb the effects of eating sea urchins, their favorite food, the spines of which are often seen protruding from their lips. Blue gropers are fond of crustaceans and molluscs as well, and are always looking for a handout.

Blue groper males are usually the most friendly. They will follow divers around, seeming curious about what the diver is doing, occasionally pushing a diver out of

A common sight these days at most New South Wales dive sites, the blue (groper) wrasse (*Acherodus viridis*) has made a remarkable comeback since becoming a protected species. *Nigel Marsh*

blue gropers in the fight for food, and the action continues until all the divers have left the water.

The eastern blue groper wrasse (*Achoerodus viridis*) is found along the entire coast of New South Wales, and into southern Queensland and Victoria. The males grow to 120 cm in length and are very distinctive with their blubber lips, bright blue body and yellow facial markings. The females are smaller and reddish-brown in color. Most males appear to have a harem of females, and on most popular dive sites in New South Wales,

the way if a tasty morsel is discovered. Be warned, though, they are rarely happy with one feed, and will chase and annoy the diver until more food is produced. If you choose to oblige, use only food that they naturally eat, and don't overfeed. At some sites divers have critically reduced the numbers of sea urchins in the area.

In the past these intriguing fish have suffered at the hands of fishermen and spearfishermen, but since blue gropers have been banned as spearfishing targets, the populations have recovered. Close encounters with these photogenic fish can be enjoyed throughout New South Wales, as they are naturally inquisitive and usually quite fearless.

Norfolk Island
Convict Hell, Diver's Heaven

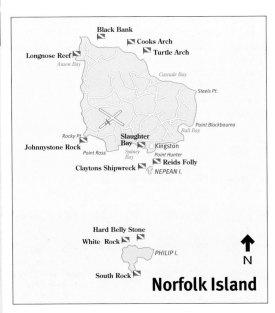

Norfolk Island

 Boat dives up to 20 minutes away

 Usually 20–30 m

 Occasional currents offshore

 Soft and hard corals

 Excellent variety of marine life and interesting terrain

 Reef and pelagic fish common

 Rocky and coral reefs

Norfolk Island was established as a penal colony in 1788, an event which turned this uninhabited island paradise into a living hell for its convict residents. After years of terrible treatment, in 1856 the convicts were transferred to the even harsher penal colony at Port Arthur, Tasmania. During those years as a penal colony, a small settlement was built along the shore at Kingston, which is now the main town.

The deserted island was subsequently given to the Pitcairn Islanders, the descendants of the Bounty mutineers, whose own island was becoming overcrowded. They have since turned Norfolk back into a paradise, and while fishing and farming are still major occupations, tourism is now the island's most important industry.

Norfolk Island today is a federal territory of Australia, with its own laws and customs. The island, located 1600 km northeast of Sydney, is regularly serviced by flights from Sydney and Brisbane. Norfolk enjoys a subtropical climate, but can be quite cool in winter, and diving in 5 mm suits is common year round. Visitors to the island enjoy its natural beauty, explore the historic ruins, shop duty free, fish, swim, snorkel, dive, and meet the descendants of the Bounty mutineers.

Norfolk and the nearby islands of Phillip and Nepean are surrounded by rocky reefs, which are covered in hard and soft corals, a refuge for many fish and endemic invertebrate species. A dive shop is based on the island and runs regular boat dives to the many outstanding dive sites in the area.

Black Bank
Black Bank is a dramatic boulder reef in depths up to 21 m. The boulders form caves, swim-throughs and gutters scattered with soft corals, sponges, sea stars, brittle stars, cowries and nudibranchs. Species of reef fish often seen include catfish, butterflyfish, wrasse, parrotfish, anemonefish, sweep, rock cod and goatfish. Kingfish and trevally in large schools and other pelagic fish are common sights.

Cook's Arch
Cook's Arch (located in Duncombe Bay where there are numerous interesting dive sites) is a huge 12 m-high curve cutting through the reef, and a drop-off to 21 m. The reef here has marine growth typical of the area—soft corals, sponges, ascidians and tubastraea coral. Schools of baitfish sometimes fill the arch and other nearby caves. Gropers, morwong, rock cod,

moray eels, lionfish, emperors and the occasional slipper rock lobster are found in the crevices and under the overhangs and ledges.

Longnose Reef

The outer side of Longnose Reef drops to 30 m, and the inner side from 5–25 m. Many caves and swim-throughs are located along the walls and provide exciting diving. A torch will reveal sponges and soft corals, lionfish, rock cod, moray eels and bizarre nudibranchs. Reef fish are common, and on occasions the reef is surrounded by larger pelagic fish.

Johnnystone Rock

The tip of this dramatic pinnacle rises 2 m above the surface of the sea, and its walls descend to 30 m below. These walls are riddled with caves and ledges sheltering baitfish, shrimp, hermit crabs, cardinalfish, rock cod, sea stars, feather stars and lionfish. Schools of kingfish and trevally circle the rock looking for a meal. Stingrays, double header wrasse, turtles and the occasional groper are usually seen in the background.

Slaughter Bay

This sheltered bay, a popular night dive, can be explored as a shore dive. Patches of hard and soft coral, nudibranchs, sea stars, anemonefish, stingrays, snake eels, butterflyfish, shrimp, goatfish and many more species thrive at a depth of 6 m. The HMS *Sirus*, the flagship of the first fleet which ran aground here in 1790, lies at the edge of the bay. This historic ship has been pounded by heavy seas for over 200 years, and little remains above the sand. However maritime archaeologists have recovered a wealth of material from the site.

Reids Folly

Located on the northern side of Nepean Island, this pinnacle drops to

24 m. The descent into a hole in the top of the pinnacle, which leads to a large archway, is an exciting dive. Hard and soft corals are numerous and the pinnacle teems with reef fish and schools of pelagics.

Clayton's Shipwreck

Located on the southern side of Nepean Island, at a depth of 16 m, this coral-encrusted reef is inhabited by damsels, anemonefish, rock cod, nudibranchs, shrimps, sea stars, butterflyfish and moray eels. The rugged terrain makes for interesting diving.

South Rock

South Rock is the best of a number of excellent dive sites found around Phillip Island. The rock, sprinkled with colonies of black coral, spiky soft corals, sponges, hard corals and ascidians, plummets into 40 m of water. Many species of colorful small reef fish and invertebrates live along the wall, while turtles, double header wrasse, trevally, sweep, kingfish, rock cod, morwong and the occasional Galapagos shark cruise the open water not far away.

Below: Often seen during the day, the hermit crab (*Dardanus* sp.) has no hard exterior carapace covering its abdomen and uses uninhabited mollusc shells as protection from predators.
Michael Aw

Lord Howe Island
The World's Southern-Most Coral Reefs

Above: One of the world's most beautiful islands, Lord Howe's incredible scenery and brilliant diving make it a diver's mecca.
Neville Coleman

Boat dives up to 20 minutes away

Generally 20–30 m

Occasional strong currents offshore

Good hard and soft corals

Interesting terrain and plenty of fish

Reef and pelagic fish common on most reefs

Rocky and coral reefs

Located 770 km northeast of Sydney, Lord Howe Island is one of the most beautiful islands in the world. Two small mountains, Mt Gower and Mt Lidgbird, tower over the island—the remains of a large volcano, thought to be 7 million years old. Many unique plants and animals have evolved here, including the endangered Lord Howe Island wood hen and the endemic kentia palm. The island was first settled in 1830, and today has a local population of 300 that earns a living mainly from the tourism industry. A good range of accommodation is available.

About 50 species of coral have been identified on the surrounding coral reefs (the most southern in the world), most of which are located in the large lagoon on the western side of the island. These reefs maintain vigorous populations of invertebrates and over 500 species of fish, including 13 that are endemic to this area. In recognition of these outstanding natural features, Lord Howe Island was inscribed on the World Heritage List in 1982.

Visitors to Lord Howe can snorkel the lagoon or Neds Beach (where thousands of fish gather to be fed), enjoy bushwalks or mountain treks (for wonderful views), observe the native wildlife (especially the nesting sea birds) or explore the island on bike (the main form of transport on this wonderful island).

Many divers return year after year, and prefer to book package deals which include diving and accommodation. The local dive shop is Pro Dive, which runs two boat dives daily to any of the 28 islands around Lord Howe, and has close to 100 dive sites to choose from.

Roach Island
Huge boulders encrusted with soft and hard corals, sponges, ascidians, and gorgonians provide interesting dive sites at depths of 18–30 m. Although invertebrates are plentiful on the fringing reef, this area will be most remembered for its fish life. Angelfish, butterflyfish, rare Japanese boarfish, anemonefish, spangled emperor, painted morwong, striped catfish, mosaic moray eels, lionfish, sweetlips, parrotfish, drummer, double header wrasse and Galapagos sharks are just some of the species found at Roach Island, and at most dive sites around Lord Howe Island.

Malabar Reef
This large, rocky reef, located off Malabar Hill in 9–18 m of water, has endless gutters, ledges and small pinnacles—all covered in excellent coral growth. Have a look among the corals for nudibranchs (including Spanish dancers), anemonefish, flatworms, shrimp, hermit crabs,

sea stars, feather stars, brittle stars, lionfish, hawkfish, gobies and painted morwong.

Comets Hole, Erscotts Hole

These 7 m-deep holes in the lagoon are usually filled with double-header wrasse, spangled emperor, butterflyfish, angelfish, morwong, wrasse, moray eels, lionfish and many more species. Nudibranchs, flatworms, crabs, shrimp, sea stars, tube worms and other invertebrate species inhabit the many hard coral formations also found in the lagoon.

Shark Reef

Many gutters, swim-throughs and ledges occur where the edge of the lagoon drops into 30 m. Macro-photographers will find many photogenic subjects here among the corals— shrimps, cowries, flatworms, nudibranchs, sea stars and abundant reef fish. The occasional school of pelagics and individual Galapagos sharks patrol the waters off the reef.

South Head

The southern end of Lord Howe Island, which drops steeply into 50 m of water, is rarely dived. Here you will see plenty of reef and pelagic fish around the walls and caves, and perhaps some fast Galapagos sharks.

Balls Pyramid

This spectacular blade of rock rises 551 m above the surface of the water and drops to 37 m below. Located 23 km southeast of Lord Howe Island, Balls Pyramid is occasionally dived and only when conditions are good. The walls and the sea bottom at the base of the monolith are sprinkled with a sparse covering of black coral trees, gorgonians, soft corals and sponges. Reef fish dart among the corals and sponges, while schools of trevally, surgeonfish, drummer and kingfish swarm in midwater.

Grey reef and Galapagos sharks are very common, and will often come in close to inspect divers.

Elizabeth & Middleton Reefs

Located 190 km north of Lord Howe Island, these Coral Sea reefs have claimed many ships. Reef fish, kingfish, sweetlips, Japanese boarfish, doubler-header wrasse, black cod, drummer, trevally and particularly sharks are abundant in this area. Dozens of grey reef and Galapagos sharks are seen on every dive, and even a few tiger sharks have been sighted. These reefs are only occasionally visited by live-aboard boats operating from Lord Howe Island.

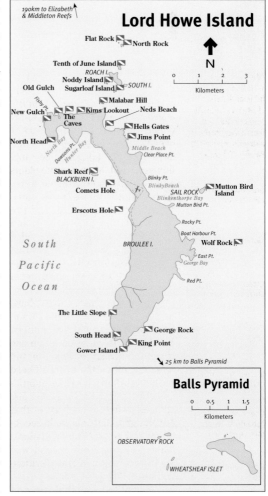

North Haven
Exploring the Titan

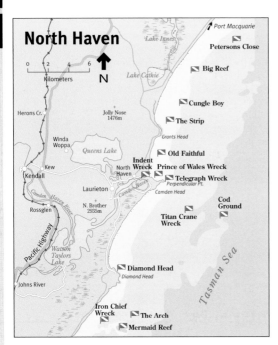

Boat dives up to 20 minutes away

Generally 15–20 m

Occasional strong currents offshore

Colorful sponge gardens

Titan crane wreck. Fish and shark action at Cod Ground

Reef and pelagic fish common

Rocky reefs and pinnacles

The *Titan*, the largest floating crane in the southern hemisphere, played an important part in the history of Sydney. In January 1992, the crane was being towed from Sydney to Singapore under controversial circumstances, as many felt that such an historic item should not be sold overseas. The crane sank off North Haven (a small holiday town 470 km north of Sydney), in 38 m of water. The Cool D Dive Shop organizes trips to the *Titan*, and a number of other exciting reefs and wrecks in the North Haven area.

Titan Crane Wreck

Diving on the wreckage of the huge crane, which now lies on its side in 28–38 m of water, is somewhat like visiting an underwater construction site. Divers can swim in and out of the crane structure and explore the deck area. The *Titan* has attracted a fantastic variety of marine life in the short time it has been underwater. Beautiful jewel anemones and encrusting sponges adorn the structure, wobbegongs rest on vacant vantage points, rock lobsters shelter in holes, and lovely nudibranchs crawl over the beams. Schools of bullseyes, yellowtail, kingfish, jewfish and trevally are always around, as well as the occasional snapper, blue groper and Port Jackson shark.

Cod Ground

The Cod Ground has a number of rocky pinnacles, in depths from 18–40 m, cut by gutters and ledges, lined with sponges, ascidians and black coral trees. While many beautiful reef fish and invertebrate species are permanent residents, the larger species dominate the scene. Grey nurse sharks gather in the gutters—sometimes over a dozen are seen at close quarters. Wobbegongs and Port Jackson sharks lie side by side under ledges, with rock lobster and rare black cod. Likely to be found hovering around the pinnacles are schools of yellowtail, pike, jewfish, kingfish and trevally.

The Cool D Dive Shop regularly visits about 20 other sites. Some are shallow dives with a good range of reef fish and invertebrates, while others are deeper dives with marine life similar to that found at the Cod Ground. A number of shipwrecks are located in the area, including the *Telegraph* in 17 m, the *Iron Chief* in 9 m, the *Prince of Wales* in 4 m, and the *Indent* in the Camden Haven River, at a depth of 6 m.

Forster/Tuncurry and Seal Rocks
Welcome to Shark City

A dive at **Big Seal Rock**, when the grey nurse sharks are in, is an unforgettable experience. Descending the rock wall, you will come upon a wide gutter at 21 m, which has a small cave cutting into the rock face. Usually schools of kingfish, drummer and trevally circle the gutter, while turtles, wobbegongs, stingrays and Port Jackson sharks can be seen resting on the bottom. Between summer and winter the gutter is often filled with dozens of grey nurse sharks. Sit on the edge of the gutter and watch these large sharks swim in figure-of-eight patterns. Grey nurse sharks are encountered on most of the reefs off Forster/Tuncurry and Seal Rocks at almost any time of the year.

There are hundreds, maybe thousands, of hidden reefs off the twin towns of Forster/Tuncurry, located 300 km north of Sydney. Divers have explored the reefs in the area for 40 years, and in that time have only scratched the surface. Three dive shops are based in the area, which run regular trips to the local reefs and Seal Rocks.

Taurus Reef

Taurus Reef, located at a depth of 9–15 m, is shallow and rocky. Although only sparsely covered with sponges and kelp, its many gutters and caves have attracted a wealth of marine life—Port Jackson sharks, wobbegongs, moray eels, lionfish, jewfish, kingfish, trevally, pike, reef fish and delicately banded coral shrimp. The best place to observe grey nurse sharks is a large cave on the southern side of the reef.

Snapper Rock

The many walls and gutters around Snapper Rock are barren in areas, but dense sponge gardens can be seen down deeper. Grey nurse sharks, stingrays, cuttlefish, wobbegongs, snapper, blue gropers and many colorful reef fish are common. This is a large reef in depths from 18–24 m, and will take many dives to explore thoroughly.

Snowflake Reef

This reef is blanketed in sponges, ascidians, gorgonians and white soft

Below: This nudibranch (*Chromodoridae* sp.*)*, a mollusc, began life with a shell which was discarded when the larva settled on the reef to metamorphose into an adult. *Michael Aw*

Boat dives up to 30 minutes away

Generally 15–20 m

Occasional strong currents offshore

Sponge gardens and a few hard corals

Grey nurse sharks at most dive sites. Many colorful reefs packed with marine life

Reef and pelagic fish common on most reefs

Rocky reefs and pinnacles

THE WORLD'S FIRST PROTECTED SHARK
The Grey Nurse Shark

FIERCE-LOOKING, BUT USUALLY QUITE HARMLESS, the grey nurse shark (*Carcharias taurus*) was blamed in the 1960s for every shark attack that occurred off the New South Wales coast. For the next two decades, spearfishermen killed thousands of these presumably menacing sharks with power-heads and strychnine nitrate needles. These people were considered heroes by the general public, even though divers soon realized that the grey nurse was not aggressive, no threat to swimmers or divers, and an easy target. The massacre continued, and the meshing catch measurements have shown that these sharks sometimes reach 3.8 m in length, but the average mature size is 2.5 to 3 m. No one knows how long they live, and little is understood about their courtship and mating rituals. Females are thought to reproduce biannually and have one or two pups per litter after an eight-month gestation period.

The grey nurse feeds on pelagic fish, small sharks, rays, squid, crabs and rock lobsters. Their long dagger-like teeth are used to grip prey, not cut, so they usually only take

Although protected by law, the grey nurse shark (*Carcharias taurus)* is still subject to injury by shark meshing nets and fishermen targeting wobbegong sharks (many grey nurse sharks have multiple hooks hanging from their jaws). This one here has survived a net with only superficial injuries. *Nigel Marsh*

sharks were eradicated on many reefs off the New South Wales coast.

By the early 1980s, grey nurse shark numbers were so low that many thought the population would never recover—ignorance had almost wiped them out in under twenty years. Alarm bells sounded through the dive industry, and a number of divers petitioned the government to protect the shark. In 1984 the grey nurse and its deep-water cousin the Herbst's nurse shark (*Odontaspis ferox*) were declared protected species in the waters off New South Wales.

The grey nurse shark belongs to the family Odontaspididae (sand tiger sharks), and is found in the temperate and subtropical coastal waters of the Atlantic, Indian and Pacific Oceans. There are four recognized species of sand tiger sharks. Beach

prey that can be swallowed whole. There are only four cases of divers being bitten—all occurred when divers were feeding sharks in aquariums.

The grey nurse is found off southern Queensland, southern Western Australia and most commonly off New South Wales. Here they migrate up and down the coast with changes in water temperature—in winter they are found in the north of the state, and in the south over summer. Since their protection, numbers appear to be increasing, and grey nurses are now seen regularly at a number of dive sites across the state.

However a new threat has appeared in the form of setlines. Professional fishermen off New South Wales use setlines to catch wobbegongs, but grey nurse sharks also take the baits. The grey nurse is often left to die. Many divers are lobbying to have setlining banned but the protests have fallen on deaf ears so far, and both the New South Wales Fisheries and the government have failed to act to save this presumably "protected" shark.

corals, hence the name Snowflake Reef. At a depth of about 20 m, the reef becomes a series of gutters, where you can always find nudibranchs, blue devilfish, hawkfish, blue gropers, morwong, leatherjackets and lionfish.

Latitude Reef

Latitude Rock, one of the best dives in the area, is a long blade of rock which drops into 20 m of water. Its many gutters are filled with blue gropers, wobbegongs, Port Jackson sharks, stingrays, cuttlefish, blind sharks, moray eels and the occasional grey nurse shark. Reef fish and invertebrate species are abundant, as are schools of pelagic fish. A resident loggerhead turtle, called Agro, can be hand fed. He's not always around, but if he is, he won't let you forget it—climbing all over you and hoping for a handout.

Pinnacles

Located a few kilometers off the coast, these rocky outcrops (rising from 45–30 m), are covered with beautiful corals and sponges. The pinnacles attract large schools of pelagic fish, including kingfish, yellowtail, sweep, bullseyes, trevally and mackerel. Port Jackson sharks, wobbegongs, stingrays, red morwong and a dozen or so grey nurse sharks can usually be seen on or near the bottom. When diving The Pinnacles, you should expect the unexpected, as bronze whalers, hammerheads, marlin and the occasional mako shark have all been sighted lurking around the rocks.

Seal Rocks

Along the shoreline near the tiny unspoiled settlement of Seal Rocks lie clean beaches, rocky reefs and a number of small islands. A rough ride over 5 km of dirt road leads to Seal Rocks, located 50 km south of Forster/Tuncurry. Dive operators run trips from the beach to the excellent sites nearby.

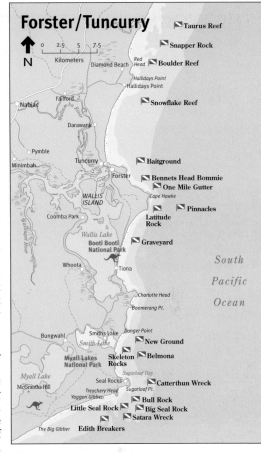

Satara Shipwreck

The SS *Satara*, a 120 m-long cargo steamer which foundered off Seal Rocks in 1910, now rests on its port side in 42 m of water. The stern section sits in an upright position, displaying the enormous prop, as well as portholes, boilers, the engine, propeller shaft, piles of chains and hundreds of plates. The wreck is covered in sponges, ascidians, anemones and black coral trees. Schools of reef and pelagic fish swarm about the wreck, and Port Jackson, grey nurse sharks, wobbegongs and the occasional bronze whaler are often sighted.

A number of other interesting sites are regularly dived off Seal Rocks, including **Skeleton Rocks**, **Little Seal Rock**, **Edith Breakers** and the 93 m-long wreck of the *Catterthun*, in 60 m of water.

Port Stephens
New South Wales' Best Shore Dives

Shore diving and boat dives up to 30 minutes away

Generally 10–15 m

Strong currents off-shore occasionally

Sponge gardens

Brilliant shore dives inside the bay. Colorful reefs and wrecks outside

Reef and pelagic fish are common

Rocky reefs

Port Stephens is a beautiful, relaxed holiday area located 230 km north of Sydney. This picturesque, blue-water bay is bordered by clean beaches, rugged bushland and a number of weather-beaten offshore islands. Diving outside the bay is fantastic, with plenty of reefs, deep drop-offs and a number of historic shipwrecks. Even inside the bay, the diving is great—the bay has three of the top shore dives on the east coast of Australia. All sites inside the bay are best dived on the turning high tide, as dirty water and strong currents can be experienced at other times.

Most of the dive shops servicing the Port Stephens area are based at Nelsons Bay, although one is located on the other side of the bay at Hawks Nest. All operators run regular shore and boat dives, as well as very popular night dives. Conditions and visibility may vary, but no matter how rough the seas are outside, divers are still able to enjoy an excellent shore dive inside Port Stephens.

Halifax Park

The rocky reef, with its huge variety of sponges, soft corals and associated inhabitants, drops straight into the main boating channel at Halifax Park (beware of passing boats), providing shore dives to 30 m. Nudibranchs, sea horses, anglerfish, sea stars, spider crabs, pineapplefish, moray eels, sea hares and many species of tropical fish are everywhere. Often the water is thick with stripeys, mado, yellowtail, bulls-eyes, blue gropers, pike, mor-wong, bream and sweep. Closer to the bottom live cuttlefish, octopi, lionfish, goatfish, leatherjackets, globefish, boxfish, catfish, wobbe-gongs, Port Jackson sharks, sting-rays and electric rays. The biological diversity of this area is so great that Halifax Park and nearby Fly Point were declared marine reserves in 1983.

Fly Point

Fly Point is a dive site that drops in a series of ledges to 24 m. Until a few years ago, the area was very rich in marine species but has since suffered from too many divers and the construction of a marina at Nelsons Bay. The marine life at Fly Point is similiar to that found at Halifax Park, with large colorful sponges being the dominant bottom feature.

The Pipeline

This pipeline, which runs deep into the bay, is overgrown with sponges, ascidians and especially soft corals—at times the marine life carpeting the bottom is even more prolific than that at Halifax Park and Fly Point. At 12 m divers are in the middle of the action. Species most commonly seen along the pipeline are nudibranchs, spider crabs, sea pens, sea horses, flatworms, feather stars, plenty of soft corals, cuttlefish, moray eels, reef fish and the occasional school of pelagic fish. Stingrays, shovelnose rays, electric rays and wobbegongs are often found resting on the sea floor.

Broughton Island

A number of fascinating dive sites have lately been discovered around Broughton Island, at depths from 12–35 m. Caves, colorful sponge gardens, walls and gutters attract masses of fish. Divers regularly see turtles, stingrays, grey nurse sharks, pelagic fish and the occasional manta ray. If conditions allow, a visit to the island is well worth the 30-minute boat ride up the coast.

Oakland Shipwreck

In 1903 the SS *Oakland* foundered off Cabbage Tree Island. The 45 m-long hull, essentially intact, still sits upright in 27 m of water, and is an exciting dive. Schools of kingfish, sweep, bullseyes, yellowtail and trevally mingle above the wreck, which shelters numerous reef fish, several resident stingrays and a couple of large wobbegong sharks.

Little Island

The rocky reef surrounding Little Island, which drops into 35 m, swarms with a great number of pelagic fish—kingfish, trevally, mackerel, yellowtail and turrum. Although there is only a sparse covering of sponges on the rocks, the fish population will be enough to entertain most divers.

Boondelbah Island

Pretty sponge gardens line the gutters, ledges and caves on the rocky reefs of Boondelbah Island, at depths from 20–30 m. A variety of reef fish, invertebrate species, wobbegongs, blue gropers, stingrays, cuttlefish and schools of kingfish are found around the island.

Shark Island

A small island off Point Stephens, Shark Island is situated where the bottom drops abruptly into deep water. The rocky reef forms walls and ledges to 35 m thick with colonies of sea whips, gorgonians, bryozoans, sea ferns, ascidians, sponges and soft corals. Reef and pelagic fish are common. Blue gropers, kingfish, red morwong, lionfish, bream, stingrays and Port Jackson sharks are regularly seen.

Opposite: During summer months, delicate juvenile lionfish (*Pterois volitans*) can be found on reefs in harbors and bays. If the temperature stays warm, these fish may survive until the next season. *Neville Coleman*

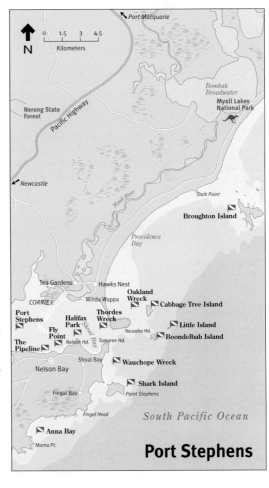

Newcastle and Swansea
Shipwreck Towns

Below: Rarely seen, the nudibranch (*Miamira sinuata*) is found on the reefs off central New South Wales. It has been recorded at Lord Howe Island in depths down to 20 meters. *Neville Coleman*

Shore diving and boat dives up to 30 minutes away

Usually 10–12 m

Occasional strong currents offshore

Sponge gardens

Good variety of shipwrecks and reefs

Reef and pelagic fish are common

Rocky reefs and pinnacles

Newcastle is an important industrial town and the sixth-largest city in Australia. Thousands of ships have visited this major port over the last 150 years, many of which have ended their days in the area—either by collison, or running aground on the notorious Oyster Banks at the entrance to Newcastle Harbour. Consequently, Newcastle is an excellent destination for those interested in wreck diving. For those more intrigued by marine life, many wonderful reefs and pinnacles are located in the area.

Uralla Pinnacle
This impressive dive site off the northern end of Stockton Beach is dived only occasionally. The top of the pinnacle, covered in kelp, is located at a depth of 6 m. The walls, blanketed with sponges, drop straight to 30 m. Kingfish, jewfish, grey nurse sharks, wobbegongs, Port Jackson sharks, eagle rays, blue gropers, samsonfish, trevally and reef fish are regular visitors.

Davenport Shipwreck
The 60 m-long *Davenport*, which rests in 12 m of water off Stockton Beach, was lost in 1943. The boiler,

prop shaft, ribs, winch and other wreckage can be seen best at high tide. Wobbegongs, blind sharks, blue gropers, morays and schools of bullseyes have moved to the area.

Signa Shipwreck
Beached in 1974, the *Signa* sits half out of the water on Stockton Beach. The bow has broken off, and divers can enter the wreck to survey the interior. The engine room and other sections of the wreck lie at a depth of 8 m, and are easily explored. Jewfish, rock lobster and globefish live in and around the remains.

Stockton Breakwall Wrecks
Oyster Banks is now a breakwall, built on top of the remains of the many ships that rest on the banks. The *Cawarra, Colonist, Wendouree, Regent Murray, Lindus* and *Adolphe* can be dived in 6–15 m of water. Many species of reef fish and invertebrates flourish in and around the shipwrecks.

Swansea
Swansea is a southern suburb of Newcastle situated at the entrance to Lake Macquarie. The lake is a

favorite of many holidaymakers, who come to Swansea to fish, sail and water ski. Each day on the low tide the lake flushes the lush sponge gardens in the Swansea Channel with nutrients.

including kingfish, jewfish, bullseyes, stingrays, Port Jackson sharks and wobbegongs. Just south of the *Bonnie Dundee* are the remains of the *Advance*, which sank in 48 m of water.

Swansea Channel
This brilliant shore dive is best done on the high tide, unless you particularly want a fast drift dive. The channel bottom and bridge pylons are encrusted with sponges, ascidians and soft corals, and the waters within the channel are rich with marine life. Nudibranchs, pineapplefish, lionfish, boxfish, goatfish, leatherjackets, anglerfish, sea stars, brittle stars, feather stars, molluscs, cuttlefish and moray eels are often found at depths of 12 m or less.

Other Shore Dives
The Swansea area offers some exciting shore dives, around the old coal loading pier in **Catherine Hill Bay**, and on the wrecks of the *Wallarah, Shamrock* and *Lubra,* in depths from 3–6 m. A great variety of marine life gathers in the bay and around the pier—from invertebrates to schools of yellowtail. The sea caves nearby, that undercut the headlands at **Fraser Park**, are not very deep, but should only be attempted on calm days because the exit can be difficult. Around **Moon Island**, extensive sponge gardens are found in depths from 12–20 m, and the many caves and swim-throughs are fun to explore. Reef fish, wobbegongs, stingrays, Port Jackson sharks, cuttlefish, blue gropers and morwong occupy the surrounding reef.

Bonnie Dundee Shipwreck
The *Bonnie Dundee*, which sank off Swansea in 1879, now lies on the sandy bottom in 34 m of water. The hull has collapsed to reveal the engine and boiler, and the bow still protrudes from the sand. An interesting assortment of marine life swarms about the wreck,

Caves Beach Shoal
Just off Caves Beach, at a depth of 13 m, is a rocky reef broken by gutters and ridges. The shoal is covered with sponges, ascidians, gorgonians and bryozoans, and shelters many larger invertebrates and reef fish. On a good day, you should see wobbegongs, stingrays, eagle rays, drummer and perhaps a turtle.

There are other interesting reefs off Newcastle, such as **Big Ben Reef** and **North Reef**, and many more wrecks, including the *Irresistable, Yarra Yarra, Southland, Mud Barge, Commodore* and *Osprey,* in depths from 20–42 m. A number of dive shops, located in Newcastle and nearby Swansea, run regular shore and boat dives to the surrounding areas.

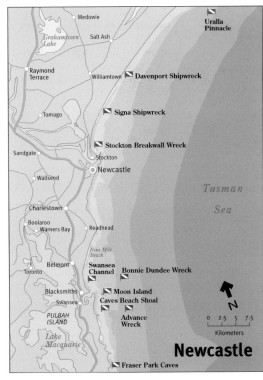

The Central Coast
A Weekend Hideaway

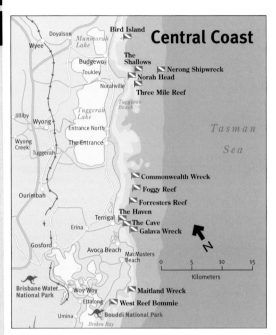

Central Coast

Shore diving and boat dives up to 30 minutes away

Generally 10–12 m

Occasional strong currents offshore

Sponge gardens

Good variety of reefs and wrecks

Reef and pelagic fish regularly seen

Coral reefs and pinnacles

The Central Coast of New South Wales, between Norah Head and Broken Bay, has always been a favorite Sydneysider holiday destination. Over the last few years large numbers of Sydney residents have moved to the area, and now commute daily to the city.

Inexpensive dive trips and an excellent range of accommodation are available. Plentiful marine life can be found on numerous sites accessible from the shore; and an endless selection of offshore reefs and interesting wrecks, in a variety of depths, can be easily reached by boat.

Divers visiting the Central Coast will find dive shops at Long Jetty, Terrigal and Umina. Local dive operators run boat dives to the best sites in the area. Being so close to Sydney, the Central Coast can be very busy on weekends and over the school holidays, so always book ahead. The best time of the year to dive is over winter, when the crowds disappear—the perfect weekend getaway.

Bird Island
Bird Island is a nature reserve to the north of Norah Head. Reef fish, numerous invertebrates, blue gropers, Port Jackson sharks, cuttlefish and stingrays are just a few of the inhabitants of the gutters and caves on the surrounding rugged rocky reef at depths from 9–20 m.

The Shallows
This large reef system has many excellent dive sites along its length. Most of the rocky reef is in 12–18 m, but some areas drop to 30–40 m. The reef has a good coverage of sponges and kelp, and plenty of reef fish. One huge, 25 m-wide canyon cuts through the reef, its sides dropping from 18–25 m. This canyon is often full of yellowtail and bullseyes. Wobbegongs, stingrays and a large family of blue devilfish can be found along the bottom.

Three Mile Reef
Located off Norah Head at a depth of 8–30 m, this large reef, also known as "The Bommies", features walls, pinnacles, caves and multi-colored sponge gardens. Pelagic fish, grey nurse sharks and bronze whalers are plentiful. Nearby—at 46m—lie the remains of the *Kiama*, which sank in 1951.

Nerong Shipwreck
The 36 m-long *Nerong* foundered off Norah Head in 1917, and part of the

hull, the engine, winches, boiler and prop shaft now lie in 42 m of water. The wreck has attracted bullseyes, yellowtail, trevally, kingfish, mackerel, wobbegongs, reef fish and even the occasional bronze whaler shark.

Commonwealth Shipwreck
The *Commonwealth*, carrying a cargo of coal, foundered off Terrigal in 1916. The remains of the 36 m-long wooden steamer—boilers, engines and other bits of wreckage—can be found scattered over the rocky bottom at a depth of 35 m.

Foggy Reef
Foggy Reef, at a depth of 30–40 m, is a wonderful boat dive. Its gutters, caves, walls and ledges are covered in sea tulips, gorgonians and ascidians. Browsing nudibranchs, molluscs, reef and pelagic fish, blue gropers, wobbegongs, cuttlefish, kingfish and grey nurse sharks over winter (particularly at Foggy Cave)—are usual sights.

The Cave
This shore dive off Terrigal is a deep gutter, about 15 m deep and 45 m long, cutting into the reef. Best attempted in calm conditions, parts of the gutter are covered by boulders, forming caves. The walls are coated with kelp, sponges, ascidians and sea squirts, and, if you look

closely, you will find nudibranchs and shrimp. Stingrays, cuttlefish, yellowtail, blue devilfish, kingfish and blue gropers are often seen.

Forresters Reef
Cuttlefish, Port Jackson sharks, stingrays, blue gropers, wobbegongs and masses of reef fish inhabit this colorful reef, which has a maximum depth of 30 m. Forresters Reef always manages to put on something special for divers, especially when washed by clear, blue ocean currents.

The Haven
The Haven is a popular location for snorkeling and open water diving. Sheltered and shallow, the rocky reef is well worth a dive as many invertebrate species, reef fish, giant black stingrays, cuttlefish, moray eels, electric rays, wobbegongs, blue gropers and Port Jackson sharks are always about.

Galava Shipwreck
In 1927, the coal ship *Galava* foundered and sank off Terrigal in 52 m of water. The 42 m-long ship has started to break up, but provides a rewarding dive for experienced divers. Similar to other deepwater wrecks, it attracts masses of fish life, typically bullseyes, kingfish, yellowtail and trevally.

Above: A common resident of reefs and sea grass meadows in sheltered bays and inlets, White's seahorse (*Hippocampus whitei)* is seen here in its orange coloration. Others can be black, white, yellow or brown with black spots.
Neville Coleman

Sydney
Diving the Harbor City

Sydney may be the largest city in Australia, and the pace of life rather hectic at times, but Sydneysiders know how to relax; and most do it on or near the water—sailing, surfing, swimming, fishing or diving. One of the major dive centers in the country, Sydney has a great deal to offer the visiting diver. Dozens of dive shops and charter boat operators offer trips to the many excellent shore dive sites, reefs and deep-water shipwrecks along Sydney's 100 km-plus coastline.

Northern Beaches

The beaches from Palm Beach to Manly are visited by thousands of people every day, who come to swim, surf, snorkel and dive. While there are some interesting shore dive sites on the northern beaches, especially around the headlands, the area is most noted for its many excellent boat diving sites on shipwrecks and reefs.

Valiant Shipwreck

A popular boat dive site, the *Valiant,* is a 22 m-long tug which sank in 1981, and now lies in 26 m of water, essentially intact. You can inspect the engine room, peer into hatchways, and swim through the bridge area. At times the wreck swarms with schools of yellowtail and sweep, while bullseyes and larger pelagic fish cruise the open water outside. Blue gropers, cuttlefish, moray eels, wobbegongs, stingrays and a number of reef fish share the protection provided by the hull.

Palm Beach Reef

This pretty reef is located off the southern end of Palm Beach, at depths from 10–16 m. Sections of the reef are accessible from shore, but the best sites are reached by boat. Extensive areas of reef are covered with sponges and small gorgonians. Weedy sea dragons are common, as are the ever-present Port Jackson sharks, stingrays, rock lobster, fiddler rays, cuttlefish and moray eels.

The Pinnacles

The Pinnacles are massive rocky outcrops which rise from 16 m, with interesting gutters and walls scattered with sponges and gorgonians. Residents include Port Jackson sharks, giant Australian cuttlefish, blue gropers, kingfish, pike, yellowtail, moray eels and lots of reef fish.

Duckenfield Shipwreck

The *Duckenfield* sank in 1889, after hitting Long Reef. The engines, boiler and other remains of this historic wreck have been recently discovered at a depth of 24 m—a haven for gropers, drummer, yellowtail, kingfish, morwong and wobbegongs.

Long Reef Wall

A number of excellent dive sites are found along the Long Reef Wall. This boulder wall, which drops from 8–20 m, supports masses of sponges, sea tulips and gorgonians. Kingfish, yellowtail, bullseyes, pike, blue gropers, surgeonfish, sweep and trevally patrol the open waters nearby. Giant cuttlefish, stingrays, fiddler rays, Port Jackson sharks, weedy sea dragons, wobbegongs and grey nurse sharks are often seen in the area.

Shore diving and boat dives up to 15 minutes away

Generally 10–12 m

Occasional strong currents offshore

Sponge gardens

Deepwater shipwrecks. Easy shore and boat dives

Reef and pelagic fish regularly seen

Rocky reefs and pinnacles

North Head

On any dive on this rocky reef, you are likely to see the remains of the several ships that have run aground on North Head. The reef is covered with invertebrates (especially sponges) and reef fish. Pelagic fish, wobbegongs, Port Jackson sharks, nudibranchs and giant Australian cuttlefish are common.

South Head

A number of brilliant shore and boat dives are found along the stretch of coast from South Head to Cape Banks. Sydney Harbour also has numerous interesting dive sites with an excellent range of reef fish and invertebrates.

Camp Cove

In 8 m of water, just off the beach at Camp Cove inside the harbor, is a rocky reef. This is an easily accessible reef is populated with pipefish, boxfish, cuttlefish, octopi, old wives, moray eels, anglerfish, morwong, brittle stars, sea stars, sea hares, nudibranchs, stingrays and other marine creatures.

Royal Shepherd Shipwreck

The 40 m-long *Royal Shepherd* sank in 1890 after a collision. The boiler, engine, prop shaft and other scattered bits of wreckage rest on the sandy bottom at 28 m. Moray eels, conger eels and numerous small reef fish live among the remains, which are often surrounded by schools of yellowtail and bullseyes.

The Gap

The Gap is an excellent boat dive to 22 m, where boulders form caves and gutters. Numerous sea stars and nudibranchs inhabit lovely sponge gardens. Divers will usually see Port Jackson sharks, blue gropers, kingfish, bonito, yellowtail, bullseyes and many reef fish along the gutters.

Below: Camp Cove, on the southern shore entrance to Sydney Harbour, is an excellent shallow-water dive site, especially for close-up photography. Through the years this area has produced many new species. *Neville Coleman*

Shark Point

Shark Point offers great shore diving. Where the reef drops into 20 m of water are lush sponge gardens, and ledges and caves. Rock lobsters, stingrays, moray eels, weedy sea dragons, pineapplefish, blue devilfish, Port Jackson sharks and cuttlefish are usually easy to find. Reef fish are plentiful, and pelagic fish school off the point. Behind Shark Point is Clovelly Bay—a natural ocean swimming pool, and a wonderful night dive in only 8 m of water.

Thomsons Bay

A popular shore dive to 14 m, Thomsons Bay also has an underwater trail. An astonishing assortment of marine species can be observed in the gutters or under the ledges and boulders, including stingrays, goatfish, electric rays, Port Jackson sharks, wobbegongs, rock lobsters, nudibranchs, moray eels, leatherjackets, lionfish, cuttlefish, sea perch, bream, flatheads and morwongs.

Long Bay

The *Malabar*, which ran aground in 1931, sank on the northern side of Long Bay. Plates and machinery from the ship lie on the boulder-strewn bottom, in depths from 6–10 m. Many species of reef fish reside in the bay, as well as wobbegongs, Port Jackson sharks, stingrays and cuttlefish.

Bare Island

A number of excellent shore dives are popular around Bare Island. The island is surrounded by pretty sponge gardens, caves, small drop-offs and gutters in depths from 9 to 18 m. Marine life found around the island includes nudibranchs, moray eels, cuttlefish, sea horses, cowries, weedy sea dragons, pipefish, Port Jackson sharks, morwongs, blue gropers, shrimp, crabs, stingrays and plenty of reef fish.

Southern Suburbs

Many excellent dive sites are located along the coastline from Botany Bay to the Royal National Park. This area has the clearest water and the most colorful sponge gardens found off Sydney.

Kurnell

Some of Sydney's best shore dives are at Kurnell. On the inside of the bay is a long pier in only 5 m of water, which shelters many different species of reef fish and invertebrates. Beautiful sponge gardens are found off both Sutherland and Inscription Point, in depths from 10 to 22 m. Plenty of reef fish and invertebrates can be found on every dive. Also usually seen are sea horses, weedy sea dragons, Port Jackson sharks, stingrays, blue gropers, cuttlefish, moray eels, blue devilfish and occasionally a school of pelagic fish.

Cape Bailey

A number of excellent boat dives are located off Cape Bailey, where the rocky bottom drops into 26 m of water. This rocky reef is blanketed with sponge gardens. Nudibranchs, sea stars, small cuttlefish, shrimps, boxfish, sea horses, reef and pelagic fish, sharks and rays, are common.

Osborne Shoals

The inner side of Osborne Shoals, which drops to 18 m, is thick with kelp. The outer side, which drops to 25 m, is overgrown with multi-colored sponge gardens, where there are good populations of reef fish, kingfish, mackerel, yellowtail, blue devilfish, cuttlefish, morwong, stingrays and Port Jackson sharks.

Shiprock

This fantastic shore dive in Port Hacking is best done on the high tide. The wall, overgrown with sponges, ascidians and soft corals, drops steeply from 6–15 m. Macrophotographers will enjoy the enormous variety—sea horses, anglerfish, pineapplefish, pipefish, nudibranchs, moray eels, sea stars, cuttlefish, octopus, tube worms and lionfish. Larger reef fish include sweep, stripey, morwong, leatherjackets, hawkfish, wrasse and old wives.

Jibbon Bombora

This rocky pinnacle, covered with a lovely sponge garden, rises from 30 m. Photographers will find many subjects here as well—sea stars, nudibranchs, cuttlefish, sea horses, shrimp, weedy sea drag-

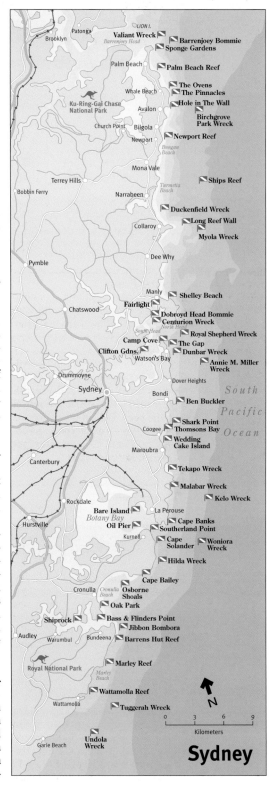

Sydney

THE FRIENDLY MOLLUSC
The Giant Australian Cuttlefish

ABOUT 10 SPECIES OF CUTTLEFISH ARE FOUND in the seas around Australia. These belong to the molluscan class, Cephalopoda, which includes cuttlefish, octopi, squid and the nautilus. Most cuttlefish are quite small and shy, however one member of the family grows to 150 cm in length and will boldly approach and interact with divers. This is the giant Australian cuttlefish—the friendly mollusc.

Often seen on reefs and wrecks from southern New South Wales to southern Western Australia, this large cuttlefish (*Sepia apama*) spends most of its day sheltering in caves or among kelp. At night it stalks reef fish, crustaceans and even other molluscs, entangling its prey in its eight arms, then devouring the victim with its parrot-like beak and rasp-like tongue. When threatened by a shark, ray or moray eel, the cuttlefish will change its color or flash warning signals by expanding and contracting pigment cells in its skin called chromatophores. It can even change its texture, to blend in with its surroundings, by controlling the tubercles that cover its skin. These devices are also employed when hunting, courting and mating. When threatened, the cuttlefish will raise two arms to threaten its attacker, and as a last resort squirt out a cloud of sepia ink to cover its getaway.

Cuttlefish are able to move slowly—by undulating their lateral fins; or rapidly—by expelling water through their siphon, a form of jet propulsion. Their porous internal bone can be filled with gas for buoyancy control. Cuttlefish have excellent eyesight, focusing their eyes by contracting muscles.

Divers are most likely to encounter this giant over winter and spring, which appears to be its mating season. During this time the male's arms enlarge, and he displays for the gathered females. Once the male has fully impressed a female, they embrace in a mass of arms, and he delivers a sperm packet to the female via a specially modified tentacle. The female later lays hundreds of large, round, white eggs on a sponge, gorgonian, cave roof or any vacant position that is well-washed by currents, to ensure an adequate supply of oxygen for the developing young. The eggs hatch after one month, and at this stage the juvenile cuttlefish, only 1 cm in length, drifts for the first part of its life with the currents, before finding a reef on which to live. The cuttlefish die after mating a few times, having lived for only one year.

Amorous males follow divers during the mating season, and attempt to mate with brightly colored strobes or regulators. On most encounters, however, cuttlefish appear to be curious of divers, and will pose for photos or come in close to study the bubble-blowing invaders.

The giant cuttlefish (*Sepia apama)* occurs from central New South Wales to south Western Australia. These molluscs are intelligent and very inquisitive. Although they appear harmless, they have a sharp, biting beak. Because of their attraction to shiny things (usually fish) one is thought to have contributed to a diver fatality, by attacking a regulator mouthpiece. *Nigel Marsh*

ons, hermit crabs and octopi. A sizable population of reef fish inhabits the Bombora, and schools of large pelagic fish are regular visitors.

Barrens Hut

A popular boat dive on a rocky reef, stepping down to 26 m. The walls and gutters are packed with sponges, sea whips, gorgonians, bryozoans and ascidians. A good variety of invertebrates and reef fish are found on the rest of the reef, as well as Port Jackson sharks, cuttlefish, stingrays and schools of kingfish.

Marley Reef

Offshore from the Royal National Park are a number of good dive sites on Marley Reef. This rocky reef has many walls and gutters, dropping to 24 m. An interesting assortment of invertebrates, including dense sponge gardens, cover the boulders. Reef fish are common—hawkfish, morwong, leatherjackets, wrasse, scorpionfish, lionfish and moray eels.

Sydney Shipwrecks

There are far too many shipwrecks found off Sydney to describe here—and new ones are discovered every few years, even in popular diving areas. Some shallow wrecks that are easily explored include the *Dunbar, Centurion, Fame, Tekapo, Belbowrie* and *Hilda*. The most exciting shipwrecks are those found in deeper water, but these are only accessible to experienced divers with adequate training and equipment. These deep-water wrecks include the *Birchgrove Park* in 50 m, the ten wrecks on the **Ships Reef** (45 m), the *Myola* in 48 m, the *Annie M. Miller* (44 m), the *Kelo* (42 m), the *Woniora* (62 m), the *Tuggerah* (45 m) and the *Undola* (45 m).

The above-mentioned are just a few of the wrecks and reefs found off Sydney. Boat dives are run every weekend, and a number of shops run mid-week trips if they have the numbers. Conditions can vary greatly, with visibility ranging from 3–30 m. By far the best time of the year for diving is during winter, as the westerly winds flatten out the seas and bring in clear blue water from the open ocean.

Above:
Distinctively patterned, the fiddler ray (*Trigonorrhina fasciata*) lives along southern coastal areas in sea grass meadows, on low profile reefs and on sandy bottom. It feeds mostly on molluscs and crustaceans but will eat other fish if the chance arises.
Nigel Marsh

Wollongong to Kiama
Rock-Hopping on the Leisure Coast

Shore diving and boat dives up to 15 minutes away

Generally 10–15 m

Occasional strong currents offshore

Good sponge gardens

Brilliant shore dives

Reef and pelagic fish common

Rocky coral reefs and pinnacles

This stretch of coastline, known as the Leisure Coast, offers plenty of leisure activities—surfing, snorkeling, diving, bushwalking in rainforest and national parks, as well as relaxing on golden beaches and at nearby lakes. Within easy reach of Sydney, the Leisure Coast is a popular destination for day trips and weekend escapees who stream down the Prince's Highway.

The area from Wollongong to Kiama has many excellent, inexpensive shore dives, known as rock hops, along the coastline. In fact around Bass Point and Kiama, divers will find some of the best rock hops in the state. Dive shops located in Wollongong and Bass Point run shore and boat dives to sites in the area.

Beaky Bay
On the northern side of Bass Point is a large bay known as Beaky Bay. You can jump in just about anywhere and have a good dive along the gutters and ledges on the rocky bottom, at a

maximum depth of about 12 m. A good range of reef fish are always around and Port Jackson sharks, cuttlefish, wobbegongs and moray eels are frequently part of the underwater scenery. A 100 m-long blue metal loader dominates the bay. The pylons are encrusted with sponges and anemones, nudibranchs and crabs. Globefish, cuttlefish, octopi, stingrays, blue gropers and schools of yellowtail and bullseyes are often found under the pier.

Bushrangers Bay
Bushrangers Bay is located at the very tip of Bass Point. On the sheltered, rocky bottom, which levels off at a depth of 15 m, are kelp beds, many colorful sponges, nudibranchs, weedy sea dragons, stingrays and lots of reef fish. The outer edge of the bay drops down to 25 m, and here divers will usually see Port Jackson sharks, wobbegongs, schools of pelagic fish and maybe the occasional turtle.

Kiama Blowhole
All around Blowhole Point are exciting dive sites, but the Blowhole itself is something magic. Its rocky walls drop straight down to 12 m, and sponges and numerous invertebrate species cling to the walls. The Blowhole is a deep cave that creates a lot of surge. Inside the Blowhole and the other nearby caves live stingrays, cuttlefish, moray eels, blue gropers, rock lobster, schools of yellowtail and pike, and a host of reef fish.

Wollongong Reef
This large, rocky reef off Wollongong, which drops from 25–40 m, is a

popular boat dive. Reef and pelagic fish share the reef with numerous invertebrates and sponge gardens.

Bombo Shipwreck

In 1949, the 45 m-long *Bombo* sank off Wollongong in rough seas, and now rests upside down in 30 m of water. Although the hull has collapsed, the wreck can be entered through various holes. The *Bombo* has a good coverage of sponges and attracts schools of reef and pelagic fish.

Gap Island

Gap Island—one of the Five Islands off Wollongong—has steep, rocky drop-offs, blanketed with thick sponge gardens. Gap Island has the most dramatic dive sites, but all the island reefs support healthy fish populations. Resident reef fish include blue gropers, sea perch, leatherjackets, wrasse, red morwong and scorpionfish. Pelagic fish regularly seen are kingfish, yellowtail, pike, sweep, bream, and occasionally salmon and jewfish.

The Humps

This sponge-covered dive site off Bass Point, known as The Humps, consists of three large, rocky pinnacles which rise from 30–10 m. Dense schools of kingfish, trevally, red morwong, yellowtail, pike, sweep, blue gropers, old wives and many other species congregate around the pinnacles. Manta rays and turtles are sometimes seen.

Lou's Reef

Directly off the front of Bass Point is a brilliant spot known as Lou's Reef, which drops steeply from 15–35 m. This reef has some of the best sponge gardens in the area, as well as gorgonians, sea whips, bryozoans, anemones, sea tulips, finger sponges, sea stars and especially nudibranchs. Reef fish are always around, and you will usually see cuttlefish, stingrays, king-

fish, moray eels, wobbegongs and blue gropers.

The Archway

This massive swim-through is located on the southern side of Bass Point. The Archway is in 25 m of water, and is covered with sponges, ascidians and anemones. Nearby are brilliant sponge gardens to about 30 m. Reef fish and invertebrates are common, as are blue gropers, giant cuttlefish, blue devilfish, stingrays and large numbers of Port Jackson sharks.

Blowhole Point

While most of Blowhole Point is accessible from the shore, the very tip is best done as a boat dive, and well worth the effort. Here the rocky reef drops to 20 m, and features an array of gorgonians, sea tulips and sponges. Kingfish, mackerel, yellowtail, bullseyes, pike and drummer gather at the point. Stingrays, eagle rays, blue gropers and Port Jackson sharks are often around.

Opposite: A common yet beautiful species, the magnificent ascidian (*Botryloides magnicoecum*) can be found in bays, estuaries and on offshore reefs. The golden yellow coloration appears stable though the patterning may vary on particular colonies from blue to purple, or dark red to black. *Neville Coleman*

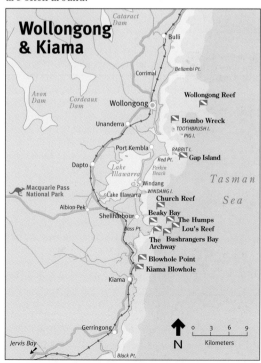

Jervis Bay
Protected for Your Enjoyment

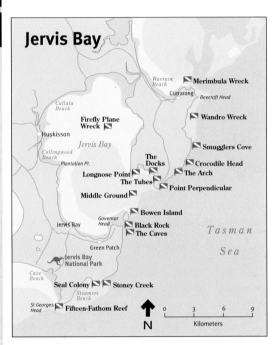

Jervis Bay

Warrain Beach
Currarong
Beecroft Head
Merimbula Wreck
Callala Beach
Firefly Plane Wreck
Huskisson
Jervis Bay
Wandro Wreck
Collingwood Beach
Plantation Pt.
Smugglers Cove
The Docks
Crocodile Head
Longnose Point
The Arch
The Tubes
Point Perpendicular
Middle Ground
Bowen Island
Jervis Bay
Governor Head
Black Rock
The Caves
Tasman Sea
Green Patch
Jervis Bay National Park
Cave Beach
Seal Colony
Stoney Creek
Steamers Beach
St Georges Head
Fifteen-Fathom Reef
N
0   3   6   9
Kilometers

Shore diving and boat dives up to 1 hour away

Usually 15–20 m

Occasional strong currents outside bay

Incredible sponge gardens

Dramatic underwater terrain and brilliant sponge gardens

Good numbers of reef and pelagic fish

Rocky reefs, walls and pinnacles

sponges and a wide variety of marine life. Some interesting shore dives lie inside the bay at **Murrays Beach** and **Green Patch**, but the best dive sites, inside and outside the bay, are reached by boat.

Boat dives depart from **Huskisson**, where all dive shops are based, to the superb dive sites (including a recently-established fur seal colony) located in and around Jervis Bay. If planning a visit during the holidays, book dives and accommodation early.

Smugglers Cave

This spectacular, wide cave is 150 m long and cuts right through the headland. The main entrance is half above water, while the boulder-lined cave floor is at a depth of 15 m. Take a good flashlight, and have a look at the many sponges and gorgonians. The cave is reasonably safe, as light from the entrances can be seen at all times, but should be avoided in big seas. You can swim through the sponge-coated cave and back around the headland, which drops into deeper water, or return via the cave.

The Arch

The Arch is a natural bridge spanning a step in the rock wall. The top of The Arch is in 28 m, the base in 38 m, and the area is alive with a profusion of colorful marine organisms. Reef fish are common, as are wobbegongs, stingrays and schools of kingfish and butterfly perch.

Point Perpendicular

Point Perpendicular drops steeply to incredible sponge gardens at 40 m, however the best diving is found around the huge boulders in the

For years conservationists campaigned against plans for the relocation of a naval base from Sydney to Jervis Bay. Such a move would have involved the dredging of significant seagrass beds within the fragile marine environment of the bay. In 1994, the Federal Government decided to protect Jervis Bay by listing it on the Register of the National Estate—especially good news for divers, as the bay has some of the best dive sites found on the coast of New South Wales.

Many thousands of visitors enjoy Jervis Bay each year, relaxing on the clean, white, sandy beaches, birdwatching, and bushwalking in the thickly-wooded forests that line the shore. Divers come to explore the underwater walls and caves below the 200 m-high cliffs which tower above the water outside the bay. These walls are crowded with

shallows, on the inner side of the point. Numerous swim-throughs are found at 15 m, encrusted with sponges and small invertebrates. Wobbegongs, stingrays, cuttlefish, Port Jackson sharks, blue devilfish and a good variety of reef fish are very common.

The Docks
Sheer walls, boulders and caves make The Docks a popular dive site. The walls drop straight to the sand in 20 m, where nudibranchs, sea stars and other invertebrates feed in the sponge gardens at the bottom of the wall. The caves shelter various reef creatures, the elusive red Indian fish, cuttlefish, weedy sea dragons, octopi, bullseyes, moray eels and blue gropers. Usually seen near the bottom among the boulders are Port Jackson sharks, blue devilfish, stingrays, grey nurse sharks (over summer) and fiddler rays.

Stoney Creek
Stoney Creek is one of the most exciting dives in the area. The site is deep (dropping from 25 m to well over 60 m), affected by currents, and is for experienced divers only. The rocky walls of Stoney Creek are overgrown with sponges, ascidians, sea whips, anemones, gorgonians and bryozoans—all competing for space. The reef is packed with invertebrate species, numerous reef and

pelagic fish, and is occasionally visited by sunfish.

Longnose Point
Some of the best places to see grey nurse sharks over summer are the gutters, pinnacles and ledges off Longnose Point, in depths from 10–25 m. Blue gropers, wobbegongs, boarfish, rock lobster, weedy sea dragons, moray eels, stingrays and giant Australian cuttlefish are found year round.

Middle Ground
This reef at the entrance to Jervis Bay reaches from 35 m to within 16 m of the surface. Apart from some brightly-colored sponges, Middle Ground is most famous for its fish life—kingfish, pike, trevally, boarfish, yellowtail, bullseyes, fiddler rays, stingrays, wobbegongs, Port Jackson sharks, butterfly perch and reef fish.

Bowen Island
Bowen Island has many excellent all-weather dive sites. The inner western side has shallow, rocky reefs to 15 m, where there is plenty of invertebrate and fish life. The northern and eastern sides, which drop into 30 m plus, are covered with a dense carpet of sponges. Kingfish, blue gropers, angel sharks, eagle rays, stingrays, wobbegongs and cuttlefish are just some of the resident species.

Below: Protection from spear fishermen over a period of years has allowed Bleeker's blue devil (*Paraplesiops bleekeri*) to build up numbers and to become used to scuba divers. *Nigel Marsh*

Ulladulla
Brilliant Reefs Close to Shore

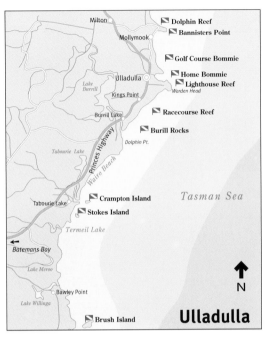

Milton

Mollymook

Lake
Burrill

Ulladulla

Kings Point

Burrill Lake

Tabourie Lake

Tabourie Lake

Termeil Lake

Batemans Bay

Lake Meroo

Bawley Point

Lake Willinga

Princes Highway

Warro Beach

Dolphin Pt.

🏴 Dolphin Reef
🏴 Bannisters Point

🏴 Golf Course Bommie

🏴 Home Bommie
🏴 Lighthouse Reef
Warden Head

🏴 Racecourse Reef

🏴 Burill Rocks

🏴 Crampton Island
🏴 Stokes Island

🏴 Brush Island

Tasman Sea

↑
N

Ulladulla

corals and sponges are sea stars, nudibranchs, basket stars, hermit crabs, cuttlefish, octopi, colorful shrimp, and the usual reef fish— leatherjackets, red morwong, scorpionfish, beardie, sea perch and old wives. The wall is an excellent gathering place for pelagic fish such as kingfish, yellowtail, bonito and trevally.

Home Bommie
Numerous boulders at depths of 15–22 m make up the dive site known as Home Bommie. Under ledges and in caves (usually overflowing with bullseyes) you will find cuttlefish and Port Jackson sharks. One wide cave houses a large anchor. Also common around Home Bommie are stingrays, giant Australian cuttlefish and a number of friendly blue gropers.

Burrill Rocks
Boulders at depths from 10–26 m form a long reef off Burrill Beach. These rocks are covered in dense sponge gardens and support an excellent variety of vertebrate and invertebrate species, including weedy sea dragons, sea horses, blue gropers, blue devilfish, stingrays, wobbegongs, green moray eels, cuttlefish, pipefish and the occasional school of pelagic fish.

Other excellent dive sites (the best of all) are located south of the harbor at Ulladulla off **Crampton Island**, **Stokes Island** and **Brush Island**. These are deep-water sponge gardens teeming with marine life. There are a few good shore dives in the area, however these are generally shallow and overshadowed by the easy boat dives.

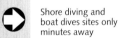
Shore diving and boat dives sites only minutes away

Generally 10–15 m

Slight currents on offshore reefs

Good sponge gardens

Many colorful sponge gardens

Reef and pelagic fish common

Rocky reefs

Located 60 km south of Jervis Bay, Ulladulla's reefs are found in shallow water, very close to shore— some only five minutes away by boat. These rocky reefs support an incredible variety of sponges, gorgonians, sea whips, ascidians, sea tulips, anemones and bryozoans, as well as numerous reef fish and invertebrates. Common and bottlenose dolphins, and humpback and southern right whales frequent the area during the winter months. Ulladulla is a fishing port and a popular holiday destination so book early during the holidays to avoid missing out.

Lighthouse Reef Wall
This rocky reef drops from the surface to 20 m, and is covered with colonies of gorgonians, sponges and sea tulips. Amid the

Batemans Bay
Rocky Reefs and Weedy Sea Dragons

Along the rocky shore from Batemans Bay to Broulee Island are numerous small islands and reefs that offer exciting diving. The area is most popular with divers from Canberra, only 85 km away. The bay was proposed as a seaport in the early days but it proved to be too shallow. Today, Batemans Bay is a popular holiday destination, with many national parks and lovely beaches in the area. Visitors will find an excellent range of accommodation and eating places to suit every budget.

Batemans Bay

Shore Diving

Around Batemans Bay are a number of shallow, shore diving sites. The most popular spot is **Guerilla Bay**, which is quite shallow and dominated by kelp. Once outside the bay, the bottom drops to 15 m and colorful sponges become more common. Marine life is abundant and divers will see nudibranchs, stingrays, electric rays, blue gropers, cuttlefish, sea stars and weedy sea dragons.

Boat Diving

The best the Batemans Bay area has to offer is accessible by boat. **The Tollgate Islands** are surrounded by rocky reefs, which attract schools of pelagic fish. The boulders are overgrown with sponge gardens hosting an excellent variety of marine life. **Black Rock** has a number of ledges and caves with cuttlefish, wobbegongs and rock lobsters. **Jemmy Island** offers interesting reefs packed with sponges, invertebrates and reef and pelagic fish. **Burrewarra Point** provides exceptional diving where the reef drops into deep

water. This rocky reef is covered in beautiful sponges and an extensive variety of invertebrates. Vertebrates are plentiful as well—stingrays, weedy sea dragons, blue gropers, boarfish, Port Jackson sharks, blue devilfish and the occasional school of kingfish.

John Penn

In 1879 the *John Penn* ran aground on Burrewarra Point, and sank in Broulee Bay after being towed off the rocks. Still an interesting wreck dive, the 50 m-long hull is encrusted with sponges and gorgonians, and alive with reef fish. Although it lies in 13 m of water and is filled with sand, divers are still able to see the engines, boiler, gunwhales and anchor.

Shore diving and boat dives up to 30 minutes away

Generally 10–15 m

Slight currents on offshore reefs

Sponge gardens

Many colorful sponge gardens and the John Penn shipwreck

Reef and pelagic fish quite common

Rocky reefs

Montague Island
Diving with Dozens of Friendly Fur Seals

Below: Montague Island is well-known for its friendly fur seas *(Artocephalus pusillus)* which can be viewed easily from a boat. *Michael Aw*

"We knew it was going to be a great dive—even while we were gearing up, there were fur seals swimming around the back of the boat. Once we were in the water and sitting on the rocky bottom at 15 m, we had dozens of seals zooming around us and putting on a fantastic show. They charged between us blowing bubbles as they went, while others played tag or just swam somersaults for the sheer joy of it. After a few minutes we all joined in—somersaulting, twisting, turning and rolling to amuse the seals. They seemed to enjoy the entertainment and performed more of their own. A few even came up to us and felt our gloves with their whiskers and noses. Some of the seals spent the whole time sunning themselves on the surface, but they at least had their heads under the water, watching the commotion below. Then a large manta ray cruised through the activities, and several seals followed it off into the distance. A few of us moved into the shallows where the seal haul-out area is located. Every couple of seconds a seal would dive into the water, glide through the thick kelp, and shoot straight past us. We could have stayed with the fur seals for hours, but had more dive sites to explore." *Neville Coleman*

Montague Island, a large rocky outcrop located 9 km off the town of Narooma, is the site of a lighthouse built in 1881, and a nesting area for thousands of sea birds, including sea eagles, terns and little penguins. A non-breeding colony of up to 400 Australian fur seals lives on the island in winter and spring, and smaller numbers can be seen at almost anytime of the year.

 Boat dives up to 30 minutes away

 Generally 15–20 m

 Slight currents around island

 Thick sponge gardens

 Encounters with fur seals, sunfish and grey nurse sharks

 Reef and pelagic fish common

 Rocky reefs, walls and pinnacles

The island is surrounded by deep water. The continental shelf, only a few kilometers away, brings clear water to the island for most of the year, and with it comes a surprising number of tropical fish. The local dive shops at Narooma and Bermagui usually run double dives to the dozens of excellent sites around the island.

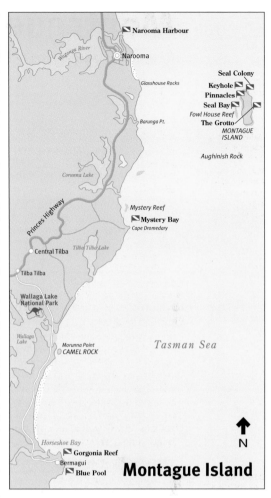

Keyhole
Similar to most of the dives around Montague Island, the Keyhole is a rocky wall that drops from 20–35 m plus. This wall is covered with multi-colored sea whips, finger sponges, gorgonians, ascidians, bryozoans and sea tulips, and the more mobile species such as feather stars, sea stars, sea urchins, basket stars, nudibranchs, octopi, shrimp and cuttlefish. Reef fish are abundant and include leatherjackets, boarfish, blue gropers, old wives, wrasse, red morwong and green moray eels. Occasionally pelagic fish are seen; also watch for giant sunfish and manta rays, which are sometimes found in the temperate waters around Montague Island.

Seal Bay
Hundreds of seals live on the boulders around Seal Bay when the colony is at its peak, and grey nurse sharks also hang out there during the summer months. The bottom of the bay is covered in boulders that form gutters, ledges and walls that drop into 30 m of water. There are a number of gutters around the island, and these are usually the best place to see the sharks hovering just above the bottom. Also found around the boulders are eagle rays, Port Jackson sharks, wobbegongs, boarfish, stingrays, fiddler rays, blue gropers and giant cuttlefish.

Other exciting dive sites around Montague Island include the Bubble Cave, The Pinnacles, The Den and The Grotto, all of which are found in depths from 20–40 m.

There is always somewhere to dive in all but the worst conditions.

Shore Diving
There are plenty of interesting shore dives in the area around Montague Island. A drift dive in the **Narooma Harbour**, at a depth of 6 m, can be fast and fun. When the water is clear, divers see numerous small fish and invertebrates. **Mystery Bay** has some interesting rocky reefs where there are plenty of fish, stingrays and nudibranchs. At **Horseshoe Bay**, off Bermagui, the rocky shore drops off steeply to beautiful sponge gardens and abundant marine life at a depth of 20 m. Check with the local dive shop for advice on shore diving the area.

Tathra
Sponge Gardens and a Great Wharf

A small fishing town, 450 km south of Sydney, Tathra is situated on the edge of a deep bay. The area round Tathra Wharf is one of the best shore dives in New South Wales, and in the waters off Tathra are reefs and pinnacles sustaining a substantial population of fish and invertebrates.

Tathra Pinnacles
Incredible sponge gardens decorate these twin peaks that drop steeply from 10–30 m. The two rocky pinnacles are covered with finger sponges, sea tulips, gorgonians, sea whips, bryozoans and ascidians. Have a close look among the sponges at the dozens of nudibranchs, sea stars, shrimps, cuttlefish and small reef fish. Schools of pelagic fish often sweep past the pinnacles.

Tathra Wharf
The 6–8 m of water under the Tathra Wharf is worth exploring. The colorful pylons are encrusted with sponges, jewel anemones and other associated marine life—blennies, shrimps, crabs and numerous nudibranchs. Moray eels, sea horses, octopi, cuttlefish, blue gropers and reef fishes also live among the pylons. From the wharf divers can swim to a rocky reef in 15 m of water, which is covered in lovely sponge gardens, with an interesting variety of reef fish and invertebrates. Divers usually see stingarees, kingfish, fiddler rays and giant cuttlefish on most dives.

Kianinny Bay
Kianinny Bay is another exciting shore dive. The bay itself is quite shallow, but out along the channel the reef drops to 18 m and is covered in lush sponge gardens. Here gutters, pinnacles and ledges are shared by wobbegongs, Port Jackson sharks and a good variety of reef fish.

Little Kangarutha
This is a boat dive on a brilliant pinnacle, with sponge gardens at its base in 22 m—a great place to see weedy sea dragons, blue gropers and just masses of colorful invertebrates.

 Shore diving and boat dives up to 15 minutes away

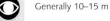 Generally 10–15 m

 Slight currents on offshore reefs

 Wonderful sponge gardens

 Tathra Wharf. Rich sponge gardens at most dive sites

 Reef and pelagic fish common

 Rocky reefs and pinnacles

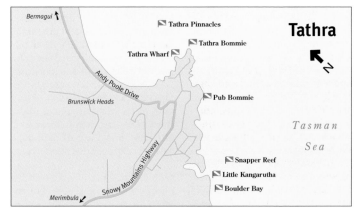

Merimbula and Eden
Adventures on the Sapphire Coast

The resort town of Merimbula and the busy fishing port of Eden are located halfway between Sydney and Melbourne. This picturesque area of rugged rocky coastline is known as the Sapphire Coast, because of its clear blue coastal waters. Both towns are popular holiday destinations offering surfing, fishing, horse riding, bushwalks and a host of other activities. Divers will particularly enjoy the great shore dives, off-shore reefs and shipwrecks in the area. Two dive operators work the Sapphire Coast area—Twofold Dive Charters based in Eden, and Merimbula Divers Lodge based in Merimbula. Both offer dive courses, boat dives and package deals on accommodation and diving.

Shore Diving

Long Point, a rocky reef off Merimbula, is the most popular shore dive in the area. Kelp dominates the shallows, the perfect habitat for weedy sea dragons, sea horses, cuttlefish and green moray eels. The kelp gives way to sponges as the rocky reef drops onto the sand at 15 m. Reef fish such as leatherjackets, cowfish, boxfish, morwongs, wrasse, scorpionfish, weedfish, old wives and perch are all common. You are also likely to see stingarees, conger eels, fiddler rays, electric rays, blue gropers, wobbegongs and perhaps an angel shark partly covered by sand. Invertebrate species are plentiful—several species of sea stars, nudibranchs, crabs and shrimp can usually be found.

There are a number of interesting shore dives around Eden, and a little further south, exciting adventure dives at Green Cape. Although

most sites at Green Cape are accessible by 4WD only, the multitude of fish and invertebrates inhabiting the rocky reefs make for rewarding dives. The area always provides an accessible shore diving site no matter what the conditions, but consult the local dive shop for advice.

Below: The propeller of the tug *Tasman Hauler* (sunk in 1988) is covered in encrusting marine life, almost as if it had been painted. *Dave Warth*

Merimbula Boat Dives

Many rocky reefs offer great boat diving just off Merimbula. **Short Point Bommie** rises from 18–5 m, and attracts large schools of pelagic fish including kingfish, bonito and clouds of yellowtail. The base of the pinnacle has brilliant sponge gardens with weedy sea dragons, blue gropers, octopi, nudibranchs, stingrays and abundant reef fish. **The Gardens** at Long Point, situated in 16 m of water, are packed with sponges, gorgonians, sea tulips, ascidians and bryozoans. This is also a good place to see reef and pelagic fish, many colorful nudibranchs, Port Jackson sharks, giant cuttlefish and sea horses. **Wonderland**, a rocky reef in 25 m of water, has a superb sponge garden—divers will find few places to settle, as the bottom is completely covered with a kaleidoscope of encrusting

Shore diving and boat dives up to 30 minutes away

Generally 10–15 m

Slight currents on offshore reefs

Beautiful sponge gardens

Empire Gladstone and The Tugs shipwrecks. Rich sponge gardens

Reef and pelagic fish common on all reefs

Rocky reefs and pinnacles

Merimbula & Eden

Bega
Tura Beach
Short Point Bommie
Tura Head
Merimbula
The Gardens
Wonderland
Long Pt.
Lochiel
Pambula
Merimbula Bay
Pambula Beach
Empire Gladstone Wreck
Greigs Flat
Haycock Pt.
Nethercote
Lennards Island
Ben Boyd National Park
Nullica
Eden
Twofold Bay
The Tugs
Tasman Sea
Boydtown
Edrom
Kiah
Mowarry Pt.
Ben Boyd National Park
Wonboyn
Disaster Bay
Green Cape

N

0   2.5   5   7.5
Kilometers

marine life, as well as stingrays, weedy sea dragons, boarfish, leatherjackets and many varieties of reef fish.

Empire Gladstone

In 1950, the 140 m-long *Empire Gladstone* hit Haystack Rock, before breaking up and sinking. Much of the wreck—the boilers, prop shaft and numerous twisted plates and ribs—can be found protruding from the kelp, in 6–12 m of water. Divers can swim inside and along the long drive shaft tube, which opens into the engine room which is usually packed with yellowtail and sweep. Pieces of wreckage lie everywhere on the rocky bottom. Wobbegongs, Port Jackson sharks, stingrays, cuttlefish, moray eels, plenty of reef fish and the occasional school of pelagic fish gather around the remains. Divers may see a fur seal as they sometimes visit the area.

Opposite: Although a sandy bottom may appear uninteresting and devoid of life to many divers, beneath the surface lies another major habitat teeming with life. This diver has found the giant sand star (*Luidia australasie*). *Nigel Marsh*

The Eden Tugs

Many interesting rocky reefs and sponge gardens are found off Eden, however the most requested dive site is The Tugs. In 1988 the local dive operator sank two 42 m-long tugs—the *Henry Bolte* and *Tasman Hauler*—to create an artificial reef. The *Tasman Hauler* sits upright in 30 m on a sandy bottom, and less than 500 m away the *Henry Bolte* rests at 26 m. After only a few years underwater, the wrecks are coated with beautiful pink jewel anemones and encrusting sponges. Many reef fish are found around the tugs, and schools of baitfish swarm about the wrecks. Although penetration diving is discouraged, divers are able to explore the massive props, masts, and superstructure, and look into the bridges and engine rooms. The wrecks lie at the entrance of Twofold Bay, in clear water, and 30 m visibility is not uncommon.

Introducing Victoria

Temperate Waters

Victorian divers are some of the keenest in Australia. On any weekend in the middle of winter, thousands of divers explore the waters around Melbourne, no matter what the conditions. These divers may seem a little "mad" to some, but after experiencing the surprising variety of sites and marine life found in the waters off Victoria, you will appreciate their enthusiasm and perhaps join in.

The second smallest state in Australia, Victoria is generally over-shadowed by the other states as a dive destination. However many excellent diving centers service the southern coastline at Wilsons Promontory, Melbourne, Port Campbell, Warrnambool and Portland. The remains of hundreds of ships (including a few submarines), colorful sponge gardens, rocky reefs, caves, pinnacles, kelp forests and piers with plenty of invertebrates and fish are found along the coast. You will also enjoy dives with fur seals and sight the occasional southern right whale.

Captain Cook first sighted Victoria in 1770, when he sailed past Cape Everard in the Gippsland region of Victoria. Although many explorers surveyed the coastline in the years that followed, and a number of sealers and whalers established small settlements, the state was not truly settled until after 1826, when a party landed at Phillip Island. The possibility of a Russian invasion in the 1880s prompted the building of forts, tunnels and gun emplacements. One of these unfinished forts in Port Phillip Bay (Popes Eye) is now a popular dive site, and part of a marine reserve.

Melbourne, the capital of Victoria, was established in 1835 after a treaty with the local Aborigines, but the population of the city and state did not increase dramatically until gold was discovered at Ballarat in 1851. The population of Victoria grew rapidly during the

gold rush that followed, and Melbourne soon rivaled Sydney as the most important city in the colony. After Federation in 1901, Melbourne was named the capital of Australia, until Canberra was founded in 1927. Victoria is now one of the most important industrial states in the nation and the base city for some of Australia's biggest companies.

The state covers an area of 227,600 sq km, which represents just 3 percent of the Australian continental land mass. Even so, Victoria has a wonderful variety of natural environments—one-third of the country's national parks are contained within its borders. Visitors are sure to enjoy the natural attractions—the snowfields, mountain ranges, rivers and lakes,

Above: One of the many back beaches located on the ocean side of Mornington Peninsula. Diving on the reefs adjacent to these beaches can only be carried out during calm conditions. *Nigel Marsh*

Opposite: Rarely observed alone, old wives *(Enoplosus armatus)* occur in pairs, small groups or large schools around jetty piles, on reefs or among kelp beds in temperate southern waters. *Michael Aw*

INTRODUCTION

VICTORIA

native bushland, lush green valleys, scrub land and deserts. Your itinerary could also include the penguins and other wildlife of Phillip Island, the spectacular scenery of the Great Ocean Road, the sheltered waters of Port Phillip Bay, the rugged beauty of Wilsons Promontory, and the endless maze of waterways of the Gippsland Lakes. The historic towns and old gold fields, the many cultural events and the famous Melbourne shopping are more big drawcards.

Victoria has a reputation for miserable weather, and while four seasons in one day may be experienced, the picture is not altogether unpleasant. During summer the state enjoys an air temperature range of 10–24° C, during winter a range of 4–14° C, and a wild fluctuation between these at any time. Summer and autumn provide the most consistently good weather, especially for divers. The seas are usually calm, the sky blue, the winds light and the temperature pleasant. The water temperature can sometimes reach 20° C, although it usually varies from 12–18° C from winter to summer.

A large number of dive shops are located in and around Melbourne, but there are only a handful of facilities throughout the rest of the state. Many excellent sites, especially along the east coast, are not accessible to most divers because of a lack of dive shops and charter boats. One of these sites is Gabo Island, with its brilliant sponge gardens, and the historic wreck of the *Monumental City.*

Numerous shore and boat dives are available along the coast of Victoria. A few live-aboard boats operate trips to Wilsons Promontory and the islands of Bass Strait. These offer some of the most exciting diving to be experienced anywhere in Australia. Visibility varies quite dramatically across the state, ranging from 5–15 m. The clearest water in Victoria can be experienced off Wilsons Promontory. On a good day visibility may be over 45 m. Divers in Victoria generally use 5 mm wetsuits in summer, and 7 mm wetsuits or drysuits in winter.

Visitors to Victoria will find an excellent range of accommodation on offer, and a number of first-rate dive lodges. Transport throughout the state is good, but if you are from outside the state and driving yourself, check the local driving regulations. Melbourne has an excellent tram (cable car) system—a popular way to explore this cosmopolitan city.

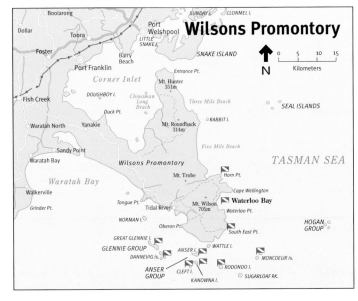

Wilsons Promontory
The Rugged World of "The Prom"

Boat dives up to 80 minutes away

Average 15–25 m

Currents on some reefs

Sponge gardens and kelp beds

Walls, pinnacles, caves and incredible marine life

Reef and pelagic fish common

Rocky reefs and pinnacles

"The Prom", as Wilsons Promontory is commonly known, is a rugged bushland peninsula featuring a wide variety of native animals—kangaroos, wombats, wallabies, emus, echidnas, platypus, koalas, fur seals, little penguins and many species of birds. Located 140 km from Melbourne, The Prom has always been considered something special, and was declared a national park in 1908.

Many thousands of people visit each year, to enjoy the many interesting bushwalks and camping areas, although access to these is limited. The main camping ground is at Tidal River, where boats can be launched across the beach. Each weekend dozens of divers explore the bays and islands at The Prom from small craft.

The striking landscape of granite headlands, boulders and islands continues underwater, forming sheer walls, caves and many pinnacles. These rocky reefs are covered in kelp in the shallows and spectacular sponge gardens in deeper water. The marine life is impressive—a remarkable variety of invertebrates, reef and pelagic fish, and numerous colonies of fur seals. The only limiting factor can be rough weather and access, as the most exciting dive sites are offshore, and best reached by a fast boat. Several charter boats run day and liveaboard trips to this area. These leave from Port Albert, Port Welshpool and Port Franklin on the eastern side of The Prom.

Horn Point
Here a steep, rocky wall drops to 20 m, covered with pretty sponge gardens. Have a close look among the sponges for sea stars, sea spiders, feather stars, basket stars and a variety of nudibranchs. The rocky and sandy bottom is alive with reef fish—morwong, perch, leatherjackets, boxfish, old wives, southern coral fish, boarfish, goatfish, as well as an occasional school of kingfish. Divers often see stingarees, Port Jackson sharks, weedy sea dragons, cuttlefish and draughtboard sharks.

Bareback Cove
At the southern end of Bareback Cove are a number of granite pinnacles which provide excellent div-

ing. The tops are coated with kelp, but as they drop deeper into 25 m the pinnacles are encrusted with sponges, ascidians, gorgonians and zoanthids. In the many caves and under edges are rock lobsters, cuttlefish, bullseyes, bearded cod, leatherjackets and blue devilfish.

Waterloo Bay
Granite boulders tumble into 40 m of water, forming fantastic walls and caves in this deep-water bay. Carpets of yellow zoanthids and sea

Above: Basket stars *(Conocladus australis)* are very common inhabitants of "The Prom". During the day they are usually found wrapped around sessile animal colonies such as sponges or sea fans. At night they move to the highest point and spread out their arms to catch plankton.
Neville Coleman

whips can be seen by flashlight in the caves, and numerous rock lobsters wave their antennae in the semi-darkness. Photographers will find an endless variety of subjects, including giant cuttlefish, draughtboard sharks, nudibranchs, sea stars, blue devilfish, long-snouted boarfish, schools of kingfish, and many over-friendly leatherjackets.

South East Point
Walls and gutters, with the usual multi-hued sponge gardens, reef fish and invertebrates, are located at depths to 28 m. Scattered along the sea floor beneath the lighthouse are piles of supplies, lost while being off-loaded from supply ships by crane.

West Moncoeur Island
A large fur seal colony on West Moncoeur Island provides hours of fun, as hundreds of seals join divers in the water. Some are curious enough to nibble on fins or fingers, usually gently. Divers can either sit on the bottom in only 10 m of water and enjoy the show, or swim with these superb acrobats. Either way, no one ever leaves till their air runs low.

Forty Foot Rocks
These two rocks rise 10 m above the surface, and drop to the sea bottom at 70 m. A gutter between the rocks lies in only 24 m of water, and everywhere around the rocks are numerous caves and ledges. Jewel anemones, sea whips, yellow zoanthids, gorgonians, ascidians, sea tulips, sponges, bryozoans and all make for brilliant photographs. Port Jackson sharks, schools of kingfish, yellowtail, bullseyes, boarfish, rock lobsters, and cuttlefish are common. A few fur seals have established a colony here.

Rodondo Island
Breathtaking is the best description of the diving at Rodondo Island. The island towers 40 m above the dive boat, and then drops straight into 50 m of water. A number of exciting sites around the island feature walls, caves, swimthroughs, gutters and ledges. Kelp dominates the upper areas of the rocks, and wonderful sponge gardens and associated marine life are found below. A variety of nudibranchs and sea stars can be seen on the reef, plus cuttlefish, rock lobsters, hermit crabs, shrimps and molluscs. Many species of reef fish are found alongside Port Jackson sharks, catsharks, kingfish, pike, trevally and schools of butterfly perch.

Cleft Island
Also known as Skull Island, Cleft Island looks as if it were created for a movie set. The island rises 113 m out of the water, has a rounded top and deep caves cut into it. Underwater, the granite pinnacle has fascinating caves and walls, to depths of 40 m.

Below: Hardly noticeable to the average diver, the sea spider (*Pseudopallene ambigua)* lives among the curly fronds of bryozoan colonies.
Neville Coleman

The northeast side offers some of the best diving, among piles of boulders covered in sponges, sea whips, zoanthids and gorgonians. Fur seals, boarfish, old wives, blue devilfish, morwong, butterfly perch, Port Jackson sharks, stingarees, boxfish, kingfish, bearded cod and scorpionfish are just a few of the animal residents.

Kanowna Island

Over 2000 fur seals have established a colony on Kanowna Island, and at times the water can be thick with these friendly animals. The action is so fast that photographers find it hard to concentrate on taking photos, especially when a curious pup swims up and stares at its own reflection in the lens, or decides that a strobe deserves a little chew. Although diving with seals is hard to beat (no matter where you dive there are bound to be seals), have a look at the numerous caves and walls around the island.

Anser Island

Anser Island offers interesting underwater caves lined with jewel anemones, encrusting sponges, ascidians and golden patches of yellow zoanthids. Make sure you take a flashlight to spot rock lobsters, conger eels, beautiful blue devilfish, scorpionfish, bearded cod and maybe an anglerfish. On the southern side of the island lie the remains of an unidentified shipwreck that has been thoroughly pounded by the sea.

Dannevig Island

The islands on the western side of The Prom all provide excellent diving. Dannevig Island is no exception, with rocky walls to 35 m, and numerous caves. Lovely sponge gardens cover the rocks beyond 15 m, and wrasse, leatherjackets, boxfish, stingarees, perch, morwong, southern coral fish, scalyfin, sweep, sea stars, catsharks and nudibranchs can always be found. Rock lobster, Port Jackson sharks, schools of pelagic fish and butterfly perch are also likely to be around.

Great Glennie Island

In rough weather many boats shelter in the bay at the northern end of Great Glennie Island. This protected area is an excellent place to dive. At depths to 18 m, along the sandy/rocky, kelp-covered bottom are fiddler rays, skates, stingarees, weedy sea dragons, draughtboard sharks, catsharks, scallops, sea pens, nudibranchs and plenty of reef fish. At the outer edge of the bay, the bottom drops to 30 m, and here the boulders are covered with a wonderful array of sessile organisms. Usually seen underneath the many ledges are kingfish, boarfish, bullseyes, pike, perch, morwong and blue devilfish.

Above: Similar to all boxfish, Shaw's cowfish (*Aracana aurita*) has a hard exoskeleton and is poisonous to eat. *Neville Coleman*

AUSTRALIAN FUR SEALS
Underwater acrobats

WHEN AUSTRALIA WAS FIRST DISCOVERED BY Europeans, hundreds of thousands of seals populated the southern coastline. Sealers soon arrived and killed countless animals for their pelts, meat and oil. Between 1798 and 1860 the sealers succeeded in wiping out the southern elephant seal colonies, and drastically reduced populations and distributions of the Australian fur seal, New Zealand fur seal and the Australian sea lion. Although fully protected since 1890, all populations are still low in number, and face new threats from oil spills, and the occasional irate fisherman with a gun.

although if the shark is seen in time it is easily avoided. Seals have even been observed harassing great white sharks.

Australian fur seals breed and pup each year in November and December. Females give birth to last season's pups, which start to eat solid food after six months. Females are rounded up by the aggressive males, and many battles take place between the males during the breeding season for control of the harems. The strongest male will then mate with the females which are in season, and after a 51-week gestation period the pup is born. Infant mortality rates are high, and the

Diving with Australia fur seals among giant kelp forests is one of the most exhilarating underwater experiences. *Neville Coleman*

The most common seal found in Victoria, Tasmania and southern New South Wales is the Australian fur seal (*Arctocephalus pusillus doriferus*). The population currently stands at 30,000. The largest colonies in Victoria are at Seal Rocks, Lady Julia Percy Island and Kanowna Island.

Extensive studies were made of the Australian fur seal in the 1960s and 1970s by the Fisheries and Wildlife Department of Victoria. Large numbers of seals at Seal Rocks and Lady Julia Percy Island were tagged, weighed and measured, including over 1000 pups born into the colonies each year. Their studies found that the seals eat reef and pelagic fish, octopi, squid, cuttlefish, rock lobsters and crabs. They may dive to depths beyond 200 m for food (the current record stands at 120 m, which was unfortunately discovered when juveniles were drowned in craypots). The seals may fall victim to killer whales and great white sharks,

average life expectancy is 20 years.

One of the most playful of all seals is the Australian sea lion (*Neophoca cinera*), which is found in South Australia and southern Western Australia. They are very friendly toward divers, and will even sit on the bottom, and pose for photographers. The population is currently around 5000, and they are considered to be one of the most endangered of all seals.

About 5000 New Zealand fur seals (*Arctocephalus fosteri*) are found in South Australia and southern Western Australia waters. This seal is fairly common in New Zealand. Occasional visitors to Australia's southern shores include southern elephant seals, leopard seals and crabeater seals which head north to escape the very cold Antarctic winter.

Melbourne
A City for All Interests

Shore and boat dives up to 30 minutes away

Summer 10–20 m
Winter 5–10 m

Currents on some reefs

Sponge gardens and kelp beds

Great shipwrecks and reef sites. Diving with fur seals

Reef and pelagic fish quite common

Rocky reefs and pinnacles

Few divers other than the locals realize that Melbourne has some of the most interesting and varied diving in southern Australia. While weather conditions might not always be brilliant, on a good day Melbourne has much to offer, whether it's exploring a submarine, coming face to face with a giant rock lobster, frolicking with fur seals or bottlenose dolphins, or just poking around under a pier.

Melbourne is the second-largest city in Australia. With two large bays and a couple of hundred dive sites to choose from—be it reef, wreck or pier—there is always somewhere sheltered to dive around Melbourne, no matter how rough the conditions. The most comfortable months for diving are from November to May, as the seas are generally calm, the water warmer (18–21° C), and the visibility consistently good within the range of 10–20 m.

In between dives, Melbourne, as Australia's most cosmopolitan city, has much to offer the visitor—sporting attractions, art galleries, wildlife parks, aquariums, historic towns and pubs, night clubs and festivals.

Western Port Bay Sites

Western Port Bay is dominated by two large islands—French Island at its center, and Phillip Island at its entrance. Phillip Island is the site of Melbourne's major tourist attraction, the nightly penguin parade, where little penguins can be seen returning to the island after a day's fishing. Visitors to this lovely island will also see kangaroos, wombats, koalas and other native animals, while divers will find it offers a good variety of dive sites.

The Pinnacle

This impressive rock tower rises from 40 m, to within 10 m of the surface. Crowned with kelp, the rock is thickly encrusted with gorgonians, zoanthids, bryozoans, anemones, ascidians and a variety of sponges. Reef fish and invertebrates are plentiful. The Pinnacle's pelagic visitors include kingfish, snapper and trevally.

Pyramid Rock

Located off the southern side of Phillip Island, Pyramid Rock can be

Below: At a bottom depth of only 4 m, the hundreds of pylons under Flinders Pier support an amazing wealth of marine life.
Neville Coleman

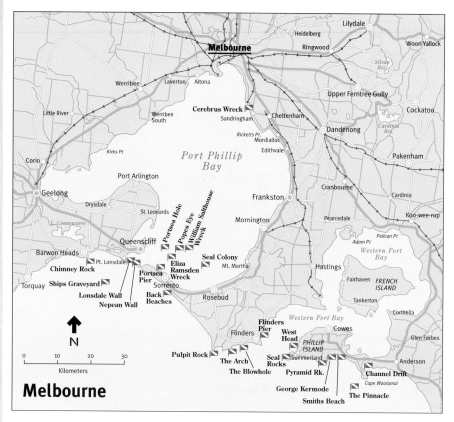

dived from the shore, but is most accessible by boat. The rock has many gutters, pinnacles, ledges and caves to investigate, at depths from 10–15 m. The reef is dominated by kelp, and may be affected by surge, but beneath the kelp canopy are sponges, sea stars, molluscs, zoanthids and gorgonians. Around the reef are Port Jackson sharks, kingfish, morwong, pike, wrasse, boarfish, old wives, catsharks, rock lobsters, bullseyes, leatherjackets and occasionally a fur seal.

Seal Rocks

The largest Australian fur seal colony in southern Australia is located at Seal Rocks. Over 5000 seals live on the rocky shore, so divers are always guaranteed of seeing at least one seal. In fact divers often have hundreds circling them as they dive the rocky reef. In clear water the experience is unforgettable, and the photo opportunities are endless. All seals are curious and will inspect divers and their gear. It is a fantastic experience when one feels your hand with its nose and whiskers.

Flinders Pier

An incredible variety of marine creatures are found under Flinders Pier, at a depth of just 4 m. The pylons are covered in weed, anemones and sponges, which shelter nudibranchs, shrimps, crabs, sea stars and weedfish. The bottom is sandy, with thick patches of weed and kelp, and the odd bit of junk. Dozens of weedy sea dragons can be found drifting among the kelp. On and around the bottom live pipefish, leatherjackets, wrasse, boxfish, goatfish, sea urchins, stingarees, cuttlefish, octopi and sometimes a red velvetfish. Schools of sweep and pike often swarm between the pylons, and divers may encounter a huge, resident stingray.

West Head

If conditions are calm, a shore dive at West Head can be spectacular. Although it's a long walk to the entry point, the trip is worth it. Caves and gutters wait to be explored, in depths from 4–10 m, and thick kelp covers the bottom. A good look among the kelp will reveal catsharks, rock lobsters, sea stars, weedfish and abalone. The small caves are lined with sponges and gorgonians, and shelter blue devilfish, cardinalfish, boarfish, perch and many rock lobsters.

The Arch

A number of interesting shallow dive sites can be found off the Mornington Peninsula. The Arch is typical of the area, being only 5–10 m deep, with lots of caves and gutters. Rock lobsters are quite common, as are catsharks, blue devilfish, sweep, cuttlefish, leatherjackets, wrasse, fiddler rays, Port Jackson sharks and a variety of invertebrates.

Port Phillip Bay Sites

The narrow entrance to Port Phillip Bay, known as The Rip, has claimed many ships over the last 200 years. Most shipwrecks in the bay are badly broken up, however the best wreck dives are on the "ships' graveyard," where over 30 ships were sunk in the 1920s. As well as shipwrecks, many reefs, walls and pinnacles can be reached by boat. Shallow reefs and colorful piers are best visited by finning out from the shore.

Back Beaches

When the conditions are calm, many dive boats head for the ocean side of the Mornington Peninsula, to catch rock lobsters—and there are some real monsters to be found! Even without the rock lobsters, diving the Back Beaches is interesting. Mostly in 5–15 m of water, the rocky terrain is riddled with caves and

swim-throughs. Many caves and tunnels are lined with gorgonians and zoanthids, and occupied by conger eels, blue devilfish, boarfish and cuttlefish. Also common on the kelp-covered reef are sea stars, nudibranchs, sweep, catsharks, morwong, perch and stingarees. The occasional Australian eagle ray is sometimes seen.

Nepean Wall

Located at the entrance to Port Phillip Bay, this wall drops from 18–66 m, and offers spectacular diving. Many caves and ledges are found along the wall, and the area is packed with sponges, sea whips, huge "lace corals" (bryozoans), zoanthids, gorgonians and anemones. Photographers will find endless subjects—nudibranchs, sea stars, reef fish, cuttlefish and sometimes schools of pelagic fish. This area can only be dived at slack tide.

Ships Graveyard

Over 30 ships were scuttled off Melbourne in the 1920s, and today they provide some of the most exciting diving in Victoria. Four J-class submarines, all originally from England and 80 m long, are the most popular dive sites. The J5 lies in 25 m, and has the best penetration diving. Since the bow is broken away, divers are able to inspect the torpedo room. The other subs (J1, J2 and J4) are found in depths from 36–39 m,

Below: The large shallow-water spider crab (*Leptomithrax gaimardi)* is frequently found among sponge beds, around pylons, alga stands and sea grass meadows. *Nigel Marsh*

Above: Common to southeastern waters, especially in the Victorian Bass Strait area, the red gurnard scorpionfish (*Helicolenus papillosus)* is a bottom-dwelling predator.
Neville Coleman

and penetration diving of these subs is considered very dangerous. Another popular site is the *Coogee*, which rests in 33 m, and is covered in sponges and zoanthids. The hull has collapsed in sections, but divers can still explore the bow, stern and engine room of this 66 m-long ship.

Lonsdale Reef

Point Lonsdale is the resting place of many ships, and when conditions are calm, the remains of the shipwrecks are accessible from the shore. The rocky reef here is covered in kelp, and only 5–10 m deep. Rising above the kelp are the ribs, beams and other wreckage from ships such as the *George Roper, Holy Head, Black Boy, Grange* and *Glaneuse.*

Lonsdale Wall

This great wall dive at the entrance to the bay drops from 12–60 m, and is covered with sedentary marine life. Throughout the numerous caves and swim-throughs are rock lobsters, boarfish, blue devilfish, nudibranchs, sea spiders, perch, morwong and many varieties of reef fish.

Eliza Ramsden Shipwreck

One of the most interesting wreck dives in the bay is the *Eliza Ramsden*, which sank in 1875. Much of the hull is still resting on the sandy, rock-strewn bottom in 18

m of water, with the bow section sitting up 7 m from the sea floor. While poking around the wreck, you will come upon kingfish, cuttlefish, leatherjackets, invertebrates and many reef fish.

Portsea Hole

Portsea Hole is only dived on the high or low tide, when water movement is least—as are most of the dive sites within the bay. Here a wall drops from 13–28 m, with many ledges and caves. Numerous sponges, ascidians, zoanthids and bryozoans cling to the wall, and among them are sea stars, nudibranchs, basket stars, shrimps, crabs and octopi. Some of the reef fish found along the wall include wrasse, leatherjackets, perch, blue devils, and morwong.

Popes Eye

Built as a fort, but never finished, Popes Eye is now part of a marine reserve, and home to numerous sea birds. The best dive is on the southern side, on the boulder wall which drops from 3–12 m. Swarms of fish surround divers, large leatherjackets peer into divers' masks, while wrasse and perch dart in and out of the kelp. Morwong, blue devilfish, boxfish, pipefish, globefish, weedfish, boar- fish, scorpionfish, scalyfin, old wives and stingarees are all common.

Portsea Pier

Used for diver training and as the departure point for many dive boats, the Portsea Pier is best dived when boating activity is at a minimum, as visibility is better. The pier is in only 6 m of water, and among its pylons live weedy sea dragons, pipefish, sea horses, cuttlefish, octopus, stingarees, large spider crabs, sea stars, boxfish, nudibranchs, wrasse, goatfish and some more unusual creatures such as goblinfish and small sea moths.

Macro-photographers will be delighted with the sponges, soft corals and ascidians which cover the pylons. To the right of the pier is a rocky, kelp-covered reef, in 8 m of water, with plenty of reef fish, giant cuttlefish, abalone and occasionally a skate.

Cerebrus Shipwreck

The *Cerebrus* was scuttled off Black Rock in 1926 to form a breakwall. The 68 m-long ship, sitting in only 5 m of water, can be easily dived from shore, as most of the ship sticks out of the water. While the hull is easily penetrated, it has deteriorated badly over the last few years, and the possibility of collapse makes it unsafe to enter. Diving around the wreck is still interesting, and nearby is a wonderful patch of reef with sea horses, stingarees, sea stars, nudi-branchs, leatherjackets, scallops, boxfish, flatheads, fiddler rays and many other reef fish.

Seal Colony

Two small groups of fur seals have established colonies on the south channel navigation towers 6 and 10, in Port Phillip Bay. Snorkel or dive with the seals, and either way have a fantastic experience. If diving, have a look at the tower structures (in 12 m and 21m of water) which are encrusted with many species of sponges and other invertebrates. Various reef fish are seen around the towers as well.

Dolphin Dives

Two pods of bottlenose dolphins reside in Port Phillip Bay, and it is possible to do snorkel dives with some of them. The boat heads out, and once the dolphins are found divers climb into the water and are towed around on a rope. This way the dolphins come in very close to the snorkelers. You may even feel them bouncing sonar waves off your body. This is an exhilarating experience that anyone will enjoy.

Divers visiting Melbourne will find dozens of dive shops offering excellent advice on where to shore dive or charter a boat. A number of shops at Queenscliff and Portsea are associated with dive lodges, and offer special package deals on accommodation and dive trips.

Below: The magnificent ascidian *(Botrylloides magnicoecum)* is among the most advanced of invertebrates. The presence of a rudimentary backbone during the larval stage indicates that they are related to vertebrates. *Michael Aw*

SOUTHERN RIGHT WHALES
On the slow road to recovery

"SNORKELING ON THE SURFACE I COULD SEE A number of small fish on the bottom 8 m below. The visibility must have been only 10 m, as I peered into the gloomy water waiting for the whale to appear. Then suddenly a large barnacle-encrusted head materialized in front of me, and the rest of the 12 m-long body slowly followed—an enormous southern right whale! I was dumb-struck, forgetting to take pictures, as I was also directly in the whale's flight path. The bulk of the creature approached, and as the head passed just below my fins, I could see the creature's small eye, its pectoral fins, then the rest of its wide body, including its 3 m-wide tail. I braced myself for the impact, as the tail appeared to be heading straight for me. But then the tail stopped, glided right around me, and continued its stroke on the other side of my body.

The whale knew exactly where I was, and

southern hemisphere, the southern right whale is making a very slow comeback. The world-wide population of southern right whales is still only a few thousand.

Every winter the annual whale migration along the Australian coastline makes the nightly news. Humpback, minke and southern right whales migrate at roughly the same time. The humpback and minke head further north into tropical seas, however the southern right whales usually go no further north than Sydney and Perth. While individual whales can turn up in almost any bay, the largest numbers are observed off Warrnambool, and the cliffs of the Nullarbor Plain.

Before protective legislation, divers used to be able to swim freely with southern right whales, and being curious creatures, they would swim right up to a diver. Looking into the eye of a whale is a humbling experi-

Southern right whales breed along the coasts of southern Australia during spring. During this time many come very close to shore and can be photographed. *Neville Coleman*

was in complete control of this wonderful encounter. For the next hour I, and another dozen snorkelers, swam with the whale, and enjoyed encounter after encounter as it sought out people to observe." *Neville Coleman*

The southern right whale (*Eubalaena australis*) used to be very common in the southern waters of Australia between June and September, when they migrated north to give birth and breed. Unlike other whales, they came into shallow bays and were an easy target for whalers. Hundreds of thousands were slaughtered, and the population dropped to critical levels before they were granted protection. Found only in the

ence—divers swear they can see the intelligent, curious mind working overtime.

Diving with whales is now restricted, to stop moronic surfers jumping onto whales, and fishermen in boats charging in for a better look. A boat must not approach closer than 100 m, and must stop its engine to observe the animal. Divers are not allowed any closer than 30 m, and must not chase the whale, but the whale is allowed to approach the diver. While most whales are generally shy, the inquisitive southern right whale will swim over to inspect people in the water. Do not abuse these regulations—a number of people have already been charged and fined. Otherwise, the government might feel compelled to introduce even more draconian laws to limit encounters with these incredible creatures.

Port Campbell
Diving the Shipwreck Coast

Shore and boat dives up to 20 minutes away

Inshore 5 m, offshore 15 m

Currents and surge on some reefs

Sponge gardens and kelp beds

Diving historic shipwrecks

Abundant reef and pelagic fish

Rocky reefs and pinnacles

One of the most spectacular drives in Australia is along Victoria's Great Ocean Road. The scenery along this stretch of coastline is breathtaking—towering cliffs, deep gorges, incredible rock pinnacles and weathered carved arches. This section of coastline was a danger to early mariners, and many a fine ship was lost after being driven into the cliffs by wild seas. Around Port Campbell are some of the area's most famous landmarks, such as the Twelve Apostles, the Arch, the Grotto and the London Bridge (now collapsed).

This area is now commonly known as the Shipwreck Coast, and although the seas are wild at times, many excellent dive sites can be explored in calm weather. Shore dives access shallow rocky reefs, with sizable populations of reef fish and invertebrates. The shipwrecks and reefs are all dived by boat, when conditions allow. Diving is centered around Port Campbell—contact Schomberg Dive Services or Port Campbell Boat Charters.

Port Campbell is a popular holiday area, and offers a good range of accommodation. Visit the Loch Ard Shipwreck Museum, which displays many fascinating items salvaged from the shipwreck.

Loch Ard Shipwreck
Built in 1873, the iron barque *Loch Ard* was on her fifth voyage to Australia when she went aground on the rocky shore of Mutton Bird Island. The 80 m-long ship was discovered by divers in 1967, and has since been declared a historic shipwreck. The wreck is scattered in depths from 10–24 m. The bow can be identified, lying on its port

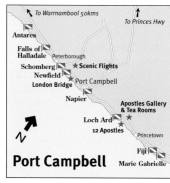
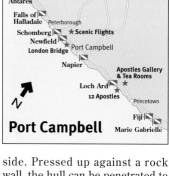

To Warrnambool 50kms
To Princes Hwy
Antares
Falls of Halladale
Peterborough
Schomberg
Scenic Flights
Newfield
London Bridge
Port Campbell
Napier
Apostles Gallery & Tea Rooms
Loch Ard
12 Apostles
Princetown
Fiji
Marie Gabrielle
Port Campbell

side. Pressed up against a rock wall, the hull can be penetrated to see the remains of her cargo—lead ingots, copper rods, railway iron, bottles, tiles, cutlery, crockery, even the bilge pump and plenty of reef fish and rock lobsters.

The Falls of Halladale Shipwreck
After running aground at full speed in 1908, *The Falls of Halladale* became quite a tourist attraction. Although abandoned, her sails were fully set for two months

Below: The Twelve Apostles stand as sentinels along one of the roughest pieces of coastline in Australia. *Neville Coleman*

before she started to break up. Today the wreck is found in 12 m of water, and is a very interesting dive. The iron hull and the cargo of slate are distinguishable, and the bow and rudder still stand upright off the bottom. There is much to see around the kelp-covered site, and since this is an historic shipwreck, no items should be handled or removed.

Schomberg Shipwreck

The 83 m-long *Schomberg* was a wooden-hulled clipper ship that sank in 1855, on its maiden voyage from England to Australia. The remains lie scattered in 3–8 m of water, and although much of the wooden hull is gone, you will see hundreds of railway irons.

Fiji Shipwreck

The scattered remains of the *Fiji* lie in only 3–6 m of water. After running aground at Moonlight Head in 1891, the *Fiji* quickly broke up in heavy seas. You can still see part of the hull, the rolls of wire that were her cargo, and other artefacts such as toys, porcelain and china.

Other Shipwrecks

Many other historic shipwrecks in the area can be dived if conditions allow. These include the *Newfield*, *Lydia*, *Children*, *Antares* and *Napier*. To dive protected shipwrecks such as *Loch Ard* and *Schomberg*, a permit is required, so contact the dive shops for details.

Shore Diving

Peterborough, 15 km west of Port Campbell, probably has the best shore diving access. The shallow reefs and bays have a thick coverage of kelp and other seaweeds. The many small ledges and caves are lined with gorgonians, sponges and zoanthids, and are occupied by rock lobsters, sea stars and other invertebrates. Common fish life includes leatherjackets, boxfish, wrasse, morwong, perch, wobbegongs, Port Jackson sharks, blue devilfish and the occasional conger eel.

Offshore Reefs

Hundreds of hidden reefs are located off this section of coastline. Depths vary from 15–25 m, and the terrain consists of gutters, caves, ledges and pinnacles. Pretty sponge gardens and fields of kelp cover the bottom. Divers usually see Port Jackson sharks, pike, sweep, morwong, boarfish, rock lobsters, snapper, leatherjackets, perch, ling cod and an interesting variety of invertebrate life.

Lake Purrumbete

For those after something a little different, Lake Purrumbete lies 50 km north of Port Campbell. A variety of fish, eels, tortoises and yabbies (freshwater lobsters) are found in this clear, freshwater lake.

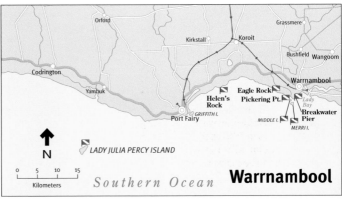

Warrnambool
A Variety of Shallow Shore Dives

In the past, many thousands of seals and whales were killed and processed here but today Warrnambool is best known as a whale watching area. Each winter the coastline is visited by southern right whales, and many thousands of people gather along the shoreline to watch these magnificent marine mammals calving and playing in the shallow water. Many divers come for the numerous excellent boat and shore diving sites in and around the area.

Breakwater Pier
Although usually considered a beginner's dive, there is always something interesting to watch under the Breakwater Pier. Around the pylons you are likely to see pipefish, octopi, cuttlefish, sea stars, boxfish, sweep, wrasse, gobies, blennies and nudibranchs, at depths from 3–9 m.

Stingray Bay
Although few stingrays have been seen here, the rocky, kelp-covered bay is always a pleasant dive. The bottom is only 7 m deep, but divers will find plenty of wobbegongs, morwong, leatherjackets, rock lobsters, abalone, perch, and a variety of invertebrates among the kelp.

Middle Island
The sheltered waters around Middle Island offer good diving in depths to 12 m. Many ledges and gutters are accessible from the shore, where rock lobsters, blue devilfish, cuttlefish, catsharks, Port Jackson sharks, morwong, wobbegongs and numerous reef fish are usually found.

Pickering Point
Similar to many of the dive sites around Warrnambool, Pickering Point provides interesting shore diving on rocky reefs to 8 m. Many local divers catch rock lobsters and abalone on these reefs, and there are always plenty of reef fish and invertebrates around.

Shore and boat dives up to 20 minutes away

5–10 m

Very little

Kelp beds

A wealth of interesting shore dives and offshore reefs

Abundant reef fish

Rocky reefs

Below: Very rare, this unidentified anemone is found on a rocky ledge at a depth of 12 m in the waters off Kangaroo Island. *Michael Aw*

WARRNAMBOOL

Above: Leafy sea dragons *(Phycodunus eques)* are a magnificent sight in their lacy "leaf-like" camouflage. *Michael Aw*

Helen's Rock
One of the most impressive boat diving sites in the area is Helen's Rock. This pinnacle rises from 24 m to almost break the surface, and is always surrounded by pelagic fish. Common are kingfish, yellowtail, trevally and the ever-present bullseyes hovering close to the walls.

Port Fairy
Located 28 km west of Warrnambool, Port Fairy is a small holiday town with numerous shore and boat diving sites on rocky reefs. A diver with a boat can organize a trip out to Lady Julia Percy Island, which is home to over 5000 Australian fur seals. There are many good dive sites around the island, and plenty of seals to swim with, but the island is rarely dived due to its remote location, and the large number of great white sharks reputedly feeding in the area.

The Warrnambool area has two dive shops which run dive charters, mainly from Port Fairy. The Flagstaff Hill Maritime Museum is a must, as the museum houses a fascinating collection of artefacts from the many ships lost along this rugged coastline.

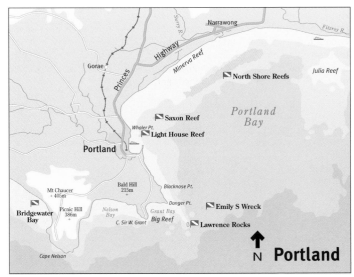

Portland
Victoria's Western Gem

Shore and boat dives up to 20 minutes away

Inshore 5 m, offshore 15 m

Currents on some reefs

Sponge gardens and kelp beds

Shore dive with fur seals. Incredible variety of dive sites

Reef and pelagic fish common on all reefs

Rocky reefs and pinnacles

Located close to the Victorian and South Australian border, Portland has some of southern Australia's best diving. There would be few other places in the world where you can dive with fur seals from the shore, explore fascinating caves and colorful sponge gardens, swim through kelp forests, drop down walls to 70 m, dive on complete shipwrecks, and find leafy and weedy sea dragons, little penguins, southern right whales, and a host of other animals—all within a few kilometers of one town.

Portland is a deep-water port, 375 km from Melbourne, best known for its commerce and industry. Tourists are slowly discovering its many attractions, especially its great diving. You can dive from the shore or try a boat dive run by Professional Diving Services. They have approximately 160 sites to choose from, so variety is the name of the game.

Bridgewater Bay

Approximately 250 fur seals are found here year round, and close encounters with seals are guaranteed on this shore dive, as these friendly animals seem to enjoy swimming with divers. The bottom of the bay (12 m deep) has areas of rocky reef, kelp and sandy patches. While the seals are the highlight of any dive, catsharks, stingarees, flounder, leatherjackets and other reef fish are also common.

Nunns Bay

Another one of the many shore dives around Portland, the rocky reef at Nunns Beach slopes down to 12 m in sheltered waters. This is a great place to see leafy and weedy sea dragons, although their natural camouflage makes them hard to find in the kelp. Also common are conger eels, sweep, perch, morwong, leatherjackets, wrasse, catsharks and a good variety of invertebrates.

Cappers Camp

The climb down a cliff face might put off some divers, but this is an excellent shore dive. Rocky pools and gutters lie in depths to 14 m, and under ledges and among the kelp are many rock lobsters, catsharks, shrimp, cuttlefish, octopi and nudibranchs. The reef has plenty of reef fish, mostly morwong, sweep, perch, leatherjackets and wrasse.

Left: Gunn's sea star (*Patiriella gunnii*) is often found beneath stones, where it resides during the daylight hours.
Neville Coleman

VICTORIA

Opposite: One of the most popular dive training areas is Portsea Pier. However, due to increased boating in the area, diving is only allowed by permit. *Nigel Marsh*

Saxon Shipwreck

Deliberately sunk to form an artificial reef, this ship is located in a sheltered bay in only 9 m of water. You can explore the bridge, wheelhouse and funnel, or the limestone reef where the wreckage lies. The wreck has attracted many reef fish, including sweep, weedfish, ling cod, bullseyes, scorpionfish, perch, morwong, boarfish and wrasse.

Emily S Shipwreck

Sunk in 1991 to form an artificial reef, this 30 m-long ship sits in 23 m of water, with the deck in 18 m. The ship is still essentially intact, and home to countless reef fish. Divers can safely enter the wheelhouse and other parts of the wreck, which are covered in jewel anem- ones and sponges.

Lawrence Rocks

These rocks offer some of the most spectacular diving off Portland. On the lee side, you have the choice of diving many different types of terrain. A lovely kelp forest lies in 5–12 m of water (which is thickest over winter), with plenty of reef fish and invertebrates. Along the sides of the rocks many ledges drop into 45 m, with pretty sponge gardens—a good place to see nudibranchs, sea stars, numerous reef fish, and schools of kingfish and mullet. Explore the gully that cuts through the rocks— when a swell is running it can be an exhilarating experience. The gully leads to an amphitheatre in 33 m of water, where you will find sponge gardens and plenty of fish. If conditions are calm enough, try a dive along the exposed side of the rocks, where the wall drops into 70 m.

Southwest Bay

A great dive site known as Shark Alley is actually a deep gutter reaching 21 m in depth. This gutter is usually packed with wobbegongs and Port Jackson sharks, resting on top of one another. The gutter can also be brimming over with fish— bullseyes, yellowtail, pike, whiting, mullet, morwong and perch. One of the gutter walls is known as the wall of gorgonians. Thousands of gorgonians line the gutter, as well as sponges, ascidians, bryozoans and zoanthids. Have a close look at the wall and you will find sea stars, basket stars, nudibranchs, shrimp, sea spiders and crabs.

Many other excellent shore and boat dives on reefs and wrecks are accessible off Portland. Over winter, southern right whales come in close to the coast to calve and mate, and this is one of the few places in the world where the rare pygmy right whale has been seen. A number of penguin colonies are found in the area—on almost any dive there is a chance of seeing a penguin in the water. Good conditions can be experienced year-round at **Portland**, and plenty of sheltered sites can be dived in windy weather.

Right: Egg cowries (*Ovula ovum*) browse on sedentary animals such as soft corals and sponges, or on encrusting algae which is scraped from surfaces with a file-like device called a radula. *Michael Aw*

Introducing Tasmania

The Wilderness State

Located in the notorious "Roaring Forties", Tasmania can experience foul winds and weather almost any time of the year. Add cold water and air temperatures, and it may not sound like a very appealing dive destination. But if you bypass Tasmania, you will miss some of Australia's greatest dive experiences. Tasmania's temperate seas are usually clear, and are full of fascinating marine creatures. Numerous species of fish and invertebrates are seen on almost every dive, and the chance of finding new species is always a possibility. Deep-water sponge gardens are plentiful, and much more colorful than any coral reef. Kelp forests, caves, pinnacles, and shipwrecks provide many memorable dives. Add to this encounters with dolphins, seals, whales and penguins, and you will begin to understand why many divers head south to Tasmania for their holidays.

Although the state is located in the roaring forties, the average day is no more windy than in most of the southern states. Temperatures vary —the average summer day ranges from 12–22° C, and in winter temperatures range from 6–14° C. Winter is the best time for diving, as the weather is quite stable (although cool), the seas are calm, and the visibility can reach 45 m.

Tasmania was first sighted by Europeans in 1642, when Dutch explorer Abel Tasman landed at Marion Bay, and named the new land mass Van Diemans Land after the Governor General of the Indies. Tasmania was thought to be connected to the mainland until 1798, when Bass and Flinders circumnavigated the island and charted much of the coastline. John Bowen, with a company of 49 convicts and

soldiers, established the first settlement at Ridson Cove, in 1803. However, conflict with the local Aborigines lead them to relocate to Sullivan's Cove, the present site of Hobart. Thousands of convicts were sent to Tasmania from 1803 to

1877, and many died in the notorious jails at Port Arthur, Macquarie Harbour, Maria Island and Sarah Island.

Tasmania makes up 1 percent of the Australian land mass, and is only 296 km from top to bottom. The state has a population close to half a million, with 40 percent of its inhabitants living in Hobart. It is the most wooded and rugged state in Australia, with many areas in the southwest still unexplored. Much of the interior is high country, with rocky mountains and large snow fields. Snow is guaranteed over winter, and unexpected falls can occur even in summer. Many unique plants and animals survive on the island due to its isolation, including the Huon pine (one of the best timbers known to man), the leatherwood tree (from which bees make the

Above: Little, or fairy, penguins *(Eudyptula minor)* as they are often called are regularly seen in Tasmanian waters. They have burrows along the coastal fringes or on offshore islands, often quite high up. *Nigel Marsh*

Opposite: The reefs in Tasmanian waters support an incredibly rich fauna, much of it unique to southern Australia. Here a diver uses hi-tech photographic gear to make the best of turbid conditions. *Michael Aw*

high-quality leatherwood honey) and the famous Tasmanian devil.

Diving in Tasmania is limited, mainly by the number of dive shops, access points and conditions. Very little diving is done on the wild west coast, except by the occasional abalone diver. One area on the southwest coast that deserves more exploration is around Port Davey. Here the dark tannen-stained surface water gives way to clear water underneath, and because of the limited light, many deep-water fish and invertebrates are found in shallow water. The wonderful variety of sites around Maria Island and Freycinet Peninsula also deserve a mention.

The areas serviced by dive shops and charter boats provide outstanding diving experiences. Bicheno has become Tasmania's most famous dive destination (the Cousteau team were so impressed they made a special about the area) and excellent diving can also be found on the Tasman Peninsula, off St Helens, Hobart, Wynyard and on the islands of Bass Strait.

Water temperature around Tasmania is no worse than Victoria, varying from 10–16° C, although cooler and warmer water can be experienced due to currents and thermoclines. Most divers use 7 mm wetsuits, or drysuits, for maximum comfort.

Tourism contributes much to Tasmania's economy. The natural beauty of Tasmania is hard to beat —rugged bushland, clean empty beaches, snow-capped ranges, clear lakes and streams, towering sea cliffs and wonderful panoramas. Visitors can explore remote wilderness national parks, raft the Gordon and Franklin Rivers, ski the highlands, tour the historic ruins at Port Arthur, visit museums and art galleries, fish for trout, observe native wildlife in the bush or in one of the many wildlife parks, take a scenic flight or buy local arts and crafts.

Accommodation ranges from hotels and motels, to bed and breakfast places. A number of dive shops have bunk-houses and package deals including accommodation and diving. Tasmania is reached quickest from the mainland by airplane, while bus, train, and hire car/caravan services are available for travel throughout the state. Tasmania is best explored by car—a vehicular ferry runs from Melbourne to Devonport if you would like to bring your vehicle from the mainland. A ferry service also runs from Port Welshpool in Victoria to George Town.

Below: Although common, the Tasmanian spotted catshark (*Parascyllium multimaculatum*) is not often seen due to the nature of its favorite habitat—the alga-covered reefs. *Neville Coleman*

Bass Strait Islands
Exploring a Graveyard of Ships

Dozens of islands and numerous reefs are scattered throughout Bass Strait, which lies between Victoria and Tasmania. These wild waters claimed over 250 ships and many thousands of lives before lighthouses were finally installed.

Tasmania's many shipwrecks have long attracted divers. Some wrecks have been salvaged, however the location of many remains a mystery, and plenty of artefacts can still be found on many regularly dived wreck sites. Today Flinders Island and King Island are the most popular dive destinations—both have dive shops and are accessible by boat or airplane. The other islands in Bass Strait are occasionally visited by liveaboard boats from Victoria and Tasmania.

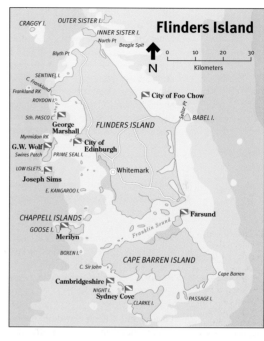

Flinders Island
Flinders Island, the largest island in the Furneaux Group, is located off the northeastern tip of Tasmania. This rugged island is 64 km long and 29 km wide, and has a number of small towns on its shores, Whitemark being the largest. The small local population survives by farming, fishing and tourism. Divers visit Whitemark to catch rock lobsters, and to explore the shallow rocky reefs and the shipwrecks, many of which are accessible from the shore.

City of Edinburgh
This ship was lost in 1840, and little remains except for the occasional bit of wreckage. Nearby the wreck is an interesting granite reef in 13 m, with caves and gutters inhabited by rock lobsters, leatherjackets, boarfish, morwong, perch and other reef fish.

Merilyn
The *Merilyn* sank in 1958, after striking a reef off Goose Island. The twisted wreckage is scattered over the rocky bottom, occupied by perch, nudibranchs, wrasse, boxfish, ling cod and lots of rock lobsters.

Cambridgeshire
The remains of the *Cambridgeshire* can only be dived in calm seas. The ship was lost in 1875, off Preservation Island. The hull, which is laid open in 10 m, makes a wonderful wreck dive.

Sydney Cove
One of Australia's oldest shipwrecks, the *Sydney Cove* was lost off Preservation Island in 1797. The

Shore and boat dives up to 30 minutes away

Summer 10–15 m, winter 20–30 m

Currents on some reefs

Kelp and sponge gardens

Hundreds of shipwrecks and rock lobsters

Reef fish abundant, pelagic fish less common

Rocky reefs and pinnacles

wreck lies in only 4 m of water on a sandy, weedy bottom. Over the years maritime archeologists have recovered many interesting items from the wreck, including cannons, Chinese porcelain, bottles, bowls and coins. Much of the wreck lies buried under the sand, which hopefully will preserve the timber hull for many years to come. The wreck is rarely dived, and a permit is required to visit the site.

King Island

King Island, approximately the same size as Flinders Island, is located off the northwest tip of Tasmania. The island has a population approaching 3000, and is most famous for its dairy products, especially cheeses. Other local industries include rock lobsters, kelp farming and tourism. Many small settlements are spread across the island's flat terrain—the largest are Grassy and Currie. Rock lobsters (some huge) are plentiful around the island. Although conditions can be rough at times, you will enjoy exploring King Island's rocky reefs and shipwrecks.

Loch Leven

The remains of the *Loch Leven*, wrecked in 1871, are found on the northern end of the island, and are accessible from the shore. Wreckage is scattered along the bottom in 6 m of water. The rocky reef is home to rock lobsters, invertebrates and many small reef fish.

Cataraqui

The loss of the *Cataraqui* and its 399 passengers in 1845 remains Australia's worst maritime disaster. Little is left of the historic shipwreck today, except an anchor, cannons, bottles and other wreckage, found in shallow water.

Brahmin

The remains of the *Brahmin*, which sank in 1842, are now scattered in 5–10 m of water. Along the weedy

bottom divers often find coins, stoneware, bowls, porcelain figurines and bottles.

Blencathra

The wreck of the *Blencathra*, which sank on her maiden voyage in 1875, is located off Currie Harbour, in 8 m of water. Clay pipes and bottles, plus rock lobsters and reef fish are found in the vicinity of the wreck.

Grassy Harbour

Off Grassy Harbour are a number of good dive sites. An interesting shore dive on a rocky reef can be accessed from the harbor. Kelp and sponges are scattered over rocky walls at 12 m. On the reef are rock lobsters, abalone, boarfish, nudibranchs, sea stars, boxfish, leatherjackets and wrasse. You may even see some little penguins, which nest on the island.

The Drop-off

This is an excellent boat dive along a wall which drops from 15–30 m. The wall is covered with sponges, sea tulips, ascidians, sea ferns, bryozoans and yellow zoanthids, and has many ledges where rock lobster, shrimp and other invertebrates shelter. A good variety of reef fish including scorpionfish, weedfish, leatherjackets and butterfly perch can be found as well.

ROCK LOBSTER AND ABALONE
Big business down under

DIVING ON A VIRGIN SITE IS ALWAYS EXCITING. One easy way to tell whether you are the first to explore any reef in southern Australia is by the number of rock lobsters and abalone to be seen. Rock lobsters and abalone were abundant in the southern waters of Australia, and divers would often see both animals packed in caves and along ledges. While both are still considered common, their numbers are low at most popular dive sites, due to over-fishing.

Several tropical species of rock lobster are found in Australian waters. The most common species taken by divers and fishermen are the southern rock lobster (*Jasus novaehollandiae*), found from New South Wales to Western Aus-

females with eggs can be taken. A permit is required in most states. For information on size and catch limits, and closed seasons, refer to the laws of each state. These regulations have been imposed to ensure the future of the rock lobster populations, so please observe the limits. Why not just take photos of those corgi-sized monsters that have eluded capture in the past?

Many species of abalone are found in shallow and deep water. Most are quite small, but the three southern species, greenlip abalone (*Haliotis laevigata*), Roe's abalone (*Haliotis roei*) and the blacklip abalone (*Haliotis ruber*) have always been a popular food for Aborigines, and now form the basis

tralia, and the western rock lobster (*Panulirus cygnus*), found in Western Australia. Both species congregate in caves and venture out at night to feed on abalone, sea urchins, other rock lobsters and dead animal tissue. Found in shallow water to depths beyond 80 m, they grow to 500 mm in length. The rock lobster breeds in winter, and females can be seen carrying eggs in October and November. After the eggs hatch, the young larvae drift with the plankton, before settling onto a reef to spend their adult life there.

Countless thousands of rock lobsters are taken each year by fishermen in a multi-million dollar export industry, but divers also take their fair share. Regulations governing rock lobster quotas vary for each state. In New South Wales and Queensland, lobsters can only be caught while free diving, and no

The cold-water conditions and rough weather create high-energy coastlines which are ideal for abalone, but not for diving as abalone divers know only too well. The life of a Tasmanian abalone diver is not an easy one, especially when working the west coast. *Neville Coleman*

of a large export industry. Australia supplies over a third of the international market for abalone. In the pioneering days, abalone divers worked long hours for little pay. These days they make millions, but to buy a license costs a great deal of money.

Abalone is collected off the coasts of New South Wales, Victoria, South Australia and Tasmania. Unscrupulous divers take undersize animals for sale on the black market, an activity which could eventually decimate the abalone population, and destroy the industry.

Wynyard
Adventure Diving on the North Coast

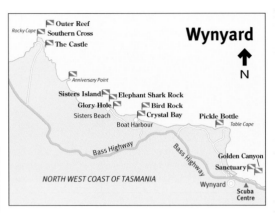

Rocky Cape
- Outer Reef
- Southern Cross
- The Castle

Anniversary Point

Sisters Island — Elephant Shark Rock
Glory Hole — Bird Rock
Sisters Beach — Crystal Bay
Boat Harbour

Pickle Bottle

Table Cape

Wynyard

↑ N

Bass Highway

Bass Highway

Golden Canyon
Sanctuary

Wynyard

Scuba Centre

NORTH WEST COAST OF TASMANIA

Shore and boat dives 5–20 minutes from boat ramp

Varies from 10–20 m

Slight currents on some reefs

Colorful sponge gardens

Variety of good shore and boat dives

Good populations of reef and pelagic fish

Rocky reefs and pinnacles

Surrounded by farmland and a rocky coastline, Wynyard is one of the few towns on the northern coast of Tasmania that has a professional dive shop. The Scuba Centre runs regular boat dives to a wide variety of reefs in the area, but those divers on a budget can explore the many interesting shore dive sites. Accommodation is limited in Wynyard, so book early.

Golden Canyon
An interesting artificial reef can be explored at Golden Canyon in depths varying from 8–21 m. Patches of sponges and zoanthids cover much of the reef, where you will find plenty of nudibranchs, sea stars, brittle stars, crabs and other invertebrates. Fish life is generally small, but leatherjackets, old wives, boar- fish, wrasse, morwong and bullseyes are common.

Sanctuary
The rocky reef at the Sanctuary has many caves, gutters and swim-throughs located at depths from 8–20 m. Around the reef are plenty of reef fish, and the occasional school of pelagic fish.

Pickle Bottle
Extensive kelp beds cover the rocky outcrop known as the Pickle Bottle, from the shallows to 25 m. Hidden under the kelp are numerous caves and swim-throughs with sea spiders, sea stars, nudibranchs and molluscs. The kelp-covered terrain also supports a large population of reef fish, including morwong, perch, leatherjackets, blennies, wrasse and scorpionfish.

Western Bay
Although a long walk, Western Bay is an excellent shore dive with lots to see. The right side of the bay is generally the most interesting. Following the reef edge, descend to 16 m, where nudibranchs, sea stars, cuttlefish, small reef fish, and sometimes rock lobsters are found along the rocky bottom.

Bird Rock
A variety of dive sites are available at Bird Rock. On the western side are several ledges; numerous pinnacles are found on the eastern side. The northern side drops off into 25 m of water, where there are pretty sponge gardens, plentiful reef fish and invertebrates, and occasionally pelagic fish.

Glory Hole
A shallow shore dive, the Glory Hole is always a good place to see reef fish. The rocky reef here varies from 4–9 m in depth, with numerous ledges and caves. Common reef fish include perch, morwong, old wives, wrasse and a wide variety of leatherjackets.

Elephant Shark Rock

Three rocks with lovely sponge gardens can be explored at Elephant Shark Rock. The depth varies from 18–25 m. Bullseyes, boarfish, leatherjackets and an occasional school of pelagic fish are usually found around here.

Sister's Island

Luxuriant sponge gardens are located in less than 14 m at Sister's Island. Macro-photographers will find nudibranchs, sea spiders, sea stars, cuttlefish and many other invertebrate subjects.

Anniversary Point

The rocky reef at Anniversary Point has many colorful sponges in depths from 10–16 m. The reef is only sparsely populated by reef fish, however, schools of Port Jackson sharks frequent the area, as do stingarees, and occasionally a draughtboard shark. The most unusual creature found here is the warty prowfish, which has brown leather-like skin (which it sheds). These lie motionless among the sponges, and are very difficult to find.

Rocky Cape

The national park at Rocky Cape offers excellent shore diving, however an entry fee must be paid to enter the park. Once at the cape, you can either dive the shallow eastern side where nudibranchs, cuttlefish and other invertebrate species can be seen, or the more rugged western side. The western side drops down to 16 m, where there are plenty of boarfish, rock lobsters, leatherjackets, perch, morwongs, wrasse and colorful invertebrates.

The Castle

This large rocky pinnacle, which rises from 14–6 m, always seems to have plenty of fish life swarming around

it—bullseyes, trevally, kingfish, boarfish, old wives, morwong, leatherjackets and wrasse. The Castle is situated off Rocky Cape, and is covered in sessile marine life and kelp.

Southern Cross Shipwreck

After disappearing in 1920, the fate of the wooden barquentine *Southern Cross* and her crew of ten was unknown for many years. The ship now lies in 8–12 m of water off Rocky Cape, and is still an interesting dive, although badly broken up. The boilers, the propeller and the prop shaft are scattered along the bottom.

Outer Reef

The most colorful, action-packed dive sites off Wynyard would have to be on the Outer Reef, which covers a large area, and drops into 35 m. Interesting diving can be found at any depth. Sponges, gorgonians, ascidians, bryozoans and zoanthids cover much of the reef, and sheltering among them are many small reef fish and invertebrates. Divers are likely to encounter cuttlefish, draughtboard sharks boarfish, Port Jackson sharks, and rock lobsters. Pelagic fish gather at the reef's edge, and it is not uncommon to be surrounded by schools of magnificent butterfly perch.

Above: Usually nocturnal, the red velvetfish (*Gnathanacanthus goetzeei*) lives among kelpcovered reefs and is not easy to find.
Nigel Marsh

St Helens
Shore Dives and Superb Seafood

Above: Common in Tasmanian waters, the banded morwong (*Cheilodactylus spectabilis*) is a large species reaching the size of 1 m. It is shown here against a background of yellow zoanthids.
Nigel Marsh

Shore and boat dives up to 30 minutes away

Summer 10–15 m winter 20–30 m

Currents offshore

Dense sponge gardens

Large number of unspoilt dive sites

Prolific reef and pelagic fish

Rocky reefs and pinnacles

Situated at the top end of Georges Bay, St Helens is a former mining town that now relies on the fishing industry and tourism for its existence. Visitors enjoy seafood meals, buy arts and crafts, explore the nearby national parks, and dive the unique marine world along the coastline.

The diving off St Helens has only really opened up since the East Coast Scuba Centre began offering boat dives, and invaluable advice on the best shore diving sites in the area.

Booker Rocks
Located 1 km off St Helens Point, this site is also known locally as the "Dough Boys". On the eastern side of the rocks, a brilliant reef drops from 10–26 m. The top of the reef has a thick blanket of kelp, which thins out further down the wall, to be replaced by colorful sponges, ascidians, bryozoans and zoanthids. The many caves and swim-throughs that cut deep into the wall are occupied by boarfish, rock lobsters, conger eels, bearded rock cod and globefish. In among the sponges are sea stars, nudibranchs, sea spiders, basket stars and other invertebrates. There are also several species of reef fish such as wrasse,

leatherjackets, cowfish, morwong and perch.

Merrick Rock
Three kilometers east of St Helens Point is a submerged reef known as Merrick Rock, the top of which lies in 4 m. The sides drop into deep water, providing spectacular diving on pinnacles, walls, caves and gutters covered with sponge gardens, and abundant reef fish and invertebrates. Divers are usually surrounded by schools of butterfly perch, and may see draughtboard sharks, tuna, kingfish and other pelagics. This reef is visited by southern right whales and dolphins during winter.

Many other excellent boat diving sites can be explored off St Helens, including Sloop Rock, Elephant Rock and St Helens Island.

Shore Diving
A good selection of shore dives are accessible off St Helen's coast. Try Binalong Bay and Grants Point, where a wide variety of fish and invertebrates are found on the reefs. In Georges Bay, some of the best diving is on the local jetties. These shelter a multitude of invertebrate life, and make great night dives.

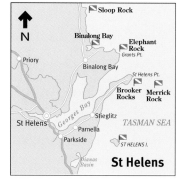

Bicheno
Diving the Governor Island Marine Reserve

The clear, temperate waters around Governor Island, Bicheno feature abundant sponge gardens, prolific fish life, caves packed with invertebrate life and impressive kelp beds. This area is so rich in marine life that 60 ha on the eastern side of Governor Island was declared a marine reserve in 1991, ensuring the future of this valued marine environment.

Bicheno is a small holiday and fishing town on the east coast of Tasmania, roughly halfway between Hobart and Launceston. This part of Tasmania's coastline, known as the Sun Coast, boasts the warmest climate and the most sunshine in Tasmania. The area around Bicheno has uncrowded sandy beaches, spectacular granite headlands and numerous rocky islands washed by the Tasman Sea.

Thousands of tourists come to Bicheno each year to fish, dive, snorkel, surf, sail, beachcomb, bushwalk or just relax. For many years abalone divers were the only people enjoying the rich diversity of marine life, however all that changed in 1983, when the Bicheno Dive Centre opened.

The shop runs daily boat dives, operates a "live" boat to avoid anchor damage to the delicate sponges, and provides basic accommodation. The operators have pioneered many excellent dive sites, and regularly visit over 30 locations.

Other attractions around Bicheno include the Sea Life Centre, East Coast Birdlife and Animal Park, and national parks. The closest national park is on Diamond Island, where hundreds of little penguins nest.

Trap Reef

Trap Reef is a pinnacle north of Governor Island located in 35 m of water. The reef here is a solid, multi-colored carpet of sponges, sea whips, ascidians, sea fans, zoanthids and bryozoans. This garden is so dense that good buoyancy control is essential, as there are few places to settle on the bottom. Banded morwong, magpie perch, jackassfish, butterfly perch, nannygai, bearded cod, Shaws cowfish and perhaps a few stingarees are permanent reef residents.

Below: Feeding conger eels in southern waters is not as hazardous as hand feeding moray eels, as the conger eels have passive natures and small teeth. Even so, this practice is not recommended. *Nigel Marsh*

Boat dives 5–10 minutes from boat ramp

Summer 10–15 m winter 20–30 m

Slight currents on some reefs

Some of the richest sponge gardens and kelp beds in Australia

Dense sponge gardens packed with marine life, incredible kelp beds

Reef fish abundant, pelagic fish less common

Rocky reefs and pinnacles

Above: Governor Island at Bicheno is a bird sanctuary and a marine reserve. *Nigel Marsh*

Rose Garden

Situated between two walls, in 36 m of water, is a valley full of sponges called the Rose Garden. This immense sponge garden is a patchwork of color—reds, oranges, yellows, pinks, purples and whites are revealed by flashlight. The fixed marine life includes rose and finger sponges, dusky sea ferns, ascidians, anemones, southern sea whips, sea fans, zoanthids, solitary corals, tube worms and bryozoans. Sea perch, rock cod, and magpie perch rest on the sponges. Long-snouted boarfish, giant boarfish, butterfly perch, bearded cod, jackassfish, scaly fin, banded morwong, Shaws cowfish, goatfish, john dory, trumpeter, gobies, blennies and many species of wrasse and leatherjacket are typical inhabitants of the valley. Basket stars and draughtboard shark eggs are sometimes found clinging to the sponges.

Golden Bommies

Bicheno's most famous dive site are these two 10 m-tall pinnacles, found in 40 m of water. Absolutely covered in sea whips, sponges, ascidians, bryozoan, and masses of yellow zoanthids, these pinnacles are a breathtaking sight. There are so many zoanthids that the pinnacles appear to give off a golden glow, even without a flashlight. You could spend hours photographing the invertebrate species—sea stars, nudibranchs, basket stars, shrimp, crabs, sea spiders, molluscs and cuttlefish. These pinnacles also attract large numbers of fish. Commonly seen are boarfish, old wives, banded morwong, pike and schools of butterfly perch.

The Castle

Two huge granite boulders jammed together form the structure known as The Castle. At the base of these boulders is a long swim-through at 30 m, which is usually packed with fish. Schools of bullseyes and cardinalfish fill the entrance, and among these are banded morwong, bearded cod, ling cod and nannygai. Shine a flashlight along the many ledges in the cave and you will see numerous red legs and antennae. Dozens of southern rock lobsters shelter in the cave, but only take photos as this is a marine reserve. Once out of the cave, there is a huge overhang to explore. The bottom here is packed with sea whips, and the ceiling is lined with yellow zoanthids. Deco stops around Bicheno are usually fun, as they can be done on the kelp-covered peaks of pinnacles. Search the kelp as abalone, crabs, sea stars, weedfish, octopi, cuttlefish and other species are plentiful in the area.

Kanuck

Kanuck is similar to many areas off Governor Island, with large boulders forming caves, gutters and walls. Dense kelp beds and sponge gardens, which support masses of reef fish and many invertebrate species, can be found at 20 m—a good place to see pot-bellied sea horses, red velvet fish, leatherjackets, cowfish, morwong and cuttlefish. Have a look in the caves for rock lobsters, shrimp, sea spiders, bullseyes, ling cod and bearded cod.

Bird Rock

Bird Rock features many interesting caves and swim-throughs in depths from 10–20m. In a cave known as The Elbow lives a 2 m-long southern conger eel that is regularly hand fed by the staff of the Bicheno Dive Centre. When a few fish pieces are produced, the eel slowly emerges, and heads for the free meal. With a powerful suck, the bait disappears into the eel's mouth. Another cave nearby is known as The Ballroom. The roof of this wide cave is completely covered in orange jewel anemones. The fish life in this cave can be quite impressive. Long-snouted boarfish, banded morwong, magpie perch, bullseyes, blue throated wrasse and chinaman leatherjackets are all common.

Alligator Rock

Granite walls, coated with an incredible collection of sponges, ascidians, zoanthids and sea whips, drop to 20 m just off Alligator Rock. The sea whips are particularly beautiful, encased in delicate, pink jewel anemones. Butterfly perch, blue-throated wrasse, sea perch, toothbrush leatherjackets and perhaps a draughtboard shark are highlights.

Muirs Rock

Outside the marine reserve are a number of interesting dive sites. Around Muirs Rock, in 15–20 m of water, lies a huge jumble of boulders, forming caves, swim-throughs and gutters. An interesting variety of marine life is found here, including cuttlefish, rock lobsters, boarfish, nudibranchs, sea stars, leatherjackets, morwong, bullseyes, abalone, sea perch and globefish.

Kelp Beds

Over winter, when the conditions are just right, a number of kelp beds can be explored around Bicheno. The most popular one lies south of the marine reserve, and stretches from 18 m to the surface. It is a surreal experience swimming through these underwater forests. The plants are usually spaced far enough apart to make entanglement a slim possibility. You are likely to see reef fish, molluscs, shrimp, sea stars and draughtboard sharks among the kelp.

Between autumn and spring the waters around Bicheno are frequently visited by Australian fur seals, humpback whales, minke whales, orcas, southern right whales and pods of bottlenose dolphins.

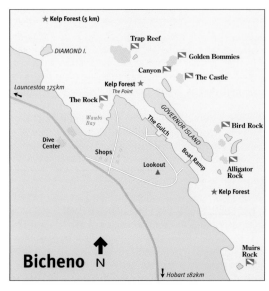

★ Kelp Forest (5 km)

Trap Reef

DIAMOND I.

Golden Bommies

Canyon

The Castle

Launceston 175km

Kelp Forest ★
The Point

The Rock

Waubs
Bay

GOVERNOR ISLAND

The Gulch

Bird Rock

Dive
Center

Shops

Boat Ramp

Lookout

Alligator
Rock

★ Kelp Forest

Muirs
Rock

Bicheno N

↓ Hobart 182km

UNDERWATER JUNGLES
The kelp forests of Tasmania

"ENTERING THE WATER, WE SLOWLY, DESCEND and swim over the rocky bottom. Suddenly a green wall looms above us, as we enter the twilight world of the kelp forest. Swimming between these towering plants is easy, and with good buoyancy control divers can explore the bushy fronds, or the base of the kelp where a mass of strands anchors the plant to the sea floor. Filtered light flickers through the canopy, and in the semi-darkness, nocturnal species roam under the cover of the kelp. Feeding on and around the kelp are nudibranchs, sea spiders, molluscs, shrimp, crabs, abalone, rock lobsters, sea stars, basket stars and a variety of reef fish.

thick rubber-like variety most common in Victoria and Tasmania. It grows to 10 m in length in shallow water, and prefers rough exposed areas. Bull kelp can be very difficult to contend with in rough conditions, but when the water is calm, a remarkable assortment of marine life can be found sheltering among the kelp. Bull kelp is harvested on King Island in Bass Strait—collected off the beaches after storms. The kelp is then kiln -dried and processed to make alginate, which is used in ice cream, beer and toothpaste.

The true kelp forests are formed by giant string kelp (*Macrocystis augustifolia*)

The giant kelp forests *Macrocystis angustifolia* occur throughout Tasmanian waters. The ones shown here, off St Helens, are not as dense as others in southern areas. *Neville Coleman*

The photo opportunities are endless—silhouettes of the dense foliage, divers surrounded by fronds or macro shots of the marine creatures that live within this incredible ecosystem." *Neville Coleman*

Kelp is a variety of brown algae, many species of which are found in the seas around Australia. The most common variety is the brown kelp (*Ecklonia radiata*), which grows to just 1 m in length, but is found from southern Queensland through to southern Western Australia. Brown kelp grows best in semi-sheltered areas, with its single stem attached to rocky bottoms.

Bull kelp (*Durvillaea potatorium*) is a

which can grow in depths to 25 m, depending on the available light. It is found off Victoria and Tasmania, but these truly exceptional forests are patchy in their distribution. The giant string kelp is anchored by strong holdfasts, while the branches stretch to the surface and are supported by gas-filled floats on each frond. The kelp grows best over winter when the seas are calm and the water clearest, and under ideal conditions can grow as much as 60 cm per day.

The giant string kelp may live for many years, and in that time lose numerous branches and fronds to molluscs, sea urchins and heavy seas. The kelp was once harvested in Australia, but is now left as an animal habitat, and for the enjoyment of those who dive.

Tasman Peninsula
Spectacular Diving on the Steamship Nord

The *Nord* was a steel steamship that sank after striking an uncharted reef off the Hippolyte Rocks in 1915. The 81 m-long ship now lies upright at a depth of 42 m, and is considered to be one of the best wreck dives in Australia. The hull of the ship is still in remarkably good condition, and although much of the deck has collapsed, the engine, boiler, prop shaft, winches and other bits of machinery are all easy to recognize. The bow section has also collapsed, but the stern and propeller still make for interesting photos. It takes quite a few dives to see all of the wreck, and if divers take their time they are more likely to come across interesting artefacts, such as bottles and plates. The hull is covered in zoanthids, sponges, sea tulips, sea whips and bryozoans. Masses of reef fish can be seen on most dives, including butterfly perch, wrasse, bullseyes, boarfish, leatherjackets, bearded cod, morwong, cowfish and an occasional draughtboard shark.

The *Nord* is just one of the excellent dive sites found on the Tasman Peninsula. This rugged projection of land with its towering cliffs has excellent shore dives on rocky reefs and piers, and boat dives on sponge gardens, pinnacles, caves and kelp forests. Because of its shape, there is always somewhere to dive no matter the conditions. Diving on the Tasman Peninsula is centered around Eagle-hawk Neck, where the Eaglehawk Dive Centre offers boat dives, and its own comfortable, hostel-style accommodation.

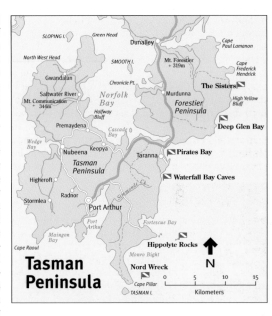

Sisters Rocks

Spectacular walls and pinnacles are found right along the eastern side of the Tasman Peninsula. At the Sisters Rocks, the walls plunge to 40 m and more, covered with finger sponges, thick beds of sea whips, bryozoans, yellow zoanthids and sea ferns. Schools of butterfly perch often engulf divers in the deeper water, and other reef fish are plentiful around the reef. Macro-photographers will find nudibranchs, sea stars, basket stars, molluscs, crustaceans and sea spiders.

Waterfall Bay Caves

This huge cave system at Waterfall Bay is regarded as Australia's best ocean cave dive. These caves undercut the sea cliffs, with Cathedral Cave being one of the most impressive. Three large openings allow access to this cave, which is about 30 m long and 21 m deep. Other caves in the area wind (100 m or more) back into the cliff, and require good cave diving training before they can be explored. All the

Boat dives 5–40 minutes from boat ramp

Summer 10–15 m, winter 20–30 m

Slight currents on some reefs

Sponge gardens and kelp beds

The *Nord* Shipwreck. Waterfall Bay Caves

Reef fish prolific, pelagic fish also seen

Rocky reefs and pinnacles

Above: In Tasmanian waters live interesting fishes that walk along the bottom on modified pectoral fins. The prickly-skinned handfish (*Brachionichthys hirsutus*) is the most common and is usually seen on soft bottom. Similar to anglerfish, these fishes have a lure to attract prey (seen here folded up). *Neville Coleman*

caves are lined with sponges and zoanthids, and are occupied by invertebrates, reef fish, and sometimes schools of bullseyes and butterfly perch.

Giant Kelp Forests
Over winter three large kelp forests are found off Eaglehawk Neck—at Shag Rock Bay, Deep Glen Bay and Fortescue Bay. These are best reached by boat, although parts of the kelp forest at Fortescue Bay can be reached from the shore. Thick jungles of *Macrocystis* kelp are found in depths from 10–30 m, and provide very exciting diving. Although swimming in and out of the forest is a novelty in itself, you will also see an impressive array of marine life—banded stingarees, leatherjackets, boxfish, wrasse, perch, morwong, trevally, pike, mackerel, draughtboard sharks, weedy sea dragons, handfish, sea horses, molluscs and crustaceans.

Hippolyte Rocks
Brilliant walls, pinnacles and caves are found around the Hippolyte Rocks in depths to 40 m. This area is densely packed with sponge gardens, and the deeper one goes, the better the marine life gets. Numerous reef fish and invertebrates species add even more color to these picturesque sponge gardens. On the northeast side of Big Hippolyte lives

a small colony of fur seals that often join divers for an entertaining swim.

Port Arthur
A number of good shore and boat dives are located around historic Port Arthur. The Port Arthur Jetty pylons are covered with sponges, nudibranchs, sea stars, shrimps, crabs, molluscs and blennies. Small reef fish are common, and on the sandy bottom occasional banded stingarees and Tasmanian numbfish can be found.

At nearby Safety Cove is a pretty rocky reef that can be explored from the shore. Morwong, leatherjackets, bearded cod, boxfish, perch and a wide range of invertebrates are found in among the rocks and weeds on the reef. One of the best boat dives off Port Arthur is the rocky reefs around the Isle of the Dead. Here the kelp forests grow in only 12 m of water. Reef fish and invertebrate species are common, as are lobster, stingarees and beautiful weedy sea dragons.

From 1830 to 1877, Australia's most infamous penal colony was located on the Tasman Peninsula. The Peninsula was a natural prison —cool waters and towering cliffs barred any escape. Today the ruins of the penal colony at Port Arthur are a popular tourist attraction. Visitors to this area enjoy the spectacular scenery, national parks and a visit to the wildlife park at Nubeena.

Hobart
Exploring Australia's Southern Seas

Divers heading for Hobart for a dive holiday have a wide variety of dive sites to choose from—shore dives on kelp beds, pretty rocky reefs, and rich soft-bottom environments, as well as boat trips to kelp forests, sponge gardens and a number of intact vessels on an artificial reef. In fact, there is great variety along this southern-most of Australian shores. Several dive shops service the area, offer boat dives and advise on the best shore diving. Although the visibility may not always be great, somewhere calm and sheltered to dive can always be found, no matter what the conditions.

Tinderbox
A wide variety of dive sites are found around the Tinderbox. A wonderful array of creatures can be found just off the boat ramp by day or night. Over and on the sea grass beds there are bound to be cuttlefish, nudibranchs, sea stars, octopi, handfish, stingarees, numbrays, hermit crabs, molluscs, sea hares, leatherjackets, cowfish, wrasse, sea perch, goatfish, boxfish and perhaps a skate or stargazer.

Piersons Point
Thick kelp forests are an interesting feature off Piersons Point, in depths to 15 m. The rocky bottom and swaying forest of kelp provide homes for a diverse range of fauna. Rock lobsters hide under ledges with abalone, boarfish, conger eels, bearded rock cod and cardinalfish. Around the kelp swim leatherjackets, morwong, wrasse, perch, and occasional rarer animals like handfish and red velvetfish.

Bligh Point
The water around Bligh Point is only 8 m deep, but the rocky reef supports plenty of marine life—kelp, sponges, nudibranchs, cuttlefish, sea stars, leatherjackets, octopi, goatfish, cowfish, pipefish, toadfish, flounder,

gobies, wrasse, morwong and boarfish. There are also a number of small caves and swim-throughs here, so take a flashlight to highlight the many colorful sponges and hidden creatures.

Cape De La Sortie
The rocky reef at Cape De La Sortie provides a good anchor for a dense kelp forest, found in depths to 12 m, where divers will find plenty of excitement swimming among the kelp. Look for the reef fish, rock lobsters, abalone, handfish, cowfish and draughtboard sharks that reside here.

Yellow Bluff
The rocky reefs that drop into 25 m around Yellow Bluff are similar to many dive sites off Bruny Island.

Below: The southern rock cod (*Scorpaena papillosa*), a popular food fish, inhabits rocky ledges in temperate waters. *Michael Aw*

Shore and boat dives up to 30 minutes away

Summer 5–10 m, winter 15–25 m

Slight currents on some reefs

Colorful sponge gardens and thick kelp forests

Brilliant variety of shore and boat dives

Abundant reef fish

Rocky reefs and pinnacles

Numerous large boulders are jumbled together on the bottom to form caves, gutters and swim-throughs. Beautiful sponge gardens with nudibranchs, scorpionfish, sea stars, basket stars, cowfish, gobies and the elusive spiny pipehorse (an animal that looks like a cross between a pipefish and a sea dragon) are found around these reefs. Boarfish, sweep, butterfly perch, banded morwong and a variety of leatherjacket species are common.

Top Slip Point

Brilliant sponge gardens cover the rocky reef off Top Slip Point. The reef drops to a sandy bottom in 25 m, where skates, stingarees, stargazers, Tasmanian numbrays, angel sharks and butterfly gurnard are often seen.

Betsey Island Artificial Reef

Eleven vessels were sunk on this artificial reef in the 1970s and 1980s. The two most interesting ships are the *William Callper* and *Macquarie*, which rest in 22 m of water. The wrecks have become an oasis for fish and invertebrates—morwong, wrasse, perch, cuttlefish, octopi, nudibranchs, sponges, zoanthids, jewel anemones and sea stars are common. The wrecks are safe for novice divers to explore as many large holes allow easy penetration of the hulks.

Betsey Reef

Located just south of Betsey Island is a small rocky outcrop, surrounded by a boulder reef in depths to 22 m. Betsey Reef is a great spot to find rock lobsters, abalone and reef fish. Watchful divers may also see weedy sea dragons, spiny pipehorses, handfish, draughtboard sharks and sea horses.

Ninepin Point

Located at the mouth of the Huon River, Ninepin Point is washed by tannin-stained fresh water, which floats on top of the salt water. Once under the dark and murky top layer of water, the sea water is clear underneath. Accessible from the shore, the rocky bottom here varies in depth from 6–10 m, and is covered with interesting varieties of sponges and kelp. Because of the darkness, there are extraordinary numbers of fish and invertebrate species, including many deep-water species. Basket stars, shrimp, brittle stars, sea spiders, morwong, nudibranchs, stingarees, sea stars, pike, leatherjackets, perch, scorpionfish, sea horses, pipefish, rock lobsters, wrasse and beautiful handfish are all common.

Opposite: Often neglected by underwater photographers, the flora of the ocean presents great opportunities, when well lit and contrasted with the color of the surrounding sea.
Michael Aw

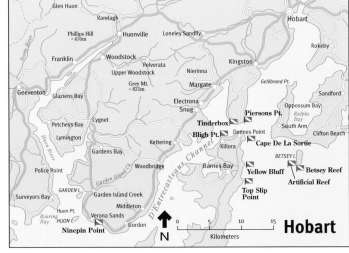

SOUTH AUSTRALIA

Introducing South Australia

Where the Currents Mix

Most overseas divers head for South Australia for one reason—to see the legendary great white shark. The countless films and documentaries produced in the waters of South Australia give the impression that thousands of white sharks patrol just off the coast. But the fact is, their numbers are low and very few divers will ever see one in the water.

South Australia has many underwater attractions apart from the great white shark. Currents from both the Indian and Pacific Oceans bring creatures typical to both eastern and western coastal zones, and the state has a few species of its own as well. Australian sea lions and New Zealand fur seals are found at many dive sites, and local divers are accustomed to having seals around during dives. Along the South Australian coast is a great place to see southern right whales, common and bottlenose dolphins, rock lobsters and unusual fish such as the multicolored harlequin fish, the western blue groper wrasse, the western blue devilfish, and weedy and leafy sea dragons.

Although South Australia's dive industry is small, many areas offer excellent diving. Mount Gambier is famous for its freshwater lakes and sinkholes—a must for those into caves or really clear water. Numerous shore and boat dives can be found at Victor Harbour, Kangaroo Island, Adelaide and along the Yorke and Eyre Peninsulas. Those who enjoy live-aboard diving can visit the hundreds of islands scattered off the

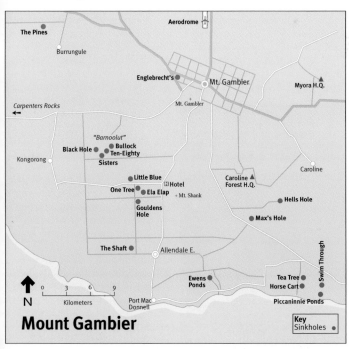

Mount Gambier

Opposite:
Kangaroo Island can be reached by a variety of vessels. Although well-known as a habitat for kangaroos, divers come to the island to have close encounters with the fur seals.
Michael Aw

Opposite: Freshwater vegetation is the main food of the freshwater cray (*Euastaceus bispenosus*), although it also scavenges and hunts other freshwater creatures.
Neville Coleman

Below: Strikingly-colorful, the blue devilfish (*Paraplesiops meleagris)* is usually seen beneath ledges and in caves.
Neville Coleman

coastline. Many locations are not mentioned in the text because of the lack of diving facilities in the area, but for the diver with his/her own boat and compressor (or a large supply of tanks), there is good diving along the east coast at Port Mac-Donnell, Beachport, Robe and Kingston. The top end of the Eyre Peninsula from Whyalla to Port Neill offers good diving when the water is clear over winter.

Along the vast stretch of coast parallel to the Nullarbor Plain—off towns like Streaky Bay, Smoky Bay and Ceduna—lie rugged reefs with rock lobsters and plentiful reef fish. Many shipwrecks and a number of artificial reefs off Adelaide have attracted plenty of fish and invertebrate life. South Australia has numerous marine reserves throughout the state, which protect the marine life at many of the more popular dive sites.

Diving conditions are often good at any time of the year, but the best weather is usually experienced over summer, when the water is clear and warm. Most local divers use a 5 or 7 mm wetsuit, as the water temperature varies from 14–20° C. The whole state is arid and dry, with the air temperature varying from 15–28° C over summer, and 6–16° C during winter.

South Australia covers an area of 984,377 sq km, about the same size as the US state of Texas. The state was officially settled in 1836, when a small town was established on Kangaroo Island. The population has since grown to 1.4 million, mostly centered around the city of Adelaide, a stately city noted particularly for its colonial architecture and its parks and gardens. Mining and agriculture make up most of the state's revenue. Wine production is a major industry—the Barossa Valley is famous for its wine varieties.

Some 250 national parks draw visitors to South Australia. The state's natural attractions include the Flinders Ranges, which are some of the most ancient mountains on earth, containing many fossils; the Lake Eyre Basin—vast inland salt flats which flood every few years, and team with bird and fish life; the desolate Nullarbor Plain bordering the Great Australian Bight, riddled with underground caves containing clear water sinkholes and Aboriginal paintings; the 1500 million year-old Gawler Ranges —huge, granite monoliths, home to unique wildlife; and the numerous marsupial and bird species that inhabit Kangaroo Island. Other attractions include the beaches, fishing, the Adelaide Arts Festival, opal mining at Coober Pedy, and the mighty Murray River, where visitors enjoy paddlewheel and house boat trips. The state promotes the natural beauty of the landscape, its history and culture, and steers away from theme parks and large resort developments. Tourism is a growing industry, worth almost A$2 billion to the economy each year.

Visitors to South Australia will find a wide range of accommodation available, and a good network of roads to most areas, although a 4WD is required to reach many of the more remote regions. Buses and trains service most of the state, and a number of state-based airlines offer flights from Adelaide to Kangaroo Island and Port Lincoln. An increasing number of divers each year visit South Australia's more than 3700 km of coastline, and hundreds of islands and reefs.

Mount Gambier
Freshwater Fantasyland

Ewens Ponds is a series of three small, incredibly clear, interconnected lakes 15 km south of Mount Gambier. The first pond is 50 m in diameter, and divers are usually able to see the far side clearly. While swimming over grasses and reeds to the bottom at 10 m, it is difficult to tell if there is any water at all—you could be flying over a rolling grassy hill. The only give-away is the occasional small fish and the bubbles rising from the vegetation—oxygen being produced by photosynthesis.

When entering the shallow channel at the far side of the pond that leads to the next pond, there is no need to fin as the strong current quickly pulls you into the second pond. This second pond (40 m in diameter) is home to a larger fish population, including black bream, tupong, pygmy perch, and a few eels. The sand at the bottom bubbles where spring water enters the pond. After a short drift through the next channel, divers are deposited in a 30 m-diameter pond, the last in the series. Small fish dart across the bottom, and at 9 m, freshwater lobsters hide on a rocky ledge. This is where most divers terminate their dive, but it is possible to follow the shallow Eight Mile Creek for another 3 km. Just remember, it is a long walk back, so arrange for a car to pick you up.

The Mount Gambier district has plenty of lakes and sinkholes—some say there are over 200 diveable holes in the area, but only about 40 are visited regularly. Located close to the Victorian border, Mount Gambier was discovered by divers in the early sixties, and a small number began exploration of its extraordinary sinkholes. As word got out, more and more divers headed to the area, and eventually lack of experience and guidance led to sev-

eral deaths. To address the problem, the Cave Divers Association of Australia (CDAA) was formed, to instruct divers on safe diving procedures, and to categorize each sinkhole. Ewens Ponds is the only lake in the area that can be dived without a CDAA permit. All other sinkholes are categorized as follows: cavern (CN), sinkhole (S), cave (C) and penetration (P). Most of the sinkholes in the area are found on private property or government land, so permission and permits must be obtained before diving. However the red tape is worth the effort.

Air fills can be obtained from a number of shops in the area. For more information on the sinkholes, closed seasons, cave diver training, and permits, contact the Cave Divers Association of Australia.

Piccaninnie Ponds (S)

The most famous and popular sinkhole in Mount Gambier is Piccanin-

 Variety of entries from the shore

 Generally 20–40 m

 Between ponds

 Grasses, reeds and freshwater sponges

 Spectacular clear-water lakes and sinkholes

 Sparse numbers of freshwater fish

 Limestone caves and sinkholes

Above: The terrapin or freshwater tortoise, found in many of the Mt Gambier sinkholes and ponds, is best observed early morning or late afternoon.
Neville Coleman

nie Ponds. After entering the water from a small landing, divers swim across a small pond and then over The Chasm. This gaping hole (about 5 m wide and 50 m long) drops to 60 m. The depths below look very inviting during the descent down the algae-covered walls, but remember the limit of 36 m on all dives in the area. At 10 m is an opening in the wall, The Cathedral, an impressive chamber 30 m high and 20 m wide, with white limestone walls. From here you can exit from a second hole at 25 m, and explore the limestone walls of The Chasm. A

variety of animals can be seen in Piccaninnie Ponds, including tortoises, freshwater lobsters, crabs, shrimp, eels, pygmy perch, diving beetles and other insects. Both divers and snorkelers will enjoy Piccaninnie Ponds, but since visitor numbers are restricted, book well ahead.

Little Blue (S)
A number of objects have been dumped in this hole over the years, including cars, which now litter the bottom at 35 m.

Gouldens Hole (CN)
Many ledges are found in depths to 25 m in Gouldens Hole. A pumping station ramp allows easy access, but watch out for duck weed and silt.

One Tree (S)
Typical of most sinkholes in the area, One Tree is a funnel-style cave, with a collapsed roof forming a rock pile 30 m below the surface. Passages lead down from the rock pile to 50 m, well beyond the safe diving limits.

The Pines (C)
The surface of this hole is covered in duckweed, but beneath the greenery lies clear water and a white limestone bottom. At The Pines there are many tunnels and caves to explore in depths to 30 m. Fossilized mollusc shells can be seen imbedded in the walls.

The Shaft (S)
Closed for 16 years after the tragic death of four divers, The Shaft is without doubt one of the most notorious holes in the area. Access is through a manhole-sized opening, with the water surface 10 m below. A rock pile is found at 35 m, and recent exploration by a film crew (using trimix) established the bottom at 87 m. Permission to dive this infamous hole, which is located on a private farm, is rarely granted.

Map

Victor Harbour

N
0 2 4 6
Kilometers

Heysen Trail
Spring Mount Conservation Park
Hindmarsh Falls
Glacier Rock
Inman River
Heysen Trail
Back Valley
Lookout
Yilki
GRANITE I.
Rosetta Head
The Bluff Lookout
The Bluff
WEST I.
Waitpinga Beach
Newland Head

Crow's Nest Lookout
Urimbirra Wildlife Park
Middleton
Nangawooka Flora Reserve
Greenhills Park
Pt. Elliot
Oliver Reefs
Whale Bone Caves
Victor Harbour
Encounter Bay
Chapel Ground
Seal Rocks

SOUTHERN OCEAN

Victor Harbour

Relaxed Atmosphere, Rugged Shoreline

Victor Harbour is a favorite holiday destination for many Adelaide residents, who enjoy the relaxed atmosphere, lovely countryside and the rugged seashore. One of the most popular attractions at Victor Harbour is Granite Island, which is situated just offshore, in Encounter Bay. The historic Screwpile Jetty links the island to the mainland—you can either walk across, or catch a ride on a horse-drawn tram. Rock wallabies and little penguins can be seen on the island, and sometimes dramatic sea spray, as massive swells crash into the island.

There are plenty of interesting dive sites and marine creatures around Victor Harbour. Although the sea is not always rough, diving in the harbor is weather-dependent. If a southerly is blowing, divers generally head for nearby Rapid Bay, but northerly winds calm the seas, especially during autumn. Servicing the Victor Harbour area are Victor Dive Charters and Victor Marine and Watersport.

Port Elliot

A variety of interesting reefs are found around the rocky shores of Port Elliot. Ledges and gutters in depths varying from 10–20 m can be accessed from the rocks. Along the bottom are sea stars, nudibranchs, sweep, leatherjackets, boxfish, wrasse, morwong, abalone, leafy sea dragons, rock lobsters and bullseyes.

Olivers Reefs and Whale Bone Caves

These two reefs in Encounter Bay offer a range of diving possibilities, at depths from 8–12 m. Thick kelp covers much of the bottom, where you are likely to see leafy sea dragons, rock lobsters, abalone and a range of reef fish and invertebrate species.

Granite Island

Granite Island can be dived from the shore, but there are more interesting sites to be explored by boat. On the southern side are boulders tumbling down to 15 m, which shelter blue devilfish, boarfish, perch, sweep and the elusive black cowrie.

Seal Rocks

Huge granite boulders surround Seal Rocks in depths down to 25 m. Sponges, gorgonians, zoanthids, bryozoans and ascidians are found around the island, along with morwong, Port Jackson sharks, rock lobsters, yellowtail, kingfish and plenty of reef fish.

The Bluff

Probably the most popular shore dive at Victor Harbour is The Bluff. Among the boulders down to 18 m are leafy sea dragons, abalone, rock lobsters, sea stars, blue devilfish, morwong, boxfish, globefish, sweep and sometimes a fur seal.

West Island

Although rarely visited by local divers, West Island is worth the trip. Surrounded by deep reefs, covered with kelp, the deep caves and fissures are alive with color, and are home to gorgonians, sponges, ascidians and an occasional black cowrie. The island has a small New Zealand fur seal colony, a little penguin colony and flocks of crested terns and silver gulls.

Shore and boat dives 10 minutes away

Generally 5–10 m

Some offshore currents

Sponge gardens and kelp

Rocky reefs with the occasional leafy sea dragon

Reef fish quite common

Rocky reefs

SEA DRAGONS
The masters of camouflage

SEA DRAGONS ARE SOME OF THE MOST BIZARRE and unique animals found in the waters of southern Australia. Only two species are known. The weedy (or common) sea dragon (*Phyllopteryx taeniolatus*), found in shallow water on kelp beds and sponge gardens from Sydney to Perth, is the most often seen. The coloration of this sea dragon is nothing short of spectacular—purple, orange and pink, with thousands of yellow polka dots. Although colorful, the animal is difficult for the untrained eye to detect, looking like a piece of kelp until exposed by a flashlight beam which reveals its array of brilliant colors.

If you think a weedy dragon is difficult to find, then forget about looking for a majestic leafy sea dragon (*Phycodurus eques*), as its bushy appendages make it a master of cryptic camouflage. Found in the shallow waters off South Australia, western Victoria and southern Western Australia, they are most common in sheltered bays—around kelp and sea grass beds. The author has spent many a dive in South Australia searching, without success, for leafy sea dragons.

Sea dragons belong to the family Syngnathidae, along with the sea horses and pipefish. They have a bony exoskeletons that offers little protection from their main predators—sharks and rays. Their best defence is their camouflage. They usually drift with the tide and move with the surge, however their small fins can carry them along at a steady pace if necessary.

Sea dragons feed exclusively on my sids (tiny shrimp-like crustaceans), which they suck up with their elongated snouts. The male sea horses, pipefish and sea dragons look after the young. The female deposits the eggs on the underside of the male's tail, then disappears. Over summer it is not uncommon to see male weedy sea dragons carrying hundreds of pink eggs. This strategy gives the young a better chance of survival than if the eggs were released directly into the water, to be eaten by other fish. After a few weeks the 3 cm-long young hatch, and are mini versions of the adults. It is not known how long sea dragons live, but both species grow to a length of 45 cm.

Subject to restrictive collection (license) and partial protection in some areas, the unique leafy sea dragon (*Phycodurus eques*) is one of Australia's most unusual sea creatures. *Michael Aw*

Encounters with sea dragons are always fascinating. They make brilliant photo subjects, but don't take your eye off them as they can quickly disappear. And don't handle them. Even though these animals have a tough exoskeleton, they are very fragile and can die of shock from rough treatment.

Although semi-protected in Australia, sea dragons are still targeted by the aquarium trade. Collectors can make money on the black market, and numbers have dropped noticeably at some dive sites over the last few years. They rarely survive capture, and die quickly in aquariums, as they only eat live mysid. Sea dragons are best enjoyed in their natural environment.

Kangaroo Island
Wildlife on Parade:
Above and Below Water

Kangaroo Island is a haven for wildlife—koalas, possums, emus, kangaroos, wallabies, echidnas and numerous species of reptiles and birds. Thousands of visitors come to this large, wooded island each year to see them, but the most memorable encounters are with the Australian sea lions found on the beach at Seal Bay. The sea lions sleep and relax on the beach during the day, and are used to humans invading their territory. People are allowed to approach within 4 m.

Divers often meet sea lions, little penguins, dolphins, New Zealand fur seals and sea dragons on the reefs around Kangaroo Island, as well as pelagic fish and plenty of reef fish and invertebrates. One of Kangaroo Island's greatest attractions is the underwater terrain along the 400-km coastline—colorful sponge gardens, rocky reefs and over fifty shipwrecks, many yet to be located.

Two local dive operators, Adventureland Diving and Kangaroo Island Dive Safaris, run regular boat dives to the best spots on the day. A good range of accommodation is available. Visitors can reach the island by plane, or by car on the passenger ferry, from Port Adelaide or Cape Jervis.

Snapper Point

This spectacular boat dive, against a towering cliff face, is best done on the high tide to avoid strong currents. The reef wall drops to beyond 40 m, and has many ledges lined with sponges, ascidians, gorgonians and soft corals. Interesting invertebrate life can be found on the bottom, including nudibranchs, sea stars, basket stars, cuttlefish, crabs and cowries. Reef fish are prolific—leatherjackets, morwong, perch, scorpionfish, wrasse, blue devilfish, old wives, sweep and beautiful harlequin fish. Here you will often see schools of yellowtail, pike and kingfish, and sometimes a seal or penguin.

Penneshaw Jetty

Although the water is only 6 m deep, a shore dive at Penneshaw Jetty can be very rewarding. The pylons of the jetty are encrusted with gorgonians, sponges, ascidians and anemones, where macrophotographers will find plenty of subjects—sea stars, brittle stars, cowries, nudibranchs, octopi and cuttlefish. The resident fish population includes goatfish, morwong,

Shore and boat dives up to 20 minutes away

Generally 10–20 m

Some tidal currents

Rich sponge gardens and kelp

Endless encounters with interesting marine life

Reef and pelagic fish both abundant

Rocky reefs

Kangaroo Island

N

0 10 20 30
Kilometers

Gulf St Vincent

Investigator Strait

Cape Torrens
Cape Cassini
Point Marsden
Cape Jervis
Fairfield
Fanny M
Fides
Western River Cove
Kingscote
Nepean Bay
Penneshaw Jetty
Cape Borda
Snug Cove
Portland Maru
Kangaroo Head
Loch Vennachar
Parndana
American River
Penneshaw
Snapper Point
KANGAROO ISLAND
American Beach
Cape Bedout
D'Estress Bay
Cape Willoughby
Mars
Point Tinline
Vivonne Bay
Seal Bay
Osmanli
Hanson Bay
Montebello
You Yangs
Cape Gantheaume
Cape du Couedic
SOUTHERN OCEAN

perch, leatherjackets, zebrafish, cowfish, wrasse and the occasional stargazer sometimes hidden on the sandy bottom.

Kangaroo Head
Probably one of the best spots to find leafy sea dragons is Kangaroo Head, however it takes a good eye to distinguish these fish from the surrounding weed and kelp. The rocky reef, with rock lobster, boarfish, perch, morwong and much colorful invertebrate life, averages 12 m deep.

Nepean Bay
A variety of dive sites found around Nepean Bay include the wreck of the *Fanny M.* The 50 m-long ship ran aground in 1885, and the scattered remains are now found in 5 m of water. You will be able to make out part of the hull, as numerous ribs protrude from the bottom. Although the occasional artefact is still found, nothing can be removed from this historic shipwreck.

Cape Torrens
One of the most colorful dives in the area is along the wall off Cape Torrens. This wall, which drops to 39 m, is packed with yellow zoanthids, gorgonians, sponges, soft corals, anemones, bryozoans and

ascidians. There are numerous invertebrates to be found, as well as blue gropers, kingfish, blue devilfish, sea dragons, boarfish, morwong, and perch. Divers have even seen seals and common dolphins here.

Western River Cove
This rocky cove is an interesting shore dive. Its outer edge drops into 18 m of water, where the reef is covered with kelp and sponges. Nudibranchs, cuttlefish, rock lobster, blue devilfish, blue gropers, cowfish and old wives are common. Sea dragons and red snappers are sometimes seen.

Loch Vennachar Shipwreck
The *Loch Vennachar* disappeared in 1905, and was not located by divers until 1976. Much of shipwreck still lies on the rocky bottom—the winch, anchor and piles of pig iron ballast.

Fides Shipwreck
The *Fides* sank in 1860, and has now broken up in 10 m of water under the cliff face. Among the wreckage are a few bits of brass, bottles and cutlery. The reef itself, occupied by a variety of reef fish and invertebrates, makes a good dive.

Snug Cove
Cliffs 200 m high tower above the waters of Snug Cove. The walls descend underwater to 20 m, with numerous gutters and ledges. Rock lobster, morwong, kingfish, boarfish, wrasse, leatherjackets, harlequin fish, cuttlefish and blue gropers are usually seen along the walls.

Hanson Bay
Located at the mouth of the South West River, Hanson Bay can be dived from the shore. Stingrays, cuttlefish, drummer, morwong, bream, pike and abundant invertebrate species are found in the bay, which is only 5–10 m deep.

Opposite: Situated some 95 km south of Adelaide, Rapid Bay Jetty is over 500 m long. One of the best jetty dives, it is only 9 m (30 ft) deep at the end.
Nigel Marsh

Below: Usually observed in schools, yellowtail kingfish (*Seriola lalandi*) are very inquisitive and will often encircle divers at close quarters.
Nigel Marsh

Adelaide
Artificial Reefs Aplenty

A few rocky reefs occur off Adelaide's coastline, however much of the shallow seabed is sandy, and offers little shelter for marine life. To address this problem, the South Australian Fisheries Department has systematically created artificial reefs off this stretch of coast. For over ten years, bundles of tires and old ships have been sunk in depths from 18–30 m. These artificial reefs have attracted a wide variety of fish and invertebrates, and many fishermen and divers visit these reefs every weekend.

The capital of South Australia, Adelaide is a well-planned city, with wide streets and numerous parks. Known as the City of Churches, the city is famous for its art festival and the great wines grown in the nearby Barossa Valley.

Many underwater attractions are accessible from the shore or by boat, such as artificial reefs, jetties, rocky reefs and a number of historic shipwrecks. The staff of the several dive shops and charter boats that service the Adelaide district are happy to share their local knowledge.

Rapid Bay Jetty
Many divers head for Rapid Bay (95 km south of Adelaide) each weekend to explore the 500 m-long jetty, known as one of the best pier dives in Australia. A wealth of marine life can be found around the hundreds of pylons. Enter at the shore or walk to the end (a bit of a hike), and climb down the ladder. The fish population is remarkable, considering the number of fishermen trying their luck above. Schools of old wives, pike, yellowtail and bullseyes swarm between the pylons. Swimming among the seaweeds on the

bottom are leatherjackets, boarfish, morwong, perch, scorpionfish, cowfish, sweep, wrasse, zebrafish, moonlighters, goatfish and southern coralfish. Also found around and on the

bottom are cuttlefish, squid, octopi, nudibranchs, sea stars, molluscs and the occasional stargazer or leafy sea dragon. Macro-photographers are advised to take a close look at the pylons, as most are covered with invertebrates. The end of the pier sits in 9 m of water, and schools of kingfish sometimes gather there. Look for fishing lines when diving the jetty—it is not uncommon to find lost squid jigs and rods.

Aldinga Reef Drop-off
The top of Aldinga Reef is only 6 m deep, but the outer edge drops into 20 m. Although silty in some areas, this 6 km-long reef has masses of colorful sponges, ascidians, gorgonians, soft corals, bryozoans and zoanthids. Cuttlefish, nudibranchs, sea stars, blue devilfish, morwong, perch, boarfish, blue gropers, old wives, wobbegongs, octopi, sting-

Shore and boat dives up to 20 minutes away

Generally 10–15 m

Little current

Sponge gardens and kelp

Brilliant shore diving at Rapid Bay Jetty and Port Noarlunga. Numerous interesting artificial reefs

Prolific reef fish and also pelagic fish

Rocky reefs

rays, and scorpionfish can be found among the boulders or under the ledges. School of kingfish, pike and sweep cruise past the edge of the drop-off.

Star of Greece Shipwreck

The 70 m-long *Star of Greece* sank in 1880, after a wild storm blew her ashore. The remains of this iron ship are now in 8 m of water, approximately 200 m offshore. Numerous twisted plates now shelter a variety of marine species.

Port Noarlunga Reef

An aquatic reserve, Port Noarlunga Reef is one of the most popular dive sites in South Australia. This rocky reef, which runs parallel to the coast for several hundred meters, is exposed at low tide. Access to the reef is via a jetty. After climbing down the ladder at the end, divers can either explore the sheltered inner reef or the more interesting outer side. The inner side of the rocky reef (9 m deep) is a good place to see schools of drummer, old wives, moonlighters, wrasse, zebrafish, scaly-fin, leatherjackets and cuttlefish. The rocky outer reef drops into 20 m, with plenty of gutters and ledges, covered in kelp, sponges, ascidians, soft corals and small gor-

gonians. Common marine life includes blue devilfish, octopi, nudibranchs, morwong, sea stars, scorpionfish, perch, cowfish, catfish, bullseyes, yellowtail, flatheads, scallops and a variety of leatherjackets.

Noarlunga Tyre Reef

An artificial reef of tires lies at 20 m, 3 km off Noarlunga. These tires shelter cuttlefish, octopi, blue devilfish, morwong, wobbegongs, bullseyes, perch and many other species. Tire reefs have also been constructed off Glenelg and Grange.

Stanvac Barges

Located in 30 m of water off Port Stanvac, two 20 m-long barges and one 50 m-long barge make up another of Adelaide's excellent artificial reefs. In and around the barges are stingrays, bullseyes, cuttlefish, blue devilfish, morwong, perch and catfish.

Stanvac Dump

A good variety of marine species can be found in a dumping area located off the Port Stanvac Oil Refinery, in 12 m of water. The pipes and the other industrial wreckage that have been disposed of here are now occupied by rock lobsters, blue devilfish, cowfish, perch, nudibranchs, morwong and various other animals.

Seacliff Reef

Seacliff Reef is only 13 m deep, but its many gutters and ledges make this rocky reef a fascinating dive site. Blue devilfish, nudibranchs, leatherjackets, bullseyes, wrasse, blue gropers and even the elusive leafy sea dragon are found among the sponges and seaweeds.

Glenelg Jetty

An abundance of small creatures can be found on every dive under Glenelg Jetty. Located in very shallow water, the pylons and scattered wreckage under the jetty shelter molluscs, nudibranchs, cuttlefish, octopi, blennies, cowfish, leatherjackets, wrasse and sea stars. Macrophotographers will have a ball, especially at night when the crabs and shrimps venture forth.

The Dredge

Sunk in 1985 as an artificial reef, The Dredge is now the most popular boat diving site off Adelaide. The wreck rests upright in 20 m of water and divers can explore the holds, the engine room and the wheelhouse, which is usually full of bullseyes. In the short time since it was sunk, The Dredge has become covered in soft corals, sponges, anemones, ascidians and bryozoans. Many reef fish are found around the wreck, including old wives, blue devilfish, morwong, perch, leatherjackets, stingrays, wobbegongs and cuttlefish. Just 80 m south of The Dredge is a hopper barge that can be reached by following a series of markers. This barge is also an interesting dive, but doesn't usually have as many fish around it.

Norma Shipwreck

After a collision in 1907, the 85 m-long *Norma* sank in 15 m of water off Semaphore Beach. Although much of the hull has broken up,

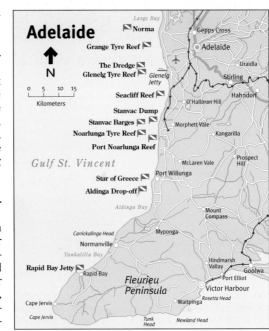

the mass of plates, masts and other fittings can still be identified. The wreck also attracts large numbers of fish, including yellowtail, bullseyes, perch, boarfish, morwong and goatfish.

Zanoni Shipwreck

Probably the most intact historic shipwreck off South Australia, the 42 m-long *Zanoni* was only discovered by divers in 1983. The ship capsized during a storm in 1867, and now lies on its port side in 18 m of water. The masts, sternposts, rudder, bow sprit, and many other fittings and artefacts are still recognizable. This is an important historic shipwreck that is currently being surveyed and studied by maritime archeologists from Adelaide.

Below: Silver sweeps aggregate in caves by day and disperse to feed on zooplankton at night. *Michael Aw*

THE GREAT WHITE SHARK
A species under threat?

BALING OUT CUPS FULL OF BLOODY BURLY AT 3 AM might not be everyone's idea of a great holiday, but for those hoping to see a great white shark it is all part of the charm of a cage diving trip. For four days we burlied the water, played cards, fished, watched the seals and waited, but no great white. We couldn't even go diving or swimming to break the monotony. It was a discouraging and expensive experience, but these are the risks divers must take to see the most notorious shark of all.

The great white shark (*Carcharodon carcharias*) is found in both temperate and tropical seas, but is mainly found in cooler waters, where it feeds on dolphins, sharks, seals, rays and pelagic fish. Also known as the white death or white shark, the great white is a member of the mackerel shark family, which includes the makos and porbeagles. Great whites have a reproductive cycle like the grey nurse shark, during which the unborn young eat extra eggs produced by the female. Litter sizes are generally under ten, and at birth the pups are 1 m long. Young white sharks have long, needle-like teeth (which are eventually replaced by the cutting, triangular teeth of the adults) and feed mainly on assorted fish.

Great whites are thought to be most common along the southern coastline of Australia. Many divers dream of seeing this incredible creature in the water, even though it has been responsible for the majority of fatal attacks on humans. The occasional white shark is seen in the wild, however the most reliable way to see these sharks is by burlying up the water. Cage diving trips are run out of Port Lincoln to Dangerous Reef and the Neptune Islands.

Divers from around the world head for Port Lincoln in hope of seeing a great white, but these sharks seem to be getting rarer and rarer. Several years ago there was a 70 per cent chance of seeing a great white, but recently the figure appears to be more like 30 per cent. Many people may be happy at the decline in numbers, but it also represents the current status of many commercial and recreational fisheries in southern Australia.

Recently protected in Queensland, New South Wales and Tasmania, the great white still faces pressure in the other states. Only a small number are taken by game fishermen for their jaws. The major threat to the population seems to come from some commercial fishermen using nets and longlines. Studies conducted by the South Australian Fisheries Research Unit have found that most tagged animals caught in commercial fishing nets are under the reproductive age.

Obtaining Australia-wide protection for the great white shark will be difficult, as most people remember *Jaws* and the media always goes into a frenzy whenever anyone is attacked—propagating myths of the rogue shark, and encouraging revenge killings. Soon the great white may only be seen in museums and old films.

The recent decision not to protect the great white shark (*Carcharodon carcharias*) throughout Australian waters means that the above practice will continue throughout the country. Big game fishing clubs and fishermen in general say that the numbers are not declining.
Nigel Marsh

Yorke Peninsula
Barren Above, Beautiful Below

Built in 1873, **Edithburgh Jetty** is 170 m long and 12 m wide, and is easily the most popular dive on the Yorke Peninsula. The depth under the pier is only 5–7 m, and each pylon is encrusted with sponges, ascidians, tube worms, bryozoans and soft corals. Among this mass of sessile marine life are nudibranchs, sea stars, spider crabs, shrimp and molluscs. Octopi, cuttlefish, squid, anglerfish, drummer, globefish, cowfish, sea horses, pipefish, goblinfish, leafy sea dragons and many more species inhabit the area underneath the jetty—a hive of activity that will delight any photographer. Edithburgh Jetty is but one of a number of brilliant shore and boat dives available around the Yorke Peninsula.

A popular destination with holidaymakers, the rather dry and barren peninsula has many wonderful beaches and small towns along its length. Charter boats and compressed air are available in a few locations on this rugged strip of land.

Map: Yorke Peninsula — Wallaroo, Kadina, Moonta, Port Wakefield, White Rock, Maitland, Ardrossan, Dublin, Spencer Gulf, WARDANG I., Moorara Wreck, Yorke Peninsula, Pine Point, Port Rickaby, Port Julia, Minlaton, Port Vincent, Gulf St Vincent, Stansbury, Yorketown, Adelaide, Port Giles Jetty, Marion Wreck, Edithburgh Jetty, Troubridge Shoal, The Gap, Stenhouse Bay, Iron King Wreck, Clan Ranald Wreck, ALTHORPE Is., McLaren Vale. N, 0 10 20 30 Kilometers.

one over 50 m long. Take a torch to reveal the colorful sponges, gorgonians and ascidians on the walls of the cave, and the resident boarfish, bullseyes, blue devilfish, morwong and wobbegongs.

Port Giles Jetty
This is another wonderful jetty dive with masses of color on each pylon, and even more fish than the Edithburgh Jetty. Commonly seen are boarfish, trevally, perch, morwong, bullseyes, yellowtail, sea horses and leafy sea dragons.

Clan Ranald Shipwreck
The battered remains of the *Clan Ranald*, which sank in 1909, now lie at 20 m. Many fish and invertebrates shelter in and around the wreckage.

The Gap
There are a number of interesting caves on this boulder reef, including

Althorpe Island
A trip out to Althorpe Island can be very rewarding when the weather allows. The rocky reefs around the island drop into 25 m of water, with many caves and gutters. Reef fish and invertebrates are abundant, and the occasional seal is seen.

Wardang Island
The remains of nine shipwrecks have been located around the island in depths ranging from 2–8 m. The *Moorara*, which sank in 1975, is the most complete. You can also explore rocky reefs and visit a sea lion colony at White Rock, at the northern end.

Shore and boat dives up to 20 minutes away

Generally 10–15 m

Tidal currents common

Rich sponge gardens

Fascinating pier dives

Good assortment of reef and pelagic fish

Rocky reefs

Spencer Gulf
Island-Hopping the Gulf

Live-aboard trip up to 12 hours offshore

Generally 15–20 m

Occasional current offshore

Sponge gardens and kelp beds

Excellent diving at Wedge and Pearson Islands

Reef fish and pelagic fish common

Rocky reefs

Numerous islands are scattered across the open waters at the southern end of the Spencer Gulf. A few of these islands are close enough to be visited on day trips, but most can only be reached by long-range, live-aboard boats. Fortunately there is such a boat—one of the most unique dive boats in all of Australia—the 35 m-long ketch *Falie*.

The two-masted ketch was built in 1919, and looks as if she just sailed out of the last century. She was brought to South Australia in 1922 to work as a general cargo ship. In 1982 she was taken out of service, and the South Australian government purchased the ship, giving her a complete refit. She now runs regular sailing and dive trips around the islands of South Australia.

Falie is available for charters to the Gambier Islands, the Sir Joseph Banks Group, the Neptune Islands (where they conduct great white shark cage trips) and the Investigator Group, way out in the Great Australian Bight.

Wedge Island
Some of the best diving in South Australia is found off Wedge Island, the largest of the Gambier Islands. Spectacular diving can be enjoyed off its rocky shores, in depths to 25 m. Countless boulders are scattered over the sea floor, forming gutters, ledges and caves. Take a flashlight to illuminate the brilliantly-colored sponges, gorgonians, zoanthids, soft corals, bryozoans and anemones which cover the walls of the caves. Blue devilfish, bullseyes, globefish and numerous species of invertebrates are often seen under the ledges and in the gutters. Leafy sea dragons, catsharks, stingrays, old wives, wobbegongs, morwong, harlequin fish, perch, wrasse, leatherjackets, seals and some large, friendly blue gropers are found on the rocky reef.

Sir Joseph Banks Group
Located only 25 km east of Tumby Bay on the Eyre Peninsula, the seventeen islands of the Sir Joseph Banks Group are best dived from a live-aboard vessel. Most of the islands offer interesting diving in depths to 20 m, and the wonderful marine life below the waves is almost matched by the animal life above. Shore visits are a must to see wallabies, Cape Barren geese, little penguins, lizards, snakes, sea eagles, ospreys, parrots and colonies of sleepy seals.

Spilsby Island
The largest island in the Sir Joseph Banks Group is Spilsby Island. The best dive sites are found on its southeastern side. Here the rocky reef supports vast numbers of fish,

including silver drummer, trevally, yellowtail, bullseyes, cowfish, blue groper, leatherjackets, wrasse, boarfish, zebrafish, sweep, blue groper and lots of morwong.

Stickney Island

The most exciting dive sites at Stickney Island are two narrow slots that cut through the center of the island. These slots are a photographer's dream—walls with sponges, gorgonians, soft corals and species such as nudibranchs, cowries, sea stars, feather stars and spider crabs. Many fish are attracted to the slot, typically morwong, bullseyes, boarfish, blue devilfish and old wives.

Pearson Island

One of the Investigator Group, Pearson Island is surrounded by wonderful dive sites in depths beyond 30 m. Countless kelp-covered boulders are found in the shallows, and sponge gardens deeper down. Seals are regularly seen, and seem to take great pleasure in accompanying divers. Harlequin fish, blue devilfish, morwong, perch, drummer, blue gropers and masses of wrasse and leatherjackets are common reef fish. You can also expect to find schools of pelagic fish, and solitary wobbegongs, rock lobsters and cat-

sharks hidden in caves and ledges. A shore visit to Pearson Island is well worth the effort. Many of the animals seen in the Sir Joseph Banks Groups are common here, plus the added bonus of seeing the rare Pearson Island wallaby, only found on this group of islands.

Langton Island

The Australian sea lions at Langton Island regularly swim with divers. Forget the scuba, as snorkeling allows more freedom when swimming with these playful creatures in only 2 m of water. Divers can perform somersaults with the seals, or play a game of chase. For really close encounters just lie on the bottom, and the seals will do the same. They may even come close enough to touch you with their whiskers.

Topgallant Island

Many walls and gutters provide exciting dive sites at Topgallant Island, in the Investigator Group. Around the rocky reef nudibranchs feed in the sponge gardens, bold blue devilfish guard their caves, rock lobsters rest, silver drummer school off the reef's edge, blue gropers look for a free feed and a marvellous variety of reef fish adds color to the seascape.

Opposite: Volutes have been heavily fished by professional shell divers in South Australia, which has led to species becoming endangered in many locations.
Michael Aw

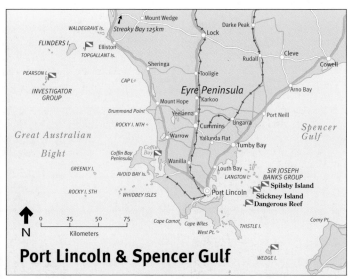

Port Lincoln & Spencer Gulf

Port Lincoln
Gateway to the "Great White"

Below: Unique to southern Australia, the weedy sea dragon (*Phyllopteryx taeniolatus*) is one of the most bizarre and unusual fishes in the sea.
Neville Coleman

Port Lincoln, famous for its tuna fleet, is a fishing town situated at the tip of the Eyre Peninsula. Many exciting dive sites can be found in the area. Don't worry about looking over your shoulder every few minutes since the chances of even seeing a great white shark are remote, unless you spearfish or catch a few rock lobsters or abalone. A number of dive shops in Port Lincoln run regular boat dives to many of the islands and reefs around the southern tip of the Eyre Peninsula.

Port Lincoln Town Jetty
Try a relaxing shore dive under the Town Jetty, in the center of Port Lincoln. Many of the pylons, in just 4 m of water, are festooned with sponges, anemones and ascidians. Typical marine life includes spider crabs, hermit crabs, octopi, sea stars, sea cucumbers, blennies, nudibranchs, shrimps, yellowtail, perch, leatherjackets, wrasse, goatfish, globefish, sweep and small

rock lobsters. A number of other jetties in the area, including the Tumby Bay Jetty, are also good dive sites. Other shore diving in the area requires a 4WD to reach the best spots, so boat dives are probably the best option.

Degei Shipwreck
This trawler lies in 11 m on the western side of Donington Island. The wreck has a good coverage of photographic subjects—invertebrates are plentiful, as well as old wives, leatherjackets, scorpionfish, boarfish, bullseyes and cuttlefish.

Taylors Island
The boulder-strewn bottom provides a number of exciting dive sites around Taylors Island. The many swim-throughs and gutters are occupied by morwong, perch, old wives, boarfish, blue gropers and rock lobsters. At a maximum depth of 12 m are many small caves lined with sponges and gorgonians.

 Shore and boat dives up to 30 minutes away

 Generally 10–15 m

 Slight currents

 Sponge gardens and kelp

 Hundreds of islands to dive

 Good numbers of reef and pelagic fish

 Rocky reefs

Hopkins Island

The shallow waters around Hopkins Island are a great place to dive with sea lions. As soon as divers arrive, many curious sea lions leave the beach, and join them in the water. Some of these magnificent animals seem to enjoy out-performing the visitors, and others are just as happy to lie on the bottom and ponder the divers. There are a number of interesting sites around Hopkins Island, including a pinnacle off the southwest tip of the island. Masses of boulders rise from 30–4 m, and form endless caves and swim-throughs. The caves are lined with particularly colorful sponges and gorgonians, and are home to old wives, bullseyes, blue devilfish and morwong.

Dangerous Reef

There is probably some excellent diving around Dangerous Reef, but for the last thirty years the only people game enough to dive here have done so in shark cages. Today many visit the reef, famous for its great white sharks, and hope to see one from the safety of the underwater viewing platform.

Cape Wiles

The spectacular sheltered lagoon at Cape Wiles, 30 km south of Port Lincoln, is accessible only by boat. The rocky bottom varies in depth from 6–15 m, and the many small caves found here are packed with invertebrate life. On the reef are rock lobsters, morwong, blue gropers, harlequin fish, drummer, cuttlefish, blue devilfish, perch and sometimes an occasional fur seal.

Coffin Bay

Located 50 km northwest of Port Lincoln are the picturesque waters of Coffin Bay. The area is best accessed by 4WD, and then explored from the shore or by boat. The rocky reefs and nearby islands support a wealth of marine life.

Elliston

The town of Elliston, located 150 km northwest of Port Lincoln, could easily be listed as a dive destination, except for the lack of dive facilities. Those with their own boat can visit the reefs, teeming with marine life, situated around the many offshore islands. Divers who have explored these report incredible underwater terrain, and regular encounters with seals, dolphins and many species of fish.

Streaky Bay

An area famous for its mainland population of Australian sea lions, Streaky Bay is located 125 km northwest of Elliston. The colony can be found at Point Labatt, which involves a climb down a cliff face, possible in scuba gear for those desperate for a dive.

WESTERN AUSTRALIA

Introducing Western Australia

The "State of Excitement"

The search for pearls lured the first divers to the waters off Western Australia. Pearl oysters thrive in the warm waters along the northern beaches of Australia's largest state, and during the last century this discovery attracted thousands of Japanese, Chinese, Filipinos and Malays to a number of towns north of Shark Bay. Broome was the heart of the pearl diving industry, and in the boom years between 1890 and 1910, over 2000 Japanese lived in the town. Many returned to Japan as wealthy men, but over 900 of the divers were not so lucky, and were buried in the Japanese cemetery in Broome. A handful of divers still work in the industry, however the great majority of pearls are now cultured, seeded by a small bead of mother-of-pearl.

Today many attractions bring divers to Western Australia—particularly the annual gathering of whale sharks off Ningaloo Reef. Other excellent dive experiences include exploration of the exceptional complex of caves under the Nullarbor Plain, the islands and reefs of Esperance and Albany, the limestone reefs and shipwrecks of Rottnest Island, the species-rich coral reefs of Ningaloo and Shark Bay, and the live-aboard diving off the Houtman Abrolhos, Monte Bello Islands and the North West Shelf. Offshore, the island territories of Christmas Island and the Cocos (Keeling) Islands have been recently opened up to visitors.

Western Australia has the most varied marine environment of all the Australian states. In the southern temperate waters grow dense, colorful sponge gardens where seals, giant cuttlefish, leafy sea dragons, harlequin fish and a host of other interesting species are found. Coral reefs and isolated atolls flourish in the warmer waters off the northern coasts, where dugongs, sea snakes, turtles, reef sharks, manta rays and a range of tropical fish and invertebrates are common. An interesting mixture of tropical and temperate species is found off the mid-coast of Western Australia, in the warm water carried down the coast by the Leeuwin Current.

Western Australia has a massive 12,500 km coastline, and covers an area of 2.5 million sq km, most of which is desert. While the southwest corner of the state is

Opposite: Although the waters off central and northwestern Australia are often clear and visibility may at times exceed 25 m, it may be somewhat less on inshore reefs depending on conditions and tidal flow. *Neville Coleman*

Below: One of the excellent dive areas around the island, Fishhook Bay at Rottnest Island is a sheltered area perfect for snorkeling or gaining experience at scuba diving. *Neville Coleman*

WEST. AUSTRALIA   INTRODUCTION

231

Above: The discovery of the local underwater flora and fauna around Esperance, Albany and Denmark has only begun. During spring the granite landscapes and long, sandy beaches are bordered by a brilliant array of native wildflowers. *Neville Coleman*

lush and green, with lovely pastures and dense forest, the rest of the state is dominated by the Nullarbor Plain, Great Victoria Desert, Gibson Desert and Great Sandy Desert. The first Europeans to explore the Western Australian coastline were the Dutch, who found the country dry and inhospitable. Settlement of the state was delayed until 1829, when a small colony was established on the banks of the Swan River, the site of present-day Perth. However, the development of the state was slow, due to its isolation and vast size. The southern town of Albany was established soon afterward, and became the first port of call for ships crossing the Indian Ocean, but the rest of the state did not expand until gold was discovered in the 1890s. Mining is still one the state's major industries.

Western Australia has a steadily growing population approaching 2 million, and because of its rela-

tive isolation, there are still endless opportunities for small business ventures. The great majority of the population lives in Perth, the state's capital, situated on the bank of the Swan River. Perth is a young city with plenty of attractions, including museums, parklands, historic buildings, the Perth Zoo, markets and beautiful sandy beaches. Travel to and from Perth is quite expensive by either plane, train or bus. While there are good sealed roads across the Nullarbor Plain and up the coastline to Darwin, the interior of the state is best explored by 4WD.

For the more adventurous, Western Australia has many spectacular national parks and rugged areas to explore. The desert (or outback) is well worth a look—especially after rain as wildflowers bloom in abundance. Caves, rainforests, low mountain ranges, deep gorges, rivers, lakes and meteor craters are found in the national parks and wilderness areas across the state.

Western Australia experiences a wide range of climatic conditions. Summer sees monsoons and cyclones in the north and warm dry conditions in the south, while winter is cool and wet in the south, but dry and warm in the north. The air temperature varies from of 10–25° C in the south to 20–35° C in the north. For divers, the best time to visit the north of the state is over winter, and the south over summer. Water temperature ranges from 13–20° C in the south to 20–28° C in the north.

The dive industry in Western Australia is still developing, and many local divers still spend most their time hunting fish and rock lobsters. Only a handful of marine parks exist in the state, but these protect some of the most popular diving areas such as Ningaloo Reef, Shark Bay, Rottnest Island, the Houtman Abrolhos and Rowley Shoals. While many dive shops and charter boats service the major centers, many small towns such as Bremer Bay and Lancelin, have exceptional dive sites offshore that are only accessible to divers with their own boats.

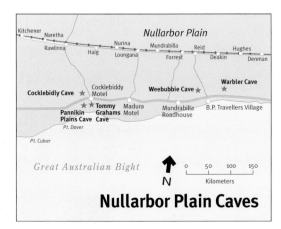

Nullarbor Plain
Under the Desert: Exciting Cave Diving

When driving from the eastern states to Perth, one has to cross the arid Nullarbor Plain. This vast dry desert is only sparsely dotted with vegetation, and is the last place anyone would expect to find caves full of clear water. But lying 90 m under the desert is a huge artesian basin offering the most exceptional cave diving in the world.

Although the location of the Nullarbor Plain caves has been known for many years by the Aborigines who decorated them with numerous rock paintings, the caves were not explored by divers until 1963. At least 11 of the caves contain water, but only eight provide exciting diving.

Diving any cave requires specialist training, and these caves are no different. Sound caving knowledge is required just to reach many of the lakes. For advice and information on diving the Nullarbor Plain caves, you should contact the Cave Divers Association of Australia (CDAA).

Cocklebiddy Cave

Undoubtedly the most famous cave under the Nullarbor Plain is Cocklebiddy Cave. Since the early seventies many expeditions have visited the cave, in an attempt to find its end. In that time several records were set for the longest cave dive in the world, culminating in 1983 when an Australian team pushed the distance traveled within the cave to the current record of 6090 m—with no end to the cave in sight. This spectacular cave has tunnels 30 m wide in places, and two dry rockpiles, where divers camp overnight. The visibility is limited only by the power of one's flashlight.

Pannikin Cave

In 1988 an expedition of Australian cave divers made headlines around the world, when they became trapped in the Pannikin Plains Cave after a freak storm. They had just located the end of the cave, 3000 m from the entrance, when the storm struck. Much gear was lost and 13 members of the expedition were trapped for 30 hours, before a new exit could be found. Luckily no one was seriously injured, but now the cave can no longer be dived because of the instability of the entrance.

Warbler Cave

A shallow cave, only 10 m deep, with large caverns and an underground air chamber.

Weebubbie Cave

Massive tunnels are a feature of Weebubbie Cave, some of which are 20 m in diameter. Two lakes have been reported and an air chamber 160 m into the cave.

Awkward descents over loose boulders

Virtually unlimited

Nil

Nil

Massive caves and clear water

Only the occasional fossil

Limestone caves

Below: Sinkholes leading down to freshwater pools and underground rivers are features along the barren but not quite treeless Nullarbor Plain. *Neville Coleman*

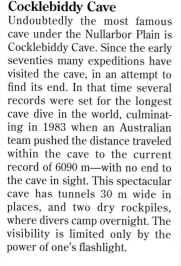

Shore and boat dives up to 1 hour away

Generally 15–20 m

Some offshore currents

Rich sponge gardens and kelp beds

Sanko Harvest shipwreck. Unlimited islands and reefs to explore

Reef and pelagic fish abundant

Rocky reefs and pinnacles

Esperance
Over 280 Islands and Twice as Many Reefs

Below: Common off southwestern Australia are the sea stars (*Nepanthia troughtoni*) and the biscuit star (*Pentagonaster duebeni*)—seen here in its orange form typical of the area.
Neville Coleman

The captain of the 33,000-ton bulk cargo ship, *Sanko Harvest*, would rather forget Valentine's Day 1991. While taking a short cut through the uncharted waters off Esperance, the ship struck a hidden reef and began to take on water. Hopes were high that the vessel and her cargo of phosphate could be saved. But when a wild storm blew up the next day, she was battered on more rocks, broke in half, and sank. Oil leaked from the wreck, polluting pristine beaches and killing dozens of sea birds and seals. However quick action from volunteers and the authorities averted a major disaster.

Today the 174 m-long wreck sits in 30–40 m of water, with the bridge resting 50 m away from the hull. Only experienced divers should attempt the dive, as one has to avoid twisted, sharp metal, dangling wires, and disorientation on this large wreck site. Divers can explore the bridge area, the engine room and the tower cranes. The hull now has a covering of kelp, anemones, sponges and sea tulips. Reef fish usually found on the wreck include boarfish, bullseyes, blue gropers, morwong, sweep, perch and yellowtail.

Esperance is located 725 km southeast of Perth. The town offers a wide range of accommodation. Servicing the area is the Esperance Diving Academy which runs regular day and live-aboard trips to the Archipelago of the Recherche and the numerous sites off Esperance.

Over 280 islands, and probably twice as many reefs, make up the Archipelago of the Recherche Nature Reserve. This mass of granite islands and reefs stretches for 230 km parallel to the coastline, and is famous for its wildlife above and below the water. While most of these islands are only accessible to a live-aboard boat, closer to Esperance are many excellent shore and boat dives.

Esperance Jetty

About 1 km in length, with a few sections missing, the Esperance Jetty provides brilliant diving in depths ranging from 6–12 m. Photographers will find an incredible assortment of photo subjects, whether using a macro or wide-angle lens. Countless small fish

swarm under the structure, including schools of old wives, leatherjackets, globefish, silver drummer, sea horses, pipefish, gobies, boxfish, anglerfish, blennies, southern coral fish, scorpionfish, wrasse and perch. Each wooden pylon is crammed with soft corals, sponges, gorgonians, and ascidians. On and around the sea floor are spider crabs, sea stars, brittle stars, flatworms, nudibranchs, shrimps, feather stars, octopi, sea cucumbers, cuttlefish and hermit crabs. A number of sea lions reside near the jetty, and will sometimes follow divers around.

Lion Island

Numerous boulders shape the terrain around Lion Island, creating gutters, swim-throughs, ledges and caves. Kelp dominates the shallows, and sponges, soft corals, sea tulips, ascidians, hard corals and gorgonians cover the bottom. Again, photographers will find many subjects—nudibranchs, octopi, hermit crabs, sea stars, rock lobsters, cuttlefish, basket stars and a wide variety of reef fish.

Cape Le Grand

Although some areas around Cape Le Grand are accessible from the shore, the tip of the cape is best dived from a boat. Here large boulders tumble down to the reef in 30 m of water. Around the boulders live leafy sea dragons, blue devilfish, boarfish, bullseyes, yellowtail, silver drummer, harlequin fish, leatherjackets, blue gropers, morwong, perch, scorpionfish and many invertebrate species.

Long Island

The most popular of a number of dive sites around Long Island is the wreck of the trawler *Lapwing*, in 30 m of water. The wreck is mostly intact and covered with soft corals and sponges. Nearby is a rocky reef with reef fish and an occasional leafy sea dragon.

Remark Island

Similar to many of the islands in the Archipelago of the Recherche, Remark Island offers a variety of diving experiences. The northern side of the island is shallow and sheltered—a haven for reef fish and invertebrates. The exposed southern side drops into 50 m of water, where you will find many ledges and caves. The terrain in deeper water has a dense covering of sponges, gorgonians, soft corals and an occasional black coral tree. Typical fish life includes blue groper, morwong, boarfish, harlequin fish, blue devilfish, silver drummer, yellowtail, bullseyes and schools of pelagic fish. Seals appear at the most unexpected times, as colonies are located on many of the outer islands. Divers may also be lucky enough to see dolphins, or a southern right whale during wintertime.

Below: Found only in south and southwest Australia, the spiny-tail leatherjacket *(Acanthaluteres brownii)* is seen regularly on the wreck of the *Cheynes III* in depths of 20–25 m. The individual shown here is male, in full-color display. *Neville Coleman*

Shore and boat dives up to 20 minutes away

Generally 15–20 m

Offshore currents

Colorful sponge gardens and kelp beds

Cheynes III wreck. Countless islands and reefs to explore

Prolific reef and pelagic fish

Rocky reefs and pinnacles

Albany
Exploring a Whale Chaser's Grave

The town of Albany, located 410 km south of Perth, was established in 1826 on the sheltered shores of King George Sound. It soon became Western Australia's premier port and the first point of call for sailing ships crossing the Indian Ocean. The port of Fremantle was opened in 1901, and the town was forgotten until 1947, when Albany became Australia's major whaling port. During the next 31 years, thousands of sperm and humpback whales were slaughtered. Whaling was banned in 1978.

Whaleworld, a museum located in the old Cheynes Beach Whaling Station, reflects on the town's whaling days. Its main attraction is the former whale chaser, *Cheynes IV*, but its sister ship is usually of more interest to divers.

The 47 m-long *Cheynes III*, scuttled as an artificial reef off the western side of Michaelmas Island in 1982, lies in 23 m of water. Around the wreck live boarfish, morwong, blue gropers, bullseyes, old wives, perch, snapper, jewfish, silver drummer, kingfish, samsonfish and leatherjackets. Although the hull is beginning to break up, you can still explore the wheelhouse and engine room. Nearly all of the structure is encrusted with sponges, soft corals, anemones and other invertebrates.

Numerous excellent dive sites can be enjoyed around Albany, on the reefs and islands that dot the coastline. The best conditions for diving are usually experienced during autumn, when the seas are calm and the water clear. This popular tourist region has an excellent range of accommodation and places to eat.

Mistaken Island
The rocky reefs around Mistaken Island provide some of the best shore dives in the area. The depth of the reef varies from 5–12 m, with the best marine life found on the deeper southern side—sponge gardens with nudibranchs, octopi, shrimp, boxfish, morwong, cuttlefish, crabs, sea stars, leatherjackets, scorpionfish, gobies, blennies, pipefish and wrasse.

Michaelmas Island
Granite boulders lined with kelp, sponges, gorgonians, sea tulips, ascidians and soft corals surround the island, and drop into depths of 20–30 m. Many reef fish and invertebrates live around the boulders—boarfish,

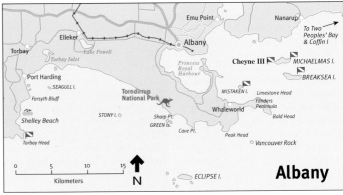

blue gropers, morwong, sea stars, nudibranchs, harlequin fish, wrasse, leatherjackets and scalyfin. Ledges shelter rock lobsters, bullseyes, blue devilfish, cuttlefish and globefish.

Breaksea Island

Most sites off Breaksea Island are similar to those found at Michaelmas Island. For those interested in an interesting deep dive, the southern side of the island plummets into 40 m of water. Along this wall are plenty of caves and dazzling sponge gardens where a few black coral trees can be found. Abundant reef fish and invertebrates are permanent residents, while regular visitors to the area include schools of pelagic kingfish, samsonfish and trevally.

Two People Bay

The beaches around Albany are absolutely fantastic, and those at Two People Bay are no exception. The best dive sites are on the boulder reefs offshore from Little Beach and Waterfall Beach. These rocky reefs drop down to 15 m, and have a surprising variety of invertebrates. Around the boulders live old wives, wrasse, leatherjackets, scalyfin, harlequin fish, morwong, perch and the occasional leafy sea dragon.

Coffin Island

Just south of Two People Bay, Coffin Island offers several dives on rocky reefs with caves, gutters, sponge gardens and abundant marine life. Divers usually come to swim with the colonies of Australian sea lions and New Zealand fur seals that reside in the sheltered areas along the island's shoreline. Although a little shy when divers first arrive, they soon zoom around the visitors, performing acrobatics and posing for brilliant photos.

Torbay Head

Similar to many dive sites in the area, the granite boulders at Torbay Head tumble into 30 m. These boulders, covered with sponges, soft coral and gorgonians, form many caves and gutters where numerous species of reef fish can be seen.

Bremer Bay

Located 180 km east of Albany, Bremer Bay has excellent dive sites, but lacks diving facilities. Trips are sometimes run to Bremer Bay, and especially to Glasse Island. The island is surrounded with colorful reefs, inhabited by masses of fish and seals.

Above: An underwater photographer scanning the sea grass meadows of Two People Bay, Albany in search of elusive sea dragons.
Neville Coleman

Augusta
A Wild and Unexplored Coast

 Shore and boat dives up to 20 minutes away

 Generally 10–15m

 Strong offshore currents

 Mixture of sponge gardens and kelp beds

 Number of untouched reefs and islands

Reef and pelagic fish common

Rocky reefs and pinnacles

The numerous islands and reefs found between Cape Leeuwin and Cape Naturaliste are packed with large fish, rock lobsters and dense, colorful sponge gardens. Because of the large swells which crash onto the rocky coastline for much of the year, this region remains one of the least explored areas of southern Western Australia. During the calmer autumn months, however, divers can enjoy the many great dive sites. Dive shops in Augusta and Margaret River offer charter trips and invaluable tips on the local dive scene.

Seal Island

The many gutters and ledges along the rocky bottom, at a depth of just 12 m, are lined with soft corals, sponges, gorgonians and ascidians. Rock lobsters, crabs, shrimp, blue devilfish, cuttlefish, nudibranch and even the elusive Western Australian jewfish are found under the overhangs. Many reef fish can usually be seen around the reef, as well as schools of pelagic visitors such as samson-fish, kingfish and trevally.

Groper Bay

One of a number of interesting shore dives in the area is the rock hop at Groper Bay. At 12 m, on a rocky reef with a thick coverage of kelp, are leatherjackets, sea stars, wrasse, morwong, scorpionfish, bullseyes, nudibranchs, globefish and a few rock lobsters.

St Alouarn & Flinders Is

A few kilometers off Cape Leeuwin, the exposed rocky outcrops known as St Alouarn and Flinders Island offer spectacular diving when conditions allow. Divers report brilliant sponge gardens surrounding the islands. Jewfish, morwong, snapper, blue gropers, samsonfish, kingfish and many other species are common. Seals occasionally visit the area, and there have been reports of bronze whalers and great white sharks as well.

Cumberland Shipwreck

Cape Leeuwin has always had a bad reputation among mariners. Shallow reefs and rough weather have claimed over a dozen ships, including the *Cumberland* (1830), the remains of which were discovered in 1981. The wreck is scattered in depths from 3–8 m on a rocky, kelp-covered reef. You will find anchors, some of the timber hull, cannons and other artifacts among the kelp.

Augusta & Geographe Bay

Cape Naturaliste
Sugarloaf Rock
The Indicators
Canal Rocks
Cape Clairault
Cowaramup
Margaret River
Prevelly Park
Witchcliffe
Karridale
Cumberland Wreck
Augusta
Grouper Bay
Cape Leeuwin
N

Geographe Bay
Eagle Bay
Busselton Jetty
Ludlow
Busselton
Jarrahwood
Margaret River
Blackwood River
Alexandra Bridge
Kudardup
Flinders Bay
Seal Island
St Alouarn Island

0   10   20   30
Kilometers

Geographe Bay
Under the Busstleton Jetty

Shore and boat
dives up to
15 minutes away

Generally 10–15 m

Some offshore
currents

Brilliant coral and
sponge gardens

Busselton Jetty

Good collection of
reef and pelagic fish

Rocky reefs

Almost two kilometers long, the **Busselton Jetty** is one of Western Australia's most popular dive sites. Diving is good anywhere along the length of the structure, but the best area is found towards the end of the jetty—which involves a long walk or a short boat ride. Once in the water, you will find a jungle of pylons in only 8 m of water. Each pylon supports a mass of colorful soft corals, sponges, ascidians, gorgonians, bryozoans and anemones. A closer inspection reveals an incredible variety of nudibranchs, shrimp, sea stars, brittle stars, feather stars, sea cucumbers, hermit crabs, spider crabs, gobies, blennies, scorpionfish, anglerfish, lionfish and boxfish. Schools of old wives, silver drummer, trevally, bullseye, and yellowtail engulf sections of the jetty, joined sometimes by larger pelagic fish. The weedy bottom supports fiddler rays, globefish, octopi, wrasse, cuttlefish, leatherjackets, flatheads, southern coral fish, stingrays and harlequin fish. If diving the jetty during the day sounds great, by night the area is a fantastic world of color and movement.

The sheltered waters of Geographe Bay, 230 km south of Perth, provide a great weekend escape with plenty of shore and boat dives. This wide bay is usually calm, except in occasional strong northerly winds during the winter months. Around Busselton and Bunbury, a favorite area with many divers, a number of dive shops offer boat trips to the best sites.

The Indicators
A number of colorful coral and sponge gardens can be found around The Indicators, in depths from 20–30 m. Walls, caves and gutters teem with a variety of reef fish and invertebrates, plus the occasional school of kingfish and samsonfish.

Canal Rocks
The inner side of Canal Rocks is accessible from the shore. Gutters and ledges at 14 m are full of small fish and invertebrates. The rocky reef on the outer side of Canal Rocks—which drops into 25 m—is best dived from a boat. Out here are sponge gardens and a good variety of reef and pelagic fish.

Eagle Bay
Numerous rocky, coral-covered reefs are scattered along the shallow bottom of Eagle Bay. From the shore, divers can access a number of these reefs, including one massive coral head at 10 m. Marine life is plentiful, and includes wobbegongs, stingrays, jewfish, cuttlefish and rock lobsters.

The Ledge
The whole of Geographe Bay is quite shallow, but a few kilometers out a ledge at 18 m runs parallel to the coast. Diving anywhere along the ledge is exciting, as masses of reef and pelagic fish gather there.

Below: The black-banded sea perch (*Hypoplectrodes nigrorubrum*) is a bottom-dwelling species which often sits out in full view during the day, relying on its immobile behavior to catch prey. *Neville Coleman*

GEOGRAPHE BAY

WEST. AUSTRALIA

LEEUWIN CURRENT
Great for diving

WHEN EXPLORING THE REEFS OFF THE SOUTHERN coast of Western Australia for the first time, most divers are surprised to see corals and tropical fish flourishing at latitudes so far south. The water may also be a few degrees warmer than one would expect, especially during winter. This is most noticeable off Perth, where the waters around Rottnest Island can be several degrees warmer than along the mainland coast. A warm ocean current—the Leeuwin Current—travels down from the tropical north, and brings many surprises to divers in the south.

Little is known about the Leeuwin Current. About 50 km wide and 300 m deep,

tropical fish rely on the warm Leeuwin Current for survival. The current also extends the range of the western rock lobster, making the lobster fishery one of the most productive fisheries in Western Australia. Turtles are found in southern waters over winter, and even sea snakes are occasionally seen. The Leeuwin Current allows dugongs to feed year round in Shark Bay, instead of having to migrate up the coast in search of warm water during winter.

While this warm current brings many tropical species to the marine environment along the southern coasts of Western Australia, it may also be responsible for the dry

The Leeuwin Current supports a diverse array of invertebrates, many of which still remain unidentified. *Neville Coleman*

it originates in Indonesian waters, and swings down the west coast in autumn and winter. The current varies in strength each year, but speeds of up to 3 knots have been recorded. The current continues for about five months, flowing down the coast between the continental shelf and the mainland, and around Cape Leeuwin to terminate in the Great Australian Bight.

This unusual current has no equal. All other continents in the southern hemisphere are influenced by north-bound currents that bring cool water, and restrict the growth of corals to the region around the equator. The only current to have a similar effect is the south-bound current from the Great Barrier Reef, which washes the eastern seaboard of Australia. However this current swings east toward New Zealand when it reaches the northern coast of New South Wales.

Many creatures such as coral polyps and

conditions that effect most of the state. Northbound cold currents help to create fogs and rain clouds off South America and Africa, however the warm waters of the Leeuwin Current do little to encourage rainfall across the state for much of the year.

The current is probably most enjoyed by divers, who experience warm, clear water during the winter months at many locations. While effects of the current can be seen off Esperence and Albany, the phenomenon is really obvious in the offshore area between Geographe Bay and Geraldton. Here exists prolific hard and soft corals, and many tropical fish and invertebrates that would usually be associated with northern waters. This little-understood current makes Western Australian diving unique.

Perth
Dive Sites for All Tastes

Shore and boat dives up to 20 minutes away

Offshore 5–15 m, inshore 5–10 m

Some offshore currents

Kelp and sponge gardens

Marmion & Shoalwater Islands Marine Parks. Soft-bottom diving in Cockburn Sound

Good collection of reef and pelagic fish

Limestone reefs

The diving off Perth is varied—a range of brilliant sites can be enjoyed along the coastline, even if the visibility is not always perfect. Offshore limestone reefs and islands are packed with colorful reef fish and invertebrates. Australian sea lions, common on some of these islands, are regularly seen at many dive sites. The reefs are littered with shipwrecks. Some, still intact, make fascinating diving. The majority of sites are located within the Shoalwater Islands Marine Park and the Marmion Marine Park, so are protected for all to enjoy. Another unique diving experience is the soft bottom of Cockburn Sound, where visibility can be quite good during autumn and winter.

Perth is a beautiful city, with a population of over 1 million, and has much to offer apart from diving. All divers should visit the Western Australian Maritime Museum, at Fremantle—on the coast 18 km west of Perth. The museum has artifacts on display, and information on the numerous shipwrecks located along the Western Australian coastline.

A number of dive shops are located in the city and suburbs of Perth, and on any weekend dozens of dive boats service the region.

Murray Reefs

A line of reefs off Mandurah, known as the Murray Reefs, offer interesting diving in depths to 6 m. Residents of these shallow limestone reefs include rock lobsters, jewfish, samsonfish, trevally, kingfish and large numbers of reef fish. The remains of the *James Service*, a three-masted barque which ran aground in 1878, are scattered over the southern-most reef in the group.

Five Fathom Bank

Running parallel to the coast for 30 km, Five Fathom Reef is another shallow reef complex, only 12 m deep, providing excellent diving. These limestone reefs have numerous caves and ledges lined with ascidians, sponges, soft corals and gorgonians—where the usual cuttlefish, octopi, nudibranchs, sea stars, leatherjackets, perch, morwong, blue devilfish, bullseyes, wobbegongs and rock lobsters can

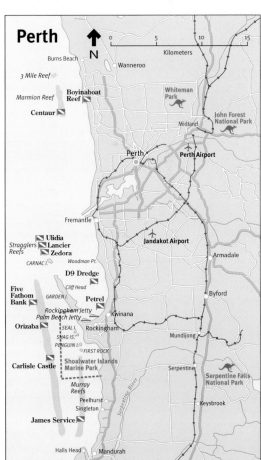

Palm Beach Jetty

Located in the sheltered waters of Cockburn Sound, the Palm Beach Jetty offers good shore diving to 5 m. Around the jetty pylons are quite a variety of small marine creatures, including spider crabs, shrimp, pipefish, blennies, boxfish, nudibranchs sea horses, and sea cucumbers.

Rockingham Jetty

Although diving under the existing Rockingham Jetty is interesting, the best diving is around the collapsed section, which drops into 18 m of water. There is also a small artificial reef here and a good variety of marine creatures. Commonly seen are stingarees, sea horses, pipefish, nudibranchs, sea stars, crabs, morwong, scorpionfish, sea pens, sea cucumbers, stripeys, anemones, blennies, globefish and southern coralfish.

Above: Common to south Western Australia, the western footballer sweep (*Neatypus obliques*) generally occurs in small schools over reefs down to 25 m. *Neville Coleman*

be found. The *Carlisle Castle* (1899) and the *Orizaba* (1886), two ships which ran aground on the reef, are now popular dive sites. Little remains of the *Carlisle Castle*, except for its cargo of bricks, an anchor and other small artifacts, however, the 140 m-long *Orizaba* is easily recognizable as a ship. Much of the hull can be explored—the bow, the boilers, the drive shaft and large sections of plates.

Seal Island

Located in the center of the Shoalwater Islands Marine Park, Seal Island is a great place for a swim with Australian sea lions. At least a dozen of these wonderful mammals live on the island, and often enter the shallow water to swim with divers. These underwater clowns make wonderful photo subjects and amusing dive companions.

Cape Peron

Shore diving is very popular at Cape Peron, on the large limestone reef offshore. There is much to see, even though the water never gets much deeper than 7 m. The reef is covered with kelp, sponges, ascidians, gorgonians, soft corals, nudibranchs, cuttlefish, sea stars, sea cucumbers, crabs and shrimp. Reef fish are generally small—species often seen include leatherjackets, gobies, wrasse, morwong, scorpionfish, bullseyes, yellowtail, boxfish and scalyfin.

MV Petrel Shipwreck

Accessible from the shore, the steam tug *Petrel* provides an interesting wreck dive. The 15 m-long ship lies in 14 m of water, and is usually surrounded by schools of yellowtail and bullseyes. Living on the soft bottom around the wreck are soft corals, anemones, sea pens, sea cucumbers, nudibranchs and other invertebrates.

D9 Dredge Shipwreck

This 30 m-long *D9 Dredge* sank in 1962, and now lies at a depth of 13 m. A popular boat dive, the dredge is essentially intact, and can be entered at a number of points, but only with the proper training and equipment. Around the dredge are cuttlefish, stingarees, globefish, sea horses, old wives, yellowtail, bullseyes, nudibranchs and shrimp. The wreck is covered in anemones, soft corals, ascidians and sponges. Watch out for the silt.

Woodman Point

Shore diving is possible on the limestone groyne at Woodman Point. The reef drops to 8 m where there are plenty of photographic subjects —sea horses, anemones, sea stars, nudibranchs, tube worms, boxfish and gobies.

Carnac Island

A number of good dive sites are found around Carnac Island in only 4–7 m of water. The reef has many caves and gutters, occupied by a wide range of reef fish and invertebrates. Divers can also dive with sea lions, as a small colony resides on the western side of the island.

Marmion Reef

One of a number of reefs in the Marmion Marine Park, Marmion Reef provides exceptional diving in depths varying from 6–10 m. The limestone reef has countless ledges and caves covered with sponges, soft coral and gorgonians. A wide variety of marine life can be found on every dive, including nudibranchs, leatherjackets, blue devilfish, sea stars, lionfish, stingarees, morwong, samsonfish, trevally, bullseyes, wrasse and

rock lobsters. At the southern end of the reef lie the scattered remains of the *Centaur*, which sank in 1874. Look among the kelp for the metal plating and ribs, and the cargo of lead ore.

Straggler Reefs

This shallow system of reefs has claimed many ships heading into Fremantle port. The *Lancier* (1839) and *Zedora* (1875) are found at 8 m. The 91 m-long sailing ship, the *Ulidia* (1893), lies at 3–6 m with the bow structure intact, and can be explored in calm conditions.

Boyinaboat Reef

This small reef has been accessible from shore, since the Hilary Boat Harbour was built in 1987. The shallow reef supports a good population of reef fish, including morwong, perch, old wives, bullseyes, leatherjackets, wobbegongs and silver drummer. This is another good spot for macro-photography, with plenty of colorful corals, nudibranchs, cuttlefish, cowries, tube worms, shrimp, crabs and sea stars. There are ten plaques placed around the reef, part of the Marmion Marine Park, to inform divers about the area.

Below: The limestone reefs located in Cockburn Sound, around Rottnest Island, and off the coast are known for their caves, swimthroughs and ledges, packed with marine life. *Neville Coleman*

Boat dives usually 15 minutes away, or 1 hr from Fremantle

Commonly 15–20 m

Slight currents and surge

Wonderful coral and sponge gardens

Numerous shallow reefs and wrecks

Good variety of reef and pelagic fish

Limestone reefs

Rottnest Island
Perth's Popular Playground

Rottnest Island is located 18 km west of Perth. About 10 km long and 4 km wide, this marine reserve is ringed by sandy beaches and sheltered bays, and is surrounded by clear, warm water for most of the year. Thousands of people visit the island each week —to dive on its numerous reefs and wrecks, relax on its clean beaches, have a look at the famous quokkas (a rabbit-sized marsupial), and enjoy the natural beauty of the island.

The island's superb sites can be dived on a day trip from Fremantle— all dive operators in Perth offer regular trips—or you can book a stay on the island. A range of accommodation is available, centered around Thomson Bay, and there are daily boat dives.

Below: One of Rottnest Island's unique shallow water sights is the large colonies of *Pocillopora* corals. This area, known as Pocillopora Reef, is showing signs of die-off, but to date the reason is unknown. *Neville Coleman*

Thomson Bay
This shallow bay, where the wreck of the *Uribes* can be seen in 3 m of water, is popular with snorkelers. The 37 m-long ship sank in 1942, and today the outline of the hull is still very distinct.

Dyer Island
When the seas are calm on the southern side of Dyer Island, the remains of the *Lady Elizabeth* can be explored. Wrecked in 1878, the 49 m-long ship is an interesting dive in 7 m of water. The bow, foremast, mainmast, bollards, winches, plates and twisted beams can still be seen. Nearby lies the wreck of the *Raven* (1891), but little remains as most of the ship lies buried under the sand.

Parker Point
Lush coral gardens are found in 3 m of water on the reef around Parker Point, as well as abundant reef fish— silver drummer, sweetlips, butterfly-fish, morwongs, wrasse and scalyfins.

Strickland Bay
One of the most exciting dives at Rottnest is on the drop-off at Strickland Bay, where the reef drops from 7–18 m, with numerous ledges and caves. Sponges, ascidians, gorgonians, soft corals and hard corals are plentiful, as well as

reef fish and many invertebrate species. Divers also usually see kingfish, boarfish, samsonfish, jewfish and occasionally a green turtle.

Cape Vlaming

When conditions allow, Cape Vlaming provides spectacular diving. The reef drops to 26 m, and numerous caves and gutters are found along the wall. Take a flashlight to see the brilliant corals covering the walls of the caves shared by rock lobsters, blue devilfish, wobbegongs, shrimp, molluscs, cuttlefish and nudibranchs. Around the reef are a good variety of fish—including morwong, bullseyes, perch, cod, kingfish and leatherjackets.

Swirl Reef

Depths around Swirl Reef vary from 4–16 m. The ledges and caves found on this limestone reef, like most in the area, are home to many invertebrate species and harlequin fish, blue devilfish, rock lobsters and even a few Port Jackson sharks. Near the reef lies the wreck of the *Mira Flores*, which ran aground in 1886. The remains of the wreck are now scattered at 12 m, and many artifacts can still be found around the stern section which stands high off the bottom.

Above: The Transit Reefs have large schools of Woodward's pomfrets (*Schuetta woodwardi*) that school in the shallow water above the kelp in the late afternoon.
Neville Coleman

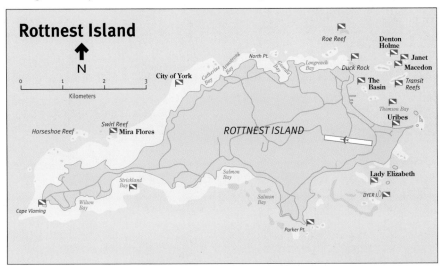

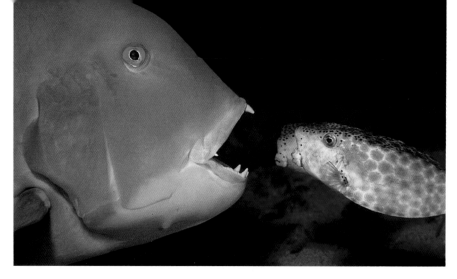

Above: A blue tusk-fish *(Choerudon cyanodus)* and a small-nosed boxfish come face-to-face. *Michael Aw*

Page 248: In the dim half-light beneath the ledges and in the crevasses live a whole range of various species of gorgonian sea fans, tunicates and sponges. *Neville Coleman*

Catherine Bay

On the numerous reefs that surround Catherine Bay, in depths to 7 m, are many caves and gutters covered in sponges and corals. Common are boxfish, wrasse, silver drummer, morwongs, lionfish, yellowtail, bullseyes, butterflyfish, blue devilfish, globefish, leatherjackets and numerous invertebrates. The remains of the *City of York* lie just off the bay in 7 m. Wrecked in 1899, much of the ship is now covered in kelp, but there is still plenty to see.

Transit Reefs

The Transit Reefs claimed three ships last century, the *Janet* (1887), the *Macedon* (1883) and the *Denton Holme* (1890). Although the reef is interesting to explore, with plenty of colorful corals and fish life, the wrecks provide the most excitement. The *Denton Holme* has broken up in 2–7 m of water, with the bow section rising high off the bottom. Pipes, bollards, masts, beams and plates lie scattered around the site. Little can be seen of the *Janet*, except for a boiler and anchor, while the 67 m-long *Macedon* is essentially intact. The hull lies in 6 m of water and makes a great wreck dive, especially when conditions are calm.

Roe Reef

In depths varying from 3–25 m are a number of interesting sites around Roe Reef. In caves and gutters, you are likely to find wobbegongs, stingrays, silver drummer, harlequin fish, cuttlefish, blue devilfish and reef fish.

Duck Rock

Many caves undercut the reefs around Duck Rock, in depths from 5–10 m. These are good places to see rock lobsters, stingrays, cuttlefish, octopi, and the occasional jewfish.

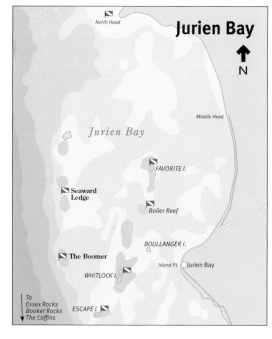

Jurien Bay

↑ N

North Head

Middle Head

Jurien Bay

FAVORITE I.

Seaward Ledge

Boiler Reef

BOULLANGER I.

The Boomer

Island Pt. Jurien Bay

WHITLOCK I.

To
Essex Rocks
Booker Rocks
The Coffins

ESCAPE I.

Jurien Bay
A Species-Rich Marine Reserve

Shore and boat dives up to 30 minutes away

Commonly 15–20 m

Slight currents

Wonderful coral and sponge gardens

Endless supply of reefs and islands

Interesting reef and pelagic fish

Limestone reefs

Since the construction of a marina complex at Jurien Bay in 1988 this large bay has really been opened up to divers. Before, the biggest challenge when diving the area was launching the dive boat on one of the many exposed ramps. But the effort was worthwhile, as Jurien Bay, just zoned as a marine reserve, boasts an incredible assortment of reefs and islands with wonderful dive sites.

This picturesque fishing port and holiday town (250 km north of Perth), offers a good range of accommodation. Jurien Bay Dive and Hire offers boat trips to the best sites in the bay.

Booker Rocks

On the limestone reefs at Booker Rocks (accessible from the shore), are reef fish, turtles, rock lobsters and the occasional sea lion, at depths from 4–10 m.

East West Edge

Some of the best coral growth in the area is found at the East West Ledge, which drops from 8–15 m. Sponges, hard corals, soft corals, gorgonians and tubastrea corals are plentiful. Reef residents also include rock lobsters, sea stars, nudibranchs, cuttlefish and a host of reef fish.

Seaward Ledge

Many large fish are attracted to the Seaward Ledge. This reef drops from 8–20 m, and has numerous caves and ledges. Commonly seen around the reef are kingfish, baldchin gropers, yellowtail, jewfish, tuna, trevally and sometimes turtles.

Below: Riotous coral growth, dominated by a magnificent plate-like species of *Acropora*. *Michael Aw*

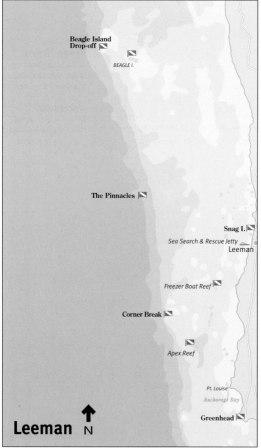

Leeman N

Boat Rock
Countless coral and sponge-lined caves inhabited by rock lobsters, stingrays and wobbegongs are found on the reefs around Boat Rock, at depths of up to 12 m.

Favourite Island
There are several great dive sites around Favourite Island. Caves and gutters, blanketed with sponge gardens and an abundance of marine life, occur in depths of 3–10 m. Sea lions live on the rocky shores and often join visitors for a swim. Turtles, gropers, rock lobsters, kingfish, jewfish, and a good range of reef fish and invertebrates are usually part of the underwater scenery.

North Head
The maze of limestone reefs off North Head can be explored from the shore or by boat. These reefs are located at 6–15 m, and have numerous caves inhabited by a wide variety of reef fish and invertebrates. A night dive in the area is magical—molluscs, echinoderms, crustaceans and sleeping fish are always seen.

Leeman

Western Australia's Next "Hot Spot"

Shore and boat
dives up to
20 minutes away

Generally 15–20 m

Slight currents

Mixture of coral and
sponge gardens

Sea lions of Beagle
Islands. Numerous
offshore reefs

Healthy populations
of reef and pelagic
fish

Limestone reefs

One of the most northern colonies of Australian sea lions is found on the **Beagle Islands**, in an area zoned as a marine reserve. This small group of islands is surrounded by limestone reefs well stocked with fish, molluscs and crustaceans, giving the sea lions a good selection of food. As soon as a dive boat pulls up near the islands, dozens of sea lions enter the water and approach the boat. Whether on snorkel or scuba, you will have a great time with the seals. The Beagle Islands are only one of the many new dive sites off Leeman, an area just recently opened up to divers.

The twin towns of Leeman and Greenhead are located 300 km north of Perth. Before the recent establishment of the Beagle Island Diving Company, few divers visited the numerous limestone reefs off this section of coastline. The dive shop now runs regular boat dives, and is part of a good self-contained holiday unit complex. Numerous excellent sites have been pioneered in the short time that trips have been organized to this fascinating maze of pretty limestone reefs.

Freezer Boat Reef

A brilliant collection of caves and swim-throughs, in only 14 m of water is located along the limestone bottom at Freezer Boat Reef. Inside the caves are gorgonians, sponges, tubastraea coral, ascidians, and the usual residents—rock lobsters, blue devilfish, bullseyes, wobbegongs and the more mobile invertebrates. Reef fish are abundant and divers are often surrounded by schools of buffalo bream.

Sea Search & Rescue Jetty

One of the best shore dives in the area is under the local rescue jetty, at only 4 m. Day or night, you will find plenty of reef fish and invertebrates. From the jetty a reef leads to Snag Island, where rock lobsters, wobbegongs and reef fish are common.

The Pinnacles

Rising from 20–10 m, The Pinnacles offer caves, ledges and swim-throughs, with rock lobsters, blue gropers, wobbegongs and baitfish. Pelagic fish constantly sweep the area, and there is a resident community of jewfish.

Beagle Islands Drop-off

Just west of the Beagle Islands, the reef drops from the surface to 25 m. Kingfish, trevally, samsonfish, snapper and other pelagic fish species are often seen along this wall, which is covered with hard and soft corals, and gorgonians—a haven for reef fish and invertebrates.

Below: Along the coast large numbers of the western rock lobster *(Panulirus cygnus)* may be seen beneath ledges and in caves. Western rock lobsters are the most prolific species of Australian rock lobster and can still be found in shallow waters.
Neville Coleman

Boat dives up to
30 minutes away

Commonly 10–15 m

Slight currents and
surge

Healthy coral and
sponge gardens

Countless unex-
plored reefs

Good variety of reef
and pelagic fish

Limestone reefs

Geraldton
Fantastic Limestone Reefs with Dramatic Caves and Crevasses

Most divers use Geraldton as a stepping stone to reach the spectacular islands and reefs of the Houtman Abrolhos. However these divers are by-passing a wealth of limestone reefs with caves and crevasses, and populations of reef and pelagic fish, rock lobsters and invertebrates. The best diving conditions occur from March to May, when the weather has settled and the seas are calm.

Point Moore
Many shore diving sites around Point Moore, on reefs at depths of 1–9 m, have moray eels, stingrays, rock lobsters, shrimp, nudibranchs, butterflyfish, cuttlefish, octopi, sea stars, coral trout, wrasse, scorpionfish and parrotfish.

Lighthouse Passage
This passage between two reefs attracts schooling fish. Regularly found in the channel are schools of buffalo bream, kingfish, trevally and samsonfish. Stingrays, turtles, gropers and a wide variety of reef fish are also often seen here. The reef at Lighthouse Passage, which drops to 18 m, is covered with soft corals and gorgonians.

Hells Gates
The reef at Hells Gates, sloping down to 18 m, is a good place to find rock lobsters, jewfish, kingfish, blue devilfish, coral trout, baldchin gropers, trevally, turtles and reef fish.

Fisherman's Wharf
A range of invertebrates and many reef fish live under the Fisherman's Wharf. Soft corals and sponges cover the pylons and the sea bed.

Breakwater
The Breakwater shelters a variety of marine creatures, including cuttlefish, octopi, sea stars, hermit crabs, butterflyfish, lionfish, moray eels, stingrays and globefish.

Shallow Reef
Typical of many of the reefs off Geraldton, Shallow Reef has many ledges and caves. Soft corals, blue devilfish, rock lobsters, pineapplefish, shrimp, coral trout, angelfish, nudibranchs and reef fish are found in depths from 4–12 m.

Mayhill Shipwreck
The *Mayhill,* almost 90 m in length, was an iron-hulled, four-masted barque that ran aground off Geraldton in 1895. The wreck lies at 6 m, with the stern standing high above the surrounding limestone reef and kelp. Parts of the hull and mast and her cargo of railway tracks lie nearby.

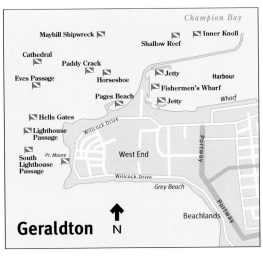

GERALDTON

Houtman Abrolhos
100 Islands Offer Outstanding Diving

Live-aboard diving

Usually 20 m

Currents common

Wonderful coral gardens

Unique mixture of tropical and temperate species on coral reefs

Plenty of reef and pelagic fish

Limestone and coral reefs

Discovered in 1617 by Dutch mariner Frederick Houtman, the low-lying islands and reefs of the Houtman Abrolhos became notorious after the sinking of the *Batavia* in 1629. The Dutch East Indian ship was bound for Batavia (Jakarta), when it ran aground at dawn. Most of the 316 people on board survived to reach Beacon Island, but few survived the mutiny that followed.

The *Batavia* was relocated in 1963, and today is one of the most important shipwrecks in Australia. Excavation of the wreck was undertaken by the Western Australian Maritime Museum, and many artifacts and parts of the hull can be seen on display at the museum in Fremantle.

Situated 60 km west of Geraldton, the Houtman Abrolhos consists of 100 islands and numerous reefs. The coral reefs found here are some of the southern-most in the Indian Ocean, and survive because of the warm Leeuwin Current which flows through the area each winter. These reefs produce the biggest catch of rock lobsters in Australia—around 200 fishermen work in the area between March and June. Fishermen have built small shacks on many of the islands, but the marine environment is still largely intact.

The islands of the Houtman Abrolhos are divided into three sections: the Pelsaert, Easter and Wallaby Groups, all of which offer great live-aboard diving. Dive sites around the islands are extremely varied, with shallow reefs, drop-offs, caves, gutters and an unusual mixture of corals and kelp. While the tropical species are common, many temperate species are also abundant. Even Australian sea lions are occasionally seen here.

A number of live-aboard boats, operating out of Geraldton, run regular trips to the Houtman Abrolhos. These vary in length from weekenders to week-long exploration trips. Diving can be good at any time of the year, however the best diving conditions are experienced in autumn and spring.

Halfmoon Reef

On and around Halfmoon Reef, divers will find spectacular fish life—morwong, jewfish, coral trout, gropers, kingfish, silver drummer, mackerel, tuna, trevally, samsonfish, yellowtail and sometimes a reef shark. Scattered across the reef are the remains of the *Zeewyk* (1727) and the *Windsor* (1908). The wreckage of the *Windsor* is the most interesting.

Pelsaert Island

A brilliant drop-off is found on the eastern side of Pelsaert Island. Try a drift dive from 5–25 m to see the

Below: This Spanish dancer nudibranch (*Hexabranchus sanguineus*) photographed at the Abrolhos Islands, is common to both the Pacific and Indian Oceans. This color variation is typical of those found in the Indian Ocean. *Neville Coleman*

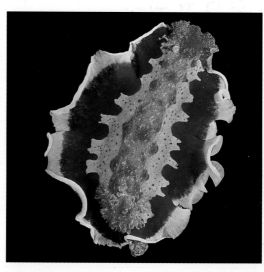

HOUTMAN ABROLHOS

WEST. AUSTRALIA

251

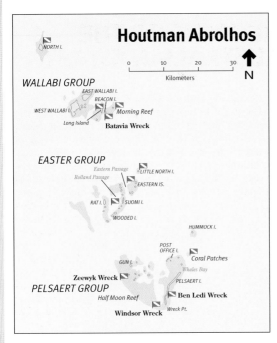

Houtman Abrolhos

WALLABI GROUP

NORTH I.

EAST WALLABI I.
BEACON I.
WEST WALLABI I.
Morning Reef
Long Island
Batavia Wreck

EASTER GROUP

Eastern Passage
Rolland Passage
LITTLE NORTH I.
EASTERN IS.
RAT I.
SUOMI I.
WOODED I.

HUMMOCK I.

POST OFFICE I.
Coral Patches
GUN I.
Whales Bay
Zeewyk Wreck
PELSAERT I.
PELSAERT GROUP
Half Moon Reef
Ben Ledi Wreck
Windsor Wreck
Wreck Pt.

0 10 20 30
Kilometers

subjects—tube worms, cuttlefish, sea stars, sea urchins, flatworms, shrimp, crabs, anemonefish, lionfish and nudibranchs.

Rolland Passage
Flourishing at depths of 5–30 m, pretty coral gardens cover the reefs in the Rolland Passage. Here butterflyfish, parrotfish, cuttlefish, angelfish, coral trout, gobies, anemonefish, damsels, rock cod, gropers and sweetlips are plentiful.

Eastern Islands
More exciting wall diving to 35 m can be enjoyed on the eastern side of the Eastern Islands. Baldchin gropers, kingfish, angelfish, snapper, stingrays, coral trout, sweetlips and many other species of reef and pelagic fish are regularly seen at this location.

Batavia Shipwreck
The remains of the *Batavia* lie in 6 m of water. Cannons, anchors and the occasional artifact can still be seen. An interesting assortment of marine life lives on the surrounding reef.

wonderful variety of corals that flourish along the wall. On the reef you can easily find rock lobsters (which cannot be removed from the area), moray eels, wrasse, parrotfish, lionfish, gropers, butterflyfish, trevally and a wide range of invertebrate species.

Below: The spangled emperor *(Lethrinus nebulosus)*, a favorite food fish, is found around weedy reef flats, lagoons and seaward reefs. *Michael Aw*

Morley Island
A variety of interesting dive sites within the lagoon or along the dropoff make a visit to Morley Island worthwhile. In the lagoon macrophotographers will find plenty of

Morning Reef
Shallow coral gardens provide pleasant diving around Morning Reef. In depths from 6–10 m are plenty of hard corals, colorful reef fish and invertebrates.

Beacon Island
Lovely coral gardens are found around Beacon Island, with staghorn and plate corals, anemonefish, octopi, rock lobsters, shrimp, butterflyfish, scorpionfish, moray eels, morwong and many other species.

Long Island
One of the best wall dives in the area is found on the eastern side of Long Island. Here the wall drops to a depth of 40 m. Sharks and pelagic fish are usual dive companions.

TREASURE SHIPS OF THE WESTERN AUSTRALIAN COAST

THE FIRST KNOWN EUROPEAN TO LAND ON THE west coast of Australia was the Dutch mariner, Dirk Hartog, who sighted the coast in the vicinity of Shark Bay in 1616, after being blown off course on his way to Batavia. Hartog climbed Cape Inscription and left an inscribed pewter plate to record his landfall. He noted that the Great Southern Land was barren and inhospitable, and was no doubt relieved that he had not been shipwrecked on this strange new continent. Several other ships were not so lucky, however, and thus some of Australia's oldest and most interesting wrecks are found off Western Australia. All are protected under the laws of the Historic Shipwrecks Act.

A section of the Zuytdorp cliffs named after the famous wreck discovered at the base in 1927, by a grazier tracking a dingo. One look at these, even from the air, shows what a daunting sight they must have been to early mariners. *Neville Coleman*

Trial (1622)
While taking a short cut, the captain of the *Trial* suddenly found his vessel aground on a reef off the Monte Bello Islands. As the vessel began to break up, the crew abandoned ship, and began the 2000 km trip to Batavia in long boats. The wreck (the oldest in Australian waters) was found in 1969, and little remains today except for cannons and anchors.

Batavia (1629)
See the Houtman Abrolhos section of this book for information on the sinking of the *Batavia* and the fate of its survivors. The *Batavia* was carrying jewels and coins, and much was salvaged at the time of her sinking. Since that time, the Western Australian Maritime Museum has recovered numerous silver coins and valuable artifacts.

Vergulde Draeck (1656)
The 42 m-long *Vergulde Draeck*, known as the Gilt Dragon, sank just north of Perth. Discovered in 1963, the wreck is scattered over a limestone reef—its cannons and anchors the most obvious relics. She was also carrying eight chests of silver coins. Many have been found, along with pipes, glass bottles, jugs, tools and brass utensils.

Zuytdorp (1712)
This ship disappeared on a voyage to Batavia. Its fate, and that of its crew, was unknown until 1927, when the wreckage was discovered at the base of a cliff just south of Shark Bay. Further investigations found silver coins in the water, and between rocks at the base of the cliff.

Zeewijk (1727)
The *Zeewijk* was carrying ten chests of silver coins when she struck a reef on the Houtman Abrolhos. Divers have discovered her anchors and cannons, but the coins were salvaged by the crew at the time of her sinking.

Rapid (1811)
The *Rapid* was an American trader on a voyage from Boston to Canton with 280,000 Spanish dollars on board, when she ran aground off Ningaloo Reef. To conceal her cargo, the ship was burnt to the water line, and most of the coins were later salvaged. The wreck was discovered by a group of spearfishermen in 1978, although her identity was a mystery for quite some time. The wreck has yielded many artifacts apart from coins, including ceramics, glassware and cannons. Part of the hull remains buried under sand.

Shore and boat dives

Commonly 5–15 m

Slight currents

Beautiful coral gardens

Encounters with dolphins, dugongs, sharks and turtles

Good variety of reef fish

Coral reefs

Shark Bay
Dolphins, Dugongs and Strange Stromatolites

One of the most primitive life forms to ever exist on earth were pillars of blue/green algae known as stromatolites—for many billions of years the planet's most abundant life form. Fossilized stromatolites have been found that date back 3.5 billion years. In 1954, a colony of stromatolites—long thought to be extinct—was discovered in Hamelin Pool, at Shark Bay. They survive in super saline sea water that few other animals can tolerate, except for the occasional mollusc and jellyfish. Found in 1.5 m of water, and exposed at low tide, stromatolites make unusual photographic subjects.

Shark Bay is probably most famous for its resident population of bottlenose dolphins, which come in for a daily feed at Monkey Mia. The dolphins first followed the fishing boats, picking up scraps, then in 1964 a few of the dolphins appeared at the beach looking for food. Others followed and today up to eighteen dolphins swim into the shallows to interact with people and pick up a few fish. Over 100,000 visitors now come to Monkey Mia to see these wonderful, intelligent marine mammals first hand.

Located at the most western point of the Australian continent, Shark Bay is enclosed by numerous islands and two long peninsulas of land. The bay covers an area of 8000 sq km, and is a World Heritage-listed site and marine park. Marine life flourishes in this shallow bay, which on average is only 10 m deep. Sharks are common, as are turtles—many turtles nest on the beaches around the bay. The bay is also home to 10,000 dugongs, which feed on the extensive sea grass beds that carpet Shark Bay. Dugongs are regularly seen by divers. Special tours are conducted to locations where people can observe and photograph the dugongs, and sometimes snorkel with them if close enough.

Shark Bay is shallow and many sites are accessible from the shore. However, some of the better locations within the bay can only be reached by boat. Most diving is restricted to inside the bay, as access and rough seas limit the diving possibilities outside.

A number of small towns are scattered around the shores of Shark Bay. The main centers are Denham and Carnarvon, where visitors will find a good range of accommodation. Diving conditions are generally best over winter and spring, when the climate is pleasant and the winds light. A number of charter boats service the Shark Bay area, and numerous boat ramps are available for those exploring the region using their own boat.

South Passage

Although the area is swept by currents and sometimes affected by dirty water, there is always something happening in the South Passage. The bottom, at a depth of only 7 m, has a sparse covering of hard

Below: Shark Bay is famous for its red cliffs, wide expanses of sea grass (supporting large dugong herds), white, sandy beaches, rugged limestone coasts, beautiful embayments, good fishing, dolphins, stromatolites and sharks. It also has some excellent diving, but most requires boat transport.
Neville Coleman

corals and other invertebrates, however much marine life shelters here. Sea snakes, turtles, reef sharks, stingrays, wobbegongs, rock lobsters, shovelnose rays, gropers and reef fish are common. Sometimes a dugong will come in close to check out a diver.

Monkey Rock

The reef around Monkey Rock steps down to 15 m, and supports an excellent variety of marine life including lionfish, wrasse, pufferfish, moray eels, parrotfish, damsels, butterflyfish, angelfish, sweetlips, surgeonfish, hawkfish, scorpionfish, nudibranchs, sea stars, feather stars, clams and other molluscs; also the occasional stingray, rock lobster, reef shark and turtle.

in Shark Bay is found in this area. Numerous hard and soft corals occupy the reefs in shallow water, as well as coral trout, batfish, reef sharks, gropers, trevally, stingrays, rock lobsters and masses of reef fish.

Above: Over 100,000 people a year make the long journey to Monkey Mia to interact with the dolphins. *Neville Coleman*

Bernier Island

Prolific fish life can be found on the reefs on the eastern side of Bernier Island. Angelfish, surgeonfish, damsels, anemonefish, boxfish, pufferfish, filefish, gobies, trevally, blennies, wrasse, rock cod, coral trout, gropers and many more species are usually seen on most dives, as well as turtles, rock lobsters, sea snakes, wobbegongs and reef sharks.

Point Quobba

At the northern end of Shark Bay are lovely shallow coral gardens, located off Point Quobba. The reef and lagoon are accessible from the shore, but since the water is only 2 m deep, the area is best explored by snorkeling. Around the hard corals that thrive here, you will usually find wobbegongs, stingrays, parrotfish, angelfish, clams, anemones, nudibranchs, sea stars, butterflyfish, pufferfish, wrasse, surgeonfish, gobies, blennies, moray eels and sometimes a turtle resting on the bottom.

Dorre Island

The eastern side of Dorre Island provides first-rate diving in depths to 20 m. Some of the best coral growth

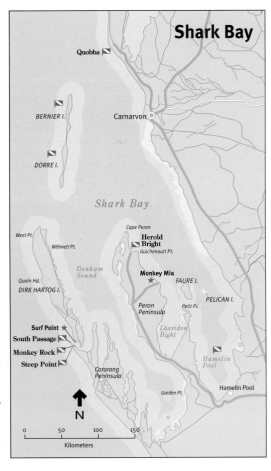

Shore dives and boat dives up to 20 minutes away

Commonly 20–30 m

Strong tidal currents inside Exmouth Gulf

Incredible coral and sponge gardens

Whale sharks from March to May. The amazing Navy Pier

Good variety of reef and pelagic fish

Coral reefs

Ningaloo Reef
A Whale Shark Stop-Over

The small town of Exmouth, located 1300 km north of Perth, sits at the top end of the barren North West Cape. The town comes to life each year in the months of March, April and May when divers and film crews descend on the town, hoping to catch a glimpse of the whale sharks, during their annual visit to the waters around the Ningaloo Reef marine reserve. These harmless giants feed on the plankton and small fishes found around the reefs during the annual coral spawning. For three months spotter planes sweep the coast and report the locations of sharks to the boats below. Swimming with these huge animals is an incredible experience that diver remember for a long time.

Ningaloo Reef runs roughly parallel to the coast, from Coral Bay north to Exmouth—a distance of over 260 km. The distance from the reef to the mainland varies from 200 m to 7 km. Many sections of the inner reef are accessible from the shore, while the outer edge is best dived from a boat.

Several dive shops and charter boats service the area year round.

An influx of dive boats arrives for the whale shark season, but the area is worth a visit any time. The best season to visit Ningaloo Reef is from autumn to spring, when the seas are calm and the winds light.

Coral Bay

Located 150 km south of Exmouth, Coral Bay is a great place to begin your exploration of Ningaloo Reef. Here the reef is dominated by hard corals. Along its edge live turtles, reef sharks, sweetlips, mackerel, gropers and schools of barracuda and trevally. On the reef fringing the shoreline, thrive many patches of coral in only 5 m of water. Big fish are uncommon, but butterflyfish, gobies, parrotfish, anemonefish, surgeonfish, angelfish and many other reef fish are often seen.

Norwegian Bay

Stingrays, turtles, sweetlips, rock cod, angelfish, surgeonfish and many invertebrate species are usually found in the many coral gardens a little further north, along the shore at Norwegian Bay.

Below: Known locally as a "toad-fish," this species from Ningaloo Reef remains unidentified. *Michael Aw*

Mandu Wall

Similar to many dive sites on the outer edge of Ningaloo Reef, Mandu Wall drops into 20 m, with only average coral growth along the wall. However, the fish life can be breathtaking. A drift dive reveals trevally, barracuda, gropers, coral trout, sweetlips, batfish, baitfish, fusiliers, unicornfish, reef sharks and countless reef fish.

Blizzard Ridge

The bottom of Blizzard Ridge, only 15 m deep, is covered with substantial colonies of colorful soft corals, sponges and gorgonians. Reef residents include wobbegongs, stingrays, coral trout, baitfish, trevally, lionfish, gropers, sea snakes and plenty of invertebrate species.

North West Reef

Many gutters, ledges and caves are part of the reef wall at North West Reef. Take a flashlight along to see the brilliant colors of the soft corals, gorgonians and other creatures that inhabit the caves. At 16 m are reef sharks, gropers, tawny sharks, stingrays, turtles, coral trout, moray eels, schools of pelagic fish and occasionally a manta ray.

Bundegi Reef

Located on the inner tip of North West Cape, Bundegi Reef is extremely rich in invertebrate life—molluscs, nudibranchs, flatworms, sea stars, sea cucumbers, feather stars, tube worms, anemones, shrimp, crabs, octopi and many colorful corals, at a depth of only 14 m. There are also plenty of reef fish in the area.

Navy Pier

Like all dive sites in the Exmouth Gulf, the 300 m-long Navy Pier can only be dived on high or low tide, because of the tidal currents. The mass of pylons and beams underneath the pier are covered in corals, and among the pylons lives an astonishing assortment of marine life—moray eels, batfish, bannerfish, nudibranchs, sea stars, flatworms, octopi, cuttlefish, gobies, shrimp, crabs, wobbegongs, rock lobsters, stonefish, crocodilefish, lionfish, butterflyfish, angelfish, boxfish, gropers, parrotfish, trevally, queenfish, perch, snapper and coral trout. Maximum depth under the pier is 17 m, and while the visibility is generally only 12 m, the abundance of marine life is great compensation. A permit is required to dive the pier, so contact the Exmouth Dive Centre at least a week in advance.

Sponge Gardens

Another spectacular dive site in the Exmouth Gulf is the Sponge Gardens. Generally done as a drift dive, the bottom at 22 m is absolutely packed with sponges, gorgonians, soft corals and sea whips. Numerous species of reef fish, moray eels, sea stars, colorful nudibranchs, clams, stingrays, wobbegongs and cowries are usually seen in the vicinity.

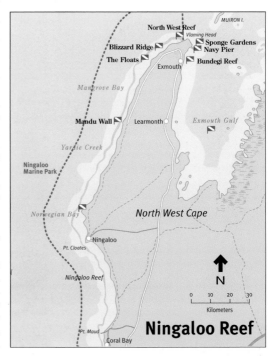

WHALE SHARKS
The giants of Ningaloo Reef

IN 1982, DR GEOFF TAYLOR MOVED TO Exmouth where he began to dive and fish around Ningaloo Reef. During that first year he was amazed to see two whale sharks on the same day, but was unable to dive with the animals. However, in March 1983, Geoff was able to dive with seven whale sharks in one weekend. Over the next few years he dived with dozens of whale sharks in the months from March to May. He knew he had stumbled onto something extraordinary, as whale sharks were generally thought to be solitary animals. He questioned why so many animals gathered each year in the one area. Were the whales migrating, breeding or feeding?

Snorkeling with the whale sharks has brought new life to the town of Exmouth, attracting visitors from around the world. *Michael Aw*

The answer became clearer when biologist Chris Simpson found that the corals on Ningaloo Reef spawned after the full moons in March and April. It was subsequently discovered that tropical krill and many other species were gathering to spawn around the reef at the same time—a thick soup of plankton was there for the taking.

Geoff Taylor has since done much valuable research on the whale sharks—conducting aerial counts, tagging, creating a photographic database on each animal, and some tracking by satellite. He has also produced a documentary, and a wonderful book titled *Whale Sharks: The Giants of Ningaloo Reef*, which is highly recommended.

Now thousands of divers head to Ningaloo Reef each year, to dive with these incredible and apparently friendly creatures.

Even though these sharks are the focus of much attention each year, very little is known about them. The whale shark (*Rhincodon typus*) is thought to grow to a maximum length of 14 m, but much larger animals have been reported. Little is known about their behavior, life cycle and migratory routes; even their reproductive cycle is still uncertain. A single egg case containing a young whale shark was once recovered by a dredge in the Gulf of Mexico, but it is more likely that the eggs hatch *in utero* just before birth, as do nurse shark eggs. The majority of sharks gathering at Ningaloo Reef are immature males, ruling out the possibility of any mating behaviour being witnessed here.

Encounters with whale sharks are breath-taking, especially if you have several swimming around you at once. With so many divers in the water, regulations were necessary, to avoid frightening off the sharks. Divers are now asked not to touch the animals, and only eight divers are allowed in the water with any one shark. Boats are also restricted in their movements, and a courtesy system exists between the boat operators, to avoid having too many boats around any one animal.

As research continues into the life of the whale shark, much more information about the largest fish in the sea is bound to be uncovered in the tropical waters around Ningaloo Reef.

The whale shark (*Rhincodon typus*) is the largest fish in the sea, growing to over 14 m. Being in the water at close range is a breathtaking experience. *Neville Coleman*

Dampier
Gateway to the Monte Bello Islands and Dampier Archipelago

In October 1952, two British warships set out for the remote Monte Bello Islands, 125 km west of Dampier, to test a nuclear bomb. The bomb, detonated on an old frigate, brought Britain and Australia into the nuclear age. This atmospheric test was followed by two more explosions in 1956. After the tests, the islands were abandoned with little concern for the devastated environment, and the islands remained closed to visitors for many years. Luckily the blasts had little impact on the marine life, and the islands have since been reopened.

Dampier is well worth a visit, as much of the area is largely unexplored and many new species have been discovered in the waters off the town. The best time for diving is over winter—the waters can get quite dirty over summer.

Monte Bello Islands
The 100 or so islands in the Monte Bello group are only occasionally visited by live-aboard vessels. Although low-level radiation can still be detected, the reefs are safe to dive. Coral reefs fringe most of the islands. Trevally, barracuda, mackerel, reef sharks, stingrays, batfish, gropers, turtles, moray eels, parrotfish and other large fish species are found on the outer reefs. In the shallow lagoon in the center of the group are numerous coral heads, where you will see plenty of reef fish, stingrays, turtles and sometimes leopard sharks. Some of the best diving is found on the northern end of North West Island, where the reef drops into 30 m, covered with gorgonians and soft corals. Cruising the drop-off are schools of pelagic fish, huge Queensland gropers and reef sharks. A tidal range of 6 m is experienced in this area, and consequently strong currents and dirty water are common off the islands. A shore visit is well worth the effort. The islands are only sparsely covered in vegetation, however there are still plenty of animals to be seen, as well as the remains of concrete bunkers from the nuclear tests.

Dampier Archipelago
Lying just off the town of Dampier are the 40-plus granite islands of the Dampier Archipelago. Turtles nest on the many beaches and the islands support abundant animal life. Even though the area is affected by large tides and occasional low visibility, many excellent dive sites are accessible on a day trip.

Enderby Island
Fringing reefs surround Enderby Island, in depths to 15 m. Butterflyfish, angelfish, parrotfish, sweetlips, stingrays, sea stars, nudibranchs, moray eels and wobbegongs are just some of the many species usually seen on the reef, which is dominated by hard and soft corals.

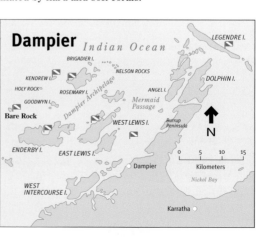

Above: Several species of the nudibranch genus *Risbecia* have an interesting habit known as tail-gating whereby one individual follows another over long distances with its front mantle touching or covering the tail of another. The nudibranch shown above is a new species from the Dampier Archipelago.
Neville Coleman

West Lewis Island

The inner islands of the Dampier Archipelago (such as West Lewis Island) have shallow fringing coral gardens around them. Common on these reefs are wrasse, anemonefish, damsels, rock cod, lionfish, butterflyfish, boxfish, pufferfish, scorpionfish, surgeonfish and many invertebrates species.

Mermaid Passage

The sandy bottom of Mermaid Passage is sprinkled with sea whips, anemones, gorgonians, sponges, soft corals and sea pens. Macro-photographers will find an interesting range of subjects here, including bizarre nudibranchs, crabs, cowries, cuttlefish, octopi, shrimp, sea stars, molluscs, flatworms, brittle stars and the occasional seahorse. Many of the species found here are rare, or have only recently been discovered.

Rosemary Island

A variety of reefs are found around Rosemary Island. The fringing reef teems with reef fish, and the sandy bays provide a protected environment for spectacular coral growth and invertebrate species. While diving any of the reefs in the area, divers may run into a dolphin, dugong or patrolling reef shark.

Bare Rock

Trevally, turtles, gropers, batfish, rock lobsters, stingrays and abundant reef fish inhabit the many gutters and ledges along the drop-off at Bare Rock, where the reef drops to 20 m.

Kendrew Island

Gutters and pinnacles can be found around Kendrew Island in depths from 10–20 m. Coral trout, angelfish and parrotfish are commonly seen on the reef, and sometimes a Queensland groper. Many reef fish gather around the scattered pinnacles, and stingrays, shovelnose rays and the occasional leopard shark can be found along the bottom.

Legendre Island

The northern side of Legendre Island has reef dropping into 30 m. Some of the best invertebrate growth in the area covers this wall—sea whips, soft corals, sponges and gorgonians. Barracuda, trevally, mackerel and batfish swirl in the currents nearby. Look along the ledges along the wall for wobbegongs, rock lobsters, coral trout, nudibranchs, moray eels, sea stars, feather stars, lionfish and maybe a resting turtle.

Port Hedland
Drift Diving Heaven

Boat dives up to
1 hour away

Varies from 2–15 m

Strong currents
from large tides

Coral and sponge
gardens

Healthy reefs
packed with marine
life

Reef and pelagic
fish common

Coral and limestone
reefs

Winter is definitely the best time to dive Port Hedland, since calmer seas mean clearer water. With 7 m tides and murky water inshore, most divers would pack away their diving gear. But travel a few kilometers offshore, and you will find exceptional diving on numerous reefs and channel markers overgrown with marine life. Big Blue Dive services the Port Hedland region, and runs charter trips to the offshore islands and reefs. Many shipwrecks are waiting to be located and explored, including the 105 m-long *Koombana,* which disappeared in 1912.

The Barges
Located in only 14 m of water, these barges sank during the construction of an iron ore facility. In the time that these wrecks have been on the bottom, they have attracted a profusion of fish species including queenfish, trevally, angelfish, butterflyfish, sweetlips, morwong and a resident groper.

24 Buoy
Some of the best diving off Port Hedland is done around the channel markers. Encrusted in corals and sponges, 24 Bouy rises from 18 m. A prodigious array of reef fish and invertebrate species gather around the buoy, and divers are likely to be engulfed by schools of trevally.

Weerdee Island Trench
Between Weerdee Island and Downer Island lies a trench which drops from 6–12 m. This trench, lined with hard and soft corals, is home to many reef fish and invertebrates, including rock lobsters.

Minilya Bank
A number of shoals are situated off Port Hedland, including Minilya Bank, at 6–12 m. Drift diving this coral-covered reef, you will see nudibranchs, stingrays, molluscs, sea stars, moray eels, wrasse, parrotfish and large schools of pelagic fish.

Little Turtle Island
The shallow coral gardens around Little Turtle Island are wonderful dive sites. Gutters and caves are found at 6–14 m. Expect to see sweetlips, morwong, batfish, parrotfish, angelfish, wobbegongs, stingrays, moray eels and perhaps a turtle.

Bedout Island
Bedout Island offers some of the area's best diving. Around the island, in depths to 30 m, are pinnacles, drop-offs, gutters, caves and ledges. Coral growth is good, and invertebrates and reef fish are plentiful. Turtles, pelagic fish, stingrays and reef sharks are common.

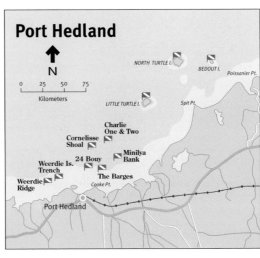

Port Hedland

↑
N

0   25   50   75
Kilometers

NORTH TURTLE I.   BEDOUT I.   Poissanier Pt.

LITTLE TURTLE I.   Spit Pt.

Charlie
One & Two

Cornelisse
Shoal

Minilya
Bank

Weerdie Is.
Trench   24 Bouy

The Barges
Weerdie   Cooke Pt.
Ridge

Port Hedland

Boat dives up to
1 hour away

Varies from 2–20 m

Strong currents
from large tides

Coral and sponge
gardens

Rich collection of
reefs and marine life

Reef and pelagic
fish common

Coral and rocky
reefs

Broome
Old Center for Pearl Diving

The first divers to explore the waters off Broome were Asian pearl divers. During the last century, thousands worked the area in less than ideal conditions—diving in standard dress diving gear, in deep, murky water and strong currents, without the benefit of diving tables. Today the pearls are cultivated.

Diving Broome is still difficult, as the 10 m tides restrict dive times. The water can be murky and box jellyfish and crocodiles must be avoided, but the rewards can be spectacular. The reefs off Broome have an excellent variety of coral, fish and invertebrate life, including many unidentified species.

Whale Rock
Angelfish, gropers, trevally, moray eels, wobbegongs, stingrays and many species of reef fish can be seen on every dive at the reef around Whale Rock, which drops to a depth of 20 m.

Swirl Rock
The reef here is covered with lovely soft corals, gorgonians, sea whips and sponges, as well as rock lobsters, scorpionfish, butterflyfish, gropers and plentiful invertebrates. Around Swirl Rock are many swim-throughs in depths to 37 m.

Battern Rock
Accessible from shore, Battern Rock is surrounded by reefs and drop-offs down to 35 m. Nudibranchs, flatworms, moray eels, stingrays, sea stars, soft corals, molluscs, anemones and reef fish will usually be sighted on day or night dives.

Disaster Rock
Schools of trevally, barracuda, tuna, mackerel, batfish, queenfish and fusiliers are the highlight of a visit to Disaster Rock. Turtles, reef sharks, stingrays, eagle rays and gropers are often around.

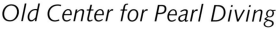

Gantheaume Bay

Whale Rock

Swirl Rock

Ganthcaume Pt.

Red Pt.

Nab Rk.

Cable Beach

+ Saddle Hill

Airport

Broome

Buccaneer Rk.

Mangrove Pt.

Dampier Creek

Inner Anchorage

+ Red Hill

Riddell Pt.

Channel Rock

Battern Rock

↑
N

Broome

Channel Rock
The Amphitheatre is one of the best of a number of good dive sites around Channel Rock. A maze of swim-throughs in depths to 25 m are inhabited by soft corals, squirrelfish, gropers, wobbegongs, rock lobsters, batfish and many small invertebrates.

Riddell Point
Numerous varieties of reef fish are residents of the coral gardens found off Riddell Point, in only 10 m of water. Hard and soft corals, sponges, clams and anemones cling to the bottom, where the abundant invertebrate life includes nudibranchs, sea stars, shrimp, crabs, molluscs and flatworms.

Northern Atoll Reefs
Tame Fish and Masses of Sea Snakes

The Great Barrier Reef may have more species of coral and fish than the Northern Atoll Reefs overall, but individually these reefs are far richer in species and variety. West of Broome lie seven large atolls similar in structure and size, although each group offers something different. The three reefs of the Rowley Shoals are known for their pelagic fish and tame potato cod, while the four northern reefs have masses of sea snakes. On all of these atolls are beautiful corals, plenty of reef sharks, manta rays, turtles and a diverse range of reef fish and invertebrates. A number of boats based in Broome run regular trips to the Rowley Shoals, and special trips to the other reef systems. Winter and spring are the best times to visit, as summer is the cyclone season.

Rowley Shoals

Situated 280 km west of Broome, the Rowley Shoals are by far the most popular dive destination of the Northern Atoll Reefs. This system is made up of three large reefs, each approximately 17 km long by 8 km wide, all offering exceptional diving. To the south lies the Imperieuse Reef; Clerke Reef is located 40 km to the north; and a further 30 km north is Mermaid Reef. Both Imperieuse Reef and Clerke Reef enjoy Marine Park protection, but sadly the natural resources of Mermaid Reef are still being exploited.

Clerke Reef

Many excellent dive sites have been found around Clerke Reef. The sheltered lagoon has scattered colonies of hard and soft coral, with a wide variety of reef fish and invertebrates. The most popular sites are on the sloping edge of the reef in depths between 20–30 m, where numerous caves, gutters and ledges are covered in superb growths of gorgonians, sea whips, sponges and soft corals. Divers often see turtles, manta rays, stingrays, moray eels, overfriendly potato cod, reef sharks and schools of pelagic fish.

Mermaid Reef

Incredible walls, plummeting to 200 m, covered with gorgonians, spiky soft corals, black corals, large sponges and masses of sea whips, are found all around Mermaid Reef. Try a drift dive along the walls to see barracuda, trevally, mackerel, tuna, reef sharks, potato cod, Maori wrasse and the occasional manta ray. The 20 m deep lagoon at the center of Mermaid Reef provides a safe anchorage.

Live-aboard trips over 14 hours offshore

Varies from 20–40 m

Strong currents common

Luxuriant coral gardens

Brilliant wall dives, colorful coral gardens. Encounters with sea snakes, sharks, gropers, and manta rays

Abundant reef and pelagic fish

Coral reefs

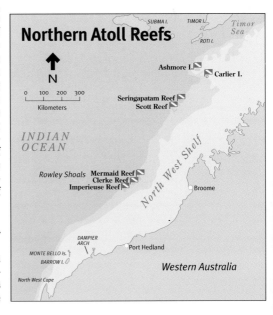

Above: The blue girdled angelfish (*Pomacanthus navachus*), one of the most spectacular of its family, was first recorded in the Australian fauna records from the Western Australian northern atoll reefs, in the 1980s.
Neville Coleman

Scott Reef

Located 400 km north of Broome is Scott Reef and nearby Seringapatam Reef. Scott Reef is split into two large reefs, North Reef and South Reef, separated by a deep-water lagoon. The first marine creatures you notice are the sea snakes—up to a dozen are seen on some dives. Diving is interesting everywhere, be it on coral outcrops in the lagoon, or on the fringing reef slopes. In a few places where the reef drops off into deep water, the walls are packed with brightly-colored invertebrates. Angelfish, turtles, butterflyfish, coral trout, trevally, barracuda, queenfish, reef sharks, and many more species are found around the reef.

Seringapatam Reef

Situated 25 km north of Scott Reef is Seringapatam Reef, an atoll 9 km in diameter, with a 30 m-deep lagoon at its center. Much of the reef slopes gently into deep water. The most spectacular diving is on a sheer wall at the northern end of the reef, which drops from 25–100 m, and always produces something special in the way of photographic subjects. Cruising the wall are dense schools of barracuda and trevally, while mackerel, tuna, rainbow runners and reef sharks are often found circling these groups. Sometimes a manta ray, a turtle, or several eagle rays are seen drifting along with the current.

Ashmore Reef

Closer to Timor than Australia, Ashmore Reef is 600 km north of Broome. This reef is rarely dived and is reported to have the largest population of sea snakes in the world. Under national park protection, the shallow reefs around Ashmore are packed with hard and soft corals, invertebrates, reef fish, turtles, manta rays, stingrays and reef sharks, and is occasionally visited by dugongs.

Cartier Island

Surrounded by deep water, Cartier Island is only 30 km east of Ashmore Reef. The dive sites here are much more dramatic. Steep dropoffs covered with soft corals, gorgonians, sponges and sea whips make up much of the reef edge. Sea snakes, moray eels, reef sharks, stingrays, turtles, pelagic fish and manta rays are common sights.

The preceeding four reefs are regularly visited by fishermen from Indonesia, and so have fewer large fish than the Rowley Shoals.

Christmas Island

Millions of Migrating Crabs

Shore and boat dives up to 20 minutes away

Varies from 20–40 m

Currents common

Rich coral growths

Highlights: Exciting wall dives

Abundant reef and pelagic fish

Coral walls

Located 2600 km northwest of Perth, Christmas Island is surrounded by spectacular walls of coral and plentiful marine life. Much of the island is heavily wooded with dense rainforest. Christmas Island has only recently been opened up to tourists, with twice-weekly flights from Perth. Most visitors come to the island to see its wildlife, particularly the annual mass migration of millions of red crabs *(Gecarcoidea natallis)*.

Perpendicular Wall

Dropping from 4–70 m, this wall attracts white-tip reef sharks, turtles, tuna, grey reef sharks, mackerel and giant Maori wrasse. Leopard sharks have also been seen here.

West White Beach

The coral gardens off the beach are popular with divers and snorkelers. Around extensive patches of beautiful hard and soft corals you will see gropers, moray eels, parrotfish, gobies, sweetlips, butterflyfish, angelfish, wrasse, triggerfish and numerous other reef fish. Whale sharks are found here from November to April.

Boat Cave

Red bass, gropers, surgeonfish, batfish, turtles, trevally, tuna, rainbow runners, giant Maori wrasse and the occasional hammerhead shark all gather off the Boat Cave wall.

Flying Fish Cove

The main settlement on Christmas Island is at Flying Fish Cove. Just off the beach are lovely coral gardens teeming with reef fish and invertebrates—fantastic shore diving.

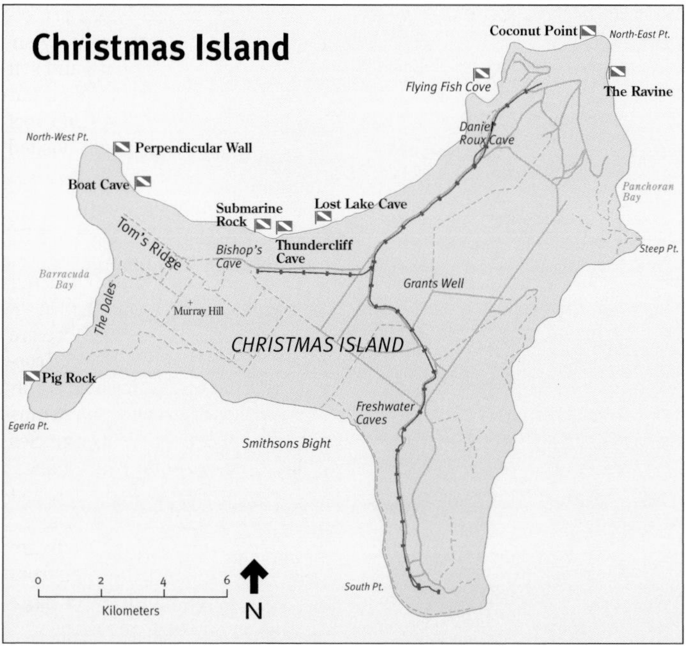

Christmas Island
Coconut Point
North-East Pt.
Flying Fish Cove
The Ravine
Daniel Roux Cave
North-West Pt.
Perpendicular Wall
Boat Cave
Panchoran Bay
Submarine Rock
Lost Lake Cave
Tom's Ridge
Bishop's Cave
Thundercliff Cave
Steep Pt.
Barracuda Bay
Grants Well
The Dales
Murray Hill
CHRISTMAS ISLAND
Pig Rock
Freshwater Caves
Egeria Pt.
Smithsons Bight
0
2
4
6
Kilometers
N
South Pt.

Some currents experienced

Colorful coral gardens

Gardens of hard coral. Encounters with manta rays and turtles

Prolific reef fish

Coral reefs

Cocos (Keeling) Islands
A Little Slice of Asia

These islands remained uninhabited until 1826 when hundreds of Asian workers were transported for the copra trade. Situated 2760 km northwest of Perth, they were brought under Australian control in 1955. The islands are slowly becoming a tourist destination, although accommodation is limited. Twice-weekly flights from Perth bring visitors to the island to enjoy the wildlife and the culture of the Cocos Malay people. The atoll is surrounded by coral gardens, drop-offs and marine life.

Opposite: Schools of crescent-tail bigeye *(Priacanthus hamur)* shelter on the reef by day and feed at night in open water. *Michael Aw*

Garden of Eden
Located on the northern side of Horsburgh Island, the Garden of Eden is a good place to see colorful corals. Divers can drift along walls dropping to 26 m, with ledges and gutters covered in gorgonians and soft corals. Reef sharks, turtles, moray eels, parrotfish, angelfish, lionfish, sweetlips and schools of pelagic fish are common here.

Cabbage Patch
Divers will enjoy exploring the dense coral gardens at the Cabbage Patch. At 20 m plentiful reef fish and invertebrates shelter among the corals.

West Island Jetty
One of the best shore dives in the area is a night dive under the West Island Jetty. At a depth of just 3 m, you will find plenty of invertebrates, sleepy reef fish and turtles.

Catalina Planewreck
This Catalina seaplane crashed in 1945, and was only recently discovered. Although badly broken up in 4–8 m of water, divers can still identify many parts.

Manta Ray Corner
Encounters with manta rays are almost guaranteed at Manta Ray Corner. The food-laden currents that flow through the channel attract manta rays, turtles, reef sharks and occasionally pelagic fish.

Emden Shipwreck
The 118 m-long German cruiser *Emden* sank many ships during World War I. She finally met her match in an exchange of gunfire with the HMAS *Sydney*, and was run aground on North Keeling Island in 1914. The shipwreck is now scattered in shallow water, and rarely dived due to her isolated location.

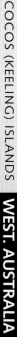

COCOS (KEELING) ISLANDS

WEST. AUSTRALIA

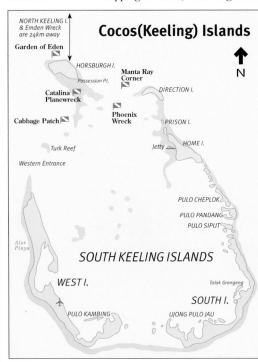

Cocos (Keeling) Islands

N

NORTH KEELING I. & Emden Wreck are 24km away

Garden of Eden

HORSBURGH I.

Possession Pt.

Manta Ray Corner

DIRECTION I.

Catalina Planewreck

Phoenix Wreck

Cabbage Patch

PRISON I.

Turk Reef

Jetty

HOME I.

Western Entrance

PULO CHEPLOK

PULO PANDANG

PULO SIPUT

Alar Pinyu

SOUTH KEELING ISLANDS

WEST I.

Tolok Grongeng

SOUTH I.

PULO KAMBING

UJONG PULO JAU

Introducing the Northern Territory
Top End Diving Down Under

Diving is a popular pastime in the Northern Territory, even though mangroves fringe the coastline, crocodiles and box jellyfish inhabit the offshore waters, and strong tidal currents and low visibility affect diving on the reefs and wrecks.

Darwin has Australia's best collection of World War II shipwrecks and planewrecks. As well, the coral reefs off the city have a rich diversity of reef fish and invertebrates. Manta rays, reef sharks, turtles, schools of pelagic fish and even whale sharks are found on the reefs off the Gove Peninsula, in quite clear water at certain times of the year.

The Northern Territory, which covers 1.4 million sq km, is a land of contrasts. Most of the Territory is hot, dry desert. The top end, however, is hot and humid, and receives a deluge of rain each summer (October to April) from the tropical monsoons. The temperature varies little—daytime temperatures are always around 30° C, while overnight temperatures range from 20–30° C. The dry interior has scorching summer days reaching 40° C, and winter days when the temperature varies from 20–30° C—however the overnight temperature can drop to 0° C.

The English attempt to settle the Northern Territory was to prevent the French and the Dutch from establishing a foothold in the Great Southern Land. Several forts were built between 1824 and 1838, but all were quickly abandoned. Darwin Harbour (named after Charles Darwin) was finally chosen as the location for a settlement in 1869. The town grew quickly after gold was discovered at Pine Creek, but

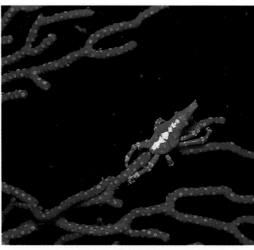

did not develop into a major port until World War II. During the war, many Allied ships and planes, involved in attacks on Japanese positions, were based in Darwin. The city was bombed by the Japanese on sixty-four occasions.

Cyclones have always been a summertime threat to Darwin. Few match the destructive force of Cyclone Tracy, which flattened much of the town on Christmas Eve in 1974. Darwin has since been rebuilt, and is now one of the most modern and cosmopolitan cities in Australia. A number of small towns are scattered throughout the Northern Territory, however the only other major town is Alice Springs, right in the heart of Australia.

Over 150,000 people live in the Territory, representing a diverse mixture of ethnic groups. It has an itinerant population although you are not considered a Territorian until you have suffered the extremes of climate for several years.

Above: The gorgonia crab (*Xenocarcinus depressus*) is a common resident on many gorgonian sea fans throughout Northern Territory waters.
Neville Coleman

Opposite: Many intertidal shorelines in Darwin Harbour have spectacularly-colored, wave-eroded rock formations—nature's stone-age art gallery.
Neville Coleman

One third of the Territory is now owned by the Aboriginal people, who make up one quarter of the population. A permit is required to enter Aboriginal land. A few tribes welcome tourists, and teach Aboriginal culture and crafts—bark painting, how to throw the spear and boomerang, and how to play the didgeridoo. Visitors can sample the native tucker (food). Aboriginal rock paintings, some of which are over 20,000 years old, can be seen throughout the Northern Territory.

Kakadu National Park, with its abundant bird and animal life, sandstone cliffs, flood plains, billabongs (water holes) and magnificent rock painting sites can be reached from Darwin. The Katherine Gorge—13 gorges on the Katherine River—is best explored by canoe. Closer to Darwin is the Litchfield National Park, noted for its springs, rainforests, waterfalls and wildlife. In the city and surrounds are crocodile farms, wildlife parks, natural springs (free of crocodiles), markets, a casino, and an excellent range of good cafes, restaurants and pubs.

Although there is plenty to see on the 1500 km drive from Darwin to Alice Springs, most tourists choose to fly the distance. Around Alice Springs are numerous national parks, including the Eastern and Western MacDonnell Ranges, which can be explored by 4WD, walking tours or camel treks. Uluru (Ayers Rock) and the equally spectacular Olgas are located 450 km west of Alice Springs. The Henburg Meteorite Crater and Kings Canyon are other places of interest.

Currently there are two diving centers in the Northern Territory—the Darwin area (which is serviced by a handful of dive shops and charter boats) and the Gove Peninsula, on the eastern tip of Arnhern Land. Diving is best enjoyed off Darwin in the dry season (from April to Septem-ber) when there is little rain, few box jellyfish and clearer water (up to 10 m on some days). The opposite is true for the Gove Peninsula, which is best dived in the wet season (September–April).

The Territory's coastal waters are always warm, ranging from 24–32° C. Divers should always wear some form of protection against box jellyfish. While there are plenty of coral reefs and marine life around Bathurst Island, Melville Island, Cobourg Peninsula and Groote Eylandt, these areas lack facilities, and can only explored by divers with their own boats.

Below: Found in coastal coral reefs and estuaries, the stonefish *(Synanceia* sp.) is among the world's most venomous fishes. Prey are sucked in during a nearly imperceptable split-second movement. Humans must be careful not to come into contact with this fish. *Michael Aw*

Darwin
Diving Australia's WWII Wrecks

During World War II, most Australian troops were sent overseas, while only a small force was left to defend the country. Attack was considered a slim possibility, until the morning of 19 February 1942, when the Japanese launched a raid on Darwin Harbour. Over 45 Allied ships were in the port when 188 carrier-borne planes (from the same fleet that attacked Pearl Harbor), and 54 land-based bombers attacked Darwin. Ten vessels and dozens of planes were destroyed, another 14 ships were damaged, and 243 people were killed in the raid.

Some of the biggest ships lost in the raid were the US destroyer *Peary*, the tanker *British Motorist*, the US transports *Meigs* and *Mauna Loa*, the US supply ships *Florence D* and *Don Isidro*, the coal hulk *Kelat*, the steamer *Zealandia* and the cargo ship *Neptuna*. The Japanese returned in 1959 to salvage the *British Motorist*, and stripped many of the other wrecks, but what they left or missed still provides some of the best wreck diving in the country.

Darwin acquired another batch of shipwrecks on Christmas Eve 1974, when Cyclone Tracy sank dozens of trawlers, ferries, and small pleasure boats. Many were later salvaged, but some of the best dive sites around Darwin are the remains of these ships. Some of the lost boats have never been located.

Several dive shops service the Darwin area, and run regular boat dives to the best sites on the day. Sites off Darwin are usually dived in less than ideal conditions. Five-meter visibility is considered good, and a huge tidal range restricts dive times to the turn of the tide. The best time of year to dive Darwin is during the dry winter months, when the seas are calm, and the visibility may even reach 10 m. During the summer monsoons, the diving can be affected by cyclones, heavy rains, bad visibility and box jellyfish. While crocodiles, stonefish and sharks are common around Darwin, the main threat to divers are the jellyfish. Divers should always wear full protection—a wetsuit or lycra suit, gloves, booties and a hood.

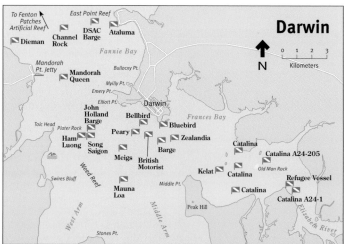

Shore and boat dives up to 90 minutes away

Summer 1–3 m, winter 1–10 m

Strong tidal currents

Diverse range of sponges and corals

Numerous ship-wrecks

Reef and pelagic fish common

Coral and sponge gardens

Kelat

Divers can explore the superstructure of 78 m-long *Kelat*, which sits at 15 m. Wobbegongs are found on the bottom, and gropers, sweetlips, batfish, trevally and mangrove jacks swim around the debris.

Mauna Loa

The remains of the 123 m-long *Mauna Loa* now lie at 18 m. A Harley Davidson motorbike, troop carriers and munitions can be seen among the wreckage. This wreck is alive with fish, including surgeonfish, barracuda, gropers and batfish.

Meigs

The remains of the 129 m-long *Meigs* can be found at 18 m. Much of the wreck was salvaged, but the bulkheads and superstructure remain. Railway tracks, munitions, cables, salvage equipment, a Bren gun carrier and a few trucks are still easy to recognize.

USS Peary

Much of the 95 m-long USS *Peary* was salvaged by the Japanese, but it still makes an interesting dive. The ship rests at 27 m, and is surrounded by schools of reef and pelagic fish. The engines are exposed and piles of ammunition, brass fittings and rifles can be found around the wreck.

Below: Darwin Harbour is fringed by mangrove forests. Numerous rivers, creeks and streams feed into it during the wet season, making diving impossible. Yet it is the very nature of the area which makes for such challenging diving during the dry season. *Neville Coleman*

Catalina Seaplanes

A number of Catalina seaplanes were lost in Darwin Harbour during the war. Most are badly broken up, but wings, engines, fuselages and the cockpit can be explored.

Zealandia

Although salvaged, there is plenty to see on the 123 m-long *Zealandia*. On an underwater junk pile are bulkheads, brass fittings, brass flashlights and piles of tiles. The ship rests at about 18 m, is covered with soft corals, and is a refuge for a variety of reef fish and invertebrates.

Bellbird

This trawler lies almost upside down at 16 m. You can swim through much of the interior of the wreck, including the engine room and cabins, but take care not to disturb the silt. An impressive array of fishlife can be seen.

Mandorah Queen

This wreck, sitting at 18 m, has attracted an unusually large population of jewfish, gropers, batfish, angelfish, butterflyfish, rock cod, coral trout and many more.

NR Dieman

One of the most intact wrecks to be found in Darwin Harbour is the *NR Dieman*. The 20 m-long trawler rests in 12 m of water, and is inhabited by a wide variety of marine life, including many small invertebrates, reef fish, wobbegongs, gropers, tuna, barracuda, trevally and rock cod.

Song Saigon and Ham Luong

These two refugee fishing boats were sunk to form part of a particularly successful artificial reef. Gropers, surgeonfish, jewfish, coral trout, batfish, parrotfish, trevally and many other species can be seen

CROCODILES
Impressive and dangerous

TWO SPECIES OF CROCODILE ARE FOUND IN THE waters of tropical Australia—the endemic freshwater crocodile (*Crocodile johnstoni*) and the saltwater crocodile (*Crocodylus porosus*), found throughout the Indo-Pacific region. While both animals are considered dangerous, the freshwater crocodile is much smaller (growing to just 2.5 m), shy, and usually harmless unless cornered. The saltwater crocodile, which grows to 7 m in length, hunts and kills large animals—pigs, cattle, horses, kangaroos, and sometimes people. These crocodiles are not restricted to saltwater, and are found along the coast from Rockhampton to Broome—in creeks, swamps, rivers, estuaries, and occasionally out to sea.

Over half a million of both species were killed this century, by hunters after trophies and their skin. Since protective legislation was passed in 1972, their numbers have increased, and now many people are calling for them to be culled. While the debate continues, tours featuring these impressive reptiles in the wild and on farms have become top tourist attractions of the north. Six crocodile farms are currently operating, which raise these reptiles for their skin and meat. Although a few people are attacked by crocodiles each year, far more people are eating crocodile than the other way around.

Crocodiles grow rapidly during the first couple of years, then more slowly, as their growth rate is dependent on the availability of food. Their reproductive cycle is similar to that of other reptiles—the female lays a clutch of eggs, which are buried and incubate within the nest. The saltwater crocodiles breed over summer, and the mother is very protective of her nest and young. After they hatch, she helps them from the nest, and guards them from other crocodiles. The freshwater crocodiles breed over winter, and are less protective of their young, since freshwater crocs rarely feed on the hatchlings.

Swimming in, or even standing near, a body of water inhabited by saltwater crocodiles is dangerous, as they are patient hunters, and can go up to a year between meals. There have been no reports of divers being attacked by crocodiles off

Each year scores of saltwater crocodiles (*Crocodylus porosus)* are removed from Darwin Harbour to reduce the risk of attacks on humans. However, the threat is always present in Northern Australia. There have been no recorded attacks, although snorkelers and swimmers have been taken in Northern Territory waters. (Pay attention to signs and be careful inshore and close to river or creek entrances.) *Neville Coleman*

Darwin, even though over 100 saltwater crocodiles are caught and removed from the harbor each year.

While a few attempts have been made to film and photograph the saltwater species underwater, divers have found that freshwater crocodiles can be cautiously approached for spectacular underwater photos. Just Add Water, a Cairns-based dive shop, currently runs weekend crocodile tours to the Mitchell River, and offers the opportunity of seeing a freshwater crocodile up close, underwater. No cage or metal suit is provided—divers and snorkelers exploring the shallow, murky water, meet fish, shrimps, tortoises and snakes—and if they are very fortunate, a 2 m-long freshwater crocodile.

on almost any dive. These small ships sit in 25 m of water and are essentially intact. Nearby is the *John Holland* barge, which also provides some good diving.

Fenton Patches Artificial Reef

This large artificial reef complex, located 28 km north of Darwin, is made up of tires, boat parts, a number of vessels and even some old bus shelters. A number of interesting sites are found around the reef, but the wreck of the oil exploration vessel *Marchart 3* is the most exciting. The wreck sits on the reef in 28 m of water, and provides some penetration diving. The Fenton Patches Artificial Reef generally has good visibility, and large schools of jewfish, trevally, batfish and other species.

Nightcliff Reef

Coral heads and dense sponge gardens are found in 6–10 m of water. Close to the bottom, you can shoot excellent photos of nudibranchs, shrimp, crabs, gobies, anemones and their resident anemonefish, lionfish, flatworms and colorful reef fish.

Mandorah Point Jetty

A rich assortment of marine life can also be found under the Mandorah Point Jetty. The pylons are coated with sponges, soft corals, ascidians, tube worms and anemones. Reef fish and invertebrates live among the tires and other rubbish under the wharf. Many large fish—including barramundi, trevally, batfish, and a resident Queensland groper—are usually found.

East Point Reef

A wide range of invertebrate species—sponges, hard and soft corals, sea whips and ascidians—cover the reef and make for interesting macro-photo opportunities, although the visibility is limited. The fish seen at East Point Reef are usually small.

Channel Rock

Exceptional marine life is found on the reefs around here. The reef rises to 12 m, with hard and soft corals, sea whips and sponges. Divers are likely to find an exceptional assortment of reef fish, including stingrays, turtles, barracuda, trevally, batfish, gropers and the occasional sea snake.

Berry Springs

A number of freshwater springs are located 100 km south of Darwin. Berry Springs is probably the most popular, and in the winter visibility can be over 10 m. Barramundi, catfish, shrimp, snakes, tortoises, archerfish, mangrove jack and sometimes a freshwater crocodile are found in depths to 7 m.

Gove Peninsula
Fantastic Fishing and Diving in the Arafura Sea

The traditional owners of Arnhem Land, one of the largest Aboriginal reserves in Australia, have lived in this area for over 40,000 years. Aboriginal communities are spread throughout the region, and many still hunt and gather. A permit is required to visit this unusual and beautiful part of Australia.

The Gove Peninsula, located on the eastern side of Arnhem Land, is washed by the warm, clear waters of the Arafura Sea. Magnificent islands and reefs surround this isolated peninsula. Fishing is spectacular in the area, and so is the diving—turtles, whale sharks, manta rays and pelagic fish are all part of the scenery. The Gove Diving Academy, which offers dive courses and organizes trips to the many offshore islands and reefs around the Gove Peninsula, is based in the bauxite mining town of Nhulunbuy.

Truant Island
Some of the most spectacular diving in the area can be found off Truant Island, quite a distance offshore and usually done as an overnight trip. Reefs with lush coral growths, reef sharks, manta rays, gropers, coral trout, pelagic fish, eagle rays, stingrays and turtles, drop into deep water all around the island. Divers may see whale sharks over summer.

Bromby Islets
On the leeward side of the Bromby Islets are a number of excellent sites on fringing coral reefs. Reef fish hover above coral gardens. On the seaward side, the reef wall drops into 35 m, covered with soft corals, gorgonians, black corals, sea whips and sponges. Occasional turtles, reef sharks, pelagic fish, manta rays, eagle rays and whale sharks cruise the water at the reef's edge.

Bonner Rocks
Coral heads, gutters, coral gardens and a shipwreck are found at depths from 7–25 m around Bonner Rocks. Angelfish, sweetlips, butterflyfish, wrasse, coral trout, rock cod, parrotfish, surgeonfish, damsels and anemonefish are common. The intact wreck of a trawler is one of the fishiest spots in the area, with gropers, wobbe-

Below: In general, great numbers of the larger fish species are not found in the harbor or around the sponge gardens and soft coral colonies. However, many colorful smaller ones, such as this scribbled angelfish *(Chaetodontoplus duboulayi)* are seen on nearly every dive.
Neville Coleman

Shore and boat dives up to 3 hour away

Summer 2–25 m, winter 2–15 m

Tidal currents common

Good coverage of sponges and corals

Adventure diving and prolific marine life

Reef and pelagic fish common

Coral gardens

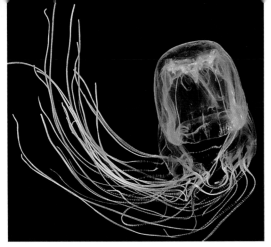

Soft corals, sea whips, sponges and gorgonians are found almost everywhere on the reefs around the island. Residents include turtles, gropers, coral trout, moray eels, manta rays, stingrays, eagle rays, trevally and masses of reef fish.

Sir Roderick's Rocks

Although a long way down the coast, Sir Roderick's Rocks are well worth the long boat ride—in good weather. Surrounding this chain of granite islands are a brilliant array of dive sites—caves and swim-throughs with tawny sharks, wobbegongs, stingrays, rock lobsters, resting turtles, moray eels, gropers and swarms of baitfish; walls to depths of 40 m, covered in soft corals, gorgonians, sea whips and sponges—with manta rays, barracuda, tuna, snapper, trevally, reef sharks, eagle rays, gropers, mackerel and an occasional whale shark cruising the deeper water; and the wreck of a trawler resting at 40 m, usually surrounded by schools of fish. While traveling to the many dive sites off the Gove Peninsula, there is always a good chance of seeing dolphins, pilot whales, whale sharks and false killer whales.

Fringing Reefs

Many fringing reefs slope down to 20 m, providing excellent shore diving off Gove, although the visibility may be reduced at times. Common species are nudibranchs, lionfish, sea stars, butterflyfish, turtles, stingrays, gobies, sweetlips, parrotfish, coral crabs and moray eels.

Town Wharf

The pylons of the Town Wharf, in 16 m of water, are covered with soft corals and sponges, and associated flatworms, decorator crabs, nudibranchs, sea stars, feather stars and other invertebrates. Gropers, trevally, queenfish, coral trout, angelfish, batfish and a variety of reef fish live beneath the structure.

Above: The months from October to May is the stinger season. When diving, swimming, snorkeling and wading in northern waters always wear protective clothing, as box jellies (*Chironex fleckeri*) are likely to be common. *Neville Coleman*

Opposite: Found in tropical reef waters, the giant Maori wrasse *(Cheilnus undulatus)* is often extremely wary, except where they are fed by divers. *Neville Coleman*

gongs, queenfish, trevally, barracuda, batfish, cobia, tuna, many reef fish and invertebrates.

Veronica Island

Some of the best diving at Veronica Island is on coral walls dropping to 30 m. Nudibranchs, flatworms, sea stars, brittle stars, shrimp, coral crabs, molluscs and fish share the reef with a wide variety of soft corals, gorgonians, sea whips and sponges.

Bremer Island

There are numerous interesting dive sites around Bremer Island—coral gardens in the shallows, walls dropping to 40 m, caves and pinnacles.

Gove Peninsula (map)

PERIPLUS TRAVEL MAPS
Detailed maps of the Asia Pacific region

This five-year program was launched in 1993 with the goal of producing accurate and up-to-date maps of every major city and country in the Asia Pacific region. About 12 new titles are published each year, along with numerous revised editions. Titles in **BOLDFACE** are already available (32 titles in mid-1996). Titles in *ITALICS* are scheduled for publication in 1997/1998

INDIVIDUAL COUNTRY TITLES
Australia	ISBN 962-593-150-3
Burma	ISBN 962-593-070-1
Cambodia	ISBN 0-945971-87-7
China	ISBN 962-593-107-4
Indonesia	ISBN 962-593-042-6
Japan	ISBN 962-593-108-2
Malaysia	ISBN 962-593-043-4
Nepal	ISBN 962-593-062-0
New Zealand	ISBN 962-593-092-2
Singapore	ISBN 0-945971-41-9
Thailand	ISBN 962-593-044-2
Vietnam	ISBN 0-945971-72-9

AUSTRALIA REGIONAL MAPS
Brisbane	ISBN 962-593-049-3
Cairns	ISBN 962-593-048-5
Darwin	ISBN 962-593-089-2
Melbourne	ISBN 962-593-050-7
Perth	ISBN 962-593-088-4
Sydney	ISBN 962-593-087-6

CHINA REGIONAL MAPS
Beijing	ISBN 962-593-031-0
Hong Kong	ISBN 0-945971-74-5
Shanghai	ISBN 962-593-032-9

INDONESIA REGIONAL MAPS
Bali	ISBN 0-945971-49-4
Bandung	ISBN 0-945971-43-5
Batam	ISBN 962-593-144-9
Bintan	ISBN 962-593-139-2
Jakarta	ISBN 0-945971-62-1
Java	ISBN 962-593-040-X
Lake Toba	ISBN 0-945971-71-0
Lombok	ISBN 0-945971-46-X
Medan	ISBN 0-945971-70-2
Sulawesi	ISBN 962-593-162-7
Sumatra	ISBN 0-945971-47-8
Surabaya	ISBN 0-945971-48-6

Tana Toraja	ISBN 0-945971-44-3
Ujung Pandang	ISBN 962-593-138-4
Yogyakarta	ISBN 0-945971-42-7

JAPAN REGIONAL MAPS
Kyoto	ISBN 962-593-143-0
Osaka	ISBN 962-593-110-4
Tokyo	ISBN 962-593-109-0

MALAYSIA REGIONAL MAPS
Kuala Lumpur	ISBN 0-945971-75-3
Malacca	ISBN 0-945971-77-X
Johor Bahru	ISBN 0-945971-98-2
Penang	ISBN 0-945971-76-1
West Malaysia	ISBN 962-593-129-5
Sabah	ISBN 0-945971-78-8
Sarawak	ISBN 0-945971-79-6

NEPAL REGIONAL MAP
Kathmandu	ISBN 962-593-063-9

THAILAND REGIONAL MAPS
Bangkok	ISBN 0-945971-81-8
Chiang Mai	ISBN 0-945971-88-5
Phuket	ISBN 0-945971-82-6
Ko Samui	ISBN 962-593-036-1

Distributed by:

Berkeley Books Pte. Ltd.
(Singapore & Malaysia)
5 Little Road, #08-01, Singapore 536983
Tel: (65) 280 3320 Fax: (65) 280 6290

PT. Wira Mandala Pustaka
(Java Books - Indonesia)
Jl. Kelapa Gading Kirana
Blok A-14 No. 17, Jakarta 14240
Tel: (62-21) 451 5351 Fax: (62-21) 453 4987

CONTENTS
PRACTICALITIES

The following Practicalities sections contain most of the practical information you need for your journey to Australia. **Travel Advisory** *provides background information about Australia.* **Transportation** *is concerned with getting to and traveling in Australia. The* **Area Practicalities** *sections focus on each destination and contain details on transport, accommodation and dive operators. These sections are organized by state and correspond to the first half of the guide.*

PRACTICALITIES

CONTENTS

VICTORIA

TASMANIA

SOUTH AUSTRALIA

WESTERN AUSTRALIA

NORTHERN TERRITORY

APPENDIX

Australia at a Glance

Covering an area of 7,682,300 sq km, Australia is the world's sixth largest country, but the smallest continent. With a population just over 17 million, the great majority of Australians live in the capital cities, or along the 36,735 km of coastline.

Last century, Australia was a group of colonies governed by England, but with Federation in 1901, the country became independent. Today, there are six states and two territories with their own governments, as well as a Federal Government, with parliamentary systems based on those of the UK. Still having constitutional ties to England, the Queen is represented in Australia by the Governor General, while the country is headed by a Prime Minister. The Federal Government is responsible for the national economy, while State and Territory governments look after transport, health, education, housing and justice. There is also a local government system which chiefly concerns itself with local issues. All governments in Australia are elected for a three-year or four-year term and voting is compulsory. Elections are contested by many political parties, but it is chiefly Labor and the Liberal/National coalition which vie for power. The nation's capital is Canberra, in the Australian Capital Territory, which is the home of the Federal Parliament.

Australia's economy has traditionally been based on agriculture and mining, and for the first half of the 20th century it was one of the wealthiest nations in the world. With the downturn in commodity prices, a depleted manufacturing sector and a rationalized economy, Australia is now importing more than it exports, and has a large foreign debt. More recently, the economy is slowing growing again and both manufacturing and tourism are playing an important part in the recovery. Australia's gross national product is about $250 billion, while the average annual income is about $30,000. The unit of currency is the Australian Dollar, with one dollar approximately equal to US$ 0.75 (May 1997).

Historical Overview

Australia has been populated for over 40,000 years. The Australian Aborigines arrived from Asia and spread throughout the land. The people lived in groups, were hunters and gatherers, and used fire as their major tool. Their culture and art is perhaps the world's oldest.

While there was much Asian contact in the north of the country, Europeans didn't discover the Great Southern Land until the 17th century. In 1606, Portuguese explorers sailed the areas around Torres Strait, and in the years that followed, many Dutch mariners landed or found themselves shipwrecked on the inhospitable west coast. Abel Tasman came across Tasmania, which he called Van Dieman's Land, in 1642. The country was often described as being unfit for human habitation, even though the Aboriginal people appeared to thrive. It was not until Captain James Cook charted the east coast in 1770, that the potential wealth of the new land could be envisaged. The English, keen to solve the problems of overcrowded prisons, sent a fleet out to establish a penal colony in 1788. From Port Jackson, at Sydney Cove, the colony of New South Wales grew slowly at first and supplies were short. The surrounding country was explored, settlers arrived, farming land was cultivated and the original inhabitants displaced and dispossessed. In the mid-nineteenth century gold was discovered, other colonies established and thousands of migrants arrived.

With Federation in 1901, Melbourne was the capital until Canberra was established in 1927. Australia maintained close ties to England, helping fight three wars, including World War II, when, with the threat of Japanese invasion, links to the USA were formed. The American and Australian troops defeated the Japanese in the Pacific, and were to become allies in the Korean and Vietnamese Wars.

After World War II, Australia opened its gates to European migrants and more recently Asian refugees and migrants have been the major newcomers. Australia is now one of the most multi-cultural societies in the world, although the process of reconciliation still continues with the Aboriginal population.

Travel Advisory
WHAT YOU SHOULD KNOW BEFORE YOU GO

What to Bring Along

This varies greatly depending on your destination and the time of the year. If heading to the Great Barrier Reef over summer, bring light clothes. But diving on the reef over winter can be quite cool, even off Cairns, as strong winds can be cold after diving, so pack a sweater and a pair of long pants. Elsewhere in Australia over summer you should be able to get away with mainly light clothes, but the further south you head, the more you should balance this up with warm clothing. Over winter bring warm clothing to explore the southern states of Australia. Although day time temperatures can be lovely, cold winds and overnight temperatures will have you wrapping up.

Most divers like to travel with their own dive gear, but for those that don't have equipment, nearly all the dive shops throughout Australia offer a good range of hire gear at competitive prices. Package deals are usually the cheapest way to hire dive gear. A dive computer is highly recommended to maximize your dive time, especially for liveaboard boats, and a few boats provide free use of dive computers. Dive gear can also be serviced at most dive shops in Australia, and all the major brands and parts are generally available.

Toiletries, slide film, print film, batteries, suntan lotion, hats, sunglasses, contact lenses, condoms, clothing, insect repellent, swimsuit, sea sickness medication and other items needed in emergencies are readily available in all cities and towns throughout Australia. Suntan lotion, a hat and sunglasses are vital and basic equipment, as the Australian sun is very fierce and is responsible for the highest rates of skin cancer in the world.

Climate

Being in the Southern Hemisphere, Australia's seasons are the reverse of those of Europe and North America. Summer is from December to February, autumn from March to May, winter from June to August and spring from September to November.

In the north, the seasons are rather blurred, especially around Darwin, as there are basically two seasons, the wet from September to April and the dry from May to August. The top half of Australia lies north of the Tropic of Capricorn, and enjoys a tropical climate for much of the year. However, temperatures and humidity here can be unbearably high in summer, so visits to the north are generally best undertaken during winter.

Southern Queensland, northern New South Wales and central Western Australia experience sub-tropical climates, with pleasant days year-round. Even though winter nights may be cool, winter days are generally sunny and warm. The southern states are at their best during summer, with hot days and calm weather. Autumn and spring can also offer many good days, but during winter, especially in Victoria and Tasmania, the low temperatures can be uncomfortable. Although the temperature rarely gets below zero, the strong winds from Antarctica are extra chilly. But winter days can be pleasant when there is no wind, and diving in Tasmania is exceptional over these cooler months.

Temperatures in the tropical north are 25–34°C (78–94°F) year-round, with nighttime temperatures varying from 20–25°C (70–78°F). In the sub-tropical regions the day time temperatures vary from 20–30°C (70–87°F), to lows of 10–15°C (50–60°F). Temperatures in the south average 15–25°C (60–78°F) over summer, but days of 30–40°C (87–105°F) are not uncommon, while night time temperatures vary from 5–15°C (42–60°F), with lows of zero over winter.

Time Zones

Australia is split into three time zones. The eastern states, Qld, NSW, ACT, Vic and Tas are 10 hours ahead of Greenwich Mean Time (GMT), while SA and NT are 9.5 hours ahead of GMT and WA is 8 hours ahead of GMT. The only problem arises over summer when a number of the states introduce daylight saving time. From October to March the country can have five different time zones with NSW, Vic, ACT, Tas and SA all putting their clocks forward 1 hour.

Money and Banking

All prices in this book are listed in Australian dollars and are only intended as a guide. The Australian dollar is widely traded and equal to roughly US$0.75. Denominations are $100, $50, $20, $10, $5 and coins are $2, $1, 50c, 20c, 10c and 5c.

There are many banks and building societies in Australia where visitors can cash travelers' checks or exchange foreign currency. These are open 9 am–4 pm Monday to Thursday, 9 am–5 pm Friday, and some are also open Thursday night until 8 pm and Saturday morning from 9 am–12 noon. In all capital cities, large towns and airports there are also currency and travelers' checks exchange centers. All popular brands of travelers' checks are accepted in Australia, and transaction fees can vary, so it may be wise to shop around.

Credit cards are widely used and accepted in Australia, the most popular cards being Visa, Mastercard, American Express, Diners Club and Bankcard, while EFTPOS is also widely available.

Tax, Service and Tipping

There is no VAT, GST or service charges on Australian goods and services, so the price shown or quoted is the price you pay.

Tipping is not expected in Australia, except in restaurants and some of the larger hotels. In restaurants it is a courtesy, but only if you are pleased with the food and service, to leave a small tip; about 5–10 per cent of the bill is sufficient. In some of the larger hotels, tips may be given to staff, but no one in Australia feels obligated to leave a tip.

Office Hours

Most government business is conducted 9 am–5 pm, Monday to Friday. Shops are open 8 am–5.30 pm Monday to Friday (until 9 pm Thursday), and 8 am–12 noon on Saturdays, while those in capital cities are open 10 am–5 pm on weekends. Supermarket late night shopping days vary from state to state. Some chemists are open 24 hours, as are large petrol stations. Convenience stores vary in hours. Some of the small family-operated ones are open 6 am–6 pm daily, while a number of the larger ones often stay open 24 hours.

Mail

To mail a standard letter or postcard within Australia costs 45c, and prices vary from 70c to $1.20, depending on the distance, to send a postcard or letter overseas. Post offices, or their agents, are found in all towns throughout the country, and are generally open from 9 am to 5 pm Monday to Friday. Stamps can also be purchased from convenience stores and newsagencies.

Telephone and Fax

Australia has an excellent telephone system which has been recently deregulated. The major phone companies are Telstra and Optus. Public phone boxes are found throughout Australia, which allow local, STD (subscriber trunk dialing) and IDD calls to be made (all the numbers listed in this book have the STD code first). A local call is 40c, while STD call rates vary with distance. Phone cards can also be purchased from shops. STD calls are cheaper on weekends and at night.

To get operator assistance on trunk calls, or to reverse the charges, dial 0101 (private phone) or 0107 (public phone). For direct access, dial the international code 0011, your country code (check the phone book for a complete listing), the city code and then the phone number. The same is true if trying to ring Australia. To contact a dive operator in, say Sydney, dial your international prefix, 61 (Australia's country code), 2 (drop the 0 from the city code) and 99123456 (the phone number). Fax machines are very common and are dialed in exactly the same way as a telephone.

Visitors to Australia will find a wealth of useful information in both the white and yellow pages of the telephone books that cover each city or area. In addition to lists of helpful phone numbers and community services, there is information on shopping, markets, history, transport, entertainments, tourist services, attractions, events and even maps.

Australia also has one of the most advanced mobile phone networks in the world, with over 90 percent of the population covered by digital and analog services. Calls to mobile phone are around the same price as STD calls.

All the phone and fax numbers in Australia are currently receiving one or two extra digits, to accommodate the increasing demand. The changes have been occurring since 1994, and will continue to the end of 1997. The phone and fax numbers that are changing in 1997 are listed in the practicalities section of the appropriate area.

Electricity
Australia runs on 220–240V, so currency converters will be required for 110V products from North America. The standard connection is a three pin, different from the British three pin. Adaptors can be purchased from hardware, luggage and airport stores.

Tourist Information
Tourist information offices are found in each state capital. These include:

Queensland Government Travel Centre, Cnr Adelaide & Edward St, Brisbane. Tel: 07-32216111.

Travel Centre of New South Wales, 19 Castlereagh St, Sydney. Tel: 02-92314444.

Victorian Tourist Information Centre, 230 Collins St, Melbourne. Tel: 03-97903333.

Tasmanian Travel & Information Centre, 20 Davey St, Hobart. Tel: 03-62308233.

South Australian Travel Centre, 1 King William St, Adelaide. Tel: 08-82121505.

Western Australian Tourist Centre, Cnr Forrest Pl and Wellington St, Perth. Tel: 0 9-94831111.

Northern Territory Holiday Centre. Tel: 1800-89621336.

Canberra Tourism Commission, Northbourne Ave, Dickson. Tel: 02-62050044.

Information is also available in some airports. Local and regional tourist offices in most towns will provide invaluable advice on accommodation, places to eat and attractions.
Before coming to Australia you may wish to contact the Australian Tourist Commission (ATC) in your country to get useful information which will help in planning your holiday. Offices include:

Canada, 10 Green Lefe Court, Eurora, Ontario L4G 6A4. Tel: 1905-7131995.

Germany, Neue Mainzerstrasse 22, D6000 Frankfurt/Mian 1. Tel: 069-204006.

Hong Kong, Suite 604, Sun Plaza, 28 Canton Rd, Tsimshatsui, Kowloon. Tel: 3-3111555.

Japan, 8th Floor, Sankaido Bldg, 9-13, Akasaka 1-chome, Minato-ku, Tokyo 107. Tel: 03-5822191.

Japan, 4th Floor, Yuki Bldg, 3-3-9 Hiranomachi, Chuo-Ku, Osaka 541. Tel: 06-2293601.

New Zealand, 15th Floor, Quay Towers, 29 Customs St West, Auckland 1. Tel: 09-799594.

Singapore, Suite 1703, United Square, 101 Thomson Rd, Singapore 307591. Tel: 2506277.

UK, Gemini House, 10-18 Putney Hill, London SW15. Tel: 071-7802227.

USA, Suite 2130, 150 North Michigan Ave, Chicago, IL. Tel: 312-7815150.

USA, Suite 1200, 2121 Ave Of The Stars, Los Angeles, CA 90067. Tel: 213-5521988.

USA, 31st Floor, 489 Fifth Ave, New York, NY 10017. Tel: 212-6876300.

Security
Australia is a safe country to travel through if you use a bit of common sense. Hitch hiking is not recommended, but is said to be as safe as hitch hiking in most other Western countries. Car theft is a problem throughout Australia, so always lock your car and put the alarm on, if it has one. The cities are generally safe and well policed, but don't walk the back streets of the cities at night by yourself. Just take the simple precautions that you would normally take at home. Lock motel doors, take advantage of safety deposit boxes to store your valuables, don't leave valuable items on display in cars, photocopy all your tickets and documents, don't carry vast amounts of cash, and don't flash your money around. You should then have a wonderful time.

Health
All travelers should take out travel insurance, not only to cover for cancellations and loss of luggage, but for medical emergencies. Aus-

tralia has a good public and private health service, with hospitals and medical centres in most towns throughout the country. In any medical emergency you will be well looked after. For minor health problems, a visit to a doctor is inexpensive and chemists (drug stores) are found in most towns. In the event of diving accidents there are recompression chambers located in most capital cities and all diving emergencies are handled by DES (Diving Emergency Service), on **1800 088 200**. Divers will find that most charter boats carry first aid kits and oxygen, but you may still prefer to travel with your own first aid kit.

There are no vaccinations required for entry into Australia, unless you have visited an infected country in the previous 14 days. AIDS and sexually transmitted diseases are under control in Australia, but condoms are recommended and needles should never be shared. While Malaria is not a major problem, Ross River Fever is carried by some of the mosquitos of tropical and sub-tropical Australia, so always wear insect repellent and cover up at night. The major problem in Australia is the sun, and it is recommended that you wear suntan lotion, a hat and sunglasses.

Accommodation

A popular tourist destination, Australia offers the visitor a wide range of accommodation to suit every budget. There are hotels, motels, holiday units, caravan parks, backpacker lodges, beach resorts, bed and breakfast places and even a number of dive lodges. Prices can very dramatically, and is not always based on style and comfort, but on availability and popularity.

Lower Priced Accommodation

Most backpacker bunkhouses are basic and share-style, with a communal kitchen, toilet and showers. These vary in price from $10 to $20 a night. A number of dive shops also offer dive lodges, which are bunkhouse style and similarly priced. While some caravan parks also have bunkhouses, most have fully self-contained vans and cabins, which can vary in price from $20 to $60 a night, but you may be able to sleep six people in some cabins for that price. Some basic motels also offer cheap accommodation, with rooms starting at $25 a night.

Medium Priced Accommodation

Holiday units, which are generally self-contained, vary in price from $30 to over $100 a day, but are generally cheaper by the week. Most motels would be in the medium price range, costing $40 to $90 a night. Bed and breakfast places and guesthouses are quite popular in the southern states, and vary from $45 to $90 a night, which also includes breakfast.

High-Priced Accommodation

Large hotels, which are generally 4 or 5-star and offer room service and a number of other facilities, range in price from $100 to $250 a room, and $200 to $1000 for a suite. Island and beach resorts usually have a variety of different rooms. These can vary in cost from $100 to over $1000 a night, but many of the island places include all meals and activities (except diving).

In the Practicalities sections a number of accommodation places are listed as a guide. For a comprehensive list of accommodation you should purchase the accommodation guides produced by the road service organizations (NRMA, RACQ, etc) in each state.

Food & Drink

Australia has one of the most ethnically diverse populations in the world, and a wide selection of foods. While the range can be limited in smaller towns, most large towns usually have Chinese, Vietnamese, Indian, Thai, French, Italian, Greek, Lebanese, Mexican and Japanese restaurants. Seafood and steak restaurants are very popular, although vegetarian places are less common. Restaurant prices vary greatly, and since some of the cheapest places have the best food, it is sometimes best to just follow your taste buds. Most restaurants in Australia are BYO (bring your own alcohol), and tipping is acceptable if you enjoyed the meal and service.

Fast foods are quite popular in Australia and there are snack bars, pizza places, hamburger joints, chicken shops and Chinese take-aways in most towns. All the major fast food companies are represented in Australia.

Most Australians enjoy a drink of beer. There are numerous brands of home-grown beer, and most popular international brands are available, except in out-of-the-way places. Australia is also one of the world's major wine exporters, and inexpensive and good quality wines are easily found.

Calendar

Australians enjoy a number of public holidays each year. The fixed national holidays are New Year's Day (Jan 1), Australia Day (Jan 26),

Easter (Good Friday and Easter Monday varies), Anzac Day (Apr 25), Queen's Birthday (2nd Monday in June), Christmas Day (Dec 25) and Boxing Day (Dec 26). Each state also celebrates bank holidays, cup days (such as the Melbourne Cup), show days and labor days, which are generally held on a Monday to give everyone a long weekend.

Australian schools generally have four terms a year, except Tasmania which has three terms. Travel during school holidays can be more expensive and sometimes booked out. School holidays are held at roughly the same time in each state, but overlap and vary by a week or two. Summer holidays are mid December to the end of January, the other holidays fall in April, late June to early July and late September to early October. It may be best to consult a calender or diary before booking, or else check with your travel agent.

Shopping

Unless buying items duty free, clothing, photographic equipment and electrical goods are generally more expensive than in Europe and North America. But some goods are worth buying in Australia, such as opals, Australian wines, Bundaberg rum, bush wear (Akubra hats and Drizabone coats) and sheep skin products.

Souvenirs naturally will depend on your own personal taste, but there are the usual range of tea towels, fluffy kangaroos, T-shirts, books, posters and postcards. Probably the best souvenirs of your trip to Australia will be Aboriginal artworks, carvings and other items.

Photography

All brands, sizes, speeds and types of films are available in Australia. Although prices are reasonable, film is best bought duty free or in bulk. Both slide and print film can be purchased throughout the country, but slide film can be harder to find in small towns. Print film can be processed just about anywhere, with prices comparable to most other countries. E6 slide film can be processed in all the capitals, and quite a few other cities. Most professional laboratories offer a 3-hour service. Kodachrome films are all sent to Melbourne for development, and turnaround time can be two weeks.

Transportation

GETTING AROUND IN AUSTRALIA

This comprehensive run-down of the wide range of travel services available will enable you to plan and budget your trip. More specific details for each area are found in the relevant Practicalities sections. Prices are in Australian dollars. Prices and schedules are given as an indication only, so check with the dive operator or your travel agent for the most up-to-date information prior to departure.

Getting to Australia

Australia is a popular holiday destination serviced by most international airlines. Flights from Europe generally come through Singapore, Hong Kong or Bangkok; flights from Asia are generally direct, and flights from North America are via Hawaii or direct from Los Angeles. Services also run from New Zealand, Africa and South America.

Sydney International Airport is the busiest airport in the country, and also the one where you are likely to experience the most delays. Most flights start or terminate in Sydney after sometimes visiting other airports around the country. Brisbane and Melbourne International Airports are the next most popular, and generally experience less delays. Cairns International Airport, placing the visitor in the heart of the Great Barrier Reef, is also quite busy. There are also international airports in Adelaide, Darwin and Perth. Canberra is only serviced by domestic flights, while Hobart is serviced by international flights from New Zealand only. Australia's two major airlines, Ansett and Qantas, offer both international and domestic flights.

Prices for flights naturally vary, with the most popular routes being the cheapest, such as London/Sydney and Los Angeles/Sydney. It is generally cheaper to land on one side of the country or the other. From Europe and Asia it is cheaper to land in Perth or Darwin, while from North America and New Zealand it is cheaper to land in Sydney, Brisbane or Melbourne. Always shop around for prices, go through a travel agent rather than direct to the airline, and keep an eye out for discount fares or special deals.

VISAS

Everyone visiting Australia, except New Zealanders, requires a visa for entry. Visas are issued by the Australian Consular Office (listed below) in your country. Tourist visas are free and available for up to six months. Working holiday visas are available for those aged 18 to 26, allowing you to work casually three months out of every 12 months. Visa extensions are possible once in Australia through the Department of Immigration, which have offices throughout the country. Extensions cost A$50, and expect to battle through a lot of red tape. All visitors will require a passport, a return or onward ticket and sufficient funds. Australian Consular Offices include the following;

Canada, Suite 710, 50 O'Connor St, Ottawa K1P 6L2. Tel: 613-2360841.

Denmark, Kristianagade 21, 2100 Copenhagen. Tel: 31262244.

Germany, Godesberger Allee 107, 5300 Bonn 2. Tel: 0228-81030.

Greece, 37 Dimitriou Soutsou St, Ambelokpi, Athens 11521. Tel: 6447303.

Hong Kong, Harbour Centre, 24th floor, 25 Harbour Rd, Wanchai, Hong Kong Is. Tel: 5-731881.

India, Australian Compound, No1/50-G Shantipath, Chanakyapuri, New Delhi 110021. Tel: 601336

Indonesia, Jalan Thamrin 15, Gambir, Jakarta. Tel: 323109.

Ireland, Fitzwilton House, Wilton Terrace, Dublin 2. Tel: 761517.

Italy, Via Alessandria 215, Rome 00198. Tel: 832721.

Japan, 2-1-14 Mita, Minato-ku, Tokyo. Tel: 52324111.

Malaysia, 6 Jalan Yap Kwan Seng, Kuala Lumpur 50450. Tel: 2423122.

Netherlands, Camegielaan 12, 2517 KH The Hague. Tel: 70-3108200.

New Zealand, 72-78 Hobson St, Thorndon, Wellington. Tel: 736411.

Philippines, Bank of Philippine Islands Blg, Paseo de Roxas, Makati, Manila. Tel: 8177911.

Singapore, 25 Napier Rd, Singapore. Tel: 7379311.

Sweden, Sergels Torg 12, Stockholm C. Tel: 6132900.

Switzerland, 29 Alpenstrasse, Berne. Tel: 430143.

Thailand, 37 South Sathorn Rd, Bangkok 10120. Tel: 2872680.

UK, Australia House, The Strand, London WC2b 4LA. Tel: 071-3794334.

USA, 1601 Massachusetts Ave NW, Washington DC, 20036. Tel: 202-7973000.

There are also smaller offices in most countries, so consult your phone book for addresses and phone numbers. (At the time of writing, Australia is implementing an electronic visa service that is completed through your travel agent in six seconds.)

Foreign Embassies
Most countries have embassies in Australia, which are located in Canberra. There are also consulate's offices in most state capitals. Consult the yellow pages phone book for a complete listing under Consulates & Legations.

Customs
Visitors to Australia can bring with them 1 litre of alcohol, 200 cigarettes, perfumes and unlimited currency or travellers checks (but you may only leave the country with A$5000). There are naturally restrictions on drugs, firearms and ammunitions, but also plant and animal products. Australia has some of the toughest quarantine laws in the world, which have kept it free of many of the diseases and pests that affect other nations, so please declare all goods.

Departure Tax
Don't forget to keep A$27 in your wallet for departure tax when leaving Australia (this is sometimes covered in the cost of the ticket).

Traveling in Australia
The two domestic airlines operating in Australia, Ansett and Qantas, both operate fleets of wide body jets and offer many daily flights to all cities around the country. Prices for flights can vary greatly, but are generally cheaper if booked ahead (at least 21 days), or picked up on stand-by. Avoid travel during school holidays as the fares are more expensive and bookings can be difficult. Airfares can be cheaper if booked outside of Australia, and there are student discounts available, but check with your travel agent for the best deal possible. Domestic flights in Australia do not have to be reconfirmed. For information or bookings contact Ansett (Tel: 131300) or Qantas (Tel: 131 313). Both these numbers can be called from anywhere in Australia for the cost of a local call.

There are many small airlines that offer regional flights within Australia (several owned by Ansett and Qantas). These airlines run flights to large towns and islands, generally on small planes. By themselves, these airfares can be expensive, but many can be combined with a package deal on accommodation which includes the cost of the airfare. Again you should check with your travel agent for the best deal on regional flights.

The Open Road
Though public transport is adequate in the cities, Australia has an automobile culture, and it can be one of the best ways to travel within a state. Australians drive on the left hand side of the road, and most road rules are quite straight-forward. Speed limit signs (in kilometers) are posted everywhere, 60 km/h is typical in built-up areas, with 100 to 110 km/h typical on highways and freeways. The use of seat belts is compulsory. Police use radar and speed cameras to catch speeding motorists, red light cameras to catch those running the lights, and random breath tests to catch drink drivers. Each state also has its own roadside service organization (NRMA, RACQ, etc), which is cheap to join, and provides free roadside assistance, and many other services. To drive a car in Australia you should obtain an International Driving Permit from your motoring organization.

Car Rental

If staying for any length of time it may be cheaper to buy a car and sell it before you leave the country, giving you the freedom to explore the country at your own pace. But if you are only on a limited stay, then car rental is a good option. Car rentals are available from airports and most towns throughout Australia. The largest companies are Avis, Budget, Hertz and Thrifty. The many smaller companies are quite competitive and some offer older cars at very cheap rates. Prices for car hire vary depending on the size of the car, the length of time required and the usage: $45 to $80 a day is average, but then you must add insurance (about $15 a day), country rates, and excess kilometer rates. Always shop around, and look out for special deals with airfares that offer free car hire for a certain number of days.

Buses

One of the cheapest ways to get around Australia is by bus. Although it can be cramped and uncomfortable on very long hauls, for example from Sydney to Perth or Melbourne to Cairns, bus travel is an excellent option for shorter trips. There are two national bus lines, Greyhound-Pioneer and McCafferty's, offering services right around the country. But many smaller companies service regional areas. Most buses are airconditioned, and have toilets and videos. They make regular stops for meals, at very odd hours sometimes, and most offer a number of different routes. Prices are listed below. Also available are Kilometre Passes, which allow you from 2000 km ($176) to 20,000 km ($1344) of travel anywhere across the country, to be used within a 12-month period. There are also a number of Aussie Passes, which allow unlimited travel for a certain number of days, these include: 7 days in 30 days ($475); 10 days in 30 days ($610); 15 days in 30 days ($710) and 21 days in 60 days ($935). For information and bookings contact Greyhound-Pioneer (Tel: 132030) or McCafferty's (Tel: 02 9212 3433).

Trains

Railways link all the capital cities and most major country areas, but the services are pretty limited along the coastline. There are a number of different classes available on most country trains, with first class and economy class sleeping berths, and first class and economy class seats only. Prices are listed below. A number of rail passes, including the Sunshine Rail Pass allow unlimited travel within Queensland priced at $267/$388 for 14 days, $309/$477 for 21 days and $388/$582 for 30 days. Austrail Pass allows travel within a 6-month period around the country with prices varying from $380/$650 for 8 days to $995/$1620 for 29 days of travel time (most of these passes are for seats only). For more information or bookings contact Rail Australia (Tel: 132232) from anywhere in Australia.

Dive Gear Hire Costs

Listed in the practicalities sections that follow are the price of boat dives around the country, some of these prices include the cost of hire gear, especially in Queensland, but most do not. The following is a rough guide to hire-gear prices on a daily basis: regulator $12, tank $10, weight belt $5, wetsuit $10, BCD $10, snorkel gear $8 and dive computer $12. These prices are much cheaper as a package or if hired for any length of time. Underwater cameras, lenses and strobes can also be hired from some operators with prices varying from $20 to $40.

Airfills in Australia vary in cost from $6 to $10, with some dive shops offering aircards, giving you, say, 10 airfills for $50.

Dive Courses

Dive courses to instructor level are offered by all the diving training agencies in Australia. Scuba experiences or introduction dives in pools are available around the country, with many dive shops giving these experiences for free or less than $20. Resort courses are popular on the Great Barrier Reef, and vary in cost from $100 to $200, depending on the boat and the length of the trip. These are just one-day courses and don't qualify you as a diver. Open water courses cost from $250 to $400, and are offered part-time or full-time over 4 to 5 days. Some of the courses on the Great Barrier Reef are more expensive as they include a number of days on a liveaboard boat (so saving on accommodation and meals). It is best to shop around, and some dive shops offer two-for-one deals over winter. To complete an open water course you will be required to undertake a full dive medical.

Divers can also do advanced, rescue, divemaster and instructor training and any number of specialty courses. Most of these vary in price from $100 to $300, but once looking at divemaster level, the prices rise, since these courses take a lot longer.

Queensland

A popular destination, millions of tourists visit Queensland each year to see the Great Barrier Reef and many other attractions. The Sunshine State has dive operators spread along the coast from Port Douglas to the Gold Coast. The Queensland dive industry is quite competitive, especially in the popular areas like Cairns and Port Douglas, however, most of the top dive sites on the Great Barrier Reef and Coral Sea are only accessible from liveaboard boats, so allow enough time and money to do these trips.

Getting there

Queensland is serviced by international airports at Brisbane, Cairns and Townsville. A number of international carriers fly directly into these centers, placing you at the heart of the Great Barrier Reef. Regular domestic flights, on either Ansett or Qantas, also provide easy access to Queensland from the other states of Australia.

Local Transport

Divers visiting Queensland will save time and money by flying directly to the area where they wish to dive, but if you want to see a variety of different dive sites and destinations, then be prepared to travel. The easiest way to move about the state is on a domestic or regional flight, since airports are found in all major centers. The airlines servicing Queensland are Ansett, Flight West, Qantas and Sunstate. If you have more time on your hands, a good network of roads links all of the towns along the coast.

Hire cars are easily obtainable at all airports and towns, the major companies being Avis, Budget, Hertz and Thrifty, and road side service is provided by the RACQ (Royal Automobile Club of Queensland). Coaches and buses run to centers right along the coastline, the service is good, but the long hours stuck in a bus (almost 2 days from Brisbane to Cairns) make it a better option for short journeys. Major buses companies servicing the Queensland coastline are Greyhound-Pioneer and McCafferty's. Queensland is also linked by a network of railways, and though more expensive than a bus ticket, an overnight journey on a train is generally more comfortable and enjoyable.

Medical and Emergencies

Hospitals and medical centers are located right along the Queensland coastline. The state's only recompression chamber is located in Townsville.

In any emergency, other than diving, ring **000**, and ask for the service you require, be it fire, police or ambulance.

For any diving accident anywhere in Australia, contact DES (Diving Emergency Service) on **1800 088 200**, state that it is a diving emergency, and give exact details of the accident and the condition of the diver.

The strict diving regulations in Queensland have made it one of the most safety-conscious industries in the world. All divers do safety deco stops and fill in log books. All charter boats, as part of their survey requirements, should carry oxygen and first aid kits, and the crew be proficient in their use.

Photographic Supplies

Both slide and print film can be purchased throughout Queensland, and a number of charter boats carry a supply in case of emergency. While print film can be processed anywhere, E6 processing is a little more restricted outside the major centres. Same day E6 processing in available in Cairns, Townsville, Airlie Beach, Rockhampton, Brisbane, Gold Coast and on a number of the larger liveaboard boats.

Note: All of the following telephone numbers are changing in November 1997; 070-xxxxxx to 07-40xxxxxx, 077-xxxxxx to 07-47xxxxxx, 079-xxxxxx to 07-49xxxxxx and 071-xxxxxx to 07-41xxxxxx.

Far Northern Reefs

The reefs of the far northern Great Barrier Reef are still largely unexplored and can only be visited by long-range liveaboard boats. A number of charter boats visit this area from April to January, departing from the Lockhart River, a small town 500 km north of Cairns. Divers fly up from Cairns by light plane, and the cost of the flight is generally covered in the cost of the trip. These trips vary in length from 7 to 10 days, and cost between $200 to $300 per day.

Charter Boats

Auriga Bay II, PO Box 274, Manunda, Cairns. Tel: 070-581408, Fax: 070-581404. For over ten years *Auriga Bay II* has pioneered trips to the Far Northern Reefs and is still exploring new areas from April to December.

Reef Explorer, PO Box 1090, Cairns, Tel: 070-939113, Fax: 070-939112. From October to January Reef Explorer runs extended trips to the Far Northern Reefs.

Mike Ball Dive Expeditions, 28 Spence St, Cairns. Tel: 070-315484, Fax: 070-315470. MBDE schedules exploratory trips to the Far Northern Reefs every few years on *Spoilsport*.

Nimrod III Dive Adventures, 46 Spence St, Cairns. Tel: 070-315566, Fax: 070-312431. *Nimrod III* occasionally offers trips to the Far Northern Reefs.

Undersea Explorer, Reef Plaza, Spence St, Cairns. Tel: 070-512733, Fax: 070-512286. Based in Port Douglas, Undersea Explorer runs exploratory trips to the Far Northern Reefs each year.

Lizard Island

Lizard Island Lodge, PMB 40, Cairns. Tel: 07-33602444, Fax: 07-33602453. Regularly visited by charter boats on their way to the Ribbon Reefs, Lizard Island is an exclusive resort island, 270 km north of Cairns. A one-hour flight from Cairns is the only official access to the island. Accommodation is in 32 villas priced from $690 to $1728 per day (including meals), and no children under

six are allowed. Facilities at the lodge include dining-room, pool, restaurant, cocktail bar and tennis court. Diving is just one of the activities that guests enjoy on the island. Also popular are game fishing, water-skiing, windsurfing, golf, bushwalking and sailing. The dive shop on the island runs dive courses and hal-day trips to local reefs at $117 and full-day trips to the Ribbon Reefs at $145. Conditions are generally good year-round at Lizard Island.

Cairns and Port Douglas

The towns of Cairns and Port Douglas are the most popular diving centers in the country. Divers can walk into just about any shop and book a dive or tour. From Cairns and Port Douglas divers can enjoy half-day trips to Green Island and Fitzroy Island for about $80, day trips to the inner and outer reefs from $100 to $200, two day trips for $250, three day trips for $350 and liveaboard trips to the Ribbon Reefs and Coral Sea with prices varying from $200 to $300 per day. Dive shops and charter boats are spread throughout this region, from Cape Tribulation in the north to Mission Beach south of Cairns. Conditions off this section of coastline can be good year-round.

Dive Operators and Charter Boats

Adventure Connections Australia, Shop 9, Paradise Village, Palm Cove. Tel: 070-591599, Fax: 070-591614. Offers day trips to the reefs off Cairns and liveaboard trips to the Ribbon Reefs and Coral Sea. Also offers dive courses and adventure tours to Cape York.

Aristocat Reef Cruises, Suite 6/8 Macrossan St, Port Douglas. Tel: 070-994544, Fax: 070-994565. Offers day trips to the reefs off Port Douglas.

Auriga Bay II, PO Box 274, Manunda, Cairns. Tel: 070-581408, Fax: 070-581404. Auriga Bay II runs liveaboard trips to the Ribbon Reefs, Cod Hole, Coral Sea and Far Northern Reefs.

Bali Hai II & Floreat Charter Boats, 15 Arnhem Cl, Cairns. Tel: 070-452649. Offers charters to the reefs off Cairns.

Cairns Dive Centre, 135 Abbott St, Cairns. Tel: 070-510294, Fax: 070-517531. CDC operates 2 to 3-day trips to the reefs off Cairns. They also run PADI and NAUI dive courses, and have retail and hire gear.

Cape Tribulation Dive Services, Cape Tribulation. Tel: 070-311588, Fax: 070-313318. Offers dive courses and day trips on the *Taipan Lady*.

Cape Tribulation H2O Dive, Mason's Store, Cape Tribulation. Tel: 070-980069.

Deep Sea Divers Den, 319 Draper St, Cairns. Tel: 070-312223, Fax: 070-311210. Operates the liveaboard charter boats, *Tropic Queen, Tropic Princess* and *Explorer II* to the Ribbon Reefs, Cod Hole and local reefs. A PADI facility, they also offer dive courses, retail and hire gear.

Dive 7 Seas, 129 Abbott St, Cairns. Tel: 070-412700.

Don Cowie's Reef Services, Shields St, Cairns. Tel: 070-311588, Fax: 070-313318. Offers day trips on *Down Under* to the reefs off Cairns and trips on *Taipan Lady* to the reefs off Cape Tribulation. They also offer dive courses, retail and hire gear.

Down Under Dive, 155 Sheridan St, Cairns. Tel: 070-311288, Fax: 070-311373. Offers daily dive trips to the reefs off Cairns on their charter boat *Scuba Roo*. They also have the tall ship SV *Atlantic Clipper* moored on the reef for extended dive trips. They also offer PADI dive courses and hire gear.

Great Diving Adventures, Wharf St, Cairns. Tel: 070-510455, Fax: 070-313753. Offers day trips to reefs off Cairns on their large catamaran, and have dive centres on Fitzroy and Green Islands. GDA have a pontoon at Moore Reef and tender boats run divers to nearby dive sites. They also offer PADI dive courses.

Haba Dive, Marina Mirage, Port Douglas. Tel: 070-995254, Fax: 070-995385. Offers day trips to the reefs off Port Douglas on their catamaran, *Haba Queen*. They also offer dive courses, retail and hire gear.

Hostel Reef Trips, 73 Esplanade, Cairns. Tel: 070-317217.

Impulse Dive, 51a Macrossan St, Port Douglas. Tel: 070-995967. Offers dive charters off Port Douglas.

John Thackrays' Diving Services, 10 Guava St, Holloways Beach. Tel: 070-559798.

Just Add Water, Shop 9, Reef Plaza, Spence St, Cairns. Tel: 070-412799. Offers dive courses, retail and hire gear, and day trips on *Front Runner* out of Port Douglas. They also offer crocodile dives in the Mitchell River.

Lady Ruby Charters, Marlin Jetty, Cairns. Tel: 070-313528, Fax: 070-313554. Offers daily and extended trips to the reefs off Cairns.

Kangaroo Explorer Cruises, 79 Wattle St, Yorkeys Knob. Tel: 070-558188. Runs extended charters to Thursday Island.

Marlin Coast Divers, Novotel Palm Cove Resort, Palm Cove. Tel: 070-591144.

Mike Ball Dive Expeditions, 28 Spence St, Cairns. Tel: 070-315484, Fax: 070-315470. MBDE offers dive courses and operates the liveaboard vessel *Supersport* on 4 day trips to the Ribbon Reefs and Cod Hole.

Nimrod III Dive Adventures, 46 Spence St, Cairns. Tel: 070-315566, Fax: 070-312431. *Nimrod III* runs charters to the Ribbon Reefs, Coral Sea and Far Northern Reefs.

Ocean Spirit Cruises, 143 Lake St, Cairns. Tel: 070-312920, Fax: 070-314344. Operate day trips on the large catamaran *Ocean Spirit* to the reefs off Cairns, and also offer PADI dive Courses.

Outer Edge Dive, Suite 6/8 Macrossan St, Port Douglas. Tel: 070-994544, Fax: 070-994565. Runs day trips to the reefs off Port Douglas.

Passions of Paradise, PO Box 2145, Cairns. Tel: 070-316465, Fax: 070-519505. Offers diving on day trips on the sailing catamaran *Passions of Paradise*.

Peter Tibb's Scuba School, 370 Sheridan St, Cairns. Tel: 070-521266.

Peter Tibb's Dive Shop, 65 Grafton St, Cairns. Tel: 070-311586.

Phantom Charters, Marina Mirage, Port Douglas. Tel: 070-941220.

Port Douglas Dive Centre, Prince's Wharf, Port Douglas. Tel: 070-995327. Offers dive courses and charters to the reefs off Port Douglas.

Poseidon Dive Charters, 10 Sonata Cl, Port Douglas. Tel and Fax: 070-985806. Operates the charter boat *Poseidon* on day trips to the reefs off Port Douglas. They also offer dive courses and hire gear.

Pro Dive Cairns, Marlin Parade, Cairns. Tel: 070-315255, Fax: 070-519955. Operates two charter boats, *Stella Maris* and *Kalinda* on 3 day trips to the reefs off Cairns. They also offer PADI dive courses, retail and hire gear.

Quicksilver Diving Services, Marina Mirage, Port Douglas. Tel: 070-995050, Fax: 070-994065. Operate 2 large catamarans which run daily to their pontoon at Agincourt Reef. They also offer helicopter flights, marine biology courses, dive courses and sailing trips.

Quintessential Diving, 8 Bradford St, Whitfield. Tel: 070-536841

Quintessential Diving, 14 Jarda St, Smithfield Heights. Tel: 070-382304.

Reef Explorer, PO Box 1090, Cairns. Tel: 070-939113, Fax: 070-939112. Operates liveaboard trips to the Ribbon Reefs, Cod Hole, Far Northern Reefs and Coral Sea.

Reef Jet Cruises, Pier Market Pl, Cairns. Tel: 070-315559, Fax: 070-315819. Operates half-day dive trips to Green Island.

Rum Runner Charters, Trinity Wharf, Cairns. Tel: 070-521388, Fax: 070-521488. Operates two liveaboards to the Ribbon Reefs, Cod Hole and Coral Sea.

Sanduria Sail & Dive, 99 The Esplanade, Cairns. Tel: 070-516950. Runs daily trips to the reefs off Cairns on their 18-m ketch.

Seastar II, 3 Leoni Cl, Cairns. Tel: 070-330333. Offers daily reef trips.

Sunlover Cruises, Trinity Wharf, Cairns. Tel: 070-311055. Runs day trips to the reefs off Cairns on their large catamaran.

S2 Dive, Shop 2 Hides Corner, Lake St, Cairns. Tel: 070-312150.

Taka Dive, Cnr Lake & Aplin Sts, Cairns. Tel: 070-518722, Fax: 070-312739. Offers dive courses, retail and hire gear and an extensive range of camera gear, and operate the liveaboard vessels *Taka II* and *Taka III* to the Ribbon Reefs, Cod Hole and Coral Sea.

Tusa Dive, Cnr Aplin St & The Esplanade, Cairns. Tel: 070-311248, Fax: 070-315221. Runs liveaboard and day trips on their 3 dive boats, as well as dive courses, retail and hire gear.

Undersea Explorer, Reef Plaza, Spence St, Cairns. Tel: 070-512733, Fax: 070-512286. Operating out of Port Douglas, Undersea Explorer runs liveaboard trips to the Ribbon Reefs, Cod Hole and Coral Sea.

Wavelength Reef Charters, Macrossan St, Port Douglas. Tel: 070-995031. Runs daily trips to the reefs off Port Douglas.

Accomodation

There are countless places to stay around Cairns and Port Douglas. Following are just a handful to give you some idea of what is on offer.

Cairns International, 17 Abbott St, Cairns. Tel: 070-311300, Fax: 070-311801. 16-storey complex located in the center of town, with rooms from $225 to $1400 per night.

Coolabah Motel, 564 Mulgrave Rd, Cairns. Tel: 070-542711, Fax: 070-335340. Rooms from $40 to $50 per night.

Sheraton Mirage Resort, Port Douglas Rd, Port Douglas. Tel: 070-995888, Fax: 070-985885. This 3-storey complex has villas and hotel units from $470 to $2100.

Port Douglas Motel, 9 Davidson St, Port Douglas. Tel: 070-995248, Fax: 070-995504. Units from $72 to $84 per night.

Fitzroy Island Resort, PO Box 2120, Cairns. Tel: 070-519588, Fax: 070-521335. Cabins at $240 to $417 per night and bunkhouses at $28 per night. They offer a range of watersports, including diving, and facilities include a restaurant, bistro and bar. Fitzroy Island is accessible via a daily express catamaran from Cairns at $22 return.

Green Island Resort, Cairns: Tel: 070-313300, Fax: 070-521511. This up-market resort has twin-share rooms, including all meals at $776 per night. The island is accessible via a launch from Cairns.

Coral Sea Reefs

Some of the most exciting diving in the world is found beyond the Great Barrier Reef deep in the Coral Sea. Over a dozen isolated reefs are found over 250 km off the mainland, spanning from Hervey Bay in the south to Cape York in the north. The more popular Northern Coral Sea Reefs are regularly visited by charter boats departing from Port Douglas, Cairns, Townsville and Airlie Beach. Trips vary in cost from $200 to $300 per day. Those to the Southern Coral Sea Reefs cost the same, but are irregular, with only a handful of charter boats visiting this region each year. Dive groups usually book the boat for the trip. Diving conditions in the Coral Sea can be good year-round, with autumn and spring offering some of the best weather.

Charter Boats
Adventure Connections Australia, Shop 9, Paradise Village, Palm Cove. Tel: 070-591599, Fax: 070-591614. Offers liveaboard trips on *Pacific Adventure* to the Ribbon Reefs and Coral Sea.

Auriga Bay II, PO Box 274, Manunda, Cairns. Tel: 070-581408, Fax: 070-581404. *Auriga Bay II* runs trips mainly to the Far Northern Reefs, but also does combined trips to Osprey Reef and the Ribbon Reefs.

Australiana, 45 Hickey Ave, Gladstone. Tel: 079-783956. Available for trips to the Swain Reefs, Capricorn and Bunker Groups and Southern Coral Sea.

Booby Bird, Marine Drv, Gladstone. Tel: 079-726990, Fax: 079-726990. Available for trips to the Swain Reefs, Capricorn and Bunker Groups and Southern Coral Sea.

Boomerang Cruises, 22 Byron St, Scarness, Hervey Bay. Tel: 071-242393. Runs trips to the Swain Reefs, Bunker Group and Southern Coral Sea.

Elizabeth E Coral Cruises, 102 Goldsmith St, Mackay. Tel: 079-574281, Fax: 079-572268. Available for charter to almost anywhere on the Great Barrier Reef and Coral Sea.

Max Allen Cruises, 7 Illawong Crt, Gladstone. Tel: 079-791377. Operates the charter boats *Kanimbla* and *Spirit of Freedom* to the Swain Reefs, Capricorn and Bunker Groups and Southern Coral Sea.

Mike Ball Dive Expeditions, 252 Walker St, Townsville. Tel: 077-723022, Fax: 077-212152. MBDE operates the catamaran *Spoilsport* and runs regular trips to Flinders Reef, Boomerang Reefs and the *Yongala*, and also does a number of extended trips deep into the Coral Sea to Herald Cays, Coringa Islets, and the Abington and Malay Reefs.

Pacific Star Charters, 48 Coral Esplanade, Cannonvale, Airlie Beach. Tel: 079-466383, Fax: 079-466901. Runs weekly and extended trips to Lihou Reef, Diamond Islets, Abington Reef, Flinders Reef, the reefs around the Whitsunday's and occasional trips to Marion Reef in the Southern Coral Sea.

Reef Explorer, PO Box 1090, Cairns Tel: 070-939113, Fax: 070-939112. Runs regular trips to Osprey Reef and the Ribbon Reefs and extended trips deep in the Coral Sea, visiting Flinders Reef, Herald Cays, Abington Reef, Lihous Reef, Diamond Islets and the reefs of the Southern Coral Sea.

Rum Runner Charters, Trinity Wharf, Cairns. Tel: 070-521388, Fax: 070-521488. Operates two charter boats to Holmes Reef, Bougainville Reef and the Ribbon Reefs.

Taka Dive, Cnr Lake & Aplin Sts, Cairns Tel: 070-518722, Fax: 070-312739. Operates two vessels year-round to Osprey Reef , the Ribbon Reefs and also to Holmes Reef.

Undersea Explorer, Reef Plaza, Spence St, Cairns. Tel: 070-512733, Fax: 070-512286. Runs weekly trips exploring Osprey Reef and the Ribbon Reefs. Also operates to Dart Reef, Bougainville Reef and the Far Northern Reefs.

Yellowfin Charters, 16 Perry St, Bundaberg. Tel: 071-516448, Fax: 071-531215. *Yellowfin* is available for trips to Capricorn and Bunker Groups, Swain Reefs and Southern Coral Sea.

Mission Beach and Dunk Island

Located 120 km south of Cairns and 160 km north of Townsville, Mission Beach is a popular tourist area with access to islands, the reef and white water rafting on the Tully River. If you don't wish to stay at Mission Beach you may choose to stay on Dunk Island. Covered in rainforests and ringed by lovely beaches, Dunk Island is a national park and part of the Bedarra Group of islands. Dunk Island is accessible by water taxi or launch from Mission Beach at $22 return, or guests can fly from Cairns or Townsville at $195 and $215 return respectively.

Dive Operators

Dale Skipper Services, 27 Holland St, Mission Beach. Tel: 070-688550. Operates charters to the reef.

Great Barrier Reef Dive Inn, The Hub Shopping Centre, Mission Beach. Tel: 070-687294, Fax: 070-687294. Offers dive courses, retail, hire gear and dive trips to the reef.

Quick Cat Dive, PO Box 208, Mission Beach. Tel: 070-687289, Fax: 070-687185. Operates the large catamaran *Quick Cat* to Beaver Reef daily. They depart Clump Point in the morning, pick up at Dunk Island and spend 3 hours out on the reef. The trip costs $110, $50 for one dive and $30 for a second dive, including all dive gear. Quick Cat Dive also offers PADI dive courses at Mission Beach and Dunk Island.

Accommodation

Great Barrier Reef Hotel Resort, Dunk Island, PMB 28, Townsville. Tel: 07-33602444, Fax: 07-33602453. Facilities at the resort include a restaurant, bistro, nightclub, squash court, golf-course, pool, spa and many activities are available. They have four styles of units, with prices varying from $340 to $534 depending on single, double or triple share, and prices don't include meals.

Around Mission Beach are resorts, motels, caravan parks and a few backpacker places.

Beachside Apartments Holiday Units, 32 Reid Rd, Mission Beach. Tel: 070-688890, Fax: 070-688898. Has units from $45 to $55 per night and $275 to $385 pw.

Mission Beach Resort, Cnr Cassowary Drive & Wongaling Beach Rd, Mission Beach. Tel: 070-688288, Fax: 070-688429. This resort has rooms starting at $80.

Orpheus Island

Part of the Palm Island Group, Orpheus Island is 80 km north of Townsville and 24 km off the mainland coast. Surrounded by fringing reef, Orpheus and the other islands of the Palm Group have good diving, with visibility varying from 8–25 m. There are coral gardens, clam beds, reef walls and a good variety of corals, reef fish and invertebrates to be seen on every dive. The only way to dive Orpheus Island is to stay at the **Orpheus Island Resort**, Private Bag 15, Townsville. Tel: 077-777377, Fax: 077-777533 This exclusive resort is very private and allows no children under 15 on the island. They offer a range of activities to guests including waterskiing, sailing, windsurfing, bushwalking, fishing, tennis, snorkeling and diving. Facilities at the resort include a restaurant and convention center. They offer four styles of accommodation with prices varying from $390 to $1030 depending on length of stay and number sharing, and prices include all meals. Daily dives are organised to the local reefs and cost $65. They also offer dive courses and trips to the reefs, and package deals are available. Orpheus Island is accessible by seaplane from Townsville or Cairns which costs $270 and $420 return respectively.

Townsville

Located 1371 km north of Brisbane, Townsville is the largest city in north Queensland. From Townsville divers can do day-trips, three-day trips and extended trips that take in both the Coral Sea, the local reefs and the *Yongala* shipwreck. Day trips cost $140 to $180, three-day trips $300 to $350, while a week or more out to the Coral Sea will vary in cost from $200 to $300 per day. Conditions are generally good off Townsville year-round.

Dive Operators

Dive Bell, 16 Dean St, Townsville. Tel: 077-211155. Offers SSI dive courses, overnight trips on *Hero*, retail and hire gear.

Duckin' N' Divin' Down Under, 7 Queens Rd, Railway Estate. Tel: 077-214089.

Mike Ball Dive Expeditions, 252 Walker St, Townsville. Tel: 077-723022, Fax: 077-212152. Operate two vessels out of Townsville, the 30-m long *Spoilsport* which does trips to the Coral Sea, local reefs and Yongala, and the 21-m long *Watersport,* which runs 2/3 day trips to the *Yongala* and local reefs. MBDE also offer dive courses, retail and hire.

Power Play Charters, Breakwater Marina, Townsville. Tel: 077-872666. Offers day trips.

Pro Dive Townsville, Shop 4, Great Barrier Reef Wonderland, Flinders St, Townsville. Tel: 077-211760, Fax: 077-211791. Operates the 17 m-long vessel *Running Free* and do 3-day trips to the *Yongala* and local reefs. They also offer PADI dive courses, retail and hire gear.

Pure Pleasure, PO Box 1831, Townsville. Tel: 077-213555, Fax: 077-213590. Operates day trips to their pontoon at Kelso Reef on the 30 m-long catamaran *2001.* They also offer dive courses and reef ecology tours.

Reef Charters, 20 Tamarind St, Kirwan. Tel: 077-733341. Offers day trips.

Reef Magic Charters, 5 Barringha Court, Mysterton. Tel: 016 782286. Run day and overnight trips to the reef and *Yongala* on their cruiser.

Scorpion Charters, 5 Sharp St, Mt Louisa. Tel: 077-797568.

Sun City Watersports, Tobruk Pool, The Strand, Townsville. Tel: 077-716527. Offers dive trips, instruction, retail and hire gear.

Tangaroa, 19 Crowle St, Hyde Park. Tel: 077-722127. Runs day and overnight dive trips.

True Blue Charters, 65 Gilbert Crs, North Ward. Tel: 077-715474.

Accommodation

Townsville has quite a good selection of accommodation on offer, from 5-star hotels to basic backpacker hostels.

Sheraton Breakwater Casino Hotel, Sir Leslie Thiess Dr, Townsville. Tel: 077-222333, Fax: 077-723488. The Sheraton is an 11-storey, 5-star hotel complex with a casino with rooms varying from $220 to $850 per night.

Townsville Travelodge, Flinders Mall, Townsville. Tel: 077-722477, Fax: 077-211263. Located in the center of town, the Travelodge varies from $160 to $200 per night.

Central City Gardens, 270 Walker St, Townsville. Tel: 077-722655, Fax: 077-211728. Located next door to Mike Ball Dive Expeditions, this is a popular motel with visiting divers. Rooms from $83 per night.

Civic Guesthouse & Backpacker Inn, 262 Walker St, Townsville. Tel: 077-715381. Rooms at $30 to $43 per night.

Magnetic Island

This lovely island sits 4 nautical miles off Townsville and is a popular holiday destination with locals and tourists. An island within the Great Barrier Reef World Heritage Area, Magnetic Island also has a number of good dive sites around its shores, although the reef and foreshore at Nelly Bay awaits restoration. On these shallow fringing reefs divers will find a range of reef fish and invertebrates, though the visibility can be limited at times. Diving Magnetic Island is done through **Magnetic Island Tropical Resort**, Yates St, Nelly Bay. Tel: 077-785955, Fax: 077-785601. They offer accommodation from $40 to $60 per night, local dives ($35 for a single dive and $55 for a double dive), arrange reef dives and SSI dive courses.

There is a wide range of accommodation on offer on Magnetic Island, but the best value places are the holiday units.

Magnetic Island Holiday Units, 16 Yule St, Picnic Bay. Tel: 077-785246. With units that sleep up to four at $65 per night, or $400 pw.

Magnetic Retreat, 11 Rheuben Tce, Alma Bay. Tel and Fax: 077-785357. With units at $50 to $80 per night.

Magnetic Island is accessible by launch or vehicular ferry, costing $19 and $85 return respectively.

Whitsunday Islands

The islands of the Whitsunday Group are popular with both tourist and divers. Centered around Airlie Beach and Mackay, the Whitsunday Islands are reached by direct flights into Hamilton Island, or by flying into Proserpine (26 km from Airlie Beach) or Mackay and then transferring to the islands by water taxi or launch (generally from Shute Harbour). A number of the islands have resorts on them and all offer diving. It is also possible to stay on the mainland and take day trips out to dive the islands or reef. Day reef trips cost around $120, and include 2 dives and all gear, while 3-day trips are priced at $375, and boat dives around the islands cost $60. Conditions are generally good year-round. Manta rays make an appearance at many dive sites over winter. Mackay is located 975 km north of Brisbane; Airlie Beach is 1125 km north of Brisbane.

Dive Operators and Charter Boats

Aquatic Centre of Education, Shute Harbour Rd, Airlie Beach. Tel: 079-467446. A PADI facility, they offer dive courses and dive trips.

Barrier Reef Diving Services, The Esplanade, Airlie Beach. Tel: 079-466204, Fax: 079-465130. Operating on Hayman Island and from Airlie Beach, they offer dive courses to instructor level, retail and hire gear and run daily and extended trips to the islands and reef.

Critical Response, 12 Apollo Dve, Mackay. Tel: 079-552986. Offers dive courses and hire gear.

Downunder Dive, 11 Iluka St, Cannonvale. Tel: 079-466869.

Elizabeth E Coral Cruises, 102 Goldsmith St, Mackay. Tel: 079-574281, Fax: 079-572268. *Elizabeth E* is a liveaboard vessel that can be hired for group charters to the Great Barrier Reef and the Coral Sea.

Hamdon Star Charters, Mackay Harbour, Mackay. Tel: 079-552490, Fax: 079-553209. Charter boat operating to the islands and the Great Barrier Reef.

High Dive The Whitsundays, 119 Whitsunday Harbour Apartments, Cannonvale. Tel: 079-467260, Fax: 079-465969.

H2O Sportz, Front St, Hamilton Island. Tel: 079-469888, Fax: 079-469888. Runs daily trips to the reef and local sites, and offers PADI dive courses, retail and hire gear.

Island Divers, Mandalay Point Rd, Airlie Beach. Tel: 079-465650.

Kelly Dive Whitsunday's, Eshelby Drv, Cannonvale. Tel: 079-466122.

Mackay Adventure Divers, 153 Victoria St, Mackay. Tel: 079-531431. A PADI dive center, they offer retail, hire gear, daily and extended trips.

Maxi Ragamuffin, 283 Shute Harbour Rd, Airlie Beach. Tel: 079-467777, Fax: 079-466941. Offers daily sailing and diving trips.

Nari Cruises, 4 Sunbird Close, Jubilee Pocket. Tel: 079-465012.

Oceania Dive, Shute Harbour Rd, Airlie Beach. Tel: 079-466032, Fax: 079-466032. A PADI facility, they run dive courses and dive trips to the local islands and reefs.

On The Edge, 402 Shute Harbour Rd, Airlie Beach. Tel and Fax: 079-467533.

Pacific Reef Charters, 48 Coral Esplanade, Cannonvale. Tel: 079-466383, Fax: 079-466901. Offers weekly and extended trips to the reefs in the Whitsunday region and to the Northern and Southern Coral Sea.

Pro-Dive Whitsunday, Shute Harbour Rd, Airlie Beach. Tel: 079-466508. Operate daily and overnight trips to the islands and reefs, conduct PADI dive courses to instructor level and have retail and hire gear.

Reef Enterprise Diving Services, 386 Shute Harbour Rd, Airlie Beach. Tel: 079-467228. Provide daily and extended trips to the islands and reef and offer dive courses.

Scuba Sport, The Esplanade, Airlie Beach. Tel: 079-466204, Fax: 079-465130. Runs daily dives to the reef on their cat and also conduct dive courses.

True Blue Dive, 364 Shute Harbour Rd, Airlie Beach. Tel: 079-466662.

Whitsunday Diving Services, 34 Manooka Drv, Cannonvale. Tel: 079-466811. Offers SSI and PADI dive courses, dive charters and also operate out of South Molle Island, Daydream Island and Hook Island.

Whitsunday Pleasure Dives, PO Box 1038, Airlie Beach. Tel: 079-465752.

Whitsunday Scuba Centre, 5 Garema St, Cannonvale. Tel: 079-466865.

Accommodation

There are a number of island resorts spread throughout the Whitsunday Group and all offer diving, bushwalking, fishing, sailing, water-skiing, archery, windsurfing, snorkeling, tennis, golf and other activities.

Brampton Island Resort, Tel: 07-33602444, Fax: 07-33602453. Two-storey resort complex with 3 styles of units, priced from $280 to $340 per night. Access via Mackay by launch service at $40 return and air service, $142 return.

Daydream Island Travelodge Resort, Tel: 079-488488, Fax: 079-488499. The resort has three styles of unit, priced from $185 to $265 per night. Access via water taxi from Shute Harbour at $22 return.

Holiday Inn Crowne Plaza Resort, Hamilton Island, Tel: 079-469999, Fax: 079-468888. This resort is quite a large complex and offers a range of accommodation from penthouse suites to basic units, with prices varying from $200 to $1675 per night. The center of activity in the area because of its airport and large marina, the resort is accessible via a launch from Shute Harbour at $32 return.

Hayman Island Resort, Tel: 079-401234, Fax: 079-401567. This is the most exclusive of all the resorts in the area. They offer penthouses, suites and units with prices varying from $395 to $1300. Access via a water taxi from Airlie Beach at $80 return.

Palm Bay Hideaway Resort, Long Island, Tel and Fax: 079-469233. This small resort has cabins and units from $129 to $284 per night. Access to Long Island is via a water taxi service from Shute Harbour at $22 return.

Whitsunday's Long Island Resort, Tel: 079-469400, Fax: 079-469555. This two-storey resort has over 140 units with rooms varying from $75 to $110 per night.

South Molle Island Resort, Tel. 079-469433, Fax. 079-469580. Six styles of units with prices varying from $190 to $370 per night, which includes all meals. Access to the island is via a launch service from Shute Harbour at $30 return.

If staying on the mainland there are a wide range of resorts, motels and caravan park units in Airlie Beach and Mackay.

Boathaven Lodge Holiday Units, 440 Shute Harbour Rd, Airlie Beach. Tel: 079-466421, Fax: 079-466421. Units from $45 to $65 per night and $270 to $390 pw.

Coral Sea Resort, 25 Ocean View Ave, Airlie Beach. Tel: 079-466458, Fax: 079-466516. Has rooms from $109 to $175 per night.

Beach Tourist Park, Petrie St, Mackay. Tel: 079-574021, Fax: 079-514551. Villas from $45, cabins from $36 and on-site tents at $16.

Coral Sands Motel, 44 MacAlister St, Mackay. Tel: 079-511244, Fax: 079-572095. Two-storey complex with rooms from $51 to $73 per night.

Keppel Islands

Located just off Yeppoon, the Keppel group of islands always seems to provide good diving year-round. It is possible to dive these islands and reefs by day trips from the mainland, or you may choose to stay on Great Keppel Island and be closer to the action. On Great Keppel there are two resorts and a dive shop. The island is accessible by a 30-minute launch ride, which costs $25 return, or there are flights from Rockhampton at $150 return. Full-day dive trips from the mainland cost about $40 for two dives, while single dives from Great Keppel also cost $40.

Great Keppel Island is 681 km north of Brisbane, and 40 km north east of Rockhampton.

Dive Operators

Capricorn Reef Diving, 189 Musgrave St, North Rockhampton. Tel: 079-227720, Fax. 079. 227933. PADI dive center, offers day trips to the Keppel Group, dive courses, retail and hire gear.

Inner Space Images, 17 Caroline St, Yeppoon, Tel. 079-393312. SSI instruction and underwater video and photo services.

Keppel Reef Scuba Adventures, Great Keppel Island. Tel: 079-395022, Fax: 079-395022. Located on Great Keppel Island, Keppel Island Dive Centre runs daily boat dives. A PADI facility, they offer dive courses, resort courses, retail and hire gear.

Keppel Isles Yacht Charters, 12 Poplar St, Cooee Bay. Tel: 079-394949. Charter trips to the Keppel Group.

Keppel Tourist Services, Rosslyn Bay Boat Harbour, Yeppoon. Tel: 079-336744. Runs the large catamaran, *Reefseeker,* on daily snorkeling and diving trips to the Keppel Group.

Rockhampton Diving, Shop 3, 61 High St, North Rockhampton. Tel: 079-280433. SSI training facility, offers Keppel and reef trips, retail and hire gear.

Tropicana Dive, 12 Anzac Pde, Yeppoon. Tel: 079-394642, Fax: 079-394662. Offers Keppel and reef trips, SSI and PADI dive courses, retail and hire gear.

Accommodation

Staying on Great Keppel Island, divers have the choice of two resorts.

Great Keppel Island Resort, PMB 8001, North Rockhampton. Tel: 079-33602444, Fax: 079-33602453. Great Keppel Island Resort is a popular tourist resort with a restaurant, night club, convention center, pool, spa, squash court, tennis court, golf course and offers a range of watersports. There are three styles of accommodation which cost from $270 to $384 per night depending on package deals and number sharing. Meals are not included in the price.

Keppel Haven Resort. Tel: 079-336744, Fax: 079-336429. Keppel Haven Resort caters for those on a budget, offering cabin and tent accommodation. The on-site tents cost $17 per night, while the self-contained cabins cost $110 per night. The resort has a restaurant, camp kitchen, barbecue and offers numerous watersports.

If staying on the mainland you have a wide range of accommodation to choose

from in the Rockhampton and Yeppoon area. There are resorts, motels, caravan parks and holiday units with prices ranging from $10 to $200 per night.

Capricorn International Resort, Farnborough Rd, Yeppoon. Tel: 079-395111, Fax: 079-395666. This large resort complex has a variety of rooms from $145 to $220 per night.

Como Holiday Units, 32 Anzac Pde, Yeppoon. Tel: 079-391594. On the beachfront, Como has units at $50 per night.

Capricorn and Bunker Groups and Swain Reefs

As with many other sites on the reef the only way to explore the Capricorn and Bunker Groups and Swain Reefs is from a liveaboard charter boat. Boats depart from the ports of Hervey Bay, Bundaberg and Gladstone, with the only regular service being day trips to Lady Musgrave Island. All of the boats listed are effectively charter boats, hired by dive shops and dive clubs for dive trips and with no set schedules. Individual bookings are possible as they just add your name to the group chartering the boat. Charters to the Capricorn and Bunker Groups vary in cost from $120 to $180 per day, while trips to the Swain Reefs vary from $150 to $200 per day. Conditions are generally good year-round to both these destinations, and while the ocean crossings can be rough, once within the reef systems there is always shelter. Gladstone is located 530 km north of Brisbane, while Bundaberg is 368 km north of Brisbane and Hervey Bay is 80 km south of Bundaberg.

Dive Operators and Charter Boats

Australiana, 45 Hickey Ave, Gladstone. Tel: 079-783956. Available for trips to the Swain Reefs, Capricorn and Bunker Groups and Southern Coral Sea.

Booby Bird, Marine Drv, Gladstone. Tel: 079-726990, Fax: 079-726990. *Booby Bird* is available for trips to the Swain Reefs, Capricorn and Bunker Groups and Southern Coral Sea.

Boomerang Cruises, 22 Byron St, Scarness, Hervey Bay. Tel: 071-242393. Runs trips to the Swain Reefs, Bunker Group and Southern Coral Sea.

Captain Cook Great Barrier Reef Cruises, Seventeen Seventy. Tel: 079-749077, Fax: 079-749505. Runs day trips to Lady Musgrave Island and dive courses.

Gladstone Reef Charters, Marine Dve, Gladstone. Tel: 079-725166. Provides island taxi service for groups wishing to camp on North West, Tyron and Masthead Islands.

Harris Undersea Services, 44 Higgins St, Gladstone. Tel: 079-722784.

Last Wave Watersports, 16 Goondoon St, Gladstone. Tel: 079-729185. Offers dive courses, dive charters, retail and hire gear.

Max Allen Cruises, 7 Illawong Crt, Gladstone. Tel: 079-791377. Operates the charter boats *Kanimbla* and *Spirit of Freedom* to the Swain Reefs, Capricorn and Bunker Groups and Southern Coral Sea.

Reef Knot Charters, 19 The Esplanade, Gladstone. Tel: 079-724129. Offers charter trips to the Swain Reefs and Capricorn and Bunker Groups.

Sewah Charters, Gayndah Rd, Oakhurst, Bundaberg. Tel: 071-213155. Runs trips to the Swain Reefs and Capricorn and Bunker Groups.

Yellowfin Charters, 16 Perry St, Bundaberg. Tel: 071-516448, Fax: 071-531215. Offers trips to the Capricorn & Bunker Groups, Swain Reefs and Southern Coral Sea.

Accommodation

Charter boats heading out to the Capricorn and Bunker Groups and the Swains generally leave overnight and return late in the afternoon. If looking for somewhere to stay you will find an endless supply of accommodation from Hervey Bay to Gladstone, including motels, holiday units, resorts and basic caravan parks, with prices ranging from $200 to $10 per night.

Heron Island

Heron Island Tourist Resort, P & O Resorts, Tel: 079-781488, Fax: 079-781457. Heron Island has always been a popular destination with divers. The diving is good year-round and divers will see plenty of marine life. Facilities on the island include a tennis court, pool, restaurant, shops and a dive shop. There are four styles of unit on the island priced from $149 to $548, and prices include all meals. The dive shop runs daily boat dives around Heron, costing $60 for two dives, while full-day adventure double dives cost $120 and night dives $55. The dive shop runs dive courses and has an extensive range of hire gear. Package deals are available on diving and accommodation, and free diving specials are sometimes offered. Heron Island is 72 km east of Gladstone and is accessible by ferry or helicopter. The ferry costs $136 return; the helicopter $364 return.

Lady Musgrave Island

Lady Musgrave Barrier Reef Cruises, 1 Quay St, Bundaberg. Tel: 071-529011, Fax: 071-524948. Lady Musgrave Island is regularly visited by charter boats exploring the Bunker Group, but it is also possible to camp on the island or visit it on a day trip. Lady Musgrave Barrier Reef Cruises operate day trips every Tuesday, Thursday, Saturday and Sunday (and on every day during school holidays). They offer semi-submersible coral viewing, glass-bottom boat coral viewing, island walks, lunch and snorkeling at $96 for adults and $50 for kids. Diving is offered in conjunction with **Salty's Dive Team**, 22 Quay St, Bundaberg. Tel: 071-534747, Fax: 071-526707. Single dives cost $35, which includes dive gear, and they offer introduction dives for $50. Salty's also offer a Fly-Dive trip. For $180 four divers are flown to Lady Musgrave Island in a seaplane, do a few dives and return to Bundaberg.

Lady Elliot Island

Lady Elliot Island Resort, PO Box 206, Torquay. Tel: 071-564444, Fax: 071-564400.

Lady Elliot Island offers great diving year-round. There is a wide range of accommodation on the island. The basic, but comfortable, bunkhouse and safari tents cost from $175 to $230 per night, while the units vary from $200 to $280; all prices include meals. Facilities on the island include an education center, dining room, bar and shop. Boat dives cost $35, and shore dives $25, but it is much cheaper to buy a package deal of 10 dives for $250. There are also specials on free diving throughout the year, so contact your travel agent to find out what is on offer. The dive shop also runs PADI dive courses, "discover scuba" pool dives, resort courses and has an extensive range of hire gear. The only way to get to Lady Elliot Island is to fly from either Hervey Bay, Bundaberg or Gladstone. The cost of the flight is always included in package deals.

Bundaberg and Hervey Bay

Bundaberg and Hervey Bay are the southern gateways to the Great Barrier Reef, with a number of charter boats offering day trips and extended trips. This area also has a number of interesting inshore dive sites, including a few shore diving areas. The local dive operators run double dives (costing about $70) to the local reefs. Conditions are generally good year-round, but the clearest inshore water is experienced over winter. Bundaberg is located 368 km north of Brisbane, while Hervey Bay is 290 km north of the state capital.

Dive Operators
Bundaberg Scuba Centre, 200 Bourbong St, Bundaberg. Tel: 071-516422. Offers boat dives, PADI dive courses, retail and hire gear.

Bernie's Dive Connection, 382 Esplanade, Hervey Bay. Tel: 071-241133. Offers SSI dive courses, boat dives, retail and hire gear.

Diver's Mecca, 472 Esplanade, Hervey Bay. Tel: 071-251626. Offers boat dives, dive courses, retail and hire gear.

Eclipse Charters, Hervey Bay. Tel: 071-287030. With a 15 m-long catamaran, Eclipse offers dive trips.

Lady Musgrave Scuba Services, 28 Holland St, Bargara. Tel: 071-592663. Offers SSI dive courses.

Maryborough Diver Supplies, 91 Wharf St, Maryborough. Tel: 071-233466. Offers equipment, sales and service.

Salty's Dive Team, 22 Quay St, Bundaberg. Tel: 071-534747, Fax: 071-526707. Runs dive trips to Lady Musgrave Island, also local boat dives, dive courses, retail and hire gear.

Spirit of Bundaberg, 39 Baldwin Crs, Bundaberg. Tel: 071-522780. Local boat dives.

Accommodation
Visitors to the Bundaberg and Hervey Bay area will find plenty of accommodation, as this region is a popular holiday destination.

Reef Gateway Motor Inn, 11 Takalvan St, Bundaberg. Tel: 071-532255, Fax: 071-532294. Units from $65 to $125 per night.

Rum City Motel, 52 Takalvan St, Bundaberg, Tel: 071-525722, Fax: 071-533964. Rooms from $40 to $55 per night.

Hervey Bay Resort, 249 Esplanade, Pialba. Tel: 071-284688, Fax: 071-284688. Three-storey complex with rooms from $60 to $200 per night.

Colonial Log Cabin Resort, Boat Harbour Drive, Urangan. Tel: 071-251844. Units from $52 per night and bunkhouses from $13 per night.

Sunshine Coast

Only 100 km north of Brisbane, numerous reefs are found off the Sunshine Coast, but diving is centered around Noosa and Mooloolaba. Double boat dives cost around $45, single dives $30, while dives in the shark tank at Underwater World at Mooloolaba cost $50. Diving can be great year-round, but with few sheltered dive sites, big seas can rule out diving.

Dive Operators
Aqua-Holic Divers, 11 Cocas Ave, Palmwoods. Tel: 07-54450789. Offers PADI dive courses.

Aqua Safari Scuba Centre, 120 Bulcock St, Caloundra. Tel: 07-54926266.

Aquatic Dive Studio, Islander Resort, Gympie Tce, Noosaville. Tel: 07-54424500. Offers boat dives, retail, hire gear and PADI dive courses.

Club Dive, 199 Brisbane Rd, Mooloolaba. Tel: 07-544447850. Runs dive charters, PADI dive courses, and offers retail and hire gear.

Dive Boatique, Cruise Terminal, Gympie Tce, Noosaville. Tel: 07-54471300. Boat dives, PADI dive courses, retail and hire gear on offer.

Scuba World, Underwater World, Parkyn Pde, Mooloolaba. Tel: 07-54448595, Fax: 07-54448596. Offers SSI dive courses, dives in Underwater World, boat dives and hire gear.

Sun Coast Fundive, Cnr Brisbane Rd & Woomba Pl, Mooloolaba, Tel: 07-54448883, Fax: 07-54781020. Offers boat dives (including night boat dives), PADI dive courses, retail and hire gear.

Sunreef Diving Services, Shop 6, 120 Brisbane Rd, Mooloolaba. Tel: 07-54445656. Offers dive courses, boat dives, retail and hire gear.

Sweetlip Dive Services, 5 Wingara St, Buddina. Tel: 07-54442033. Dive charter boat service.

Accommodation
Being a popular holiday destination, there is an unlimited supply of accommodation on the Sunshine Coast. There are hundreds of motels, holiday units, caravan parks, backpacker lodges and upmarket resorts.

Bayviews Apartments, 9 Douglas St, Mooloolaba. Tel and Fax: 07-54440966. Units from $40 to $115 per night and $275 to $850 pw.

Mooloolaba Motel, 46 Brisbane Rd, Mooloolaba. Tel: 07-54442988, Fax: 07-54448386. Two-storey complex with rooms from $48 to $105 per night.

Noosa River Beach Holiday Units, 281 Gympie Tce, Noosaville. Tel: 07-54497873. Units from $40 to $90 per night and $220 to $550 pw.

Brisbane
While the diving off Brisbane is generally brilliant year-round, the distance one has to travel to the dive sites can make it expensive. Day-trips from the mainland cost about $80, this includes two dives and lunch. It works out cheaper to do a liveaboard trip over a weekend, these cost about $200, depart on Friday night and return Sunday afternoon, allowing up to 8 dives to be done. The other option is to stay on Moreton Island or North Stradbroke Island, since both have dive shops and easier access to the dive sites. Dives cost $35 for a single dive off Moreton (inside bay) and $40 for a single dive from "Straddy", but package deals including accommodation are available. Diving conditions can be good year-round off Brisbane, but big seas limit diving to inside Moreton Bay.

Dive Operators
Adventure Sports, 119 Logan Rd, Woolloongabba. Tel: 07-33913766, Fax: 07-33917804.

Adventure Sports, 151 Caxton St, Paddington. Tel: 07-33681288. Both Adventure Sports stores offer NAUI, PADI & AUSI dive courses, boat dives, retail and hire gear.

Bribie Island Scuba Centre, 1467 Bribie Is Rd, Ningi. Tel: 07-54976088. Offers boat dives, NAUI dive courses, retail and hire gear.

Brisbane Dive Systems, 536a Rode Rd, Chermside. Tel: 07-33593925. Offers boat dives, SSI dive courses, mixed gas, retail and hire gear.

Brisbane Scuba School, 2422 Logan Rd, Eight Mile Plains. Tel: 07-33419733. Offers dive courses, retail and hire gear and boat dives.

Dive Biz Underwater Adventures, Mahogany Rd, Munruben. Tel: 07-32970169. Offers dive trips, dive courses, retail and hire gear.

Get Wet, Tangalooma Moreton Island Resort, PO Box 1102, Eagle Farm, 4009. Tel: 07-32686333, Fax: 07-34082666. Offers dive trips, dive course, accommodation, retail and hire gear.

Moreton Academy of Diving, 132 Braun St, Deagon. Tel: 07-32698400. Offers PADI & NAUI instruction, boat dives, retail and hire gear.

Nautilus Scuba Centre, 520 Lutwyche Rd, Lutwyche. Tel: 07-38571440, Fax: 07-38576141. Offers boat dives, dive courses, retail and hire gear.

Point Lookout Scuba Dive, Nth Stradbroke Is. Tel: 07-38430543. Runs charter boat *Sport Diver* and offers hire gear and accommodation.

Pro Dive Milton, Cnr Milton & Baroona Rds, Milton. Tel: 07-33683766, Fax: 07-33683025.

Pro Dive Mt Gravatt, 21 Mt Gravatt-Capalaba Rd, Upper Mt Gravatt. Tel: 07-33438866. Offers PADI dive courses, boat dives, retail and hire gear.

Redland Scuba Centre, 6/1 Dan St, Capalaba. Tel: 07-32451008. Offers boat dives, dive courses, retail and hire gear.

South Bank Dive and Hire, South Bank Parklands, Sth Brisbane. Tel: 07-38447160, Fax: 07-38441351. Offers boat dives, PADI dive course, retail and hire gear.

Stradbroke Island Scuba Centre, 1 East Coast Rd, Pt Lookout, Nth Stradbroke Is. Tel: 07-34098715, Fax: 07-34098715. Offers NAUI dive courses, boat dives, on site accommodation, retail and hire gear.

Accommodation

If you wish to stay in Brisbane there is a wide range of accommodation on offer, especially around the new international airport and in the city. But for a real holiday, you will enjoy a stay on Moreton Island or North Stradbroke Island.

Moreton Island

A 4WD is required to explore Moreton Island. A vehicular ferry service departs from Whyte Island (bookings Tel: 07-38951000) or visitors can take the passenger launch from Holt St Wharf Pinkemba (bookings Tel: 07-32686333).

Tangalooma Moreton Island Resort, PO Box 1102, Eagle Farm, 4009. Tel: 07-

32686333, Fax: 07-32686299. Holiday units from $140 to $250 per night with full resort facilities and activities plus nightly hand-feeding of wild dolphins.

Bulwer Holiday Flats. Tel: 07-32036399. Basic units from $60 per night.

Camping information and permits: contact State Government Department of Environment & Heritage, 160 Ann St. Brisbane. Tel: 07-32278186.

North Stradbroke Island

A large road network and several small towns make Straddy a bit more accessible for those without a 4WD. Access to the island is via vehicular ferry (bookings Tel: 07-32862666) or by passenger ferries (bookings Tel: 07-32862192 or 07-32862666) from Cleveland. There are a number of caravan parks and motels at Amity Point and Dunwich, but Point Lookout is the best place to stay because of the beaches, bushland and easy access to the dive shop.

Anchorage Village Beach Resort, 25 East Coast Rd, Point Lookout. Tel: 07-34098266, Fax: 07-34098304. Resort units from $80 to $130 per night.

The Islander Holiday Units, East Coast Rd, Point Lookout. Tel: 07-34098388. Units from $50 to $120 per night.

Stradbroke Island Guest House, 1 East Coast Rd, Point Lookout. Tel: 07-34098888.

Gold Coast

Diving the Gold Coast is relatively easy as dive shops are spread right along this busy tourist strip. For cheap dives there are a number of shore diving sites on the Gold Coast. Boat dives generally cost $50 for a double dive, and $30 for a single dive. Diving conditions can be good year-round, but winter brings the most stable weather and less crowds. The Gold Coast is found 100 km south of Brisbane.

Dive Operators

Aqua'Nuts, 32 Strathaird Rd, Bundall. Tel: 07-55316511. Offers PADI dive course, boat dives, retail and hire gear.

Coolangatta Scuba Centre, Cnr Wharf St & River Tce, Tweed Heads. Tel: 07-55369622. Provides boat dives, SSI dive courses, retail and hire gear.

Diver Training Services, 55 Queen St, Southport. Tel: 07-55710106.

Gold Coast Dive Centre, 20 Railway St, Southport. Tel: 07-55328088. Offers boat dives, PADI dive courses, retail and hire gear.

Gold Coast Underwater Club, 1 Fifteenth Ave, Palm Beach. Tel: 07-55353696. Runs boat dives and PADI dive courses.

Kirra Dive Centre, Cnr Creek & South St, Kirra. Tel: 07-55366622, Fax: 07-55368882. Offers PADI, NASDS and NAUI dive course, boat dives, retail and hire gear.

Ocean Dive & Photographics, PO Box 887, Coolangatta. Tel & Fax: 07-55981568. Charter boat for hire to dive shops, singles, groups and dive clubs, also offer hire gear.

Pacific Ocean Divers, 55 Carrington Crt, Mudgeeraba. Tel: 07-55303295. Offers PADI dive courses and boat dives.

Palm Beach Dive Centre & Underwater Photographics, 13 Palm Beach Ave, Palm Beach. Tel: 07-55982638, Fax: 07-55983977. Hires and sells underwater photographic equipment and offers E6 processing, boat dives, PADI dive courses and hire gear.

Southport Marine & Dive Centre, 95 Marine Pde, Southport. Tel: 07-55312333, Fax: 07-55911421. Offers boat dives, PADI dive course, retail and hire gear.

Surfers Paradise Divers, Berth 75, Mariners Cove, Seaworld Drv, Main Beach. Tel: 07-55917117, Fax: 07-55917119. Floating dive center that offers boat dives, PADI dive courses, retail and hire gear.

The Aussie Dive Store, 22 Tedder Ave, Main Beach. Tel: 07-55916133, Fax: 07-55314708. Provides PADI and SSI instruction, boat dives, retail and hire gear.

Tropic Diving Services, 23 Seabeach Ave, Mermaid Beach. Tel: 07-55725807.

Tweed Dive, 17 Tawarri Crs, Burleigh Heads. Tel: 07-55357510.

Accommodation

A popular holiday destination with a good range of accommodation from luxury 5-star resorts to basic backpacker bunk houses. But the place can be booked out and overcrowded during school holiday periods.

Greenmount Beach Resort, 3 Hill St, Coolangatta. Tel: 07-55361222, Fax: 07-55361102. 10-storey complex with rooms from $120 to $260.

On The Beach Holiday Units, 118 Marine Pde, Coolangatta. Tel and Fax: 07-55363624. 16 holiday units from $45 per day and $280 pw.

Ramada, Gold Coast Hwy, Surfers Paradise. Tel: 07-55793499, Fax: 07-55920026. 36-storey complex with rooms from $165 to $215.

New South Wales

Most of the New South Wales coastline is diveable. From the coral reefs off the north of the state to the colorful sponge gardens off the southern coast, New South Wales has always been a popular dive destination because of the variety and abundance of marine life. Dive shops and charter boats, found in all major, and quite a few minor, centers along the coast, provide relatively inexpensive boat dives.

Getting There

Divers from abroad wanting to explore the New South Wales coast can arrive on an international flight through Sydney or Brisbane airports. Most international carriers provide regular services to these airports, giving quick access to a number of areas throughout New South Wales. Divers already in Australia can use regular domestic flights from other state capitals on Ansett and Qantas.

Local Transport

One of the most popular ways to explore the New South Wales coastline is on a dive and drive trip. With so many good destinations close together, it is possible to dive several centers in your holiday, say two to three days in each location. Hire cars are available in all towns and airports. The major hire companies are Avis, Budget, Hertz and Thrifty, with roadside service provided by the NRMA (National Roads & Motorists Association). To get straight to your destination, a regional flight is fast, but expensive. Most regional centers are serviced by Qantas, Ansett and Hazelton. The New South Wales coastline is covered by a good network of bus and coach companies that offer regular scheduled services to most centers. The major bus companies are Greyhound-Pioneer and McCafferty's. The New South Wales rail service is quite good, but only runs from Murwillumbah to Nowra.

Medical and Emergencies

For any diving accident anywhere in Australia contact DES (Diving Emergency Service) on **1800 088 200**. State that it is a diving emergency, the details of the accident and the condition of the diver.

New South Wales has two recompression chambers located in Sydney, while hospitals and medical centers are located right along the coastline in all towns. All charter boats must carry oxygen as part of their survey requirements, and most boat crews are proficient in the use of first aid.

In any emergency, other than diving, ring **000**, and ask for the service you require, be it fire, police or ambulance.

Photographic Supplies

There are camera stores and film processing shops throughout New South Wales. Buying print and slide film is generally not a problem, except in some of the smaller towns. While print film can be processed just about anywhere, E6 slide processing is only possible in the larger centers, such as Sydney, Coffs Harbour, Newcastle, Wollongong, Central Coast and Canberra.

Byron Bay

Located 790 km north of Sydney, and only 200 km south of Brisbane, Byron Bay is one of the most popular diving destinations in New South Wales. Several dive shops are based in this lovely beachside town, which run daily charters to the Julian Rocks Marine Reserve and other sites. Boat dives cost about $35 for a single dive, and package deals are available if staying for several days. Conditions can be favorable at Byron year-round, and rarely is a dive canceled due to rough weather.

Dive Operators

Bayside Scuba, Cnr Lawson & Fletcher St, Byron Bay. Tel: 02-66858333, Fax: 02-66855750. Offers boat dives, SSI dive courses, retail and hire gear.

Byron Bay Dive Centre, 9 Lawson St, Byron Bay. Tel: 02-66857149. Runs daily boat dives and also offers retail, hire gear and dive instruction.

Byron Dive Downunder, Myocom Rd, Ewingsdale. Tel: 02-66847446.

Sundive Australia, Middleton St, Byron Bay. Tel: 02-66857755, Fax: 02-66858361. A PADI facility, Sundive offers daily boat dives, retail, hire gear and accommodation.

Accommodation

As a popular holiday destination Byron Bay has a wide range of accommodation on offer.

Byron Bay Holiday Inn, 45 Lawson St, Byron Bay. Tel: 02-66856373, Fax: 02-66856373. On the beachfront and with rooms at $85 to $145 per night, and $595 to $910 pw.

Cape Byron Van Village, Ewingsdale Rd, Byron Bay. Tel: 02-66857378. Cabins at $33 to $60 per night and at $96 to $140 pw.

Pacific Apartments, 62 Lawson St, Byron Bay. Tel: 02-66857597. Three-storey complex on the beach with rooms at $80 to $150 per night and $375 to $1300 pw.

Ballina

Not generally well known as a diving destination, Ballina has many interesting boat and shore diving locations, and conditions are generally good year round. One of the larger towns on the northern New South Wales coastline, Ballina is located 753 km north of Sydney.

Dive Operators

Alan Jarrett's Divers World, 29 Cherry St, Ballina. Tel: 02-66863985. Located in Ballina for 19 years, Allan Jarrett's Divers World of-

fers NASDS dive courses (part time), retail and hire gear, and will soon have a boat running weekend charters.

Accommodation

Though not well known to divers, Ballina is a favorite holiday destination with a good variety of accommodation.

Ballina Beach Resort, Compton Dve, Ballina. Tel: 02-66868888, Fax: 02-66868897. A two-storey complex with rooms from $79 to $180.

Ballina Travellers Lodge, 36 Tamar St, Ballina. Tel: 02-66866737, Fax: 02-66866342. Units from $41 to $90 a night.

Brooms Head

Brooms Head Dive Centre, 92 Ocean Rd, Brooms Head. Tel and Fax: 02-66467160. Brooms Head Dive Centre has really opened up the diving in the area and offers a complete dive holiday package. They are a PADI facility, and offer dive courses, retail and hire gear and daily double boat dives at $40 to Buchanan Reef, $60 to Sandon Shoals and $80 to Pimpernel Rock. They also have five self-contained holiday units, which sleep up to six and are priced at $12 per person per night. A small holiday town 732 km north of Sydney, Brooms Head is diveable year round.

Coffs Harbour

Lying off the coast of Coffs Harbour is a group of islands known as the Solitary Islands. This group offers some of the best diving in New South Wales and the area was recently declared a marine reserve. Access to the islands is from Coffs Harbour and Mullaway, 40 km to the north. Dive shops in both these areas offer boat dives to the reserve, costing $30 for a single dive and $60 for a double dive (which includes the second tank). Coffs Harbour is a busy tourist area, 543 km north of Sydney, that is blessed with lovely beaches and nice weather year round.

Dive Operators

Coffs Harbour Charter Boat Services, 17 Melittas Ave, Coffs Harbour. Tel: 02-66511434. Offers dive charters on MV *Laura E.*

Dive Quest, 30 Mullaway Dve, Mullaway. Tel: 02-66541930, Fax: 02-66540328. Dive Quest runs daily boat dives to the Northern Solitary Islands. They also offer dive instruction, retail, hire gear and can arrange accommodation.

Divers Depot, Showground, Pacific Hwy, Coffs Harbour. Tel: 02-66522033. Offers charters to the Southern Solitary Islands and dive instruction.

Island Snorkel & Dive Charter, 27 Carrington St, Woolgoolga. Tel: 02-66542860. Runs dive charters to the Northern Solitary Islands.

Jetty Dive Centre, 398 High St, Coffs Harbour. Tel: 02-66511611, Fax: 02-66525702. Servicing the Southern Solitary Islands, Jetty Dive provides daily boat dives, dive course, retail and hire gear.

Accommodation

Holiday makers flock to the Coffs Harbour area, where there is a wide selection of accommodation on offer.

Aanuka Beach Resort, Firman Dve, Diggers Beach. Tel: 02-66527555, Fax: 02-66527053. This resort complex has a range of units from $75 to $385 per night.

Coffs Harbour Motor Inn, 22 Elizabeth St, Coffs Harbour. Tel: 02-66526388, Fax: 02-66526493. Units from $55 to $103 per night.

Sunseeker, 7 Prince St, Coffs Harbour. Tel: 02-66522087. Holiday units priced from $40 to $80 per night and $230 to $550 pw.

South West Rocks

Located 466 km north of Sydney and on the mouth of the Macleay River, South West Rocks is a favorite area with holiday makers and divers alike. Diving is good year-round off South West Rocks on a number of offshore islands and reefs. Both dive shops based in this small town run regular boat dives, with single dives costing $35 and double dives $60. They also offer package deals on diving and accommodation.

Dive Operators

Fish Rock Dive Centre, 328 Gregory St, South West Rocks. Tel: 02-65666614, Fax: 02-65665585. Offers daily boat dives, PADI instruction, on-site bunkhouse accommodation at $15 per night, retail and hire gear.

South West Rocks Dive Centre, 98 Gregory St, South West Rocks. Tel: 02-65666474, Fax: 02-65666959. Offers dive courses, daily boat dives, retail and hire gear, and on-site bunkhouse accommodation at $15 per night.

Accommodation

If you don't wish to stay in the accommodation provided by the dive shop, there is still a wide range to choose from.

Horseshoe Bay Beach Park, Livingstone St, South West Rocks. Tel: 02-65666370, Fax: 02-65666302. Cabins and vans from $25 to $55 per night and $140 to $390 pw.

Ocean View Apartments, 2 Gregory St, South West Rocks. Tel: 02-65666313, Fax: 02-65666356. Units at $50 per night and $290 pw.

Port Macquarie

With a pleasant climate year-round, Port Macquarie is one of the busiest holiday centers on the New South Wales coast. Located 398 km north of Sydney, Port Macquarie can be packed with holiday makers, especially during school holidays. Divers will find a visit to the town is well worth the effort as many hidden reefs lie off this section of coastline.

Dive Operator

Port Macquarie Dive Centre, Port Marina, Park St, Port Macquarie. Tel: 02-65838483. A PADI facility, Port Macquarie Dive Centre offers dive charters at $30 for a single dive and $55 for a double dive, retail and hire gear.

Accommodation
There is definitely no shortage of accommodation around Port Macquarie.

Beachfront Regency Motor Inn, 40 William St, Port Macquarie. Tel: 02-65832244, Fax: 02-65832868. A three-storey complex with rooms from $55 to $75 a night.

Central View Holiday Units, 2 Clarence St, Port Macquarie. Tel: 02-65831171, Fax: 02-65831171. Units from $45 to $110 per night and $300 to $900 pw.

Sails Resort, Park St, Port Macquarie. Tel: 02-65833999, Fax: 02-65840397. Rooms from $150 to $400 per night.

Norfolk Island

Although Norfolk Island is better known as a tourist destination, it is surrounded by coral reefs and offers excellent diving. Diving is generally good year-round, but over summer the water is clear and warm. This historic island is 1676 km north east of Sydney and is serviced daily by two-and-a-half hour flights (costing around $600 return) from Sydney and Brisbane.

Dive Operator
Norfolk Island Bounty Divers, Village Centre, Norfolk Island. Tel: 0011-672-3-22751, Fax: 0011-672-3-23375. PADI dive courses; daily charter dives at $45 for a single dive and $70 for a double dive; retail and hire gear.

Accommodation
There are close to 50 places to stay on a visit to Norfolk Island.

Daydreamer Holiday Units. Tel: 0011-672-3-22114, Fax: 0011-672-3-23014. Units from $93 to $100 per night.

South Pacific Resort Hotel, Taylors Road. Tel: 0011-672-3-23154, Fax: 0011-672-3-22166. Rooms from $140 to $195 per night and $965 to $1350 pw.

Viewrest Inn, Grassy Rd. Tel: 0011-672-3-22269, Fax: 0011-672-3-22376. Units at $90.

Lord Howe Island

Located 700 km north east of Sydney, Lord Howe Island is a tropical paradise surrounded by the most southern coral reefs in the world. The diving is spectacular all around the island, and conditions can be good year round, but summer provides the clearest water and most stable weather. The island is accessible by a two-hour flight from Sydney or Brisbane. The airfare to the island is very expensive if purchased on its own, but is less if purchased in conjunction with a package deal on accommodation and diving.

Dive Operator
Sea Life International, Middle Beach, Lord Howe Island. Tel: 02-65632154. Sea Life runs daily boat dives at $55 for a single dive, and also offers dive courses.

Pro Dive Travel, Shop 620, Royal Arcade, 255 Pitt St, Sydney. Tel: 02-92649499, Fax: 02-92649494. Booking agents for the diving on Lord Howe, offering package deals on diving, airfare and accommodation.

Accommodation
With a maximum of 400 guests, there is a limited amount of accommodation on Lord Howe Island. About half a dozen holiday unit complexes are found on the island.

Blue Lagoon. Tel: 02-65632006, Fax: 02-65632150. Offers rooms from $190 to $290.

Broken Banyan. Tel: 02-65632024, Fax: 02-65632201. Units from $90 to $134 per night and $630 to $938 pw.

Leanda Lei Apartments. Tel: 02-65632195, Fax: 02-65632095. Units from $130 to $260.

Lorhiti Apartments. Tel: 02-65632081, Fax: 02-65632118. Units from $90 to $220 per night and $630 to $1540 pw.

Mary Challis Cottages. Tel: 02-65632076, Fax: 02-65632159. Prices from $65 to $110.

Somerset Holiday Accommodation. Tel: 02-65632061, Fax: 02-65632110. Units from $109 to $165 per night and $763 to $1155 pw.

North Haven

Located 400 km north of Sydney, North Haven has only recently been opened up to divers, but is proving a popular destination. Diving conditions are good year round off this small coastal town, and blue currents can wash in at any time.

Dive Operator

Cool D Dive Shop, 615 Ocean Drive, North Haven. Tel and Fax: 02-65597181. Cool D offers daily boat dives at $30 for a single dive and $50 for a double dive, PADI dive courses, retail and hire gear, and package deals on accommodation and diving.

Accommodation

There are only a few places to stay when visiting North Haven.

Jacaranda Caravan Park, 85 The Parade, North Haven. Tel: 02-65599470, Fax: 02-65598604. Park cabins from $30 to $120 per night and $160 to $720 pw.

North Haven Motel, 506 Ocean Dve, North Haven. Tel: 02-65599604. Rooms at $38 to $65 per night and $250 to $380 pw.

Forster/Tuncurry and Seal Rocks

The twin towns of Forster/Tuncurry are a very popular holiday area, and with wonderful beaches and a range of activities it is easy to see why the crowds are drawn here. For divers this area provides some of the most exciting diving in New South Wales, with numerous reefs and wrecks, and plenty of grey nurse sharks. Single boat dives cost around $30 and double dives $60 to local dive sites, and single boat dives run off the beach at Seal Rocks cost $30. Located 300 km north of Sydney, this area is perfect for a weekend escape or an extended holiday.

Dive Operator

Action Divers, 17 Manning St, Tuncurry. Tel: 02-65554053. A PADI facility, Action Divers offers daily boat dives, dive courses, retail and hire gear.

Blue Water Divers, Wharf St, Forster. Tel: 02-65547478. Offers dive instruction, boat dives, retail and hire gear.

Forster Dive Centre, 15 Little St, Forster. Tel: 02-65545255. Forster Dive Centre runs daily boat dives, and offers dive courses, retail and hire gear.

Accommodation

The range of accommodation available is extensive around Forster/Tuncurry.

Bellevue, Manning St, Tuncurry. Tel: 02-65546577, Fax: 02-65556078. Offers units from $38 to $76 per night.

Forster Motor Inn, 11 Wallis St, Forster. Tel: 02-65546877, Fax: 02-65545061. Units from $56 to $140 per night.

Forster Waters Caravan Park, Tea Tree Rd, Forster. Tel: 02-65548903, Fax: 02-65555511. Cabins from $25 to $70 per night and $175 to $480 pw.

Port Stephens

Only 200 km north of Sydney, Port Stephens has some of the best shore and boat diving in New South Wales. The shore diving will cost you the price of an air fill, while boat dives cost $30 for a single dive and $55 for a double dive. Conditions along this section of coastline are generally good year round. Port Stephens is also a busy holiday area and finding a room during school holidays can be impossible if you haven't booked ahead.

Dive Operators

Dive Nelson Bay, Nelson Towers Complex, Victoria Pde, Nelson Bay. Tel: 02-49812491. Offers PADI instructions, daily boat dives, retail and hire gear.

Hawks Nest Dive & Fishing Centre, Tuloa Ave, Hawks Nest. Tel: 02-49970442.

Kunara Charters, Halifax Park Kiosk, Little Beach, Nelson Bay. Tel: 02-49811054. Offers dive charters.

Myall Diving, 82 Port Stephens, Tea Gardens. Tel: 02-49971557.

Pro Dive, D'Albora Marinas, Nelsons Bay. Tel: 02-49814331, Fax: 02-49814763. Pro Dive provides daily boat dives, PADI dive courses, retail and hire gear.

Accommodation

With diving at Port Stephens possible on either side of the bay, divers have a wide range of accommodation to choose from. On the northern side of the bay are Tea Gardens and Hawks Nest, and on the southern side Nelson Bay, Shoal Bay, Anna Bay and many other good dive spots.

Club Inn Tea Gardens, Yalinbah St, Tea Gardens. Tel: 02-49970911, Fax: 02-49970910. This complex has rooms from $68 to $98 per night.

Hawks Nest Beach Caravan Park, Booner St, Hawks Nest. Tel: 02-49970239. Adjacent to the beach, with cabins from $35 to $65 a night.

Nelson Lodge Motel, Government Rd, Nelson Bay. Tel: 02-49811705, Fax: 02-49814785. Offers rooms from $75 to $160 a night.

Shoal Bay Flats, 50 Ronald Ave, Shoal Bay. Tel: 02-49811259. Offers units from $30 to $75 per night and $125 to $550 pw.

Newcastle & Swansea

Newcastle is one of the largest towns in New South Wales and is 150 km north of Sydney, while Swansea is 35 km south of Newcastle. The Newcastle coastline is littered with reefs and shipwrecks. Shore diving is possible all along the coastline here. Boat dives cost about $30 for a single dive and $50 for a double dive. Diving conditions can be good year round, but winter westerly winds bring clear water and calm seas.

Dive Operators

Action Divers, 194 Maitland Rd, Islington. Tel: 02-49616111. Offers PADI dive courses, retail and hire gear.

Asumco Diving Academy, 136 George St, East Maitland. Tel: 02-49342211.

Bluewater Diving Academy, 28 Watt St, Raymond Terrace. Tel: 02-49831344.

Charlestown Diving Academy, 36 Smart St, Charlestown. Tel: 02-49421412. Offers dive courses, retail and hire gear.

Dive Addicts, Fairfax Rd, Warners Bay. Tel: 02-49586527. Offers PADI dive courses, retail and hire gear.

Divercity Newcastle Swansea Dive Charters, 37 Ridge St, Merewether. Tel: 02-49633793. Runs daily dive charters.

Lets Go Diving, 59 Georgetown Rd, Georgetown. Tel: 02-49688744. Offers dive courses, retail and hire gear.

Scuba Professionals, 430 Pacific Hwy, Belmont. Tel: 02-49453676. Has retail and hire gear and run PADI dive courses.

Scuba Shack, 114 Maitland Rd, Mayfield. Tel: 02-49682977. Provide PADI and NAUI dive instruction, retail and hire gear.

Swansea Diving Services, 18 Southern Cross Dve, Booragul. Tel: 02-49505215.

The Dive Shop, 708 Hunter St, Newcastle. Tel: 02-49294234, Fax: 02-49264617. Offers dive charters, dive courses, retail and hire gear.

Accommodation

There is a wide range of accommodation in the Newcastle and Swansea area.

Blue Pacific Motel, 82 Pacific Hwy, Swansea. Tel: 02-49711055, Fax: 02-49711296. Rooms at $56 to $72 per night and $380 to $560 pw.

Newcastle Harbourside Motel, 107 Scott St, Newcastle. Tel: 02-49263244, Fax: 02-49263013. Rooms from $50 to $71 per night.

Travellers Motor Village, 295 Maitland Rd, Mayfield. Tel: 02-49681394, Fax: 02-49688230. Cabins at $58 per night and $350 pw.

Central Coast

Only 100 km north of Sydney, the Central Coast has always been a popular holiday destination. There are countless beaches and a wide range of attractions, including some first class diving. Shore and boat dives are possible off the Central Coast; single boats dives cost around $25. Clear water and calm seas can be experienced off the Central Coast at anytime of the year, but winter provides some of the best conditions.

Dive Operators

AJ's Scuba Centre, 350 Main Rd, Toukley. Tel: 02-43971901. Offers PADI dive course, boat dives, retail and hire gear.

Aquatic Dive Charters, RMB 3390 Wisemans Ferry Rd, Somersby. Tel: 02-43721502. Run dive charters from Terrigal Haven.

C Breeze Dive Centre, 352 Main Rd, Toukley. Tel: 02-43961155, Fax: 02-43961177. Offers daily boat dives, PADI dive courses, retail and hire gear.

Central Coast Charters, 38 Mirreen Ave, Davistown. Tel: 02-43631221.

Gosford Diving Services, 310 Trafalgar Ave, Umina. Tel & Fax: 02-43421855. Runs boat dives, dive courses, and has retail and hire gear.

Orca Dive, 254 Lakedge Ave, Berkeley Vale. Tel: 02-43891728.

Pro Dive The Entrance, 96 The Entrance Rd, The Entrance. Tel: 02-43341559.

Pro Dive Norah Head, 15 Mitchel St, Norah Head. Tel: 02-43963652. Both Pro Dive stores provide PADI dive courses, boat dives, retail and hire gear.

Terrigal Diving School, The Haven, Terrigal. Tel: 02-43841219. Established 28 years ago, the Terrigal Dive School offers NASDS dive courses, retail, hire gear and dive charters.

Accommodation

There is plenty of accommodation to be found on the Central Coast. From Norah Head to Umina, are motels, holiday units, beach resorts, caravan parks and houses to rent.

Beachcomber Resort, 200 Main Rd, Toukley. Tel: 02-43971300, Fax: 02-43971167. Has rooms from $105 to $185 per night.

East Ocean Beach Caravan Park, Sydney Ave, Umina. Tel: 02-43411522, Fax: 02-43414855. This caravan park has cabins at $35 to $90 per night and $210 to $540 pw.

Norah Head Tourist Park, Victoria St, Norah Head. Tel: 02-43963935. Offers park cabins from $50 to $80 per night and $300 to $550 pw.

Terrigal Beach Motel, 1 Painter Lane, Terrigal. Tel: 02-43841423. Rooms at $40 to $75 per night.

Sydney

A great deal of diving can be enjoyed around Sydney, including shore dives and boat trips to reefs and shipwrecks. Dive shops are found throughout the harbor city, and offshore trips are possible midweek and on weekends. Boat dives around Sydney are $25 to $30 for a single dive and $40 to $50 for a double dive. While conditions can be good at anytime of the year off Sydney, winter brings the calmest seas and clearest water when the westerly winds are blowing.

Dive Operators

All the dive shops listed here offer boat dives, dive courses, retail and hire gear.

Ace Bondi Diving Academy, 25 Park Pde, Bondi. Tel: 02-93693943.

Aqua Sports, 430 Hume Hwy, Yagoona. Tel: 02-97082826.

Aquatic Explorers, 7 Beach Park Ave, Cronulla. Tel: 02-95271518.

Aquatic Explorers, 11 Bridges St, Kurnell. Tel: 02-96689207.

Area North Shore Scuba School, 22 Frederick St, Hornsby. Tel: 02-94776982.

Atlantis Divers, Barrenjoey Boathouse, Palm Beach. Tel: 02-99744261.

Cannell Diving, 20 Benelong St, Seaforth. Tel: 02-99495173.

Cape Baily Diving Service, Tonkin St, Cronulla. Tel: 02-95404454. Dive Charters.

Coastline Dive, 93 Bundeena Dve, Bundeena. Tel: 02-95442668.

Deep 6 Diving, 1057 Victoria Rd, West Ryde. Tel: 02-98584299.

Dipper Diving. Tel: 02-43842607. Sydney dive charters.

Dive Centre, 40 Kingsway, Cronulla. Tel: 02-95237222.

Dive Centre Manly, 10 Belgrave St, Manly. Tel: 02-99774355.

Dive Site, Castle Pl, Castle Hill. Tel: 02-98945560.

Dive 2000, 2 Military Rd, Neutral Bay. Tel: 02-99537783.

Diver Transport, 166 Powderworks Rd, Elanora Heights. Tel: 02-99138721.

Fathom Diving, 176 Sydney Rd, Fairlight. Tel: 02-99487221.

Frog Dive Guildford, 395 Guildford Rd, Guildford. Tel: 02-98923422.

Frog Dive Maroubra Junction, 687 Anzac Pde, Maroubra Junction. Tel: 02-93496333.

Frog Dive Willoughby, 539 Willoughby Rd, Willoughby. Tel: 02-99585699.

Fun Dive Centre, 255 Stanmore Rd, Stanmore. Tel: 02-95500830.

Go Dive, 192 Bondi Rd, Bondi. Tel: 02-93693855.

Hills District Scuba School, 257 Annangrove Rd, Annangrove. Tel: 02-96791098.

Mike Scotland's Dive School, 36 Tulong Pl, Kirrawee. Tel: 02-95217720.

North Narrabeen Dive Centre, 1457 Pittwater Rd, North Narrabeen. Tel: 02-99137199.

Pacific Coast Divers Bondi, 16 O'Brien St, Bondi. Tel: 02-91303323.

Pacific Coast Divers Clovelly, 355 Clovelly Rd, Clovelly. Tel: 02-96657427.

Pacific Coast Divers Manly, 169 Pittwater Rd, Manly. Tel: 02-99775966.

Pro Aquatics, 25 Dumaresq St, Campbelltown. Tel: 02-46272351.

Pro Dive Chatswood, 67 Archer St, Chatswood. Tel: 02-94195557.

Pro Dive Coogee, 27 Alfreda St, Coogee. Tel: 02-96656333.

Pro Dive Drummoyne, 227 Victoria Rd, Drummoyne. Tel: 02-98197711.

Pro Dive Head Office, 330 Wattle St, Ultimo. Tel: 02-92816166.

Pro Dive Hornsby, Hornsby. Tel: 02-94821045.

Pro Dive Manly, Manly. Tel: 02-99763499.

Pro Dive Parramatta, 7/2 O'Connell St, Parramatta. Tel: 02-98919110.

Pro Dive Penrith, 97c Henry St, Penrith. Tel: 02-47312866.

Pro Dive Sydney, 478 George St, Sydney. Tel: 02-92646177.

St George Underwater Centre, 458 King Georges Rd, Beverly Hills. Tel: 02-91500268.

Scuba Afloat, 2 Tonkin St, Cronulla. Tel: 02-95274730.

Scuba Cruise, 15 Meig Pl, Blacktown. Tel: 02-98316088.

Scuba Warehouse, Horwood Pl, Parramatta. Tel: 02-96891389.

Sea Quest Divers, 167 Old South Head Rd, Bondi Junction. Tel: 02-93872743.

Shiprock Dive, 617 Port Hacking Rd, Lilli Pilli. Tel: 02-95262664.

Snorkel Inn, 49 President Ave, Kogarah. Tel: 02-95881152.

Southern Cross Divers, The Spit Bridge, Mossman. Tel: 02-99695072.

Sub Aquatics, 484 King Georges Rd, Beverly Hills. Tel: 02-95704222.

Wats on in Diving, Campbelltown. Tel: 02-46251425.

Wilderness Sea 'n' Ski Dee Why, 868 Pittwater Road, Dee Why. Tel: 02-99711100.

Wilderness Sea 'n' Ski Liverpool, 137 George St, Liverpool. Tel: 02-98224112.

Accommodation

If staying in Sydney just to dive, you may find it best to stay in one of the areas that dive charter boats depart from. These suburbs are Palm Beach, Narrabeen, Manly, Rose Bay, Botany Bay and Cronulla. In these areas, and throughout Sydney, you will find a wide range of accommodation.

Barrenjoey House, 1108 Barrenjoey Rd, Palm Beach. Tel: 02-99744001, Fax: 02-99545008. Rooms from $60 to $130 per night.

Cronulla Motor Inn, 85 Kingsway, Cronulla. Tel: 02-95236800, Fax: 02-95230314. Rooms from $84 to $107 per night.

Lakeside Caravan Park, Lake Park Rd, Narrabeen. Tel: 02-99137845, Fax: 02-99706385. Cabins at $58 to $88 per night and $300 to $720 pw.

Manly Beach Resort, 6 Carlton St, Manly. Tel: 02-99774188, Fax: 02-99770524. Rooms from $70 to $95 per night and $476 to $546 pw.

Sante Fe Holiday Units, 46 Victoria Pde, Manly. Tel: 02-99775213. Offers units at $69 to $180 per night and $15 to $1260 pw.

Wollongong and Bass Point

Wollongong is only 80 km south of Sydney and easily accessible on a day trip, but you will need more than a day to explore all this stretch of coastline. From Wollongong, 40 km south to Gerroa, are countless shore and boat diving sites, including Shellharbour, Bass Point and Kiama. A number of dive shops in the area run dive charters, with single dives costing $20 to $25. Diving conditions can be good year round along this section of coast; summer brings clear, warm water, and winter calm blue seas.

Dive Operators

Coastwide Diving Services, 41 Addison St, Shellharbour. Tel: 02-42964266. Runs daily boat dives and offer PADI dive courses, retail and hire gear.

Dive Time, Novotel Northbeach, North Wollongong. Tel: 02-42265066. Offers PADI dive courses, retail and hire gear.

Illawarra Aqua Centre, 235 Windang RD, Windang. Tel & Fax: 02-42964215. Offers boat dives, retail, hire gear and PADI dive courses.

Pro Dive Shellharbour, 17 Addison St, Shellharbour. Tel & Fax: 02-42963644. A PADI facility, providing boat dives, retail and hire gear.

Subdive Australia, Albion Park. Tel: 02-42716488.

United Divers, 6 Victoria St, Wollongong. Tel: 02-42285962. Provides boat dives, dive instruction, retail and hire gear.

Accommodation

There is a wide range of accommodation on offer from Wollongong to Gerroa, including:

Novotel Northbeach, 2 Cliff Rd, Wollongong. Tel: 02-42263555, Fax: 02-42291705. This 10-storey complex has rooms from $145 to $800 per night.

Ocean Beach Motel, 2 Addison St, Shellharbour. Tel: 02-42961399. Rooms from $40 to $80 per night and $423 to $462 pw.

Shellharbour Beachside Tourist Park, John St, Shellharbour. Tel: 02-42951123. Cabins from $48 to $105 per night and $330 to $630 pw.

Surfside Motel, Harbour St, Wollongong. Tel: 02-42297288, Fax: 02-42289418. Rooms from $73 to $115 per night and $385 to $441 pw.

Jervis Bay

The most popular diving destination south of Sydney, Jervis Bay attracts hundreds of divers each weekend to explore the endless range of dive sites inside and outside this massive bay. Divers have the choice of doing single dives (around $30), double dives (around $50) or liveaboard trips of 2 to 5 days (varying from $295 to $500). Diving conditions can be great at Jervis Bay year round, with blue water in summer and winter depending on the winds, currents and seas. Located 180 km south of Sydney, Jervis Bay is also a favorite destination of many holiday makers, so book early over summer and school holidays.

Dive Operators
Aquatique, 88 Worrigee St, Nowra. Tel: 02-44218159. Retail, hire gear and dive instruction.

Delphinus Diving Services, 335 Elizabeth Drv, Vincentia. Tel: 02-44416232. Offers liveaboard trips on the 18m catamaran *Ocean Trek*, as well as dive instruction.

Jervis Bay Liveaboard Charters, Jervis Bay. Tel: 02-44417107. Runs liveaboard trips on the vessel MV *Victory*.

Jervis Bay Sea Sports, 47 Owen St, Huskisson. Tel: 02-44415012, Fax: 02-44416723. Offers PADI dive courses, retail, hire gear and daily boat dives.

Pro Dive Jervis Bay, 64 Owen St, Huskisson. Tel: 02-44415255, Fax: 02-44417113. Runs daily boat dives and provides PADI dive courses, retail and hire gear.

Accommodation
There is a plentiful supply of accommodation around Jervis Bay, but most of the diving is centered around Huskisson.

Bayside Motor Inn, Bowen St, Huskisson. Tel: 02-44415194, Fax: 02-44417142. Offers rooms from $50 to $140 per night and $360 to $850 pw.

Huskisson Beach Tourist Park, Beach St, Huskisson. Tel: 02-44415142, Fax: 02-44415142. Cabins at $38 to $120 per night and $228 to $840 pw.

Jervis Bay Hotel, Owen St, Huskisson. Tel: 02-44415781, Fax: 02-44417072. Offers rooms from $55 to $95 per night.

Ulladulla

The fishing port of Ulladulla is 210km south of Sydney has many excellent dive sites. Just minutes from the harbor are dozens of hidden reefs packed with fish and invertebrates. Diving conditions can be good year round off Ulladulla, but during summer and autumn the coast is washed with warm blue water.

Dive Operator
Ulladulla Divers Supplies, Shop 10 Wason St, Ulladulla. Tel: 02-44555303, Fax: 02-44552695. Runs daily boat dives at $25 for a single dive and $20 for your second dive of the day. Offers dive courses, retail and hire gear.

Accommodation
There is good range of accommodation on offer around Ulladulla, including:

Marlin Hotel, 110 Princes Hwy, Ulladulla. Tel: 02-44551999. Offers rooms from $20 to $60 per night.

Top View Motel, 72 South St, Ulladulla. Tel: 02-44551514, Fax: 02-44551400. Units priced at $38 to $115 per night.

Ulladulla Tourist Park, South St, Ulladulla. Tel: 02-44552457, Fax: 02-44552457. Cabins from $30 to $115 per night and $180 to $805 pw.

Canberra and Country Areas

The nation's capital is not really a dive destination, but a number of dive shops based in Canberra, and other country areas, run dive trips to many locations on the New South Wales coast.

Dive Operators

Aqua-Medium Dive Centre, 43 Colbee Crt, Phillip. Tel: 02-62823919. Offers NASDS dive courses, retail, hire gear and dive trips.

Argonaut Dive, Reed St, Tuggeranong. Tel: 02-62932955. Offer PADI instruction, dive trips, retail and hire gear.

Descend Diver Education, 826 David St, Albury. Tel: 02-60411406. Provides dive courses, retail and hire gear.

Lady of the Sea Diving Academy, Collyburl Crs, Isabella Plains. Tel: 02-62925773. Runs dive trips, PADI dive courses and have retail and hire gear.

Quantum Scuba Diving, Western Creek. Tel: 02-62886111.

Scuba Store, 7 Lansdale St, Braddon. Tel: 02-62474911. Provides dive instruction, dive trips, retail and hire gear.

Snowline Caravan Park, Jindabyne. Tel: 02-64562180. Offers accommodation from $12 to $80 per night, air fills and information on diving the sunken township of Lake Jindabyne.

The remains of the town are found in 2 to 40 m of water and are said to be quite eerie. The township is best dived over summer, and is only for experienced divers as the visibility is low and the altitude is high.

South West Aquatic Services, 34 Graham St, Wagga Wagga. Tel: 02-69225003. Offers retail, hire gear and dive courses.

Batemans Bay

Batemans Bay and the surrounding towns offer the diver brilliant shore and boat diving at anytime of the year, but autumn and summer can provide the best conditions. The local dive shops run single boat dives at $25 and double dive trips at $50. Located 275 km south of Sydney, Batemans Bay is a popular holiday town and can be quite busy with holiday makers over summer, so book ahead if possible.

Dive Operators

Aqua-Medium, 5/33 Orient St, Batemans Bay. Tel: 02-44729930. Offers NASDS dive courses, boat dives, retail and hire gear.

Malua Bay Dive Shop, 8 Kuppa Ave, Malua Bay. Tel: 02-44711858. Runs dive charters and offer retai and, hire gear and dive courses.

Accommodation

Batemans Bay is a very busy area during school holidays, with holiday makers descending on the town from Sydney and Canberra. An excellent range of accommodation on offer.

Abel Tasman Motel, 222 Beach Rd, Batemans Bay. Tel: 02-44726511, Fax: 02-44724027. Rooms from $45 to $125 per night and $245 to $616 pw.

Easts Riverside Holiday Park, Wharf Rd, Batemans Bay. Tel: 02-44724048. Offers cabins from $35 to $100 per night and $210 to $770 pw.

Malua Bay Inn, 4 Kuppa Ave, Malua Bay. Tel: 02-44711659. Units at $45 to $90 per night and $190 to $600 pw.

Montague Island

Montague Island offers excellent diving year round, and is accessible from the towns of Narooma and Bermagui. Located 345km south of Sydney, Narooma is a fishing port and popular holiday town, while Bermagui is a fishing town 30 km south of Narooma. Double dives out to Montague Island cost about $60, which usually includes the second tank.

Dive Operators

Bermagui Dive & Boating, 8 Bunga St, Bermagui. Tel: 02-64934184. Runs dive charters, dive courses and provide retail and hire gear

Darryl's Tackle & Dive, 66 Princes Hwy, Narooma. Tel: 02-44762111. Offers dive courses, dive charters, retail and hire gear.

Ocean Hut Fishing & Dive Centre, 110 Main St, Narooma. Tel/Fax: 02-44762278. Offers dive charters, PADI dive courses, retail and hire gear.

Accommodation

Divers wishing to dive Montague Island will find a range of accommodation at both Narooma and Bermagui, which includes:

Amooran Court, 30 Montague St, Narooma. Tel: 02-44762198. Rooms from $45 to $80 per night and $200 to $510 pw.

Horseshoe Bay Motel, Lamont St, Bermagui. Tel: 02-64934206, Fax: 02-64934859. Units from $30 to $40 per night and $80 to $385 pw.

Surf Beach Caravan Park, Ballangalla St, Narooma. Tel: 02-44762275. Offers cabins at $30 a night and $180 to $300 pw.

Tathra

Tathra offers the diver a range of wonderful shore and boat diving experiences. Located 440 km south of Sydney, Tathra has good diving year round, but over summer brings magic days when clear warm water washes the coast.

Dive Operator

Sea Trek, 7 Beach St, Tathra. Tel: 02-64941799. Sea Trek run daily boat dives at $35 to $45 for a single dive and $50 to $60 for a double dive depending on the distance to the dive sites. They also offer dive instruction, retail and hire gear.

Accommodation

Tathra is a lovely seaside town and holiday destination with a range of accommodation.

Seabreeze Holiday Park, Andy Poole Dve, Tathra. Tel: 02-64941350. Offers cabins at $40 to $120 per night, and on-site vans at $25 to $55 per night.

Tathra Motel, Bega St, Tathra. Tel: 02-64941101. Units from $35 to 105 per night and $150 to $650 pw.

Merimbula and Eden

Located on the New South Wales and Victorian border, Eden is a busy fishing town 475 km south of Sydney. Merimbula is more of a holiday town, 20 km north of Eden, but both offer exceptional diving. Either from the shore or by boat divers will be able to explore a range of reefs and a number of shipwrecks on this section of coastline. Boat dives cost $35 for a single dive, and while conditions are generally good year round, over summer blue warm water makes the diving something special.

Dive Operators

Merimbula Divers Lodge & Dive School, 15 Park St, Merimbula. Tel: 02-64953611, Fax: 02-64953648. MDL has on-site bunkhouse accommodation at $20 per night, retail and hire gear and run boat dives and dive courses.

Twofold Dive Charter Eden, 28 Bass St, Eden. Tel: 02-64963384. Offers dive courses, dive charters, accommodation, retail and hire gear.

Accommodation

Both Merimbula and Eden have a good range of accommodation on offer if you don't wish to stay in that provided by the dive shops.

Eagle Heights Holiday Units, 12 Yule St, Eden. Tel: 02-64961971. Units from $45 to $75 per night and $230 to $700 pw.

Isabellas Holiday Flats, 2 Wonga St, Merimbula. Tel: 02-64951171. Rooms at $40 $80 per night and $250 to $650 pw.

Victoria

Diving in Victoria is full of surprises for the first-time visitor to this southern state. A number of dive shops and charter boats operate around Melbourne, and a wealth and variety of marine life is found offshore. With dive shops spread throughout most of the state, it is possible to dive along much of the coastline of Victoria except for sections of the eastern coastline, which not yet serviced by professional dive operators.

Getting There

Many international carriers provide regular flights into Melbourne International Airport, which places the diver in a good position to explore east, west, or Melbourne itself. Dozens of daily Ansett and Qantas domestic flights from other state capitals arrive at Melbourne Airport.

Local Transport

Driving is probably the best option when exploring Victoria since it is such a small state. Hire cars are available at airports and in most towns; the major companies are Avis, Budget, Hertz and Thrifty, while roadside service in Victoria is provided by the RACV (Royal Automobile Club of Victoria). Most of Victoria is also linked by a good rail network, providing inexpensive transport to most of the diving centres. Victorian towns are also accessible by regular bus services provided by Greyhound-Pioneer and McCafferty's. For those with limited time the best option is a regional flight. Ansett, Kendell and Qantas service most centers in Victoria and also the islands of Bass Strait.

Medical and Emergencies

Hospitals and medical centers are found throughout Victoria. Victoria's only recompression chamber is located in Melbourne. For any diving accident anywhere in Australia contact DES (Diving Emergency Service) on **1800 088 200**, and state that it is a diving emergency, the details of the accident and the condition of the diver.

In any emergency, other than diving, ring **000**, and ask for the service you require, be it fire, police or ambulance.

All charter boats operating in Victoria carry oxygen and first aid kits, and most boat crews are trained in their use.

Photographic Supplies

Visitors to Victoria will find they can purchase slide and print film in all large towns, but slide film may be hard to find in some of the smaller ones. Print film can be processed in just about any town in Victoria, but E6 slide film can only be developed in Melbourne and Geelong.

Wilsons Promontory

Diving The Prom is possible on single dives costing $55, double dives costing $70, or by live-aboard boat. Located 230 km southeast of Melbourne, Wilsons Promontory is the perfect destination for a weekend trip or longer.

Dive Operators

Cross Diving Services, 48 Bailey St, Bairnsdale. Tel: 03-51524666. Provides dive courses, retail and hire gear, and dive charters to Cape Conran at $25 a dive and to The Prom..

SEAL Diving Services, 29 Church St, Traralgon. Tel/Fax: 03-51746216. Offer PADI dive courses, retail and hire gear.

Seawork, Tarraville Rd, Port Albert. Tel: 03-51832401.

Southern Star Boat Charters, 23 Wattletree

Crs, Morwell. Tel: 03-51346484. Departing from Port Welshpool, *Southern Star* is a 12-m cat that runs liveaboard trips around The Prom and the islands of Bass Strait; priced at $1400 per day for groups of up to 10 divers.

Strzelecki Dive Services, 9265 Invermay Rd, Jumbuk. Tel: 03-56276474. Offers NASDS dive courses, dive charters, retail and hire gear and accommodation.

Accommodation

There is a varied range of accommodation in the towns around Wilsons Promontory, at Port Albert, Port Welshpool and Port Franklin, and at the holiday park at Tidal River right on The Prom.

Long Jetty Caravan Park, Lewis St, Port Welshpool. Tel: 03-56881233. Offers cabins from $35 to $56 per night.

Port Albert, Wharf St, Port Albert. Tel: 03-51832212. Rooms at $36 to $50.

Inverloch

Though not included in the main text of this book, Inverloch has many wonderful dive sites that are located within the Bunurong Marine Park. This section of coastline can be explored by boat or from the shore, and a wealth of marine life will be seen on every dive. Diving conditions can be good year round, but summer brings calm seas and clear water. Charter boats running out of Inverloch generally run double dives which cost around $45. Located 143 km south east of Melbourne, Inverloch is a farming area.

Dive Operators

Island Divers, 16 Short St, Inverloch. Tel: 03-56741848.

Lex Thorbecke, 26 Park St, Inverloch. Tel: 03-56742382. Offers dive charters around Inverloch and Phillip Island; retail and hire gear, and NASDS dive courses.

Accommodation

Though the area around Inverloch is farmland, the town itself is a popular holiday area and boasts a number of motels and caravan parks.

Broadbeach Caravan Park, Esplanade St, Inverloch. Tel: 03-56741447, Fax: 03-56742695. Has park cabins at $40 per night.

Inverloch Motel, Bass Hwy, Inverloch. Tel: 03-56743100, Fax: 03-56742146. Rooms from $38 to $65 per night.

Melbourne

Divers visiting Melbourne will find no shortage of dive shops or charter boats. Weekend and weekday charters cost $20 to $25 for a single dive and $35 to $45 for a double dive.

All of the following dive shops offer either dive courses, dive charters, retail and hire gear, or all of the above.

Dive Operators

AB Ocean Divers, 237 East Boundary Rd, Bentleigh East. Tel: 03-95792600.

Adventure Down Under, 604 Mountain Hwy, Bayswater. Tel: 03-97295811.

Aqua Blue Scuba Instruction, 120 Thomas St, Dandenong. Tel: 03-97948136.

Associated Divers, 1292 Centre Rd, Clayton. Tel: 03-95449002.

Australian Diving Instruction, Lot 13 Tolson St, Geelong. Tel: 03-52815410.

Bay City Scuba, 146 Ormond Rd, Geelong East. Tel: 03-52291281.

Deep Sea Charters, 27 Fyans St, Geelong. Tel: 03-52222181.

Dive & Dive, 11/6 Rebound Crt, Narre Warren. Tel: 03-97966944.

Dive Experience, 8 Wharf St, Queenscliff. Tel: 03-52584058.

Dive Experience, 82 Ferguson St, Williamstown. Tel: 03-93975139.

Dive Under, 49 Peninsula Ave, Rye. Tel: 03-59856999.

Diveline, 6 Young St, Frankston. Tel: 03-97837166.

Diver Instruction Services, 8 Mitchell St, Doncaster. Tel: 03-98407744.

Diver Instruction Services, 3752 Nepean Hwy, Portsea. Tel: 03-59843155.

Diving Headquarters, 436 High St, Prahran. Tel: 03-95109081.

Geelong Dive & Outdoor Centre, 178 Learmonth St, Geelong. Tel: 03-52213342.

In Depth Scuba, 357 Lt Bourke St, Melbourne. Tel: 03-96425422.

In Depth Scuba Queenscliff, 37 Leermonth St, Queenscliff. Tel: 1800 814200.

Interdive, 1242 Burwood Hwy, Upper Freentree Gully. Tel: 03-97588333.

John's Diveshop, 294 St Kilda Rd, St Kilda. Tel: 03-95341471.

Melbourne Diving Services & School, 157 Whitehorse Rd, Blackburn. Tel: 03-98940012.

Melbourne Diving Services & School, 144 Bell St, Heidelberg West. Tel: 03-94594111.

Melbourne Diving Services & School, 3755 Nepean Hwy, Portsea. Tel: 03-56843666.

Ocean Graphics, 47 MacBeth St, Braeside. Tel: 03-95870953.

Oceanic Diving Australia, 123 Hotham Rd, Sorrento. Tel: 03-56844770.

Paradise Divers, 114 Carlton Rd, Dandenong North. Tel: 03-97935248.

Peninsula Diving Instruction, 33 Cook St, Flinders. Tel: 03-56890900.

Peninsula Diving Instruction, 10 Main St, Mornington. Tel: 03-56756865.

Rye Scuba Centre, 2137 Nepean Hwy, Rye. Tel: 03-59854637.

San Remo Dive Charters, 10 Wynne Ave, San Remo. Tel: 03-56785426.

Scuba Pac, 114 Kings Rd, St Albans. Tel: 03-93665434.

Simply Scuba, Box Hill. Tel: 03-98887322.

Skin & Scuba Sports, Paul Crt, Dandenong. Tel: 03-97922605.

Springvale Dive Centre, 131 Springvale Rd, Springvale. Tel: 03-95460905.

Southern Cross Divers, 92 Pakington ST, Geelong West. Tel: 03-52224899.

Take 2 Diving, 6 High St, Cranborne. Tel: 1800 811063.

Vision Divers, 96 Fletcher St, Essendon. Tel: 03-93261713.

Watersports Sea To Snow, 83 Hardware St, Melbourne. Tel: 03-96060149.

West Coast Diving, 25 Rodney Rd, Geelong North. Tel: 03-52785426.

Western Diving, Spotswood. Tel: 03-93991941.

Accommodation

Melbourne covers a large area and has plenty of accommodation available, including motels, hotels, holiday units, backpacker lodges and caravan parks. Divers visiting Melbourne may find it more convenient to stay around the Mornington Peninsula or Bellarine Peninsula, where most of the charter boats depart. A number of dive shops offer cheap bunkhouse accommodation, but you could also try:

Beacon Resort, 78 Bellarine Hwy, Queenscliff. Tel: 03-52581133, Fax: 03-52581152. Has rooms from $70 to $89 a night, and cabins from $37 to $70 per night.

Bell's Hostel, 3 Miranda St, Sorrento. Tel: 03-59844323. Bunkhouse-style accommodation from $13 per night.

Oceanic Motel, 234 Ocean Beach Rd, Sorrento. Tel: 03-59841417. Rooms from $40 to $75 per night.

Country Victoria

Although there is little diving in country Victoria, except the odd splash in a river or lake, there are a few dive shops that offer dive courses and trips to sites on the coast.

Dive Operators
Deep Down Diver Education, Sale. Tel: 03-51446957.

Skin Ski & Surf, 88 Bridge Mall, Ballarat. Tel: 03-53314178.

Skin Ski & Surf, Bendigo. Tel: 03-54416337.

Wetsports, 14 Bridge Mall, Ballarat. Tel: 03-53317727, Fax: 03-53322590.

Port Campbell

Off the coast of Port Campbell lie numerous shipwrecks that provide interesting diving, and there are also a number of reefs that are home to reef fish and invertebrates. Located 250 km west of Melbourne, Port Campbell is a small town that is popular with tourists.

Dive Operators
Port Campbell Boat Charters, Great Ocean Rd, Port Campbell. Tel: 03-55986411. Operates boat dives at $35 for a single dive and $60 for a double dive.

Schomberg Dive Services, 29 Lord St, Port Campbell. Tel: 03-55986499. Offers dive instruction, retail, hire gear and charter bookings.

Accommodation
The small coastal town of Port Campbell has about half-a-dozen places that offer accommodation, these include:

Loch Ard Motel, Lord St, Port Campbell. Tel: 03-55986328. Rooms from $50 to $85.

Port Campbell Caravan Park, Morris St, Port Campbell. Tel: 03-55986369. Offers cabins from $35 to 50 per night.

Warrnambool

Warrnambool is blessed with a variety of interesting dive sites that are accessible from the shore or by boat. Diving can be reasonable anytime off Warrnambool, but summer provides the best conditions. A busy holiday town, Warrnambool is located 260 km west of Melbourne.

Dive Operators
Warrnambool Diving Services, 223 Lava St, Warrnambool. Tel: 03-55621685. Provides dive courses, retail and hire gear.

Shipwreck Coast Diving & Charters, 457 Raglan Pde, Warrnambool. Tel: 03-55616108. Offers dive charters at $25 for a single dive and $50 for double dives (mainly to the reefs around Port Fairy), hire gear and dive instruction.

Accommodation
A popular holiday area, divers will find no shortage of accommodation around Warrnambool, including:

Colonial Village Motel, 31 Mortlake Rd, Warrnambool. Tel: 03-55621455, Fax: 03-556 13445. Rooms from $40 to $85 pernight.

Surfside Holiday Park, Pertobe Rd, Warrnambool. Tel: 03-55612611. Has a range of cabins from $40 to $85 per night.

Portland

Located 360 km west of Melbourne, Portland is close to the border of South Australia. Around Portland are an abundance of dive sites, accessible from the shore and by boat.

Dive Operators
Duck Dive Scuba, 57 Bentick St, Portland. Tel: 03-55235617.

Professional Diving Services, 14 Townsend St, Portland. Tel: 03-55236392, Fax: 03-55217255. Offers boat dives at $20 to $25 for a single dive, NAUI dive courses (including cavern and sinkhole courses), retail and hire gear.

Accommodation
A wide selection of accommodation can be found in and around Portland, which includes:

Mariner Motel, 196 Percy St, Portland. Tel: 03-55232877. Has rooms from $40 to $47 per night.

Portland Haven Caravan Park, 76A Garden St, Portland. Tel: 03-55231768. Cabins from $28 to $40 per night.

Tasmania

The cool, temperate waters of Tasmania provide some of the most interesting and varied diving in Australia. Although the water may be cold at times, the variety of marine species and diverse underwater habitats make any discomfort worthwhile. Visitors will find charter boats and dive shops operating in many locations around this island state.

Getting There

Tasmania is accessible by air or sea. International flights are only possible from New Zealand through Hobart Airport. Domestic flights from the other states in Australia arrive in Launceston and Hobart daily via Ansett and Qantas Airlines. The other option is to take your car across Bass Strait on one of the regular ferries operating from Melbourne to Devonport or Port Welshpool to George Town, costing from $194 to $316 return per person and $250 return per car.

Local Transport

Once in Tasmania, getting around this small state is easily achieved by car.

If you haven't brought your own, hire cars are available at the airports and most towns. Some of the dive shops offer a pickup and return courtesy bus as part of a package deal, so check with the shops for details. Buses service all the towns in Tasmania, making local transport quite easy. There is also a good but limited rail network. For those on a really tight timetable, or wanting to visit the islands of Bass Strait, regional flights service most centers through Kendell Airlines, Australian Air Charters and Airlines of Tasmania.

Medical and Emergencies

A recompression chamber is located in Hobart and in the event of any dive accident contact DES (Diving Emergency Service) on **1800 088 200**. State that it is a diving emergency, the details of the accident and the condition of the diver.

In any other emergency, other than diving, ring **000**, and ask for the service you require, be it fire, police or ambulance. Visitors to Tasmania will find hospitals and medical centers throughout Tasmania.

Most charter boats carry oxygen and first aid kits and are generally proficient in their usage.

Photographic Supplies

Buying and processing of print film is possible in just about every town in Tasmania. While visitors will be able to purchase slide film throughout the state, the only laboratories that process E6 slide film are in Hobart and Launceston.

Bass Strait Islands

Scattered between Victoria and Tasmania are the many scenic islands of Bass Strait. Diving is good around most of the islands, however, many of the sites are only accessible by a liveaboard boat. The other option is to stay on King Island or Flinders Island and dive on their many reefs and wrecks. Flights to King Island are possible from Melbourne ($132 one way) and Bernie ($119 one way) via Kendell Airlines, or Australian Air Charters. Flights to Flinders Island depart from Melbourne ($130 one way) and Launceston ($110 one way). While diving may be good at anytime, the best conditions in Bass Strait are in summer and autumn.

Dive Operators

Flinders Island Dive, PO Box 115, Whitemark, Flinders Island. Tel: 03-63592124. Offers dive charters at $30 for a half day (2 dives) and $50 for a full day (2 to 3 dives). Hire gear and package deals for extended visits.

King Island Dive Charters, 15 Boronia Dve, Grassy. Tel: 03-64611133, Fax: 03-64611293. Runs single boat dives at $45, day dive trips at $90, and dive package deals.

Southern Star, 23 Wattletree Crs, Morwell. Tel: 03-51346484. Offers the occasional liveaboard charter to the islands of Bass Strait from Port Welshpool, Victoria, for groups of up to 10 divers at $1400 per day.

Accommodation

There is quite a good range of accommodation on offer on both King and Flinders Island, including:

Bluff House, Whitemark, Flinders Island. Tel: 03-63592034. Rooms at $33 a night.

Bulloke Holiday Units, Butter Factory Rd, Whitemark, Flinders Island. Tel: 03-63599709. Units at $60 a night and $420 a week.

King Island Gem Motel, 95 North Rd, Currie, King Island. Tel: 03-64621260, Fax: 03-64621563. Rooms from $60 to $80 per night.

The Cottage, Naracoopa, King Island. Tel: 03-64611385, Fax: 03-64611273. Units at $80 per night and $480 pw.

Wynyard

Located 345 km north west of Hobart, Wynyard is a farming area that is also popular with tourists. There are many activities to be enjoyed in the area, including diving. Diving off Wynyard is best over summer and autumn, but can be quite good at any time of the year.

Dive Operator

Scuba Centre, 62 Old Bass Hwy, Wynyard. Tel: 03-64422247, Fax: 03-64422623. Runs daily boat dives from $20 for a single dive, also offers dive courses, retail and hire gear.

Accommodation

A good range of accommodation can be found in the area around Wynyard.

Leisure Ville Holiday Units, 145 Scenic Hwy, Wynyard. Tel: 03-64422291, Fax: 03-64423058. Units from $52 to $75 per night and $240 to $400 pw.

Wynyard Caravan Park, Esplanade, Wynyard. Tel: 03-64421998. Backpacker accommodation from $12 per night.

Wynyard Motor Lodge, Esplanade, Wynyard. Tel: 03-64422351, Fax: 03-64423749. Has rooms from $52 to $60 a night.

Launceston

The largest city in the north of Tasmania, Launceston is located 200 km north of Hobart and over 50 km from the coastline. A number of dive shops are based here and run dive trips to the coast.

Dive Operators

Charlton's Scuba Education Services, 155 Brisbane St, Launceston. Tel: 03-63318322. Offers dive courses, retail and hire gear.

Scuba Ski & Tackle, 120 Hobart Rd, Kings Meadows. Tel: 03-63449411. Provides PADI dive courses, hire gear and retail. A range of accommodation is available in Launceston..

St Helens

Though not well known, there are many interesting dive sites off St Helens. Similar to many locations on the east coast, diving St Helens is possible year round, but is at its best in autumn and winter. Boat dives cost $25 for a single dive. Located 253 km north east of Hobart, St Helens is also a popular holiday town.

Dive Operators

East Coast Scuba Centre, 28 Cecilla St, St Helens. Tel: 03-63761720. Provides NAUI dive instruction, boat dives, retail and hire gear.

Norseman Charters, 149 Stoney Rise Rd, Devonport. Tel: 03-64246900. Offers dive charters from St Helens (Nov-May) and Pirates Bay (Apr-July).

Professional Charters, 18 Chimney Heights Rd, St Helens. Tel: 03-63763083. Dive charters.

Accommodation

The largest town on the east coast of Tasmania, St Helens is a busy holiday town with a broad range of accommodation on offer.

Anchor Wheel Motel, 61 Tully St, St Helens. Tel: 03-63761358. Has rooms at $35 to $60.

Binalong Bay Character Cottages, Main Rd, Binalong Bay. Tel: 03-63768262, Fax: 03-63768306. Ocean front units from $50 to $60 a night.

St Helens Caravan Park, Penelope St, St Helens. Tel: 03-63761290, Fax: 03-63761514. Offers cabins at $45 per night.

Bicheno

Located 180 km northeast of Hobart and 160 km southeast of Launceston, Bicheno is Tasmania's number one dive destination. Diving the area is possible year round, but autumn and winter is definitely the best time to visit. The water is cool, but the seas are calm and the water very clear.

Dive Operator

Bicheno Dive Centre, 4 Tasman Hwy, Bicheno. Tel: 03-63751138. Has on site accommodation at $18 for night in a bunkhouse that sleeps up to 6 people. Daily dive charters costing $24 for a single dive, and package deals on diving and accommodation. Also offers dive courses, retail and hire gear.

Accommodation

A popular holiday town, divers not wanting to stay at the dive center will find a diverse range of accommodation on offer in Bicheno including:

Beachfront Motel, Tasman Hwy, Bicheno. Tel: 03-63751111, Fax: 03-63751130. Has rooms from $70 to $80 a night.

Bicheno Cabins & Tourist Park, 4 Champ St, Bicheno. Tel: 03-63751117, Fax: 03-63751355. Cabins from $65 to $70 per night.

Coles Bay

Not mentioned in the main text, Coles Bay is the gateway to the wonderful diving around the Freycinet Peninsula. Here you will be able to dive on colorful reefs, see an amazing array of marine life and even enjoy the company of fur seals. Though diveable year round, the best conditions on the Freycinet Peninsula are experienced in autumn and winter. Coles Bay is located 205 km northeast of Hobart.

Dive Operator

Freycinet Sea Charters, The Jetty, Coles Bay. Tel & Fax: 03-62751461. Available for dive charters at $650 (for groups up to 10 divers) for double dives.

Accommodation

Coles Bay Caravan Park, Coles Bay Rd, Coles Bay. Tel: 03-62570100, Fax: 03-62570270. Has vans at $30 a night and a backpacker section at $14 a night.

Freycinet Lodge, Freycinet National Park. Tel: 03-62570101. Cabins from $120 to $160 a night.

Orford

Located 80 km north east of Hobart, Orford is a small coastal holiday town with a charter operator but no dive shop. It is the gateway to Maria Island, which has a variety of wonderful dive sites, including kelp beds and sponge gardens. Maria Island offers good diving year round, but ideal conditions are experienced in autumn and winter.

Dive Operator

Deep Sea Charters, Shelly Beach, Orford. Tel: 03-62571328. Available for dive charters to Maria Island for groups of divers.

Accommodation

Visitors to Orford will find quite a good selection of accommodation, including:

Blue Waters Motel, Tasman Hwy, Orford. Tel: 03-62571102. Rooms from $35 to $50 a night.

Sea Breeze Holiday Units, Rudd Ave, Orford. Tel: 03-62571375. Units from $35 to $40.

Tasman Peninsula

Diving on the Tasman Peninsula is centered around Eaglehawk Neck, which is located 80 km southeast of Hobart. Offering some of the most spectacular diving in southern Australia, the Tasman Peninsula is diveable year round, but is at its best over autumn and winter when clear water washes the coastline.

Dive Operators

Eaglehawk Dive Centre, Pirates Bay Dve, Eaglehawk Neck. Tel: 03-62503566, Fax: 03-62652251. Runs daily boat dives from $25 to $50 for a single dive (depending on the distance to the dive site). Offers dive courses, retail and hire gear, and has package deals.

Norseman Charters, 149 Stoney Rise Rd, Devonport. Tel: 03-64246900. Offers dive charters from St Helens (Nov-May) and Pirates Bay (Apr-July).

Accommodation

There are numerous places to stay on the Tasman Peninsula, but with the diving centered around Eaglehawk Neck, you can try:

Lufra Country Hotel, Arthur Hwy, Eaglehawk Neck. Tel: 03-62503262. Offers rooms from $25 to $70 per night.

Pirates Bay Motel, Blowhole Rd, Eaglehawk Neck. Tel: 03-62503272, Fax: 03-62503519. Has rooms from $60 to $70 per night.

Hobart

There are a wide variety of accessible dive sites in the Hobart area and while condi-tions can be good at anytime of the year, the clearest water is experienced over winter. A number of dive shops and charter boats service Hobart and run dive trips over a wide area of coastline, with single dives starting from $25.

Dive Operators

Aqua Scuba Diving Services, Market Pl, Hobart. Tel & Fax: 03-62345658. Offers PADI dive courses, retail and hire gear.

Blue Fin Charters, 1246 South Arm Rd, Sandford. Tel: 03-62489462. Dive charters.

Diversified Diving Services, 32 Gordon St, Sorell. Tel: 03-62652251.

The Dive Shop, 42 Bathurst St, Hobart. Tel: 03-62343428. Offers retail and hire gear, PADI dive courses and runs daily boat dives and weekend trips.

Accommodation

A good range of accommodation is on offer in Hobart and its surrounding suburbs.

Bowen Park Holiday Village, 673 East Derwent Hwy, Risdon Cove. Tel: 03-62439879. Cabins from $40 per night to $240 pw.

Sandy Bay Motor Inn, 429 Sandy Bay Rd, Sandy Bay. Tel: 03-62252511. Offers rooms from $69 to $85 per night.

Sheraton Hobart, 1 Davey St, Hobart. Tel: 03-62354535, Fax: 03-62238175. A 5-star hotel with rooms from $230 to $950 per night.

South Australia

Many exciting dive destinations await the diver in South Australia. From the capital of Adelaide to areas east and west, you can explore the coast from both boat and shore. Although many regions of the state haven't been opened up to divers, the existing charter boats and dive shops will help facilitate your dive plans.

Getting There

A number of international carriers fly into Adelaide Airport. Domestic flights link Adelaide with all other capital cities across Australia, with Ansett and Qantas providing the major service.

Local Transport

There are a number of options for travel within South Australia. The quickest way to get around the state is on a regional flight; though expensive, the service is fast and efficent. Airlines operating in South Australia include Kendell Airlines, Emu Airways, Eyre Commuter, O'Conner Mt Gambier Airlines and Lincoln Airlines. Regular bus and coach services operate to most towns throughout the state; the major bus companies are Greyhound-Pioneer, Firefly and McCafferty's. The railways in South Australia don't link much of the coastline, so are a poor option. One of the best ways to see the state is by car. Hire cars are available in all towns and airports; the major companies are Avis, Budget, Hertz and Thrifty. The roads are quite good in South Australia and road side service is provided by the RAA (Royal Automobile Association of South Australia).

Medical and Emergencies

Hospitals and medical centers are found throughout South Australia, and in any emergency, other than diving, ring **000**, and ask for the service you require, be it fire, police or ambulance.

For any diving accident anywhere in Australia contact DES (Diving Emergency Service) on **1800 088 200**. State that it is a diving emergency, give the details of the accident and the condition of the diver.

South Australia's only recompression chamber is located in Adelaide, and you will find that all charter boats carry oxygen and first aid kits.

Photographic Supplies

Photographers will find a ready supply of print film and slide film in most towns throughout South Australia. While processing of print film is possible anywhere in the state, E6 slide film can only be processed in Adelaide.

Mount Gambier

Located 440 km southeast of Adelaide, and about the same distance from Melbourne, Mount Gambier is surrounded by the finest collection of caves and sinkholes in Australia. These clear freshwater caves are diveable year round, but should only be dived by those with the proper training. Many of the caves and sinkholes are located on private property and government land, so permits and permission are generally required.

Dive Operators

Allendale General Store, 50 Bay Rd, Allendale East. Tel: 08-87387274. Provides airfills.

Blink Bonney Lodge, Wandillo Rd, Mount Gambier. Tel/Fax: 08-87230879. Provides air fills and accommodation from $10 per night.

Cave Divers Association of Australia (CDAA), PO Box 290, North Adelaide, S.A. 5006. For information on cave diving, training or permits contact the CDAA.

Accommodation

A good variety of accommodation is available in the Mount Gambier area.

Mt Gambier Central Caravan Park, 6 Krummel St, Mount Gambier. Tel: 08-87254427. Has cabins from $28 to $40 per night.

Presidential Motel, Jubilee Hwy West, Mount Gambier. Tel: 08-87249966, Fax: 08-87249975. 4-star motel with rooms from $74 to $130 a night.

Victor Harbour

The coastline around Victor Harbour is dominated by granite headlands and islands which provide many wonderful dive sites. You will be able to explore this fascinating coastline by shore or boat, with boat dives costing $25 for a single dive and $50 for a double dive. Located 85 km south of Adelaide, Victor Harbour is at its best from autumn to spring.

Dive Operators

Victor Harbour Boat Charters, PO Box 830, Victor Harbour. Tel: 08-85527475. Runs dive charters.

Victor Marine & Watersports Centre, 160 Hindmarsh Rd, Victor Harbour. Tel: 08-85524757. Offers dive courses, retail and hire gear.

Accommodation

A busy holiday area, divers will find no shortage of accommodation in the Victor Harbour area.

City Motel, 51 Ocean St, Victor Harbour. Tel: 08-85522455, Fax: 08-85525583. Offers rooms from $45 to $60 per night.

Victor Harbour Holiday Centre, Bay Rd, Victor Harbour. Tel: 08-85521949. Cabins and units from $56 to $68 per night.

Kangaroo Island

Located 110 km south of Adelaide, Kangaroo Island is one of South Australia's most popular holiday destinations. The island is accessible via flights from Adelaide, or by car ferry from Adelaide, Cape Jervis or Port Lincoln. Surrounding the island are many excellent dive sites. Boat dives cost around $40 for a single dive and $80 to $105 for a double dive. Kangaroo Island is washed by clear water for much of the year.

Dive Operators

Adventureland Diving, Beach Crs, Penneshaw, Kangaroo Island. Tel: 08-85531072, Fax: 08-85531002. Runs dive charters, dive courses. Provides accommodation at $15 per night. Hire gear and offer package deals.

Cape Jervis Charter & Marine Services, 27 Darkana Way, Cape Jervis. Tel: 085-980222. Offers dive charters to Kangaroo Island.

Kangaroo Island Diving Safaris, Gosse. Kangaroo Island, Tel/Fax: 08-85593225. Provide dive charters and dive courses, also limited accommodation at $55 per night (including all meals), hire gear and package deals.

Accommodation

Those divers not choosing to stay in the accommodation offered by the dive shops, divers will find a good range of accommodation around Kangaroo Island, especially in the main centers of Kingscote and Penneshaw.

Island Resort, 4 Telegraph Rd, Kingscote. Tel: 08-85522100, Fax: 08-85522747. Rooms from $60 to $70 per night.

Parade Units, The Parade, Kingscote. Tel: 08-85522394. Units at $45 a night.

Sorrento Resort Motel, North Tce, Penneshaw. Tel: 08-85531028, Fax: 08-85531204. Offers units from $58 to $92 per night.

Adelaide

Many dive shops and charter boats operate around Adelaide. Dive charters off the Adelaide coastline cost $25 for a single dive and $50 for a double dive. Conditions off this section of coast are generally good year round, and there is nearly always somewhere to dive no matter what the conditions are.

Dive Operators

Adelaide Gulf Charter Services, Henley Beach. Tel: 08-82352988. Runs dive charters.

Adelaide Skin Diving Centre, 7 Compton St, Adelaide. Tel: 08-82316144, Fax: 08-82125887. Offers dive training, retail and hire gear.

Adelaide Skin Diving Centre, 180 Main North Rd, Prospect. Tel: 08-83444456. Has retail and hire gear.

Aldinga Bay Sport & Leisure, 2 Aldinga Beach Rd, Aldinga Beach. Tel: 08-85566226.

Dangle & Dive Fishing Tackle & Scuba Centre, 71 St Vincent St, Port Adelaide. Tel: 08-83220177.

Diveden, 35 Clacton Rd, Dover Gardens. Tel: 08-83771624.

Diver Service, 80 Grange Rd, Welland. Tel: 08-83463422. Provides dive charters, NASDS & NAUI dive courses, hire and retail gear.

Falie Charters, 27 North Pde, Port Adelaide. Tel: 08-83412004, Fax: 08-83411810. The 35m long ketch, *Falie,* runs liveaboard trips (at $140 per day) to the island groups of the Spencer Gulf.

Glenelg Scuba Diving Centre, Patawalonga Frontage, Glenelg North. Tel: 08-82947744. A PADI facility that offer dive courses, boat dives, retail and hire gear.

McQ Diving, 8 Baanga Rd, Morphett Vale. Tel: 08-83846373. Runs PADI dive courses.

Pearce Scuba Instruction, 2 Eliza St, Williamstown. Tel: 08-85246287.

Port Noarlunga Dive & Snorkel Centre, 9 Saftleet St, Port Noarlunga. Tel: 08-

83266989. A NASDS facility providing courses, retail and hire gear.

Scuba Designs, 155 Burbridge Rd, Hilton. Tel: 08-82341244.

Scuba Scene, 509 Portrush Rd, Glenunga. Tel: 08-83798188. Offers boat dives, NAUI dive courses, retail and hire gear.

Southern Diving Centre, 1 Roy Tce, Christies Beach. Tel: 08-83821322, Fax: 08-83821509. Offers PADI dive courses, retail and hire gear.

Super Elliots Dive Centre, 200 Rundle St, Adelaide. Tel: 08-82232522, Fax: 08-82323403. Offers NASDS dive courses, retail and hire gear.

The Dive Shop, 111 Main South Rd, O'Hallaran Hill, Tel: 08-83220177. Offers dive courses, retail and hire gear.

Underwater Sports Diving Centre, 1198 Grand Junction Rd, Hope Valley. Tel: 08-82232522. Offers dive charters, NASDS dive courses, retail and hire gear.

Accommodation

A wide variety of accommodation can be found in Adelaide and its surrounding suburbs. Convenient places for divers to stay are located from Adelaide south to Aldinga Beach, including:

Aldinga Caravan & Holiday Park, Cox Rd, Aldinga Beach. Tel: 08-85563444. Cottages and cabins from $45 to $55 per night and $330 to $385 pw.

City Central Motel, 23 Hindley St, Adelaide. Tel: 08-82314049, Fax: 08-82314804. Rooms from $49 to $54 per night.

Hilton International Adelaide, 233 Victoria Sq, Adelaide. Tel: 08-82170711, Fax: 08-82310158. 5-star hotel with rooms from $185 to $700.

Port Noarlunga Motel, 39 Saltfleet St, Port Noarlunga. Tel: 08-83821267. Rooms from $45 to $55 per night.

Yorke Peninsula

The Yorke Peninsula provides the diver with many exciting dive sites, but is sadly lacking in dive facilities. Though conditions can be good year round, the best diving on the Yorke Peninsula is experinced over winter and spring. Dive charters cost from $60 to $80 for a double dive trip. Diving on the peninsula is centrered around Edithburgh, which is 233 km west of Adelaide.

Dive Operators

Braund & Sons, 2 Stansbury Rd, Yorketown. Tel: 08-88521005. Offers air fills, retail and hire gear.

Wallaroo Bay Yacht Charter, Wattlebrae, Moonta. Tel/Fax: 08-88256235. Offers dive charters.

Accommodation

Many towns provide a wide range of accommodation on the Yorke Peninsula. Edithburgh is the most popular dive center and accommodation includes:

Edithburgh Caravan Park, O'Halloran Pde, Edithburgh. Tel: 08-88526056. Has cabins at $30 to $40 per night.

Edithburgh Seaside Hotel Motel, Blanche St, Edithburgh. Tel: 08-88526172, Fax: 08-88526047. Rooms from $48 to $58 a night.

Port Lincoln and Sir Joseph Banks Group

A wide variety of dive sites are found around Port Lincoln and the many islands of the Sir Joseph Banks Group. These dive sites provide good diving year round, but especially in summer and winter. Dive charters are generally based on group bookings; day trips cost from $60, extended liveaboard trips around $140 per day, while shark cage trips cost from $1500 to $2000 per day for dive groups. Quite a large town, Port Lincoln is located 672 km west of Adelaide.

Dive Operators

Calypso Star Charters, 5 Willowbridge Grove, Burnside. Tel: 08-83644428, Fax: 08-83411810. Offers dive charters and shark cage trips.

Dangerous Reef Explorer II Cruises, 112 London St, Port Lincoln. Tel & Fax: 08-86822425. Offers day and extended dive charters, including shark cage trips. Also provides accommodation at **Westward Ho Holiday Units** from $45 to $100 per night.

Falie Charters, 27 North Pde, Port Adelaide. Tel: 08-83412004, Fax: 08-83326360. The 35m long ketch, *Falie,* runs liveaboard trips to the island groups of the Spencer Gulf and Sir Joseph Banks Group.

Flinders Diving Services, Lincoln Cove 9 North Quay Blv, Port Lincoln. Tel: 08-86824140.

Port Lincoln Skindiving Centre, 73 Mortlock Tce, Port Lincoln. Tel/Fax: 08-86824428. A PADI facility that offers dive charters, hire gear and retail sales.

Accommodation

A broad range of accommodation is on offer in the Port Lincoln area, including:

Blue Seas Motel, 7 Gloucester Tce, Port Lincoln. Tel: 08-86823022, Fax: 08-86826932. Rooms from $45 to $50 per night.

Port Lincoln Caravan Park, Lincoln Hwy, Port Lincoln. Tel: 08-86843512. Cabins from $32 to $51 per night.

Western Australia

The largest state in Australia, Western Australia provides some of the most impressive diving destinations in the whole country. The great majority of the Western Australian coastline is diveable, with dive shops and charter boats found from Esperance in the south to Broome in the north.

Getting There

Perth International Airport is the first port of call for many international airlines entering Australia, especially from Asia and Europe. Perth is also regularly serviced by domestic flights from the other state capitals of Australia, with Ansett and Qantas the major airlines. For rail buffs there is the famous Indian-Pacific train journey which is quite an experience as it crosses the Nullarbor Plain on the straightest section of rail line in the world.

Local Transport

Since Western Australia is such a large state, the easiest way to get around is on regional flights. Airlines include Ansett, Qantas and Skywest. Those who want to explore the coastline will find hire cars available at airports and most towns. The major hire companies are Avis, Budget, Hertz and Thrifty. Roadside service is provided by the RACWA (Royal Automobile Club of Western Australia). Buses provide services to all major towns along the coastline, although the trip can be uncomfortable on very long runs. The main bus companies are Greyhound, McCafferty's and South West Coach Lines. While the rail lines link many areas in the southwest corner of the state, areas north of Geraldton are not accessible.

Medical and Emergencies

For any diving accident anywhere in Australia contact DES (Diving Emergency Service) on **1800 088 200**. State that it is a diving emergency, the details of the accident and the condition of the diver.

Western Australia's only recompression chamber is located in Fremantle. Divers will find that all charter boats carry oxygen and first aid kits, and the crews are generally proficient in their usage.

There are hospitals and medical centers located in most of the larger towns in Western Australia, and in any emergency, other than diving, ring **000**, and ask for the service you require, be it fire, police or ambulance.

Photographic Supplies

Photographers will find they can buy print and slide film in most large towns throughout Western Australia. Print film can be processed anywhere, however, E6 slide film may only be processed in Perth.

Nullarbor Caves

The caves of the Nullarbor Plain are centered around the town of Cocklebiddy, 1160 km east of Perth. To dive these caves you will require all your own equipment, especially a compressor and fresh water. Diving the caves of the Nullarbor Plain should only be attempted by qualified cave divers with the experience and backup to attempt such an endeavour.

Diving Information

Cave Divers Association of Australia (CDAA), PO Box 290, North Adelaide SA 5006. For all information and permits required to dive the caves of the Nullabor.

Accommodation

Choice of accommodation is rather limited around Cocklebiddy, but there are also motels at Eucla, Mundrabilla, Madura and Caiguna.

Wedgetail Inn Motel Hotel, Eyre Hwy, Cocklebiddy. Tel: 08-90393462, Fax: 08-90393403. Rooms from $58 to $76, and sites for caravans at $6 to $12.

Esperance

Surrounded by hundreds of islands, Esperance provides some of the best diving in southern Western Australia. Located 720 km south east of Perth, Esperance is a popular holiday town, especially over summer. Diving can be good at any time of the year, but the best conditions are generally experienced in summer and autumn.

Dive Operator

Esperance Diving Academy, 3/56 The Esplanade, Esperance. Tel: 08-90715111, Fax: 08-90715550. Day and extended trips aboard the 15-m long vessel *Southern Image*. Prices vary from $100 for a day trips (two dives) and $1000 per day for extended trips (for groups up to 20). They also provide retail and hire gear, and dive courses.

Accommodation

Visitors to Esperance will find a broad range of accommodation on offer.

Bayview Motel, Dempster St, Esperance. Tel: 08-90711533, Fax: 08-90714544. Rooms from $45 to $65 a night.

Esperance Backpackers Lodge, 14 Emily St, Esperance. Tel: 08-90714724. Lodge from $12 to $26 a night and $75 to $170 pw.

Albany

The old whaling port of Albany is now one of the busiest holiday areas in Western Australia. Located 410 km south east of Perth, Albany has a wide variety of dive sites on its doorstep. Dive charters start at $25 for a single dive. Diving is possible year-round, how-

ever, Albany is at its best in autumn, when light winds prevail.

Dive Operators

Albany Scuba Diving Academy, 3/21 Sanford Rd, Albany. Tel: 08-98423101. Provides dive courses, retail and hire gear, and dive charters.

Southern Ocean Charters, 84b Serpentine Rd, Albany. Tel: 08-98417176. Offers dive charters, gear sales and hire.

Accommodation

There is rarely a shortage of accommodation in Albany, with hotels, motels, holiday units, caravan parks and backpacker lodges.

Albany Backpacker Lodge, Stirling Tce, Albany. Tel: 08-98418848. Has rooms from $28 to $30 per night.

Esplanade Hotel, Flinders Pde, Albany. Tel: 08-98421711, Fax: 08-98421033. 5-star hotel with rooms from $159 to $229 a night.

Travel Inn Motel, 191 Albany Hwy, Albany. Tel: 08-98414144, Fax: 08-98416215. Rooms from $72 to $119.

Augusta

Situated on the edge of Flinders Bay, Augusta offers a variety of interesting shore and boat diving locations. One dive shop operates in Augusta, and another in the nearby town of Margaret River. Dive charters off this section of coastline cost $50 for a single dive and $85 for a double dive. Located 320 km south of Perth, Augusta can be dived at anytime of the year, but is at its best in autumn.

Dive Operators

Augusta Hardware & Scuba Supplies, 2/91 Blackwood Ave. Augusta. Tel/ Fax: 08-97581770. Provides airfills, retail and hire gear.

Margaret River Dive Centre, 193 Auger Way, Margaret River. Tel: 08-97573880.

Seafari Charters, RMB 268A, Margaret River. Tel: 08-9772724. Offers dive charters.

Accommodation

Augusta Motel Hotel, Blackwood Ave, Augusta. Tel: 08-97581944, Fax: 08-97581227. Rooms from $40 to $93 per night.

Doonbanks Caravan Park, Blackwood Ave, Augusta. Tel/Fax: 08-97581517. Has park cabins from $25 to $45 per night.

Geographe Bay

The diving in Geographe Bay is centered in the towns of Busselton and Bunbury, both of which have a number of dive shops and charter boats. Dive trips to the reefs of Geographe Bay cost $25 for a single dive or $50 for a double dive. For those on a budget there are also a number of excellent shore diving sites. Diving is brilliant in the bay for most of the year, except over winter when strong winds dirty the water. Busselton is situated 230 km south of Perth, while Bunbury is 180 km south of Perth.

Dive Operators

Bunbury Dive & Outdoor, 32 Clifton St, Bunbury. Tel: 08-97914449.

Busselton Dive Academy, 64 West St, Busselton. Tel/Fax: 08-97524074. Runs daily dive charters and offers SSI dive courses, retail and hire gear.

Dunsborough Diving Academy, 26 Dunn Bay Rd, Dunsborough. Tel: 08-97553397, Fax: 08-97559730.

Naturaliste Dive Centre, 103 Queen St, Busselton. Tel: 08-97522096, Fax: 08-97522457. A NASDS facility that offers dive charters, retail and hire gear.

Ocean Probe Dive, 61 Albert Rd, Bunbury. Tel: 08-97911996. Provides dive courses, gear sales and hire.

Sportsmarine Sportslocker, 113 Victoria St, Bunbury. Tel: 08-97214961, Fax: 08-97911445. Offers dive instruction, retail and hire gear.

Accommodation

Geographe Bay is a favorite holiday area, which is reflected in the range of accommodation.

Clifton Beach Motel, 2 Molloy St, Bunbury. Tel: 08-97214300, Fax: 08-97912726. Rooms from $70 to $150 a night.

Geographe Bay Holiday Park, 525 Bussell Hwy, Busselton. Tel: 08-97524396, Fax: 08-97524396. Cabins from $40 to $75 per night and $200 to $515 pw.

Paradise Motel, Pries Ave, Busselton. Tel: 08-97521200, Fax: 08-97541348. Rooms from $45 to $59 a night.

Perth and Rottnest Island

Numerous good dive sites are found off Perth and Rottnest Island, and dive shops and charter boats can be found north and south of the city. Dive charters vary in cost. Double dives trips to Rottnest Island start at $45, while single dives to local reefs cost $25. With so many dive sites there is nearly always somewhere to dive no matter the weather or time of year. The reefs of Mandurah and Rockingham are brilliant over summer and autumn, Cockburn Sound is clearest in autumn and winter, while Rottnest can be good at any time of the year, especially in spring and autumn.

Dive Operators

All of the following dive shops offer dive courses, boat dives, retail and hire gear.

Allsports Distributors, 44 Hutton St, Osborne Park. Tel: 08-94449633.

Aquaventure Diving Services, 6/15 Prindiville Dve, Wangarra. Tel: 08-93092910.

Australasian Diving Centre, 259 Stirling Highway, Claremont. Tel: 08-93843966.

Barrakuda, 1 Cantonment St, Fremantle. Tel: 08-93358292, Fax: 08-93353271.

Barrakuda, 67 McCoy St, Myaree. Tel: 08-93171755, Fax: 08-93171286.

Barrakuda, 131 William St, Perth. Tel: 08-93213724, Fax: 08-93213746.

Charter 1, 20 Richardson Rd, Coogee. Tel: 08-94342999. Dive Charters.

David Budd Watersports & Diving Academy, Shop 3, The Plaza, Mandurah. Tel: 08-95351520.

Dive Ski & Surf, Thomson Bay, Rottnest Island. Tel: 08-92925167, Fax: 08-92925120.

Dive Ski & Surf, 413 Hay St, Subiaco. Tel: 08-93812744, Fax: 08-93881602.

Divelink, 22/92 Mallard Way, Cannington. Tel: 08-94513649.

Diver Downunder WA, 9 Wattleup Rd, Wattleup. Tel: 08-94371919, Fax: 08-94371580.

Diving Ventures, 384 South Tce, Fremantle. Tel: 08-94305130.

Diving Ventures, 37 Barrack St, Perth. Tel: 08-94211052.

Dolphin Scuba Diving, 129 Welshpool Rd, Welshpool. Tel: 08-93532488.

Freedom Scuba Academy, 24 Templemore Dve, Heathridge. Tel: 08-94013717.

Jack Sue, 6 Helena St, Midland. Tel: 08-92502737, Fax: 08-92502739.

Jazz II, 1 Blencowe St, West Leederville. Tel: 08-93881414. Dive charters.

Malibu Diving, 43 Rockingham Rd, Rockingham. Tel: 08-95279211, Fax: 08-95275892.

Mandurah Diving Academy, 1/17 Sholl St, Mandurah. Tel: 08-95813224.

Mindarie Diving Academy, Mindarie Keys Marina, Mindarie. Tel: 08-93057113.

Nautilus Diving, 71 Stirling Hwy, North Fremantle. Tel: 08-93359097.

Neptune Scuba Centre, 379 Hay St, East Perth. Tel: 08-92215780, Fax: 08-92212392.

Perth Diving Academy, 5 Rous Head Rd, North Fremantle. Tel: 08-94306300.

Perth Diving Academy, 283 Wanneroo Rd, Balcatta. Tel: 08-93441562.

Scuba Education Australia, 4/9 Loftus St, Leederville. Tel: 08-93882431.

Scubanautics Diving Academy, 8/31 Dixon Rd, Rockingham. Tel: 08-95274447.

Sorrento Quay Dive Shop, 3/6 Hillary Boat Harbour, Sorrento. Tel: 08-94486343.

Sunset Dive, 3 McWhae Rd, Hillarys. Tel/Fax: 08-94020104.

Take Five Scuba School, 70 Marine Tce, Fremantle. Tel: 08-93354465.

The Force Marine Charter, Claremont. Tel: 08-94306166. Dive charters.

Top Gun Fishing & Charter, 2 Wanndina Ave, Dianella. Tel: 08-93751585. Dive charters.

Watersports West, 787 Canning Hwy, Applecross. Tel: 08-93647878.

West Australian Scuba Centre, 6/2 Carson Rd, Malaga. Tel: 08-92491535.

West End Charters, 182 Preston Point Rd, East Fremantle. Tel: 08-93191194, Fax: 08-93191270. Dive charters.

Accommodation

Dive shops and charter operations are spread throughout Perth and its surrounding suburbs, so you will find a wide selection of accommodation to choose from, including:

Budget Backpackers International Hostel, 342 Newcastle St, Northbridge. Tel: 08-93289468. Bunkhouse at $12 a night.

Leisure Inn Motel Hotel, Read St, Rockingham. Tel: 08-95277777. Units at $55 a night.

Tradewinds Hotel, 59 Canning Hwy, Fremantle. Tel: 08-93398188, Fax: 08-93392266. Rooms at $100 per night.

Just 18 km off the coast, Rottnest Island is accessible by plane or regular water taxi service. There is a limited range of accommodation on Rottnest Island, including a hotel, cottages, hostel and camping area.

All Seasons Rottnest Lodge Hotel. Tel: 08-92925161, Fax: 08-92925158. Units from $118 to $135 per night.

Rottnest Island Authority Cottages. Tel: 08-93729729, Fax: 08-93729715. Cottages from $176 to $658 pw.

YHA, Kingston Barracks. Tel: 08-93729780. Hostel accommodation at $10 per night.

Jurien Bay

Located 266 km north of Perth, Jurien Bay is best dived in autumn and spring, but diving can be good at any time of the year.

Dive Operator

Jurien Bay Dive & Hire, 7 Shearwater Dve, Jurien. Tel/Fax: 08-96521534. Operates boat dives at $55 for a single dive and $70 for a double dive. Also offers retail and hire gear, and dive instruction.

Accommodation

The town of Jurien is quite small, with only half a dozen places to stay.

Jurien Bay Holiday Flats, Grigson St, Jurien. Tel: 08-96521172, Fax: 08-96521366. Units from $40 per night and from $110 to $210 pw.

Jurien Bay Motel, Padbury St, Jurien. Tel: 08-96521022, Fax: 08-96521425. Rooms from $50 to $65 per night.

Leeman

A small fishing town 295 km north of Perth, Leeman offers exceptional diving along its coastline. Although diveable year round, Leeman is best in autumn and spring when winds are light and clear water washes the coastline.

Dive Operator

Beagle Island Diving Company, 1 Tuart St, Leeman. Tel/Fax: 08-99531190. Provides NASDS dive courses, boat dives at $35 for a single dive and $55 for a double dive, retail and hire gear. Also offers the best accommodation in town (there is also a caravan park) as the dive operation is based at the **Tamarisk Court Holiday Units**. Fully self-contained holiday units from $15 per night

Geraldton & Houtman Abrolhos Islands

Located 420km north of Perth, Geraldton is the center of Western Australia's rock lobster industry. Just off the coastline of Geraldton are countless limestone reefs that can be dived year round, but are at their best in autumn (local dives cost around $60). Geraldton is also the gateway to the Houtman Abrolhos Islands, which provide some of the most interesting diving off Western Australia. Situated 60 km west of Geraldton, this island group is regularly visited by liveaboard boats during in autumn and spring, with dive trips costing from $150 to $200 per day.

Dive Operators

Batavia Coast Diving Academy, 153 Marine Tce, Geraldton. Tel: 08-99214229. Offers dive courses, boat dives to local reefs and Houtman Abrolhos, retail and hire gear.

Kalbarri Sports & Dive, Shop 1 Kalbarri Arc, Kalbarri. Tel: 08-99371126, Fax: 08-99371665. Provides air fills, retail and hire gear.

Sea Trek, 384 South Terrace, Fremantle. Tel: 08-94305130, Fax: 08-94305641. 18-m vessel surveyed for 14 passengers that operates charters to Houtman Abrolhos, Shark Bay, Ningaloo Reef and Monte Bello Islands.

Top Gun Fishing & Charter, 2 Wanndina Ave, Dianella. Tel: 08-93751585. 18 m-long *Top Gun* offers dive charters off Perth from Nov to April, and Shark Bay and Houtman Abrolhos from April to Oct.

Accommodation

A popular winter retreat, Geraldton has a good range of accommodation on offer to the visitor, including:

Batavia Motor Inne Motel, 54 Fitzgerald St, Geraldton. Tel: 08-99213500, Fax: 08-99641061. Rooms from $55 to $65 per night.

Grantown Guest House, 172 Marine Tce, Grantown. Tel: 08-99213275. Rooms from $20 to $50 per night.

Sun City Tourist Park, Bosely St, Sunset Beach. Tel: 08-99381655, Fax: 08-99381850. Park cabins at $30 to $75 per night.

Shark Bay

The largest town on Shark Bay is Denham, located 830 km north of Perth. Shark Bay is generally dived from liveaboard boats, which cost from $150 to $200 per day. Visitors to Shark Bay will find the diving is generally at its best over winter and spring.

Dive Operators

Sea Trek, 384 South Terrace, Fremantle. Tel: 08-94305130, Fax: 08-94305641. 18-m vessel surveyed for 14 passengers that operates charters to Houtman Abrolhos, Shark Bay, Ningaloo Reef and Monte Bello Islands.

Shark Bay Charter Service, 105 Knight Tce, Denham. Tel: 08-99481113. Provides dive charters.

Top Gun Fishing & Charter, 2 Wanndina Ave, Dianella. Tel: 08-93751585. 18 m-long *Top Gun* offers dive charters off Perth from Nov to April, and Shark Bay & Houtman Abrolhos from April to Oct.

Accommodation

With the popularity of the wild dolphins at Monkey Mia, visitors to Shark Bay will find a good selection of accommodations around Denham.

Denham Holiday Village, Sunter Pl, Denham. Tel: 08-93355550. Units from $70 to $85 a night and from $350 to $480 pw.

Monkey Mia Dolphin Resort. Tel: 08-99481320, Fax: 08-99481034. Cabins at $80 a night and $480 pw, vans from $25 to $60 per night, and a backpacker lodge at $12 a night.

Ningaloo Reef

Ningaloo Reef stretches off the coast of Western Australia from Coral Bay in the south to Exmouth in the north. Diving the reef usually costs $110 for a double dive, while whale shark trips cost around $250 per day, and are

soon booked out. Exmouth is located 1260 km north of Perth, while Coral Bay is 160 km south of Exmouth.

Dive Operators

Coral Bay Adventures, Robinson St, Coral Bay. Tel/Fax: 08-99425955. Offers dive charters.

Coral Dive, 49 Robinson Rd, Coral Bay. Tel: 08-99425940. Offers dive charters, dive courses, retail and hire gear.

Exmouth Diving Centre, Payne St, Exmouth. Tel: 08-99491201, Fax: 08-99491680. Operates 6 charter boats, runs PADI dive courses and offers retail and hire gear.

Exmouth Sea Charters, Murat Rd, Exmouth. Tel: 08-99491094, Fax: 08-99491818. Dive charters.

Ningaloo Adventures, 15 Maidstone Cres, Exmouth. Tel: 08-99491990, Fax: 08-99491199.

Ningaloo Reef Dive, Payne St, Exmouth. Tel: 08-99491999. Dive charters.

Sea Trek, 384 South Terrace, Fremantle. Tel: 08-94305130, Fax: 08-94305641. 18-m vessel surveyed for 14 passengers that operates charters to Houtman Abrolhos, Shark Bay, Ningaloo Reef and Monte Bello Islands.

Accommodation

A good range of accommodation is available in Exmouth, although Coral Bay is a little more limited. Accommodation includes:

Coral Bay Lodge Holiday Units, Coral Bay, Tel: 08-99425932. Units from $80 to $100 per night and from $460 to $515 pw.

Exmouth Cape Tourist Village, Murat St, Exmouth. Tel: 08-99491200. Cabins from $32 to $60 per night.

Potshot Hotel Resort, Murat Rd, Exmouth. Tel: 08-99491200. Homesteads, resort rooms, $60 to $115 per night.

Dampier

Located 1555 km north of Perth, Dampier is the gateway to the many islands and reefs of the Dampier Archipelago and Monte Bello Islands. The Dampier Archipelago is accessible on day trips costing around $60 (2 dives), while liveaboard trips to the Monte Bello Islands are priced at $150 to $200 per day. These areas are best dived in winter and spring.

Dive Operators

Divcon Australia, Mermaid Supply Base, Dampier. Tel: 08-91444193.

Karratha Dive & Hire, 1441 Sharpe Ave, Karratha. Tel: 08-91851957, Fax: 08-91854401. A PADI facility that offers dive charters, retail and hire gear.

Monte Bello Island Safari's, PO Box 152, Onslow. Tel: 08-91846181, Fax: 08-91846254. Extended dive trips to the Monte Bello Islands.

Sea Trek, 384 South Terrace, Fremantle. Tel: 08-94305130, Fax: 08-94305641. 18-m vessel surveyed for 14 passengers that operates charters to Houtman Abrolhos, Shark Bay, Ningaloo Reef and Monte Bello Islands.

Accommodation

Around Dampier and the nearby town of Karratha the limited range of accommodation includes:

Karratha International Hotel, Millstream Rd, Karratha. Tel: 08-91853111. Rooms from $110 to $175 a night.

Mermaid Hotel, The Esplanade, Dampier. Tel: 091-831222, Fax: 08-91831028. Units from $75 to $85 per night.

Port Hedland

Not well known as a dive destination, Port Hedland will surprise most people with the richness of its reefs and marine life. Situated 1635 km north of Perth, Port Hedland is best dived in winter and spring. Expect large tidal currents on the neap tides.

Dive Operator

Big Blue Dive, 5 Wedge St, Port Hedland. Tel: 08-91733202. Offers dive charters at $60 for a double dive, PADI dive courses, gear sales and hire.

Accommodation

A range of accommodation is available in Port Hedland.

Dixons Caravan Park, North-West Coastal Hwy, Port Hedland. Tel: 08-91401233, Fax: 091-723778. Chalets from $55 to $65 and on-site vans at $35.

Hedland Hotel, Lukis St, Port Hedland. Tel: 08-91731511, Fax: 08-91731545. Rooms from $45 to $95 a night.

Broome

A town with a colourful history and a tropical climate, Broome, located 2240 km north of Perth, has some fascinating dive sites. Diving off Broome is usually limited to the neap tides, and although murky at times, is best in winter and spring. A number of charter boats operate out of Broome, with double dive trips costing $80 ($120 with all gear supplied).

Dive Operators

Broome Fishing & Dive Charters, Farrell St, Broome. Tel: 08-91936339. Dive charters.

Broome Time Charters, 29 Dampier Tce, Broome. Tel: 08-91921764. Dive charters.

North Star Charters, 119 Walcott St, Broome. Tel: 08-91935599. Charters to Rowley Shoals.

Northwest Tackle & Sports, Dampier Tce, Broome. Tel: 08-91921669, Fax: 08-91936073.

Pearl Sea Coastal Cruises, 161 Herbert St, Broome. Tel: 018-947953. Dive charters.

Workline Divers Supply, Short St, Broome. Tel: 08-91922233, Fax: 08-91935839. Offers recreational and commercial dive courses, retail, hire gear and dive charters.

Accommodation

A wide range of accommodation to suit every budget, from 4-star hotels to backpacker lodges.

Broome Backpackers Bunkhouse, 1852 Lulifitz Dve, Broome. Tel: 08-91935050. Dormitory rooms at $15 a night and $80 pw.

Cable Beach Club Hotel, Cable Beach Rd, Broome. Tel: 08-91920400, Fax: 08-922249. Rooms from $266 to $461.

Palms Resort Motel, Hopton St, Broome. Tel: 08-91921898, Fax: 08-91922424. Rooms from $85 to $180 per night.

Rowley Shoals and Northern Atoll Reefs

A number of charter boat operators run liveaboard trips to the Rowley Shoals and the other atoll reefs found over 300 km west of Broome. These reefs are best dived in winter and spring when the winds are lighter. Liveaboard trips of generally a week or longer cost about $200 to $250 per day.

Dive Charter Boats

Broome Fishing & Dive Charters, Farrell St, Broome. Tel: 08-91936339.

Broome Time Charters, 29 Dampier Tce, Broome. Tel: 08-91921764.

North Star Charters, 119 Walcott St, Broome. Tel: 08-91935599.

Pearl Sea Coastal Cruises, 161 Herbert St, Broome. Tel: 018-947953.

Christmas Island

Located 2623 km northwest of Perth, Christmas Island is slowly growing in popularity as a diving destination. Twice-weekly flights arrive from Perth. Though brilliant for diving year-round, in August cooler currents come from the Java Trench. December to April is the season for ocean swells, but also the time for whale sharks.

Dive Operators

Indian Ocean Diving Academy, PO Box 340, Christmas Island. Tel/Fax: 08-91648090. Offer dive charters at $100 for a double dive, NASDS dive courses, retail and hire gear.

Genesis Travel, 49 Phillimore St, Fremantle. Tel: 08-94306166, Fax: 08-93353188. Booking agents for the diving and accommodation on both Christmas Island and Cocos Islands. Offers great package deals on diving, airfares and accommodation.

Accommodation

There is a limited range of accommodation on Christmas Island, but the following can be booked through Genesis Travel:

Christmas Island Resort. This resort and casino has rooms from $165 per night and suites from $245.

Christmas Island Lodge. Twin-share rooms at $85 and family rooms at $105.

Cocos (Keeling) Islands

Twice-weekly flights from Perth have made the Cocos (Keeling) Islands more accessible to divers. The flights cost $819, but are much cheaper with a package deal on diving and accommodation. Excellent diving on coral reefs and wrecks year-round. Cocos is located 2770 km northwest of Perth.

Dive Operators

Cocos Tackle and Dive. Run daily boat dives at $50 for a single dive and $100 for a double dive. They also offer NASDS dive courses and hire gear.

Genesis Travel, 49 Phillimore St, Fremantle. Tel: 08-94306166, Fax: 08-93353188. Booking agents for the diving and accommodation on both Christmas Island and Cocos Islands. Offer great package deals on diving, airfares and accommodation.

Accommodation

The range of accommodation on Cocos Islands is limited to just one place, which can be booked through Genesis Travel.

West Island Lodge. With rooms from $35 to $70 a night.

Northern Territory

Diving in the Northern Territory is restricted, due to coastal topography, limited visibility and the lack of facilities. However, divers heading to this fascinating region of Australia will find a number of dive shops and charter boats operating in Darwin and on the Gove Peninsula.

Getting There

International flights are possible through Darwin Airport, especially from Asia. Darwin and Alice Springs are also serviced by domestic flights from the other state capitals of Australia, with Ansett and Qantas running many flights each week.

Local Transport

Travel within the Northern Territory can be limited at times. Driving is not recommended during the wet season when torrential rains flood the rivers and close roads. Hire cars are available, with a 4WD being the best option to explore the often rough roads of the Territory. Roadside assistance is provided by the AANT (Automobile Association of Northern Territory), except in remote areas, but the people of the Territory are very friendly and always ready to lend a hand. Flying is the easiest way to get around, with regional flights provided by Airnorth, Arnhem Air Charter and Brolga Air. While the rail network is rather restricted, buses service many areas, the main companies being Greyhound-Pioneer and McCafferty's.

Medical and Emergencies

In the event of a diving accident anywhere in Australia contact DES (Diving Emergency Service) on **1800 088 200**. State that it is a diving emergency, give the details of the accident and the condition of the diver.

In any other emergency ring **000**, and ask for the service you require, be it fire, police or ambulance.

Hospitals and medical centers are located in most large towns throughout the Northern Territory, and there is a recompression chamber in Darwin. First aid kits and oxygen are carried by most charter boats and their crews should be proficient in their application.

Photographic Supplies

Print film is processed in most towns in the Northern Territory, but E6 slide film can only be processed in Darwin. Buying slide and print film is generally not a problem, but is best purchased from a camera store.

Darwin

Diving Darwin is limited in some aspects by reduced visibility and large tidal movements, but over winter the diving can be quite reasonable on the many wrecks and reefs in the area. A number of dive shops and charter boats in Darwin can organize diving throughout most of the year. Dive charters generally cost $30 for a single dive, but there are package deals available.

Dive Operators

Coral Divers, 42 Stuart Hwy, Stuart Park. Tel: 08-89812686.

Cullen Bay Dive Centre, 66 Marina Blvd, Larrakeyah. Tel: 08-89813049, Fax: 08-89814913. Offers dive charters, PADI dive courses, retail and hire gear.

Darwin Diving Academy, 17 Wilmot St,

The Narrows. Tel: 08-89812598.

Fathom Five Pro Charters, 13 Sabine Rd, Miner. Tel: 08-89854288, Fax: 08-89480258. Runs dive charters and offers retail and hire gear and dive courses.

Sandpebbles Dive Shop, 21 De Latour St, Coconut Grove. Tel: 08-89480444. Provides PADI dive instruction, boat dives, retail and hire gear.

VJ Fishing and Charter, Mahaffey Rd, Howard Springs. Tel: 08-89831213. Offers dive charters.

Accommodation

Darwin offers the visitor a wide range of accommodation.

Banyan View Lodge, 119 Mitchell St, Larrakeyah. Tel: 08-89818644. Rooms from $25 to $40 per night and bunkhouse at $15 per night.

Coconut Grove Holiday Apartments, 146 Dick Ward Dve, Coconut Grove. Tel: 08-89850500, Fax: 08-89850591. Rooms from $58 to $118 per night.

Plaza Hotel Darwin, 32 Mitchell St, Darwin. Tel: 08-89820000, Fax: 08-89811765. 5-star hotel with rooms from $205 to $1100 per night.

Gove Peninsula

Located over 600 km east of Darwin, the Gove Peninsula provide the most exciting diving in the Northern Territory. The coral reefs in the area are best dived from September to April when clearer water washes much of the coastline. Diving the Gove Peninsula is centered around Nhulunbuy. Although accessible by 4WD in the dry season, the peninsula is most easily accessed by flights from Darwin and Cairns.

Dive Operator

Gove Diving Academy, Arnhem Rd, Nhulunbuy. Tel/Fax: 08-89873445. Offers half-day dive trips at $40 (single dive), full-day trips at $80 (two dives) and overnight trips to Truant Island at $100. Also runs PADI dive courses and has retail and hire gear.

Accommodation

A limited range of accommodation is available in Nhulunbuy.

Hideaway Safari Lodge, Nhulunbuy. Tel: 08-89873933. Rooms from $60 per night.

General Diving Information

Diver Training Organizations

A number of dive training organizations exist within Australia, these include;

ANDI Australia, (American Nitrox Divers International) 10 Belgrave St, Manly NSW 2095. Tel: 02-99763297, Fax: 02-99773664.

AUSI (Australian Underwater Scuba Instructors) PO Box 202, Queenscliff Vic 3225.

CDAA (Cave Divers Association of Australia), PO Box 290, North Adelaide SA 5006.

IANTD Australasian (International Association Nitrox & Technical Divers), 255 Stanmore Rd, Stanmore. Tel: 02-95500830.

NASDS (National Association of Scuba Diving Schools) 396 Scarborough Beach Rd, Osborne Park, WA. Tel: 08-92424492, Fax: 08-92425380.

NAUI Australia (National Association of Underwater Instructors) PO Box 183, Capalaba Qld 4157. Tel: 07-33903233, Fax: 07-33903159.

PADI Australia (Professional Association of Diving Instructors), 372 Eastern Valley Way, Chatswood, NSW. Tel: 02-94172800, Fax: 02-94171434.

SSI (Scuba Schools International) PO Box 662, Balgowlah NSW 2093. Tel: 02-99070322, Fax: 02-99070416.

Dive Travel Companies

While most dive shops can book and arrange dive travel within Australia and overseas, there are a few companies in Australia that specialize in this service.

Always Dive Expeditions, 168 High St, Ashburton, Melbourne, Vic. Tel: 03-98858863, Fax: 03-98851164.

Dive Adventures Australia, 32 York St, Sydney, NSW. Tel: 02-92994633, Fax: 02-92994644.

Dive Adventures Australia, 464 St Kilda Rd, Melbourne, Vic. Tel: 03-98665738, Fax: 03-98209275.

Dive Travel Australia, 3/50 Kalang Rd, Elanora Heights, NSW. Tel: 02-99706311, Fax: 02-99706197.

Genesis Travel, 49 Phillimore St, Fremantle, WA. Tel: 08-94306166, Fax: 09-3353188.

PADI Travel Network, 372 Eastern Valley Way, Chatswood, NSW. Tel: 02-94172800, Fax: 02-94171434.

Pro Dive Travel, Royal Arcade, 255 Pitt St, Sydney. NSW. Tel/Fax: 02-92649499.

Sea New Guinea, 100 Clarence St, Sydney, NSW. Tel: 02-2675563, Fax: 02-92676118.

Ski & Sea Travel, PO Box 662, Balgowlah NSW 2093. Tel: 02-99070322.

Camera Servicing and Repairs

The following companies provide specialized servicing and repairs to underwater photographic equipment.

Brisbane Photographic Repairs, 33 Steptoe St, Chapel Hill, Brisbane, Qld. Tel: 07-33784862.

Camera Clinic, 19 Peel St, Collingwood, Melbourne, Vic. Tel: 03-94195247.

Hartland Cinemex Photographic Repairs, 89 Edward St, Perth. Tel: 08-93283499.

Poraday, 936 Anzac Pde, Maroubra, Sydney, NSW. Tel: 02-93497174.

Diver Accident Services

Divers in Australia and overseas can be covered for dive accidents by becoming a member of **DAN** (Divers Alert Network) South East Asia, PO Box 134, Carnegie Vic 3163, Tel: 03-95631151, Fax: 03-95631139. This membership covers the diver for all costs for transport and treatment of a dive accident. DAN works in association with **DES** (Diving Emergency Service) who arrange the transport and treatment of dive accident victims in Australia.

Diving events

There are a number of events that the diver may wish to attend in Australia each year.

SCUBA EXPO is on in July each year. Venues may change so check with Dive Australia.

South Pacific Divers Underwater Photographer of the Year, the largest photographic competition in Australasia culminates in a wonderful presentation night each year in Sydney, usually on the first weekend in August.

Cairns Dive Festival, a week of diving and talks with dive personalities, held each year in October as part of the Cairns 'Fun in the Sun Festival'.

Heron Island Dive Festival, now held every second year in November, the festival is a week of diving, talks and experiences with dive personalities from around the world.

Underwater Hazards

Conditions

A range of diving conditions are experienced in Australia. While the Great Barrier Reef waters are usually clear and warm, there are also strong currents in many places and rough seas in open water. At times in southern Australia, divers will have to handle dirty water, large swells, surge, currents, thermoclines, rough seas and strong winds. Always assess the conditions and dive because you want too, not because of someone else. Dive within your ability and abort the dive if uncomfortable or apprehensive; you can always dive another day.

The biters

The chances of being bitten by any animal when diving is remote; the general rule is leave sea creatures alone and they will leave you alone.

SHARKS

Australia has a reputation for shark attacks, but with only one or two attacks each year, there is far more chance of being struck by lightning. You can reduce your chances of being attacked by avoiding close contact with the following species. The Great White (*Carcharodon carcharias*) is very rare, but most likely to be encountered around seal colonies. When diving with seals don't float around on the surface, go straight to the bottom, and vacate the water if a shark is seen or the seals depart. Tiger sharks (*Galeocerdo cuvieri*) are more common in tropical seas, especially around turtle breeding areas. Although generally shy of divers, it may be best to leave the water if a tiger is seen cruising along the reef. The whaler shark family, which includes the grey reef shark (*Carcharhinus amblyrhynchos*), silvertip (*Carcharhinus albimarginatus*), bull shark (*Carcharhinus leucas*) and bronze whaler (*Carcharhinus brachyurus*), are fast moving, territorial and have bitten divers in the past. These sharks are usually shy, but do get excited in a shark feed. The great hammerhead (*Sphyrna mokarran*) grows to 6 m in length and is sometimes aggressive towards divers. Avoid annoying wobbegong sharks (*Orectolobus* sp.). Although though they look docile and lazy, they have a nasty set of jaws and have latched onto many divers in the past. Angel sharks (*Squatina australis*) also have a nasty set of teeth, but generally prefer to flee than use them. Always face any approaching shark, and never panic.

FISH

The most aggressive fish encountered in Australia is the damsel fish. When guarding eggs they will fearlessly attack other fish and divers, giving repeated bites to hands, head and other body parts. The titan triggerfish (*Balistoides viridescens*) is also very aggressive when guarding its large nest during the breeding season. Gropers can be quite aggressive when being fed, especially the potato cod (*Epinephelus tukula*) at the Cod Hole. Divers have to let go of food quickly to avoid hands disappearing into a cavernous mouth. Another animal that is more likely to bite when being fed is the moray eel. A number of species are found around Australia, and while generally harmless, they are still wild animals and can give a nasty bite when after food.

OTHER ANIMALS

Saltwater crocodiles (*Crocodylus porosus*) are best avoided. Stay away from mangroves, creeks and murky water in northern Australia. Seals can also give a nasty bite if their territory is threatened, but they also tend to play by gently holding objects with their teeth, so don't panic by ripping your hand or foot away.

Venomous creatures

Australia has an over abundance of venomous creatures on the land and underwater, but luckily most are shy and retiring, and are quite harmless if left alone.

VENOMOUS FISH

All species of stingray, stingaree and eagle ray have one or more spines on their tail that should be avoided. Though the venom is not fatal, a number of people have been killed by the spine cutting an artery, so take care around rays. A number of deaths have occurred from contact with stonefish. They have a row of spines along their back and with their cryptic camouflage are hard to see. Avoid contact with any stonefish or its relatives (scorpionfish, lionfish and firefish) by staying off the bottom. If stung by a ray or stonefish, immerse the wound in hot water, treat for shock and get immediate medical attention. Any fish with spines, such as catfish, should be avoided.

SEA SNAKES

A number of species of sea snakes live in tropical Australian waters. Although highly venomous, sea snakes are generally quite docile and easy to a avoid. If bitten, restrict circulation and seek medical attention.

ECHINODERMS

Sea urchins are quite common in the seas around Australia, and most have very sharp spines that are best avoided by staying off the bottom. While a number of sea stars and brittle stars should not be handled with bare hands, the most venomous is the notorious crown-of-thorns (*Acanthaster planci*). Their spines cause very intense pain, and are capable of penetrating a wetsuit. You may think you are doing your bit for the environment by lifting them off the coral, but the crown of thorns is best not handled.

MOLLUSCS

Australia is the home of the deadly, blue-ringed octopus (*Hapalochlaena* sp.), of which there are several species in tropical and temperate seas. Although small (around 100 to 200 mm), their bite is deadly, so don't touch any small octopus with blue bands or blue rings. There are also numerous species of cone shells (*Conus* sp.) that shouldn't be handled. Cones inject a venomous dart to immobilize their prey, but this venom can be highly toxic to humans.

SEA JELLIES, CORALS & ANEMONES

Avoid all contact with sea jellies. Most give a nasty sting, but especially avoid swimming in murky water in tropical Australia from October to May as this is when box jellies are most common. Hundreds of people have died from the stings of box jellies, so cover up to protect yourself. Most anemones are quite harmless, but a number can cause quite bad reactions on contact with bare skin. Corals should generally be avoided, not only because a number of species can cut and sting, but to reduce damage to the corals.

Poisonous creatures

Seafood is very popular in Australia, but there are a few simple rules to follow. Don't eat boxfish (fish with a hard outer casing), pufferfish or porcupine fish (fish with a number of spines over their bodies), moray eels or reef crabs with black nippers. These animals are poisonous. Don't eat shellfish from areas with heavy industry, pollution or sewerage discharge. Many of these areas are signposted to stop people collecting these animals.

While it is possible to get food poisoning from almost any seafood if it hasn't been refrigerated, the major danger is ciguatera poisoning. Caused by toxic chemicals from algae being passed down the food chain, the poison is concentrated in larger reef fish. Not all fish carry the poison, but avoid eating the following tropical reef fish: any gropers, large rock cods, or triggerfish, the paddle tailfish (*Lutjanus gibbus*), chinaman fish (*Symphorus nematophorous*), longnose unicornfish (*Naso unicornis*) and the bohar snapper (*Lutjanus bohar*).

Cuts and scrapes

It is always advisable to wear full protection when diving, be it wetsuit or lycra suit and gloves, to avoid cuts and scrapes, especially in the tropics. If you do get a coral cut, scrub it clean and disinfect the wound as soon as possible. Shipwrecks are always fun to dive but watch out for sharp or twisted metal, also watch your head, as many a diver, myself included, have banged their heads inside a shipwreck. There are also oysters and hydroids commonly growing on shipwrecks in tropical Australia, so be careful with hand placement. Don't grab sleeping fish or fish in the coral—it may be a surgeonfish which have razor sharp blades on its tail that cut easily through gloves and skin.

Shocks

There are several species of electric rays found in the waters of Australia, two of which are most likely to be encountered. The most common is the short tailed electric ray (*Hypnos monopterygium*) found in most southern waters, while the Tasmanian electric ray (*Narcine tasmaniensis*) is more common around the island state. Both lie hidden under the sand, and if you suddenly receive 200 volts, you know you have found one.

Further Reading

There are any number of books on Australia's underwater world. Many, unfortunately, are out of print. The following books can be read for further information.

Australia A Travel Survival Kit. Lonely Planet Publications, 1996. The best guide to travel in Australia.

Australia Down Under by Christine Deacon & Kevin Deacon. Doubleday, 1986. A wonderful book on Australia's varied marine environments.

Australian Fish Behaviour by Neville Coleman. Sea Australia Resource Centre, 1993. A natural history book.

Australian Shipwrecks Volume 4 1901-1986 by Jack Loney. Marine History Publications, 1987. A complete listing of shipwrecks from 1901 to 1986.

Australia's Underwater Wilderness by Roland Hughes. Weldons, 1985. Stunning photos and informative text about the marine environments of Australia.

Cave Diving In Australia by Ian Lewis & Peter Stace. Lewis & Stace, 1981. Detailed information about the cave diving in Mount Gambier.

Coastal Fishes of Tasmania & Bass Strait by G Edgar, P Last and M Wells. Cat & Fiddle Press, 1982. Beautiful photos of the fishes of Southern Australia.

Christmas Island Naturally by Howard Gray. Howard Gray, 1981. The natural history of this amazing island.

Discover Underwater Australia by Neville Coleman. National, 1994. A lovely coffee table book that gives an introduction to the varied marine environments of Australia.

Dive Australia by Peter Stone. Ocean Publication, 1990. A brilliant overview of the Australia dive scene.

Dive Western Australia by Jeff Mullins. Reef Images, 1992. Invaluable book for anyone diving in Western Australia.

Diving Southern Queensland by John Wright. Sunmap Publications, 1990. Information on the top 40 dive sites in Southern Queensalnd.

Down Under at the Prom by Marg O'Toole & Malcolm Turner. Field Naturalists Club of Victoria, 1990. Comprehensive guide to marine life and dive sites at Wilson's Promontory.

Encyclopedia of Marine Animals by Neville Coleman. Angus & Robertson, 1991. A guide to the marine life of the world.

Great Barrier Reef by Isobel Bennett. Lansdowne Press, 1981. A natural history guide to the Great Barrier Reef and its islands.

Guide to Sea Fishes of Australia by Rudie H. Kuiter. New Holland, 1986. A comprehensive reference book for divers and fishermen.

Hazardous Sea Creatures by Neville Coleman. Sea Australia Resource Centre, 1993. A comprehensive guide to the animals to avoid when diving in Australia.

Nudibranchs of the South Pacific by Neville Coleman. Sea Australia Resource Centre, 1989. A must for anyone fascinated by nudibranchs.

Queensland Accommodation & Touring Guide. RACQ, 1996. Guide to accommodation in Queensland.

RACQ Interstate Accommodation Guide. RACQ, 1996. Guide to accommodation in Australia (except Queensland).

Readers Digest Book of the Great Barrier Reef. Readers Digest, 1990. One of the most comprehensive guides ever produced on the Great Barrier Reef.

Readers Digest Motoring Guide To Australia. Readers Digest, 1990. Maps, distances and information for anyone driving anywhere in Australia.

Reef Fishes of the World by E. Lieske and R. Myers. Periplus Editions, 1994. A comprehensive identification guide.

Reef Sharks & Rays of the World by Scott Michael. Sea Challengers, 1993. The ultimate guide for anyone with an interest in sharks or rays.

Scuba Divers Guide to Australia's Central Great Barrier Reef by Tom Byron. Aqua Sports Publications. Detailed look at the dive sites in this region.

Scuba Divers Guide to Australia's Southern Great Barrier Reef by Tom Byron. Aqua Sports Publications. Comprehensive guide to dive sites in this area.

Scuba Divers Guide to Cairns & Australia's Northern Great Barrier Reef by Tom Byron. Aqua Sports Publications. A guide to all the popular dive sites in these areas.

Scuba Divers Guide to Jervis Bay by Tom Byron. Aqua Sports Publications. Wonderful guide to the best dive sites around Jervis Bay.

Scuba Divers Guide to New South Wales by Tom Byron. Aqua Sports Publications. A guide to most dive sites in New South Wales.

Scuba Divers Guide to the Whitsunday Islands by Tom Byron. Aqua Sports Publications. A must for anyone visiting the Whitsundays.

Sea Fishes of Southern Australia by Barry Hutchins and Roger Swainston. Swainston Publishing, 1986. Wonderful illustrations and information on the fish of Southern Australia.

Sea Stars of Australasia and their Relatives by Neville Coleman. Sea Australia Resource Centre, 1994. Full-color guide to Australia's echinoderms.

Sharks & Rays of Australia by Peter Last & John Stevens. CSIRO, 1994. The bible for anyone interested in the sharks and rays found in the waters of Australia.

Shipwrecks 1656-1942 by Sarah Kenderdine. Western Australian Maritime Museum, 1995. A guide to the wealth of shipwrecks around Perth.

Index

Map Index